PRAISE FOR *The Rise and Fall of Violent Crime in America*

"*The Rise and Fall of Violent Crime in America*, dealing mostly, but not entirely, with the period from World War II to the present, is a rare combination of sophisticated analysis and compelling prose. Professor Latzer convincingly cuts through the prejudices, passions, and politics surrounding both popular and scholarly explanations of this controversial subject. A magnificent achievement."
—Roger Lane, Professor Emeritus of History, Haverford College

"Violent crime rates have varied greatly in America over the past seventy-five years, and their fluctuations have been entangled in the complex politics of race, ethnicity, and class. Latzer takes us on a well-documented journey through these developments and provides a balanced account of the trends and their correlates—a welcome approach to an issue that is often contentious."
—Gary LaFree, Department of Criminology and Criminal Justice, University of Maryland

"[Latzer] insists that quantitative criminology cannot 'replace a deep knowledge of a society, its particular history, and the workings of its criminal justice system.' That deep knowledge is on display in this impressive volume."
—Joseph M. Bessette, Alice Tweed Tuohy Professor of Government and Ethics, Claremont McKenna College

"A masterfully researched and written work that capably demonstrates the importance of history in the study of crime. Professor Latzer is to be commended for developing an exhaustively researched yet eminently readable account that should be mandatory reading for any scholar of crime and violence in the United States."
—Samuel Bieler, Urban Institute

The Rise
and Fall
of Violent Crime
in America

The Rise
and Fall
of Violent Crime
in America

BARRY LATZER

Encounter Books
New York • London

First American edition published in 2016 by Encounter Books, an activity of Encounter for Culture and Education, Inc., a nonprofit, tax exempt corporation.
Encounter Books website address: www.encounterbooks.com

Manufactured in the United States and printed on acid-free paper. The paper used in this publication meets the minimum requirements of ANSI/NISO Z39.48–1992 (R 1997) (*Permanence of Paper*).

First paperback edition published in 2017.
Paperback edition ISBN: 978-1-59403-929-4

THE LIBRARY OF CONGRESS HAS CATALOGUED
THE HARDCOVER EDITION AS FOLLOWS:

Latzer, Barry, 1945–
The rise and fall of violent crime in America / Barry Latzer.
pages cm
Includes bibliographical references and index.
ISBN 978-1-59403-835-8 (hardcover : alk. paper) —
ISBN 978-1-59403-836-5 (ebook)
1. Violent crimes—United States—History. 2. Crime—United States.
I. Title.
HV6789.L38 2015
364.150973'090945—dc23
2015010962

PRODUCED BY WILSTED & TAYLOR PUBLISHING SERVICES

To Sandra,
for her infinite love
and patience

In memory of
Gene Plotnik and Marc Raeff,
who never saw it completed

Contents

Preface

Violent crime, especially after the late 1960s, was one of the most significant domestic issues in the United States. Aside from the civil rights movement, the campaign for women's rights, and structural changes in the economy, it is hard to think of a phenomenon that had a more profound effect on American life in the last third of the twentieth century. After 1965, crime rose to such heights that it frightened virtually all Americans and prompted significant alterations in everyday behaviors and even in lifestyles. The risk of being mugged became an issue for Americans when they chose homes and schools, selected commuter routes, and planned leisure activities. In some urban locations, people were afraid to leave their dwellings at any time, day or night, even to go to the grocery store. During the worst of the post-1960s crime wave, Americans spent part of each day literally looking back over their shoulders.

Their fears were fully justified. More Americans were murdered in the great crime tsunami than perished in World War II, the Korean War, the Vietnam War, and the conflicts in

Iraq and Afghanistan combined. Between 1970 and 1995, a staggering 540,019 Americans were murdered. War fatalities totaled 507,340. And if we compare the number of war-wounded to the number of people injured in criminal assaults, the toll of the crime tsunami is even more shocking. Fewer than 1 million service personnel suffered nonfatal injuries in the foreign conflicts above, whereas 2.2 million Americans *per year* were injured by violent crime. Over 6 million of the injuries suffered from 1973 to 1991 were considered serious, as they involved gunshot or knife wounds, broken bones, loss of consciousness, dislodged teeth, and internal injuries. Many crime victims required hospitalizations lasting two or more days. These losses do not address the financial costs, which ran into the billions of dollars and usually had to be borne by the victims.[1]

Crime stimulated billions of dollars in government expenditures and millions more in civilian attempts to harden targets with private guards, alarms, and locks. Crime and the interrelated illegal-substance problem provoked a massive buildup of the nation's criminal justice apparatus and the incarceration of millions of offenders. Crime also exacerbated racial and ethnic conflicts, largely because of the association of African Americans and other minority groups with disproportionate offending.

Inevitably, politicians responded to public fears, and violent crime became a political issue.[2] In the 1988 presidential campaign, to take a particularly vivid example, Republican George H.W. Bush successfully attacked his Democratic opponent, Michael Dukakis, governor of Massachusetts, for being "soft on crime." Bush ran the famous (or, if you prefer, infamous) Willie Horton advertisement that became a campaign flash point. The ad featured a convicted African American murderer who had been furloughed from the Massachusetts correctional system for a weekend and, instead of returning to prison, broke into a couple's home, bound and stabbed the husband, and raped the wife. Bush took forty states with 53.4 percent of the popular vote.

In the mid-1990s, after roughly two and a half decades, the crime tsunami finally began to ebb. By the turn of the century, the crime issue started to drop off the public agenda. In 1992, nearly nine in ten Americans thought that crime had gotten worse during the previous year. By 2001, only four in ten thought the same.[3]

In 2008, Barack Obama, the son of a black father and white mother, was elected president of the United States, and many people believed his success as a candidate was a by-product of the decline in anxieties over urban violence.[4] Those anxieties were rekindled by a fatal encounter between a white police officer and a young black man in Ferguson, Missouri, in August 2014. When a grand jury failed to indict the officer the following November, protests and riots erupted across the country, and the subject of crime resurfaced as part of the discussion about relations between African Americans and the police.[5]

Protesters adopted the phrase "Black Lives Matter" and campaigned to reduce police shootings and alleged overincarceration of African Americans. Media reports of several unjustified shootings lent support to the BLM narrative, but tallies of police shootings revealed that half of those shot were white and roughly one-quarter were black.[6] During the height of the protests in the summer of 2016, five police officers were murdered by a sniper in Dallas, followed by the assassination of three more officers in Baton Rouge just ten days later. The protests and shootings seemed to demoralize the police, resulting in less discretionary—and perhaps less effective—police work.[7]

As for the excessive incarceration claim, it will be difficult to reduce African American imprisonment, because 79 percent of black state prisoners are held for violent crime (58 percent); serious property offenses, such as burglary (16 percent); or weapons violations (5 percent). If all drug prisoners, regardless of race, were removed from state prisons, the black inmate population would drop only 0.36 percent, from 39.06 percent of state prisoners to 38.7 percent.[8]

Whether or not these public concerns have staying power, the time seems ripe for a searching, long-term examination of the rise and fall of crime in the United States.

◆   ◆   ◆

This book begins with the 1940s, but in some respects, this is the middle of the story. To fully understand violent crime, its genesis and development must be studied within the context of the nation's history. The forces that shaped contemporary America began to fall into place about 135 years ago, in the 1880s, when the United States developed an industrial economy, formed great metropolitan centers, received massive influxes of immigrants from all over the world, and first experienced migrations of African Americans from the South to other regions of the country.

The study of crime going back to the late nineteenth century gives us a different perspective on its causes. Some of the factors that loomed large in recent decades—poverty, economic downturns, urban environments, and ethnic and racial bias—begin to diminish in importance. By contrast, long-term analysis reveals that the propensity for violence of various subcultures, whether they be ethnic, racial, religious, or regional, seems to generate high violent crime rates over fairly long time periods. For instance, white and black southerners, each of which has a distinctive culture, have had high rates of interpersonal violence for well over a century. In the case of southern whites, violent tendencies can be traced back to the eighteenth-century Scotch-Irish migration. For African Americans, the pivotal period for the increase in violent crime was between 1880 and 1900, the notorious Jim Crow era.

Other cultural groups that immigrated to the United States have had quite variable records in terms of violent crime. In the nineteenth century, crime rates were high for the Irish and Chinese, but low for German and Scandinavian immigrants. Eastern European Jews and southern Italians, who arrived at roughly the same time, between 1900 and 1910, and settled in the same place, New York City, had very different rates of violence. Likewise, in the 1920s, Mexican migrants had elevated violent crime rates, while Japanese entrants did not.

Given that nearly all of these cultural groups arrived in poverty and suffered shameful mistreatment because of their race, religion, or national origin, the variation in violent crime rates is puzzling. It raises profound questions regarding the standard assumptions about crime and suggests that cultural influences may be more important than social deficits in explaining high or low levels of violence.

The examination of crime over the course of U.S. history also raises doubts about the role of cities in crime. In the 1890s, when American cities underwent massive growth, violent crime was relatively low, despite dilapidated urban housing, the ghettoization of immigrants and the poor, abuse by police who lacked any professional training, and thoroughly corrupt municipal governments. Violent crime rates were much lower than they would be a century later, when conditions were far better.

Finally, the long-term history of crime teaches us that economic downturns and upswings are inconsistently related to violent crime. During the low-crime 1890s, the United States was buffeted by an economic recession second only to the Great Depression in its toll on American citizens. On the other hand, crime soared in the economic boom period of the 1920s. Following the 1920s, moreover, crime kept rising right through the worst years of the Depression and began descending only when Roosevelt's New Deal commenced in 1934. And yet, if the federal safety net caused the downturn in crime, what was the explanation for the continued decline when the economy significantly worsened in 1937 and '38? American history, both before and after World War II, raises profound questions about what we know—or think we know—about crimes of violence.

◆ ◆ ◆

As with any major social development, violent crime has in-spired countless scholarly and journalistic analyses. Books and articles have focused on homicide alone,[9] on particular or es-pecially sensational cases,[10] on violence in general,[11] and violent crime in specific cities.[12] Several studies tried to explain the de-cline in crime after 1995.[13] Somewhat surprisingly, however, the literature does not include a comprehensive history of violent crime in the United States over the last six decades of the twen-tieth century and the beginning of the twenty-first. The mission of this work is to fill that gap.

The Rise and Fall of Violent Crime in America is a synthesis of history and criminology, drawing on insights from both disci-plines. The definition of violent crime used here is the standard one adopted by criminologists. Violent crime encompasses four different offenses: criminal homicide (murder and so-called "voluntary" manslaughter, which is killing caused by reckless rather than intentional or merely negligent behavior), robbery (forcible theft, as opposed to nonviolent larceny), rape (not in-cluding statutory rape, which may be consensual, though the consent is invalid), and assault (particularly aggravated assault, which involves serious physical injury). Excluded are kidnap-ping, which, although violent, is very rare, and arson and bur-glary, which are mainly considered property crimes.

Violent crimes don't occur with equal frequency: assault and robbery are much more common than rape and murder or manslaughter. Since victims underreport assault, rape, and robbery, analysts focus on criminal homicides, which provide the most accurate data. By relying on death records prepared by coroners (today's medical examiners), historians are able to collect data on killings during periods in which other crime sta-tistics are unavailable or unreliable. Fortunately, there is a cor-relation between the incidence of criminal homicide and other crimes of violence, so by studying murder and manslaughter alone, scholars acquire a good sense of the magnitude of violent crime. One shortcoming of this methodology is that homicide figures do not include robberies unaccompanied by murder, and the massive increase in urban robbery was one of the most important developments in the twentieth-century history of crime.

Another criminological convention adopted for this book is the differentiation between organized (or "mob") crime, even though it sometimes produces significant violence, and ordinary (or "street") crime. Organized crime and street crime are motivated by different concerns. The former seeks to enhance and perpetuate the illegal organization; the latter is born of impulsive anger and personal disputes. In addition, organized crime's victims are usually rival gangsters and not, except inadvertently, members of the general public. Consequently, organized crime doesn't generate the same public fear as street crime. It is often said, at least anecdotally, that residents of neighborhoods in which mob leaders reside feel perfectly safe, even in periods of high crime.

Organized crime is discussed in this book, especially in chapter 4, which examines the brutal crack cocaine gang warfare. But the main focus is common crimes of violence committed by individuals operating alone or in small ad hoc groups—acts motivated by pedestrian causes, such as sexual gratification or jealousy, avarice, personal offense, and the like.

Finally, the issue of rape probably deserves more attention than it receives in this book. Unfortunately, this offense has been so underreported that statistics on long-term developments are hard to trust. A major current concern is "acquaintance rape," especially on college campuses. Around 80 percent of all sexual assaults, on and off campus, involve assailants known to the victim, so the focus on acquaintances is not misplaced. But the campus may not be the locus for most attacks. An extensive survey by the federal Bureau of Justice Statistics found that female students are less likely to be victimized or to report sexual assaults than women ages 18 to 24 who are not enrolled in college.[14]

◆ ◆ ◆

In recent decades, criminological research has benefited from the application of sophisticated statistical techniques, such as multiple regression analysis. This methodology enables researchers to isolate causal factors and determine the extent to which each one has influenced the particular effect under study. For example, one can determine whether unemployment rates had an impact on the amount of violent crime, holding constant other apparently relevant factors, such as changes in police force staffing, criminal conviction rates, or the length of prison sentences. This book has taken full advantage of this research, while avoiding any discussion of methodological issues that would be difficult for the general reader to grasp.

Sophisticated statistical analysis has become so important in the criminology field that, unfortunately, significant avenues of study, particularly in the history of crime, have been foreclosed for want of data considered suitable. In addition, some of the quantitative studies have little utility as they are too narrow in focus and not clearly linked to theoretical explanations for crime. Although these sophisticated quantitative techniques are an advance, they do not replace a deep knowledge of a society, its particular history, and the workings of its criminal justice system.

◆ ◆ ◆

The United States is currently in a crime trough—a period of relatively low violence. How we got here and what happened before we did are questions this work can answer. What will happen next remains much more of a mystery. We grapple with this latter question at the end of chapter 5.

The Rise
and Fall
of Violent Crime
in America

Does war favor or check criminality?
The answer is we do not know.

—PITIRIM SOROKIN

Here lies a black man
killed fighting a yellow man
for the protection of a white man.

—EPITAPH OF THE 1940S

CHAPTER I

World War II and Its Aftermath

Crime in the 1940s

INTRODUCTION

There were more American casualties in World War II than in any other foreign conflict in U.S. history. Over 405,000 soldiers died, and more than 670,000 were wounded.[1] And yet, looking at the broad sweep of things, the war was good for America. After Pearl Harbor, there were no other attacks on American soil during the conflict. The horrific death and destruction suffered in Europe, Russia, China, and Japan were unknown here. The postwar weakness of the other combatant nations left the United States the unrivaled power in the global arena. Domestically, the war was tonic. For one thing, it ended the Great Depression and dispelled the gloom that had hung like a pall over the country. The world war restored the American economy and the nation's confidence in itself, rekindling its ebullient spirit.

Mobilization for the war jolted America's productive energies, spurring on young industries, such as airplane manufacturing, and encouraging the development of new consumer products, such as nylon stockings. Productivity improved, and the national wealth was vastly enlarged. From 1940 to 1945, real GDP per capita rose an extraordinary 63 percent, while the average laborer's wages climbed 58 percent.[2] The mobilization created so many jobs that no one could seriously claim that crimes of violence—which remained stable until the end of the conflict—were attributable to unemployment. In the 1940s, anyone who wanted to work could find a job.

Of even greater significance for the history of crime, the war boom inspired huge internal migrations as Americans flooded into the states and cities that produced war goods. The entire country seemed to be in motion, moving to either war production sites, military bases, or the battlefront itself. Home front historian Allan Winkler estimated that a remarkable 20 percent of the American population moved from one place to another during the conflict. On the West Coast, the population increases were enormous. "It was as if someone tilted the country," wrote historian Richard White, and "people, money, and soldiers all spilled west." By the end of the war, the population of Southern California alone exceeded that of thirty-seven states combined.[3]

For the South, which plays such an important role in America's crime story, the changes were historic. "The Second World War," historian Dewey Grantham exclaimed, "was a transforming experience for the South and a catalyst in altering its role in the nation." As federal money poured into southern war industries and the many southern military bases, the economy of the region was utterly transfigured. The South became more fully integrated into the national economy, and wealth disparities between southerners and nonsoutherners narrowed. Agriculture was totally restructured as mechanization replaced most manual labor, and southern cities grew enormously as the excess farm labor population quit rural areas altogether. It is no exaggeration to say that the dynamic Sunbelt was born during the Second World War.[4]

Insofar as crime is concerned, no event aside from the

buildup of the armed forces itself was as significant as the vast migration of workers. However, military service and migrations, as we shall see, had different effects on crime. Removing young men from civil society to domestic military camps and overseas units helped reduce stateside criminal violence. But luring them to work in war industries in cities that were totally unprepared for them and their families may have driven up crime. Overall, the military call-up appears to have had the greater impact, because national crime rates diminished right up until the end of the war, when the "boys" came home.[5]

For African Americans, the enormous demand for wartime labor meant a resumption of the Great Migration, which had gone into hiatus during the Depression. An estimated 1.45 million blacks migrated between 1940 and 1950, and most of them abandoned the South altogether. Especially significant was the rise of the black metropolitan "proletariat"—impoverished farm laborers turned big-city slum dwellers—in a process that had already begun in the 1920s. This group would bring high levels of black-on-black interpersonal violence to the cities of the North and West. By 1940, even before the war fully impacted mobility, over one million black southerners, two-thirds of all southern-born blacks living outside the South, were calling eight big metropolitan areas home: New York City–Newark, Philadelphia-Camden, Chicago-Gary, Detroit, Cleveland, Saint Louis, Los Angeles–Long Beach, and San Francisco–Oakland. The war was responsible for the final transformation of the African American from a southern rural farm laborer to a multiregional urban wage worker. This, however, is only a part of the story. Also traceable to the 1940s are the role the military played in transforming the lives of African American men and the rise of a new black assertiveness—culminating in the epochal civil rights movement of the 1960s.[6]

The following discussion describes conditions in the United States during World War II, the social and economic backdrop to the crime of the era. It then segues into a detailed treatment of violent crime in the 1940s, with special attention to the impact of the mobilization of the armed forces and the widespread migrations sparked by the war buildup. The chapter concludes with an analysis of the effect of wars in general on violent crime.

MOBILIZATION

When the German blitzkrieg quickly overran much of western Europe in the spring of 1940, the American mood changed from a fierce determination to stay out of another overseas war to shock and the fear that we could be next. "Suddenly, the country felt naked and vulnerable," wrote Roosevelt historian William Leuchtenburg, for as everyone now realized, "only the British stood between Hitler and the United States." Still, Americans were neither mentally nor materially prepared for war. The country had a total of 350 tanks, 2,800 planes, and less than 200,000 men in the army when the Germans attacked. The United States launched a billion-dollar military buildup and its first-ever peacetime conscription in 1940, but there would be no direct military engagement for another year. In the interim, we provided military and economic aid to England and the continental democracies, using naval convoys to protect the transports. Then came the attack on Pearl Harbor on December 7, 1941, which killed 2,400 servicemen and destroyed or disabled 19 ships and 150 planes, and the entire nation mobilized for all-out warfare.[7]

Presiding over the war, as he had over the Great Depression, President Franklin D. Roosevelt once again provided the extraordinary leadership that united the country. He asked Congress to establish new government bureaucracies, such as the War Production Board (succeeded by the better-run Office of War Mobilization), tasking them with managing the mobilization. Private industry, fearing loss of profits, was initially reluctant to convert to war production. Automobile factories, for instance, which were essential for the manufacture of planes and tanks, turned out nearly a million *more* cars in 1941 than in 1939. It wasn't until 1942 and 1943 that FDR created enough incentives and tax breaks to get business fully on board. An example is the cost-plus-fixed-fee system under which the government guaranteed all development and production costs and paid a percentage profit for all wartime goods produced. Business couldn't lose under such an arrangement, as the government assumed all the risks.

Once industry was committed, the pace of war production was dazzling. In 1941, Ford built a huge factory in Willow Run, thirty-five miles from Detroit. The sixty-seven-acre plant employed over 42,000 people in the production of bombers. (After the war, the plant was sold to General Motors, and following GM's decline in 2009, most of it was demolished.) Over on the West Coast, Henry J. Kaiser, shipbuilder extraordinaire, turned out tankers, troop ships, landing ships, and destroyer escorts— nearly one-third of the fleet called into service in 1943—at an amazing clip. His prefabrication methods dramatically reduced production time from nearly a year to under two months. Only one year after the attack on Pearl Harbor, the United States had produced more war materiel than had all of its enemies combined. Even Stalin toasted American production, expressing his special admiration for the astonishing rollout of 10,000 aircraft per month, over three times the Soviet output.[8]

Superheated war production completely wiped out the unemployment that plagued the Depression years. In 1939, there were 9.5 million jobless people in the United States, but by 1943, a mere 670,000 were without work, for an unemployment rate of only 1.2 percent. Of course, by 1943, over 9 million Americans were in the armed forces.[9] There were, in fact, labor shortages throughout the war, and, as Winkler observed, "jobs [were] available to virtually anyone who wanted to work."[10]

The war was good for organized labor as well as big business. Union membership went up 40 percent during the war years, by the end of which 45 percent of the workforce was covered by collective bargaining agreements. Wages rose steadily. Manufacturing wages went from $32.18 to $47.12 a week—up 65 percent—in the forty months after December 1941. Real earnings after inflation climbed 27 percent. The increases were due in part to the longer workweek as factories ran at full tilt to meet wartime production targets. Some plants went to 50- to 60-hour weeks, paying time-and-a-half for overtime.

This did not mean that labor unrest was eliminated. Despite the increase in wages, which the government tried to cap, the cost of living continued to rise, and the unions pressed for more compensation. There were, in fact, over 14,000 work stoppages during the war years, although most of them lasted only a few days. The bitterest dispute was over coal miners' pay, and the doughty John L. Lewis, no friend of FDR's, led his United Mine Workers in four strikes. Ultimately, Roosevelt nationalized the mines but nevertheless caved in to Lewis's demands.

Productivity rose dramatically in the war years, increasing 25 percent per annum (compared with the typical 1.9 percent annual increase). Output per worker was one-third higher in 1943 than in 1939, and the index of industrial production rose 239 percent over that of the prewar years.[11]

Still, there were shortages during the war—the most worrisome being those in petroleum and rubber, both essential to the military. The Roosevelt administration banned automobile production and launched rationing programs and drives to collect scrap metal and rubber. The government spent $700 million to build fifty-one synthetic-rubber plants, and the program was a success: by 1944, the United States was producing over 800,000 tons of synthetic rubber per year.

There were shortages in consumer goods as well, such as butter, sugar, and meat; clothing made of wool or nylon; and, of course, tires and gasoline. Fearing shortages and inflation, FDR created the Office of Price Administration, which had the authority to freeze retail prices, control rents, and ration scarce products. The rationing, which was heavy-handed, was wildly unpopular, but inflation was checked. Unfortunately, black marketeering flourished. The administration tried to limit wage increases as well, establishing a National War Labor Board to regulate war-related industries, such as steel. The unions complained, but they pledged not to strike (which didn't prevent wildcat actions), and wages rose 24 percent during the war.[12]

The agricultural sector also thrived in the 1940s. The farming population dropped nearly 20 percent as men joined the army or went north to work in war-production factories. Those left behind prospered, as demand for food led to the end of 1930s crop restrictions. New agricultural equipment and technologies expanded yields, and per capita farm income tripled. Farmers reduced their debts, terminated farm tenancies, and built new farmhouses. Some said it was a "second American agricultural revolution."[13]

Compared with the other combatant nations, America had it good. There was no fighting or bombing on U.S. soil, the economic disaster of the 1930s was now a bitter memory, and a tremendous patriotic esprit de corps swept the nation. People eagerly collected their tin cans, pots, pans, and razor blades for conversion to tanks, ships, bullets, and hand grenades. They donated millions of dollars to war bond drives. Singer Kate Smith's 1943 radio broadcasts alone were said to have raised $39 million. Americans even planted enough Victory Gardens to produce one-third of all vegetables grown in the United States in 1943.[14]

Despite liquor shortages and a federal amusement tax, entertainment became popular again in the 1940s—especially compared with the 1930s, when there was little money for frivolousness. Americans flocked to movies (ninety million tickets sold each week), racetracks, and nightclubs. They danced to big band music and swooned over Frank Sinatra. Golf and beach vacations had wide appeal. Baseball truly became the national pastime, even though the military took 4,000 professional players out of the leagues, including some of the most popular heroes, such as Joe DiMaggio, Bob Feller, and Ted Williams.

To compensate for their absence, chewing-gum magnate Philip Wrigley started a women's league, the All-American Girls Professional Baseball League, immortalized by the 1992 movie *A League of Their Own*. The paperback book came into its own during the war, and comics were hugely popular with children. About seventy million Americans read the newspaper "funny pages," following the exploits of Joe Palooka and Dick Tracy, both of whom "enlisted." It should be noted that Superman sat out the war because his alter ego, Clark Kent, failed the eye exam: his x-ray vision caused him to read the wrong eye chart—the one in the next room.[15]

Over 16 million men—one-third of all males aged 17 to 35—were in the military during World War II (table 1.1). Ten million had been drafted. Nearly three-quarters of the soldiers served overseas for an average tour of sixteen months. As noted, over 400,000 men never returned alive, and more than 670,000 were wounded.

Such a massive removal of young males had a predictable impact on civilian crime, a matter to be discussed shortly. It should also be no surprise that many of these men committed crimes while on active duty. Thousands of American soldiers were charged with offenses by U.S. military authorities, although we lack the complete records needed to pinpoint an exact number. A count of men confined by the army on a single day in 1945, the highest figure during the war years, totaled 32,253. How many of these were serious crimes as opposed to mere violations of military regulations is not clear.

Table 1.1 American servicemen in the armed forces during World War II (annual average)

1940	540,000
1941	1,620,000
1942	3,970,000
1943	9,020,000
1944	11,410,000
1945	11,430,000
1946	3,450,000
1947	1,590,000

Source: U.S. Department of Commerce, Bureau of the Census, *Historical Statistics,* part 1, series D 1–10, 126.

In an enumeration by the navy of courts-martial prisoners, the peak incarceration count, also for 1945, came to 16,000. In addition, from 1941 to 1950, 148 men were executed by military authorities. Needless to say, these figures do not reflect unreported killings, assaults, and rapes of civilians and enemy soldiers by U.S. servicemen, a controversial matter little explored by historians.[16]

Another effect of male mass enrollment in the military was to move females into previously male-only activities. This was less a matter of ideological commitment to sexual equality than wartime necessity. The government encouraged women to work in order to keep production up, and at one point, they comprised 36 percent of the civilian workforce. In fact, nearly half of all American women were employed at some time during 1944. Interestingly, more than seven out of ten working women were married, and married women with husbands in the armed forces were much more likely to work. Women also enlisted in the armed forces—over 300,000 served in every capacity except combat soldier. When the war ended, however, women employees were let go in large numbers, demonstrating that hiring was not motivated by feminist principles. Winkler reports that by the war's end, the proportion of female jobholders in the Detroit auto industry fell from 25 percent to 7.5 percent.[17]

MIGRATION

World War II triggered what one historian called "the greatest spacial reorganization of Americans in the nation's history."[18] Fifteen million Americans crossed county lines in the war years, and eight million traversed state boundaries. Some were servicemen's families following inductees to military bases, often located in the South to take advantage of year-round outdoor weather. Others relocated to war factories in the big manufacturing cities or shipbuilding operations on the coasts.

The West and urban areas were the big gainers in population, and rural farm areas were the big losers (although not financially). California acquired 2.3 million new inhabitants, a remarkable increase of 34 percent. The population of Los Angeles alone grew by 440,000. Hundreds of thousands of people flooded into the Detroit area to work in airplane factories and converted automobile plants. In just two years, between 1940 and 1942, Michigan's population grew by 234,000. Populations in southern seaports also swelled: Mobile, Alabama, by 65 percent; Hampton Roads, Virginia, 45 percent; and Charleston, South Carolina, 38 percent. Even Washington, D.C., beset by new government workers, added 210,000 inhabitants by 1943.[19]

Migrants, especially those moving to the big cities, faced difficult situations. Host locales were unprepared for such enormous population influxes. Housing, hospitals, and schools were woefully inadequate. Families were forced to crowd into single rooms or live in trailers or shantytowns without proper sewage. In 1942, FDR created the National Housing Agency to find and build temporary residences. Urban housing projects, first started in the 1930s, increased during and after the war.[20] There is some evidence, detailed below, that the urban influx and grim living conditions generated crime.

Certainly, family life was difficult in the war years. Dislocations, long separations of husbands and wives, and deaths and injuries in battle contributed to family breakups. Divorce climbed from 16 percent in 1940 to 27 percent in 1944.[21] But, judging by the number of homicide victimizations, spousal abuse did not rise. Female homicide victimization rates, at 2.5 per 100,000 for most of the decade, dropped to 2.1 per 100,000 in 1943 and 1944. Undoubtedly, the decline in wife killing was due to the same factor that had increased divorces: the lengthy separation of spouses.[22]

The war years were a pivotal period for African Americans. The mobilization kindled an even more massive migration to urban areas than had occurred in the 1920s (fig. 1.1). Although a great deal of this movement flowed to southern cities, blacks abandoned Dixie in record numbers. Over one-third of young blacks in Alabama, Georgia, Mississippi, and South Carolina went north in the 1940s.[23] The proportion of African Americans living in the South dropped from 77 percent in 1940 to 68 percent in 1950. At the same time, the black population of other regions increased dramatically: up 47 percent in the Northeast, 57 percent in the Midwest, and 234 percent (albeit from a low baseline) in the West.[24]

As wartime jobs opened in metropolitan areas, African American migrants moved there in huge numbers. The remarkable growth in the black population of big cities is depicted in table 1.2. At the same time that blacks moved to cities, they, perforce, abandoned farmwork and joined the urban labor force. In short, the war was changing African Americans from a rural, southern, agricultural people into a metropolitan, multiregional, non–farm working population. Insofar as crime is concerned, the effect was to transport high levels of black violent crime to the big cities of the United States, with profound

Figure 1.1   Black migration from the South, 1900–2000

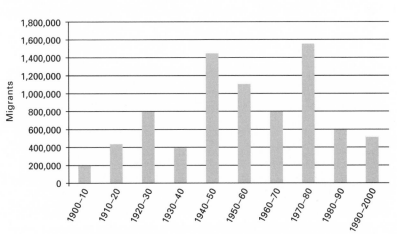

Source: Gregory, *Southern Diaspora*, 330.

consequences for urban black communities and, ultimately, for the entire nation.

Black economic mobility was as significant as geographic mobility. "Blacks not only shared in the rising prosperity of the war and the immediate postwar years," wrote Thernstrom and Thernstrom, "they advanced more rapidly than whites."[25] In fact, the economic gap between the races narrowed more in the 1940s and '50s than in any comparable time since—including the civil rights era. Economists found a decadal increase of 24 percent in the ratio of average weekly wages of blacks to whites. This growth was due to migration to higher-wage regions, to the increase in wages for all low-wage workers, and to the opening to blacks of better-paying positions formerly denied them. These gains were, as was the case of employment for women, less a matter of enlightenment than wartime necessity.

Table 1.2 Black population changes in selected cities, 1940–50

	1940		1950		
	City population	Black population (%)	City population	Black population (%)	Change 1940–50 (%)
New York	458,444	6.1	747,608	9.5	+63
Detroit	149,119	9.2	300,506	16.2	+102
Philadelphia	250,880	13.0	376,041	18.2	+50
Gary, Indiana	20,394	18.3	39,253	29.3	+93
Chicago	277,731	8.2	492,265	13.6	+77
Los Angeles	63,774	4.2	171,209	8.7	+169
San Francisco	4,846	0.8	43,502	5.6	+798
Baltimore	165,843	19.3	225,099	23.7	+36
Washington, D.C.	187,266	28.2	280,803	35.0	+50

Source: U.S. Census Bureau, *Demographic Trends in the 20th Century,* table 8, A-21.

But even after the war, demand for labor remained high, so black economic gains continued into the 1950s.[26]

White racial attitudes hadn't changed much in the 1940s, despite the blatant illogic of warring for freedom overseas while maintaining Jim Crow at home. Only 46 percent of whites surveyed in 1942 opposed separate sections for blacks on streetcars and buses. Eighty-six percent favored racially distinct residential neighborhoods. And only 42 percent said blacks should have the same opportunity as whites to get a job; a majority thought whites should get the first chance at any job opening.[27]

The military reflected prevailing attitudes, reinforced by the disproportionate number of top-ranking officers from Dixie. Both the army and navy were segregated, and initially blacks were barred from the air force and marine corps. Black officers generally were assigned to noncombat units, reducing opportunities for advancement. Black enlisted men usually were given unskilled assignments, such as mess duty or loading and unloading trucks, partly due to bias, but also because black performance on the Army General Classification Test was very poor—the result of inferior education for blacks, especially in the South. Humiliations at military bases were frequent in the South, and the American Red Cross even kept blood plasma from white and black donors separate. This last affront was an especially bitter irony, because the techniques for developing large-scale blood banks were developed by Charles R. Drew, a black physician. Notwithstanding the indignities, over one million African Americans served in the armed forces. Black enrollment, however, was much below that of whites and below the proportion of military-age males in the African American population. While three out of every four white men of service age wore a uniform, only half of black men in the same age category did.[28]

The military experience was a beneficial one for African Americans. Forty-one percent of black soldiers surveyed thought they would be "better off" as a result of service, a figure that jumped to 55 percent for southern blacks with no more than a grade-school education (which was two-thirds of all southern blacks). Only 25 percent of whites said that they would be "better off" when asked the same question. The response of black soldiers appears to have been prescient. A survey of blacks in elite jobs some decades after the war found that 68 percent had had military experience.[29]

Exposure to northern blacks who had little acquaintance with the southern Jim Crow system made southern black soldiers and migrants more assertive. Moreover, northern black servicemen sent to southern bases were outraged at their mistreatment. A spontaneous Double V Campaign—victory at home and abroad—swept through northern black communities. The war thus sparked increased black efforts to achieve equality, efforts encouraged by the First Lady, Eleanor Roosevelt, but not her husband, whose entire focus was on winning the war. When African American labor leader A. Philip Randolph threatened to organize a march on Washington, D.C., FDR, fearing violence and bad press, agreed to issue an executive order barring employment discrimination "in defense industries or government." The order established the Fair Employment Practices Committee, but lack of funding and staff limited its effectiveness.[30]

The combined effect of mass migrations by southerners of both races, more aggressive black demands for equal rights, and the persistent racism of whites, especially in military installations and war industries, helped touch off a series of incidents. There were interracial disturbances in Fayetteville, North Carolina; Mobile, Alabama; and El Paso, Texas; along with twenty-one race-related disturbances or mutinies in southern military facilities.

The bloodiest racial episode was in 1943 in Detroit, where 34 people died, 433 people were injured, and two million dollars' worth of property was destroyed. Details of the riot reveal a lot about wartime conditions and attitudes. In the early 1940s, about 450,000 whites, apparently a good many of them southerners, and 50,000 southern blacks "flooded Detroit for defense work and overtaxed its already inadequate, depression-wracked living conditions and social services."[31] Heightened racial tensions first centered on federally built defense housing, where blacks clashed with Polish Detroiters in 1942, resulting in 220 arrests and 40 injuries. One year later, in early June 1943, racial fighting was sparked by a "hate strike"—a wildcat walkout by white workers at Packard Motor Company to protest the upgrading of black workers to hitherto white jobs, which management undertook in response to pressure from the federal government. Later that month, black youth seeking revenge for the Packard incident provoked fights with whites on Belle Isle, the city's main recreation area. The fighting quickly spread to the mainland. By early the next morning, with wild rumors of atrocities flying around the city, looting erupted in black neighborhoods, and interracial clashes soon ensued. (Detroit thus earns the distinction of having the nation's first "commodity riot," in which the predominant activity is looting and destroying shops.) A subsequent study of arrested black and white rioters found, unsurprisingly, that they were overwhelmingly young males with a median age of 26, but, unexpectedly, that they tended to be longtime residents of the city.[32]

Detroit wasn't the only scene of violence in 1943, which seems to have been a year of racial strife despite widespread enthusiasm for the war. One report tallied 242 racial incidents in forty-seven cities, including a significant riot in Harlem that left six blacks dead and two million dollars in damaged property. The Harlem riot was more a black rampage than interracial violence, as it scarcely involved whites at all. In that respect, it presaged the terrible disturbances of the late 1960s.[33]

Perhaps the strangest of the 1943 incidents was the "zoot suit riot," a series of planned interethnic assaults. A zoot suit was a man's suit with a long full-cut jacket with padded shoulders and wide-legged pegged trousers. The suit was a mark of nonconformity popular with young men of Mexican and Italian extraction as well as blacks; but some people saw it as an unpatriotic waste of scarce material in wartime.

The assaults reflected tension between military personnel who had flooded into Southern California and local residents, in this case, mainly Mexican Americans. Roughly two-thirds of the ethnic Mexicans in Los Angeles were long-term residents of the United States or American citizens, while one-third were temporary residents from Mexico who came to Southern California to work on fruit and vegetable farms. (For this discussion, both will be referred to as "Mexicans.")

The incidents began with several acts of harassment of sailors from a nearby naval training school who frequented the bars and shops of downtown Los Angeles during shore leave. The locals, mainly young Mexicans sporting their zoots, resented the intrusion into their "turf." After several escalating incidents, about fifty sailors, determined to teach the Mexicans a lesson, marched downtown and accosted zoot suiters wherever they saw them, tearing off their clothes and leaving them bruised and humiliated. Over the next week, military men, nearly all white, swarmed into Los Angeles, attacking and stripping zoot suiters, while the local police, claiming lack of jurisdiction, ignored the assaults. The incidents ended when the military command terminated shore leaves. No deaths or serious injuries were reported.[34]

One who recalls the sharply escalating racial disturbances and soaring violent crime of the late 1960s and early 1970s may think the two social phenomena are related. And perhaps they are. But before we draw any such conclusion, we must examine in detail crime during the war years.

VIOLENT CRIME IN THE 1940s

During the second half of the 1930s, violent crime had declined sharply. The decade had begun with homicide rates above 9 per 100,000 and closed with rates just above 6. The decline from 1930 to 1939 was over 30 percent.

For the 1940s, the overall picture is as follows. The first half of the decade, dominated by the war, continued with the same relatively low violent crime rate of the late 1930s. When the war ended and the servicemen returned home, violent crime spiked, but the increase to 6.4 per 100,000 homicides in 1946 was short-lived, and the decade ended as it had begun, with modest rates (fig. 1.2).[35]

Other crimes of violence—dominated by robbery and aggravated assault, the most frequent violent offenses—present a pattern comparable to that of homicide, except that their rates remained elevated in the postwar years (fig. 1.3).[36]

Still, *elevated* is a relative term, and violent crime was not a national menace at any time during the 1940s. Indeed, by looking at homicide rates for 109 years, we find that the entire decade (even with the postwar spike) was part of a homicide trough, a great crime slide that began in the mid-1930s and ended in the late 1960s (fig. 1.4).

As for the end-of-war upsurge, criminologists are confident that males under the age of 35 are responsible for the vast bulk

Figure 1.2 Homicide victimization rates, 1940–49

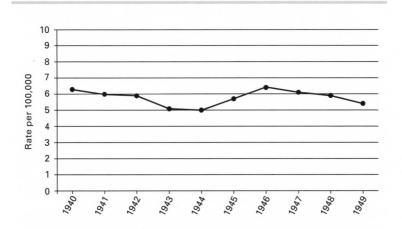

Source: U.S. Department of Justice, Bureau of Justice Statistics, "Homicide Rate Trends."

Figure 1.3 Four violent crimes known to police, rate per 100,000, 1940–49

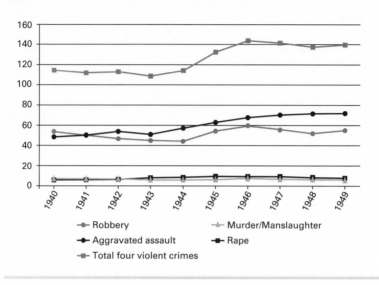

Source: U.S. Office of Management and Budget, *Social Indicators, 1973*, table 2/1, 64.

of violent crimes, and given that millions of that very group of young men demobilized when the war ended in 1945, the cause of the spike seems obvious. In 1945, there were 11.4 million Americans (overwhelmingly young men) in the armed forces, but by 1946, the figure had dropped to 3.4 million, and declined even further in 1947 to 1.6 million.[37] Given the massive size and rapidity of the demobilization, an increase in violent crime seems inevitable.

With so many firearms-trained young men returning from the battlefield, guns may be expected to have played a significant part in the violent crime rise. "The gun culture . . . flowered spectacularly in the years following World War II," two experts observed, "[there being] considerable pent-up demand in a civilian market that had been neglected for nearly a decade." Moreover, they added, "Some twelve million men had received military training and [had] some familiarity with firearms, and

Figure 1.4 Homicide victimization rates, 1900–2013

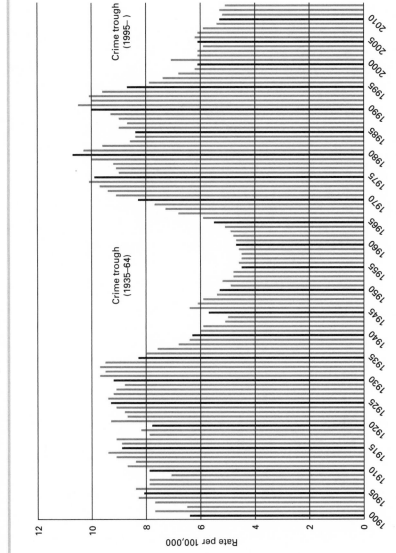

Sources: For 1900–1932, see Eckberg, "Estimates of Early Twentieth-Century U.S. Homicide Rates," 13. For 1933–2013, see U.S. Department of Justice, Bureau of Justice Statistics, "Homicide Rate Trends"; National Center for Health Statistics, *Deaths: Preliminary Data for 2009*, table 2, 43.

many of them returned to civilian life with a continuing interest in weaponry."[38]

Firearm homicides did rise at the end of the war (as did homicides in general), but they quickly leveled off. Furthermore, when we examine the proportion of homicides attributable to guns, we find that the postwar years were less the launch of a new era of gun warfare and more a return to "normalcy." The percentages of gun killings had dropped during the war years (1942–44), undoubtedly because weapons were channeled to the military campaign. But when the percentage of firearms homicides increased during and immediately after demobilization, it rose merely to prewar levels (fig. 1.5 and table 1.3). In other words, the sudden availability of guns and men to fire them had no lasting effect on postwar homicide rates.[39]

We must add a word on juvenile delinquency, which had become a multinational concern during the war years. The FBI's Uniform Crime Reports provide arrest data by age, and the results for violent crimes show a steady upward trend in juvenile

Figure 1.5   Firearm homicide rates, 1940–49

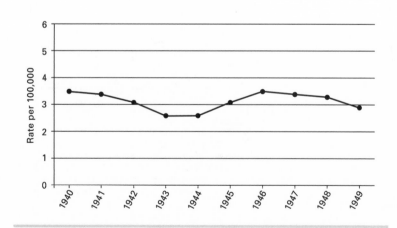

Source: National Center for Health Statistics, *Vital Statistics*, table 65, 594, 603.

Table 1.3 Firearm homicides, 1940–49

	All homicides (total)	Firearm homicides (total)	Firearm homicides (% of total homicides)	Firearm homicides (rate per 100k)
1940	8,208	4,655	56.7	3.5
1941	7,929	4,525	57.1	3.4
1942	7,743	4,204	54.3	3.1
1943	6,690	3,444	51.5	2.6
1944	6,553	3,449	52.6	2.6
1945	7,412	4,029	54.4	3.1
1946	**8,784**	**4,966**	**56.5**	**3.5**
1947	8,555	4,922	57.5	3.4
1948	8,536	4,894	57.3	3.3
1949	7,904	4,235	53.6	2.9
Average	7,831	4,332	55.15	3.14

Sources: U.S. Department of Commerce, Bureau of the Census, *Vital Statistics of the United States: 1940*, part I, table xi, 32; *1941*, part I, table xi, 32; *1942*, part I, table 2, 102. Federal Security Agency, U.S. Public Health Service, *Vital Statistics of the United States, 1943*, part I, table 4, 146. U.S. Department of Commerce, Bureau of the Census, *Vital Statistics of the United States, 1944*, part I, table 7, 88; *1945*, part I, table 4, 51; *1946*, part I, table 5, 108; *1947*, part I, table 5, 114; *1948*, part I, table 5, 116; *1949*, part I, table 6, 106.

Figure 1.6   Arrests for violent crimes, persons under age 18, 1940–49

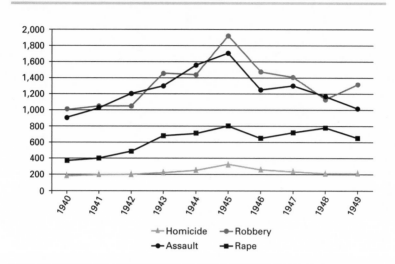

Sources: Federal Bureau of Investigation, *Crime in the United States*, Uniform Crime Reports: 1940 (table 56, 111, table 72, 143, table 93, 207); 1941 (table 55, 122, table 92, 205); 1942 (table 40, 89); 1943 (table 38, 92); 1944 (table 39, 96); 1945 (table 45, 117); 1946 (table 45, 121); 1947 (table 46, 119); 1948 (table 47, 117); 1949 (table 47, 115).

arrests from the first half of the decade to a peak in 1945, followed by a downturn during the rest of the decade (fig. 1.6).

The most obvious explanation is that the turmoil of the war years, when fathers went off to war and families were dislocated, was unsettling for youth. This is speculation, of course, but the simultaneous rise in delinquency in war-torn Europe tends to support the hypothesis and so does the postwar decline in juvenile violence in the United States. Criminologist Thorsten Sellin, who lived through the period, described the effect on youth.

> Many children were deprived of the supervision that their fathers or older brothers would ordinarily have given them. Other youngsters worked in war plants and received wages that were fantastic by peacetime standards. They

had the money, and they thought they had the right, to amuse themselves in any way they saw fit. Many children quit school at the earliest possible moment to try for some of the "big money" and thereby were exposed to temptations they would not otherwise have encountered.[40]

Juvenile rates of violence hint at a bigger issue. They rose throughout the war years, when homicide and other violent crime rates for adults were flat or declining. This suggests that the domestic crime picture may have been more nuanced than is indicated by figures for the entire country. For instance, those adult males who were not in the armed forces may have been committing crimes at higher rates than is apparent from the nationwide figures, but their offenses were masked by rate reductions attributable to military enlistments. It seems likely that a portion of those men rejected by the military had criminal records and repeated their offenses.

By looking at state and city rates, we get a better picture of crime on the home front. A perceptive article by sociologist Austin L. Porterfield found that when comparing rates of serious crimes in 1943 to rates from the prewar years 1937 to 1939, serious crime declined in 31 states but rose by double digits in 13 other states. Significantly, the states that suffered the crime growth also experienced a population increase of nearly 3.2 million people, while the other 31 states lost over 1 million people. In Porterfield's words, the high-crime states "experienced an influx of population from other states great enough to overcome the absence of young men in the military."[41]

In table 1.4, states are ranked in ascending order by an index of crime, indicating the percentage in 1943 of each state's prewar (1937–39) crime rate and population. For example, North Dakota's 1943 crime rate declined to 55 percent of its prewar rates, and its 1943 population declined to 84 percent of its prewar numbers. But note the 13 states at the bottom of the table, starting with Louisiana. All of these states suffered 10 percent

Table 1.4 Serious crime and population changes, by state, ranked by index of shift in crime, 1937–39 to 1943

	Crime	Population		Crime	Population
North Dakota	55	84	Wisconsin	93	97
Minnesota	59	93	Alabama	95	103
Iowa	59	92	Washington	95	121
Idaho	71	98	South Dakota	96	89
Tennessee	71	103	Connecticut	96	105
Montana	75	88	New Hampshire	94	105
Florida	76	132	Virginia	100	117
Kentucky	79	97	South Carolina	100	107
West Virginia	80	94	*United States*	*102*	*103*
Georgia	80	103	Missouri	103	99
Kansas	80	97	Arizona	107	149
Massachusetts	80	98	Louisiana	111	111
North Carolina	82	105	Rhode Island	114	107
Pennsylvania	83	96	Nebraska	115	93
New York	83	95	Colorado	102	104
New Jersey	84	102	Maine	124	97
Arkansas	84	97	Michigan	125	108
New Mexico	85	104	Maryland	126	118
Ohio	87	100	California	126	125
Oklahoma	89	93	Oregon	130	117
Illinois	89	98	Delaware	138	107
Vermont	89	92	Mississippi	150	105
Wyoming	90	104	Nevada	153	136
Texas	91	111	Utah	154	119
Indiana	92	100			

Source: Porterfield, "Decade of Serious Crimes," 47.

or higher *increases* in crime along with, in most cases, rising populations. (The populations of Nebraska and Maine did not increase.) This supports the hypothesis that the war migration host states experienced crime upturns even in the face of flat or declining nationwide rates.[42] (See figure 1.3 for nationwide crime rates during the 1940s.)

To further test Porterfield's hypothesis, wartime crime rates in California and Michigan (in particular, the cities of Los Angeles, Detroit, and Ypsilanti), which absorbed sizeable population increases, are examined. California seems to have grown more than any other state during the war years, gaining an astonishing 2.4 million people for an increase of 34 percent. Los Angeles grew over 14 percent from 1940 to 1945 and 27 percent by the decade's end. Detroit's gains—7 percent by mid-decade and 12.5 percent by 1949—are almost unimpressive by comparison.

Detroit gives qualified support to the hypothesis that wartime migration increased crime. As figure 1.7 shows, homicides rose in 1943 and then remained fairly level at a modestly high rate in excess of 6 per 100,000. Note that the spike occurred in 1943, the year of race riots in Detroit, Harlem, and other parts of the country. It is possible that the racial tension encouraged crime, but the spike is likely explained by the inclusion of the thirty-four riot deaths (not ordinary crimes) in Detroit's homicide count. Of course, the large migration to Detroit of white and black southerners played an important part in that city's violence. Nevertheless, one might consider Detroit a special case because of the riot and not satisfactory proof that wartime migration in general raised crime rates.[43]

Ypsilanti, Michigan, which experienced high wartime growth and concurrent crime increases, suffered no riot as did Detroit. But a long-term study noted one effect of the war: a nearly sixfold increase in arrest rates. Arrest rates per 100,000 skyrocketed during the war years to 10,804, declining to 4,764 during the postwar period from 1946 to 1955. Nearly 47 percent

Figure 1.7   Homicide victimization rates, Detroit, 1940–49

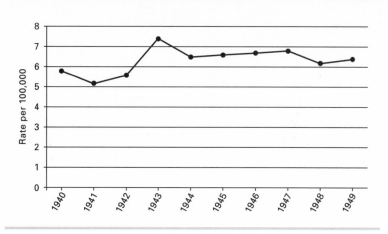

Source: Boudouris, "Trends in Homicide," table 14, 137.
   Note: Rates calculated by author.

of those arrested were born in another state, and almost 60 percent of that out-of-state group hailed from the South. Unfortunately, we do not know how many of these arrests for "assorted crimes" were for acts of violence. So while it seems apparent that crime in Ypsilanti increased during the war years, we cannot count this as proof that *serious* crime rose.[44]

The West Coast situation also provides partial support for Porterfield's thesis. In California, in the face of the explosive population growth, homicide rates rose steadily after 1943 and did not decline until 1948; nevertheless, they remained at or below the national average in each of those years (fig. 1.8). In Los Angeles, rates climbed after 1944 and, despite a dip in 1946, exceeded both state and national figures (fig. 1.9). Once again, the evidence suggests that the huge population influx brought with it violent crime.

The huge absorption of young males into the military probably would have reduced violent crime even more than the national data indicate had there not been countervailing forces

Figure 1.8 Homicide victimization rates,
California and United States, 1940–49

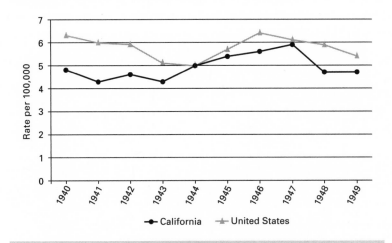

Source: U.S. Department of Justice, Bureau of Justice Statistics, "Homicide Rate Trends";
National Center for Health Statistics, *Vital Statistics*, table 66, 662.

Figure 1.9 Homicide victimization rates,
Los Angeles and United States, 1940–49

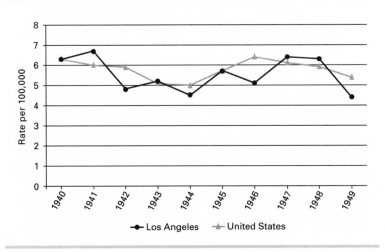

Source: Monkkonen, "Homicide in Los Angeles"; U.S. Department
of Justice, Bureau of Justice Statistics, "Homicide Rate Trends."

pushing rates up. The Porterfield data and the juvenile arrest results testify to that and, to a lesser extent, so do the California and Los Angeles homicide rates.

AFRICAN AMERICAN CRIME DURING THE WAR

For African Americans, the 1940s was a period of expanding migration, increasing employment and earnings, and growing demands for greater equality. Given improved conditions and better opportunities—there was virtually full employment during the war years—one might have expected a significant crime decline. And, in fact, there was a decline in black homicide victimizations, but it was a downturn that had begun in the middle of the 1930s and had continued, as it had for whites, into the early 1940s. As is obvious from figure 1.10, the problem was that black homicide rates, decline notwithstanding, were more than ten times higher than rates for white homicides—a situation that would persist for decades.

Figure 1.10 Homicide victimization rates, males, by race, 1940–49

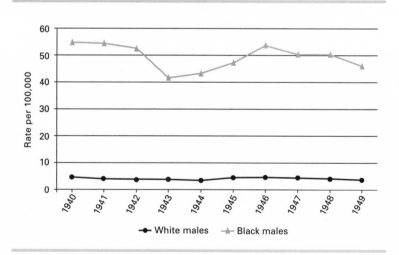

Source: National Center for Health Statistics, *Vital Statistics*, table 63, 540, 541.

Table 1.5   Homicide victimization rates, males, by race, 1940–70

	1940	1950	1960	1970
Black (rate per 100k)	54.4	47.0	42.3	78.2
White (rate per 100k)	4.9	3.8	3.9	7.2
Black/white ratio	11.1	12.4	10.9	10.9

Sources: Data for 1940, without age adjustment: National Center for Health Statistics, "Death Rates by Age," table 2; data for 1950–70, with age adjustment: National Center for Health Statistics, *Health, United States, 2006,* table 45.

Table 1.5 shows the persistence of the racial divide in homicides over a forty-year period. A comparably wide gap existed in the 1920s, when black rates were approximately seven times those of whites, and in the 1930s, when there was a roughly eightfold difference. Clearly, the war did nothing to alter the relative standing of blacks and whites with respect to murder.[45]

Despite the differences in rates between the races, blacks and whites may have had similar responses to common influences. Figure 1.11 plots white and black homicides on two different *y* axes, clearly showing corresponding oscillations. Note that both rates declined in the early 1940s, presumably reflecting the military buildup. Likewise, both manifested a postwar spike followed by a downturn as the decade ended. The message here is that despite marked differences in the magnitude of violent crime between racial groups, both blacks and whites seemed to be influenced by certain shared experiences, namely the full-throttled mobilization for war.

In the long term, however, the magnitude of black violence combined with enormous migration rekindled by the war had the profoundest impact on the United States. As African Americans continued their northward and westward trek throughout the 1940s, the demography of crime began to change. Previously, black residence and therefore black violence was overwhelmingly a southern phenomenon, and southern

Figure 1.11 Homicide victimization rates, males, ages 25–34, by race, 1940–49

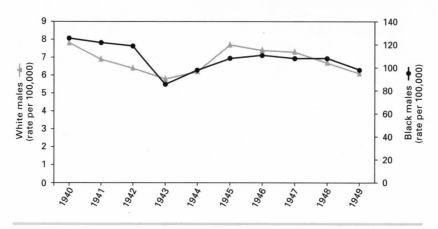

Source: National Center for Health Statistics, "Death Rates by Age, Race, and Sex," table 2.

cities, with their outsized black populations, had the highest homicide rates in the nation. Starting in the 1940s, however, the southern model of urban homicide—with its enormous black-on-black rates—began to morph into a nationwide archetype. Several city-level studies of the period drive home the point.

Take Birmingham, Alabama, for example. The 1940 population of Birmingham was over 267,000, and roughly 40 percent of it was black. An examination of coroner's files uncovered 500 homicide victims in the city between 1937 and 1944. An astonishing 427 of those killed (85.4 percent) were black. What is more, 418 of the killers (84.9 percent) were African American.[46] For southern cities, which had large black populations, this was old news. The same phenomenon had manifested in Memphis and other cities in the South during the 1920s. But for northern urban areas before the war, with relatively small numbers of black residents, such figures would have been impossible. By the 1940s, however, black migration was changing the demography of the North. Blacks were becoming sizeable minorities in many of the big northern cities, and the proportion of black homicides in these cities was rising rapidly.

Consider these northern urban homicide figures from the war and immediate postwar period.[47]

- In Saint Louis, Missouri, an "almost southern" city, African Americans accounted for less than 18 percent of the 1950 population. In 1949, a year earlier, African Americans had comprised an astonishing 81 percent of the city's homicide victims. Ninety-five percent of the perpetrators in these black victim cases were African Americans.[48]

- In Cleveland, Ohio, which was 16 percent black, African Americans were the victims in 70.6 percent of the felonious homicide cases from 1947 to 1953. Whites were accused in 6 of these cases; blacks, in 320 of them.[49]

- In New York City during the 1940s, the black population and black homicide victimization rose in tandem, 55 and 53 percent, respectively. By the end of the decade, African Americans were a mere 6 percent of the city but were nearly 60 percent of those killed through acts of violence.[50]

- In Detroit, at the start of the 1940s, blacks were about 9 percent of the population and 50 percent of its homicide victims. By decade's end, they were 16 percent of the residents and 72 percent of the victims.[51]

Thus, notwithstanding the advantages of the North—the freer environment, the greater earnings, the potential for education, and the job opportunities created by the war—African American homicides in southern and nonsouthern locations continued to occur at shockingly high rates. As a consequence, the face of urban violent crime throughout the United States was changing: it was becoming increasingly black.

We can see this clearly as we look back at the 1940s, but at the time, it was shrugged off. The reasons for the indifference are threefold. First, violent crime was not very high by American standards; indeed, it was relatively low and part of the great crime trough shown in figure 1.4. Second, Americans were enjoying post-Depression prosperity and were fixated on winning the war. Violent crime was low on the agenda. Third, whites were not terribly exercised by black victimization. So long as the assaults took place within the black urban enclaves, whites were indifferent. Within a few decades, however, these restraining circumstances would change dramatically—crime would go through the roof, and blacks would menace whites in increasing numbers—and the nation would declare a "war on crime."

WAR AND VIOLENT CRIME

Analysts have not successfully generalized about the relationship between war and crime. American sociologist Pitirim Sorokin concluded that there probably are no universal generalizations, because, for one thing, wars vary immensely. Some are protracted, dragging on for many years, and others are brief. Some, such as World War II, require maximum mobilization of a society's manpower and economic resources, and others, such as recent U.S. conflicts in Iraq and Afghanistan, may be conducted with volunteer armies and only minor economic and social strains. Wars fought on home territory, such as the U.S. Civil War, may have a different impact on crime than those conducted entirely overseas. Military engagements may be popular, as was World War II, creating a sense of national pride and purpose. Or they may generate protests and domestic turmoil, as did the U.S. war in Vietnam. Finally, whether or not the outcome of a war is successful for a country may be highly significant, as it could determine the very nature of the postwar governing regime as well as the boundaries of the nation.[52]

The problem is even more complex than specifying precisely the nature of the military conflict. Not only do wars vary, but the impact on crime of different war-related phenomena—from armed forces mobilization to economic and political mobilization—also varies. For one thing, the effects seem to differ depending on the war and the nations involved. Consequently, analysts often draw contradictory conclusions. As Edwin Sutherland, one of the luminaries of American criminology, noted, "One theory states that war produces an increase in crimes because of the emotional instability of wartime and another states that wars produce a decrease in crimes because of an upsurge of national feeling. One theory states that crimes of violence increase in wartime because of the contagion of violence, and another that they decrease because of the vicarious satiation of the need for violence."[53]

In addition, some of the assumed war-related phenomena, such as economic booms, widespread migrations, and waves of nationalism, also occur in peacetime. A crime upsurge (or decline) during hostilities, therefore, may not have been caused by the war in and of itself, but rather by social conditions triggered by the war—conditions that also occur in times of peace.

Ultimately, the effect war has on crime must be analyzed from the standpoint of the impact of a specific war on a specific nation. Below, the relationship between war and crime in the United States is examined from four different perspectives: 1) armed forces mobilization, especially the widespread induction of young men; 2) home front mobilization to support the war; 3) postwar military demobilization; and 4) the long-term effects of military service. The discussion is limited to major military conflicts, starting with the Civil War.

1. Armed Forces Mobilization

Getting a good fix on crime at the time of the American Civil War (1861–65) is difficult, but the consensus among historians is that the war's vast call to arms reduced criminality.[54] There was a significant decline in the number of civilian prisoners during the war years, but so many young offenders were allowed to enlist instead of going to prison that it is unclear whether crime actually went down or army service simply had become the alternative to confinement. Conversely, the incarceration of women and juveniles rose during the war, partly due to an increase in abortion, which was a criminal offense, and perhaps partly due to the departure of fathers, the primary breadwinners, which in turn prompted more theft. Tables 1.6 and 1.7 show incarceration figures in the North with particularly sizeable drops in 1864.[55]

Homicide historian Randolph Roth said that "during the first years of the Civil War homicide rates held steady throughout most of the South," but he added that in the borderland areas from north Texas to Missouri, where the Confederacy was unable

Table 1.6 Total population of prisons in four northern states, 1860–70

	Massachusetts	New York*	Ohio	Michigan†
1860	510	2,662	—	535
1861	520	2,824	924	621
1862	506	2,712	768	531
1863	431	2,300	740	410
1864	377	2,044	624	333
1865	359	1,898	655	292
1866	470	2,537	860	315
1867	537	2,910	1,001	502
1868	546	2,985	—	582
1869	569	2,800	—	622
1870	594	2,698	—	644

Source: Abbott, "Civil War and the Crime Wave," 217.
  * Average number of commitments.
  † Number of convicts in prison at beginning of year.

Table 1.7 Persons committed to prisons in four
northern states, new admissions, 1860–69

	Massachusetts	New Hampshire	Vermont	Pennsylvania
1860	144	—	41	413
1861	197	31	44	295
1862	102	22	42	225
1863	108	22	22	272
1864	79	9	17	223
1865	129	60	31	407
1866	249	45	51	644
1867	247	46	43	—
1868	128	39	29	—
1869	180	32	42	—

Source: Abbott, "Civil War and the Crime Wave," 217.

to establish full control, homicides rose to extremes of 100 to 200 per 100,000 people. Much of this border violence, however, was due to political conflict and not crime in the ordinary sense. The overall picture in both the South and the North suggests that military induction reduced crime during the Civil War.[56]

Moving on to World War I, the induction of young men reduced violent crime in 1918, but that reduction was relatively small when compared to drops in violence during other wars. Note that the First World War was relatively short for the United States (lasting about nineteen months) when compared with the length of the war in Europe, and mobilization involved a smaller percentage of young men (about 52 percent) than were involved in the Civil War or World War II. In addition, wartime prohibition reduced alcohol consumption, making it difficult to disentangle the relative crime-inhibiting effects of induction and prohibition.

Regarding World War II, the claim that the military buildup impacted crime is stronger. Over 72 percent of the male population between ages 20 and 29, an extraordinary figure, were inducted into armed service. Crime declined overall throughout the war years despite some increases due to war-related migrations. Homicide victimization rates went from 6.3 per 100,000 in 1940 to 5 per 100,000 in 1944, for a drop of 21 percent. And rates of violent crimes known to the police declined modestly during the war or held a steady course. Not only did the crime downturn coincide with the military buildup, but demobilization synchronized perfectly with the postwar crime spike. This enormous military conflict makes the strongest case yet for the hypothesis that induction reduces crime.

The Korean War (1950–53) and the Vietnam War (1964–73) are a study in contrasts as far as crime is concerned. First, neither buildup to these wars had the magnitude of the buildup to World War II. Indeed, the two engagements together involved fewer men than were involved in the Second World War, even though the population of the country had increased (thereby diminishing the proportion of the population affected by induction). Over 5.7 million people served in the armed forces during the Korean conflict, and more than 8.7 million served during the Vietnamese; but together they involved 1.65 million fewer American soldiers than in World War II.

Second, homicide rates went in opposite directions during these wars: they held steady during the Korean War, starting at 5.3 per 100,000 and ending at 5.2, and they went steadily up during the Vietnam War, from 5.1 per 100,000 to 9.7. Notably, the Korean War mobilization seems to have produced a brief one-year downturn in violent crime.

Third, there was so much dissension and violent protest in the United States during the Vietnam War—over the appropriateness of the conflict and as part of the black civil rights movement—that the crime-lessening effects of the military buildup, if any, are difficult to discern. Whatever the positive effects might have been, they were swamped by other developments. In short, whereas the military buildup for the Korean conflict might have produced a small crime decline, the impact of mobilization for the war in Vietnam is unclear.[57]

In summary, most American wars reduced crime by removing young males from the civilian population, but the impact appears to have depended on the magnitude of the induction in proportion to the size of the young male population as well as the length of the conflict.

2. Home Front Mobilization

Viewed broadly, home front mobilization encompasses rationing, industry conversion, civilian population migration (to support war production), and what may be called public opinion mobilization (which, in cases of widespread antiwar protest, may be ineffectual).

With respect to the Civil War, we have far too little information to assess the impact of war mobilization. We know that the war touched off a huge draft riot in New York City in 1863, and, as already noted, borderland areas not under the full control of the Confederate government were very bloody. Historian Randolph Roth asserts that such conflicts and divisions increase everyday criminal violence, but that connection requires closer examination (provided in chapter 3). In New York City, incidentally, there was a homicide spike during the Civil War, but it occurred one year *after* the Draft Riot.[58]

Regarding World War I, if we count alcohol prohibition begun during the war as a measure to reserve grain for food, then mobilization probably reduced crime. However, that conclusion is attenuated by the fact that crime went up even though the alcohol ban was extended after the war.

During the Second World War, domestic mobilization had a mixed effect on crime. On the one hand, full employment may have been a crime inhibitor, although this book presents historical evidence that cuts both ways. Roth considers positive fellow feeling and confidence in government to be restraints on crime. Racial conflict notwithstanding, such positive conditions were widespread during the war. On the other hand, as we saw previously, mass migrations to wartime production areas unprepared for such influxes may have increased law-breaking.

Given the post–World War II military resources of the United States and the relatively small size of the conflicts, neither the Korean nor the Vietnam War required full-scale domestic mobilization. Both wars suffered from flagging public support as the conflicts dragged on without clear victory, but loss of public support and protest against the war were far greater during the Vietnamese engagement. Some of the protests were illegal as well as violent, but the relationship between such protests and violent crime of the everyday variety remains uncertain. At least one analyst suggested that the Vietnam War stimulated crime increases by undermining the norms against law-breaking. "Each year," said Raymond Tanter, referring to the Vietnam War era, "brings an increase in the number of crimes committed and also in the rate at which the number is increasing. This may suggest that as the war continues, it facilitates a state of 'normlessness' in which traditional strictures against criminal acts lose their effectiveness."[59]

All told, war mobilization is a wild card. It may reduce crime by putting people to work, taking away their alcohol, or uniting them against a foreign foe. It may, however, encourage crime by stimulating population relocations without proper preparation or by triggering violent opposition to the war itself. And it may do none of the above.

3. Postwar Military Demobilization

Demobilization may cause more crime than is inhibited by troop call-ups. Not only do the young men return, but they sometimes return to housing and job scarcities and social conflicts that are either long-standing or by-products of the war. And veterans come home with greater comfort handling firearms.

At the end of the Civil War, scarcity was hardly the only problem. The Reconstruction South degenerated into near anarchy in several places, and "the surge in homicides," Roth says, "was overwhelmingly the work of former Confederates."[60] Violence wasn't restricted to the South. "Immediately after the establishment of peace there was a great increase in crime and disorder," wrote Edith Abbott, "not only in the South, where conditions were abnormal, but throughout the North as well. And a very large proportion of the new offenders in the northern states were the men who had 'worn the blue.'"[61] The late Eric Monkkonen was skeptical, pointing out that there were no national data to support the proposition that demobilization made crime rise and, in any event, that crime never spiked in New York City.[62]

In 1919, when most of the soldiers who fought in World War I came home, there was a minispike in violent crime, but perhaps the violence would have been worse had there not been an extension of the wartime ban on alcohol. Nationwide mortality rates went from 7.9 per 100,000 in 1918 to 8.2 in 1919, while in Chicago, murder rates jumped to 11.3 per 100,000 in 1919, having been at 8.6 the year before.

In 1945, at the end of World War II, after Germany surrendered in May and Japan capitulated in August, 8 million American soldiers returned to the United States. The following year, another 1.8 million were reunited with their families. It was the biggest demobilization in American history. The average homicide rate, which had been less than 5.7 per 100,000, shot up to 6.4 in 1946, a 12 percent increase. In 1947, the rate declined to 6.1, whereupon it dropped back to a little above 5 per 100,000 as the decade ended. FBI data on violent crimes known to the police told a similar tale, with four types of violent crime spiking in 1946 and remaining at that level for the rest of the decade. The conclusion seems clear: demobilization produced a short-term escalation in violent crime.[63]

The termination of the Korean War, by contrast, seems to

have had no impact on crime rates. Indeed, homicide rates were lower at the end of the war (4.8 per 100,000 in 1953) than at the start (5.3 in 1950). But it must be remembered that this was a relatively small demobilization, mainly because the United States kept troops stationed abroad after the war as part of its Cold War strategy. The Vietnam War ended with much higher homicide rates: they averaged 5.1 per 100,000 in 1964 and ended at 9.7 in 1973. But whether this was attributable to returning troops or to other factors during those turbulent years is a matter of considerable debate.

A multination study by Dane Archer and Rosemary Gartner merits consideration. This study compared prewar and postwar homicide rates for 44 nations (29 belligerents, including the United States, and 15 nonbelligerents) for five-year periods on either side of the two world wars. The authors found that average postwar homicide rates increased (compared with prewar averages) for 19 combatants and decreased for 6, while rates declined for 10 noncombatants and increased for 5. They also observed that many belligerent nations suffered demobilization crime bursts despite massive war losses. For example, homicide rates increased 108 percent in Germany at the end of World War I despite a loss of over 15 percent of the young male population. Archer and Gartner's analysis, which includes the United States, gives compelling support to the conclusion that demobilizations may be dangerous—even if only in the short term.[64]

4. Long-Term Effects of Military Service

The United States was terribly fortunate to avoid full-scale warfare at home in armed conflicts subsequent to the the Civil War. By contrast, some of our World War II allies and enemies suffered grievously from warfare on their own soil. Germany, for example, was devastated, with massive numbers of casualties, widows and orphans, and migrants and refugees. Its economy was in ruins—its homeland occupied by foreign armies and divided. For the men who survived, the war was horribly damaging, disrupting their families, schooling, and careers and leaving them without work in the ravaged postwar economy. For Americans, by contrast, the Second World War was by and large a positive experience, and the postwar economic boom along with the G.I. Bill certainly eased the adjustment to peacetime. Any generalizations one makes about war and crime must take into account both the location of the fighting (at home or abroad) and the outcome (victory or defeat).[65]

Sociologists and psychologists have studied the long-term effects of service in the armed forces using the "life course" approach, a perspective that focuses on the behavior of people affected by significant historical events. Glen Elder's work on the Depression and World War II generation pioneered these efforts in postwar scholarship.[66] Nearly all of the work on war and crime has focused on recent U.S. conflicts, beginning with the Vietnam War, undoubtedly because of the paucity of information, especially quantifiable data, for earlier wars. Even the long-term studies by Sheldon and Eleanor Glueck of delinquent boys born between 1924 and 1935 (two-thirds of whom served in World War II, overseas during the postwar period, or in the Korean War) paid little attention to the impact of military service on their subsequent criminal behavior.[67]

As for the relationship between service in Vietnam and crime (and even that has been underexamined), evidence suggests that males with juvenile delinquency records, especially those with serious delinquencies, were more likely to desist from crime if they had served in the military.[68]

For World War II veterans with a history of juvenile delinquency and Depression-era poverty, military service was often a life-changing event. Faced with huge wartime manpower demands, the army was pretty unselective, and it commonly accepted applicants with criminal records or delinquencies.[69] In fact, thousands of prisoners were paroled to the armed services. One study of such parolees found not only a positive adjustment to the military, but also a much lower recidivism rate after service. Eight years after their crimes, these offenders recidivated at a 10.5 percent rate, which was said to be one-sixth the rate of the average parolee at the time.[70]

On the other hand, the delinquent subjects of the Glueck study fared poorly. Over 60 percent of the sample of 500 males with prewar delinquency records faced charges in the military, whereas only 20 percent of the control group with no past delinquencies ran into such trouble. Moreover, 30 percent of the delinquent group received dishonorable discharges, which were rather rare during World War II, compared with 4 percent of the control group. The delinquent group continued to commit crimes into their late forties, but there seem to be no studies correlating military service in World War II with offending.[71]

What we *do* know is that the violent crime trough continued in the United States through the 1950s, when men of the Greatest Generation were most likely to commit crimes. If a male was 18 years old in 1941, when U.S. military recruitment shifted into high gear, he would have reached age 35 in 1958, which means that his most criminogenic years occurred in a time period with some of the lowest homicide rates in the twentieth century. It's a fair inference that such a life-changing event as service in World War II put a lot of these young men on a law-abiding path. If so, this might help to explain the relatively low crime rates that emerged in the 1950s.

Gee, Officer Krupke, we're very upset.
We never had the love that every
Child oughta get.
We ain't no delinquents,
We're misunderstood.
Deep down inside us there is good!

—WEST SIDE STORY

CHAPTER 2

The Golden Years

Violent Crime in the 1950s

INTRODUCTION

To its critics, the 1950s was an age of conformity, of ennui, of embarrassing commercialism. It was a time of rampant suburbanization and a stultifying Red Scare. It began with a hot war in Korea, but an anxiety-inducing Cold War pervaded the entire period. There was insufficient sensitivity to the rights of African Americans (though that would quickly change) and even less concern for the rights of women. But even if the decade's critics were totally correct, a complete picture of the 1950s would still be mixed. For one thing, the economy scarcely could have been better. The gross domestic product soared, and unemployment stayed low the entire time and right through the 1960s. Americans ate better, lived longer, attended school more, and performed less backbreaking labor for more pay than ever before in their history. And to a crime historian, it was a golden age: violent crime in the United States was as low as it would get in the twentieth century. In fact, the crime ebb, measured from the brief spike at the end of

World War II to the surge that commenced in the mid-1960s, lasted eighteen years.

The reasons why crime was so low are not readily apparent. The most obvious explanation—that the healthy economy reduced incentives to criminality—is difficult to square with events before and after the 1950s. We know that crime dropped during the terrible economic downturn of the 1890s, rose exceptionally high in the Roaring Twenties, sank during the last years of the Great Depression, and soared in the midst of the late-1960s boom. If a fizzing economy had been all that was needed to defeat violent crime, the great crime surge of the late 1960s never would have happened. But if the economic boom didn't reduce crime, what did?

HISTORICAL BACKGROUND

Three major historical developments in the 1950s had an enormous impact on the United States for the rest of the twentieth century and beyond. The first was a booming economy and the great affluence it produced. The postwar boom not only eased the historical struggle to provide necessities for oneself and one's family, it also transformed the United States into an overwhelmingly middle-class country in which most of the inhabitants were affluent enough to transcend the quest for necessities and seek ever higher standards of living. The poor, increasingly a minority of the population, came to be seen as a "social problem," one that was becoming associated with African Americans, though the white poor far outnumbered them. Moreover, since middle-class people usually are nonviolent, the crime problem and the poverty problem were fused.

Second, much of America's growth went into, and was at the same time driven by, suburbanization. The suburbs provided the opportunity to own a single-family home on a small plot of land, where the crowds, noise, smells, and dirt of the city could be left behind, and where the neighbors were quiet, hardworking, church-going folks—the new Eden for the burgeoning middle class. Moreover, being thoroughly middle-class, suburbs were low-crime zones, leaving the inner cities as increasingly dangerous centers of lawlessness.

The third development was the continuing migration of southern rural blacks to big cities in- and outside the South, which, combined with the middle-class and overwhelmingly white urban flow to the suburbs, left America's central cities increasingly African American. The violence that had long been a problem for the black lower class—especially for its black lower-class victims—was becoming an urban dilemma throughout the United States. In the late 1960s, the situation would, quite literally, explode. But in the 1950s, black homicide rates declined, while white rates held steady. Ominously, however, African American homicide death rates remained ten times those of whites, a state of affairs that continued up until the 1980s.[1]

RISE OF THE MIDDLE CLASS

Of the myriad statistics that could be brought to bear on the impact of the economic boom, one in particular captures the growth of the American middle class.[2] In 1947, just after the end of the war, 57 percent of American families earned less than $5,000 a year, and nearly half of those families were taking in less than a paltry $3,000 (fig. 2.1). Only 22 percent of 1947 families had annual incomes exceeding $7,000. Just thirteen years later, in 1960, these figures were dramatically different. At the low end (under $5,000 a year), the proportion dropped to 36 percent of families, whereas in the $7,000-plus category, the proportion nearly doubled, to 43 percent. The United States, in short, had become a middle-class country.[3]

If we look at poverty figures (defined by the Census Bureau as family income below some low threshold adjusted for inflation), we see another extraordinary change during the postwar period. The proportion of persons in poverty in the United States declined by over 45 percent in the decade ending in 1959 and

Figure 2.1 U.S. family income, by income category, 1947 and 1960

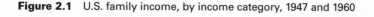

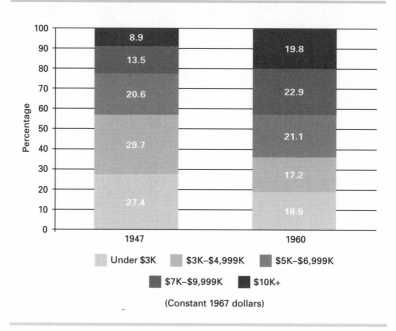

Source: U.S. Department of Commerce, Bureau of the Census, *Historical Statistics,* part 1, series G 16–30, 290.

dropped by an amazing 64 percent between 1949 and 1969. The proportion of the population in poverty, which had been 40.5 percent in 1949, stood at only 14.4 percent twenty years later.[4]

"Class" is often defined not only by income or wealth but also by the nature of work and level of education. These additional criteria provide more evidence that the American middle class was rapidly expanding. In the late 1940s, nearly half the U.S. workforce toiled in demanding manual labor jobs on farms and construction sites or in factories and mines.[5] But by 1960, over 46 percent of the employed were engaged in white-collar work, and fewer than 8 percent worked in agriculture. Among whites in 1960, six times as many held white-collar positions as did farmwork. Even among African Americans, white-collar work was growing in importance: in

1964, it accounted for nearly 19 percent of all black workers.[6] Likewise, white ethnics, such as Italian Americans, who had been slow to move up the occupational ladder, shared fully in the new prosperity. A study in the early 1960s found that 48 percent of the Italian American respondents held white-collar jobs compared with only 26 percent of their parents.[7] "Today," wrote Glazer and Moynihan in 1963, "the grand-children of the [Italian] immigrants are moving into the professions and higher white-collar fields."[8]

As for education, public-school spending in the United States skyrocketed from $48 per pupil in 1948 to $112 per pupil in 1960, a 133 percent increase. More 17-year-olds than ever were graduating from high school: over 63 percent received diplomas in 1960, which was up from 53 percent in 1948. And the G.I. Bill sparked a major leap in college education in the United States. Just after World War II, fewer than 15 percent of young adults were enrolled in post–secondary degree programs, but by 1960, over 22 percent of 18- to 24-year-olds were enrolled—a 51 percent jump.[9]

The implications for crime of such remarkable changes in the country's class structure are examined at the end of the chapter. In the meantime, here is a question to ponder: If violent crime is committed overwhelmingly by the lower class, then shouldn't it have declined simply by dint of the reduction in the size of that stratum?

SUBURBANIZATION

This brings the discussion to the second great development of the 1950s: suburbanization. Moving to the outer reaches of cities was nothing new in the United States. In the late nineteenth century, newly developed electric streetcars enabled the upper classes and then the "older" German and Irish immigrants to leave the city center for the more desirable environment on the urban periphery. In the vacuum left behind, more recent immigrants and the early black migrants packed into the wooden shanties and tenements near the waterfront and factories at which they worked. Gradually, the modern metropolis developed, and with it came new opportunities for crime. Robbery and larceny were facilitated by suburban commuters who, laden with cash and valuables, headed to the central city to work, and by the new urban downtown, with its tempting array of goods on display in the newly invented department store.

What was different in the mid-twentieth century was the enormous size of the suburb-bound population and the transportation technology that enabled it, namely, the automobile. Cities expanded farther than ever before beyond their urban cores. The consequence of that expansion was that the inner city became the new epicenter for violent misconduct.

The automobile, in many ways, was the key component of both the economic expansion and suburbanization. Americans, now enjoying postwar prosperity, were hungry for new cars and other consumer goods. Oil was cheap and plentiful in the 1950s, and new-car sales skyrocketed from 2.1 million in 1946 (when industry was still converting from war to peace production) to 6.7 million in 1950 and 7.9 million in 1955. General Motors and Ford completely dominated the market, and foreign-made vehicles were rare. A new car sold for around $1,300, or 40 percent of the median annual family income. One car per household was now commonplace, as indicated by the fact that as early as 1950, 59 percent of families owned an automobile. Within five years, the figure was 70 percent.[10]

Automobiles stimulated road building, another vital development in the exodus to the suburbs. The move to the 'burbs, in turn, triggered a huge residential housing construction boom. The federal government promoted both the highway and the housing surges. It subsidized road building through the Federal-Aid Highway Act of 1956, which created a national network of highways. And it financed new-home purchases by making mortgage loans through the Federal Housing Administration (FHA) and the Veterans Administration (V.A.). The federal income tax also encouraged home buying by allowing a deduction for the interest on a loan.[11]

A crucial role in the great suburbanization was played by entrepreneurs such as the Levitt brothers, who figured out how to mass-produce homes on vast suburban tracts. Derided for their cookie-cutter sterility, the Levittowns and other new suburbs gave millions of Americans exactly what they wanted: new, well-built, and affordable homes in a quiet landscaped space with neighbors just like themselves. The home-building boom boosted the economy and further accelerated the massive movement to the suburbs. By 1960, one-quarter of all homes in the United States had been built during the decade just ended, and 11 million of the 13 million homes constructed between 1948 and 1958 were located in suburbs. Eighty-three percent of the population growth in the United States was suburban, and by 1960, one-third of all Americans lived in suburbs.[12]

The suburbs seemed ideal for families, and the postwar era saw a big surge in marriage, also part of the bourgeoisification of America. In 1900, six out of every ten young men between the ages of 25 and 34 were married; in 1940, the figure had risen to seven out of ten. But in the 1950s and '60s, roughly 80 percent of all young men were married. Marriage, children, the suburbs, and higher incomes all combined to reduce the population at risk for violent crime. As one expert put it, "Families constrain violent and disorderly male behavior."[13]

As with all big social changes, there were winners and losers. Beneficiaries of the suburban boom were the automotive and allied industries, suburban shopping malls (over 4,000 were built by the late 1950s), and construction businesses. The big losers were the cities, especially their downtown retail districts, and also their municipal services, such as transit systems, which were funded by an eroding urban tax base.[14] The loss of financial support occurred at the same time that lower-status populations heavily dependent on municipal services, including large numbers of African Americans, continued to flood into cities.

BLACK URBANIZATION

While whites were moving to suburbs, the African American exodus to urban areas, originally stimulated by war production in the 1940s, continued. Over 1.1 million blacks moved out of the South into predominantly urban areas in the 1950s. Given that even poorly educated blacks earned 55 percent more per year in the North than in the South, continuing migration was understandable. Confined to low-paying farmwork in Dixie, blacks had a lot of catching up to do, and the economic gap between white and black workers, while narrowing, remained significant. For instance, annual wages for black males in 1960 were 58 percent of those of white males.

Still, measuring from the black economic position before the war, the gains were phenomenal. In 1940, 10 percent of black men held a white-collar or skilled manual-labor job; by 1960, 23 percent did. Earnings for black males, up 75 percent in the 1940s, rose another 45 percent in the 1950s, bringing salaries to 250 percent of their prewar level. Even white earnings didn't rise as steeply. Thirty-eight percent of black dwellings were owner-occupied in 1960, while only 23 percent had been in 1940. Life expectancy rose by 10.5 years, and, as Thernstrom and Thernstrom observed, the quality of life for African Americans improved in myriad ways.

> More dollars meant better housing and clothing, better diets, greater access to medical care—a variety of material comforts previously far out of the reach of most black Americans. The shift from sharecropper or farm laborer to factory worker also meant shorter hours, less sheer drudgery, and much greater freedom to engage in social and political activity. It was the equivalent of being liberated from serfdom.[15]

At the bottom of the ladder, the proportion of black male household heads in poverty also shrank in the 1950s—by over 35 percent—but the income gap between whites and blacks grew larger as the white poverty class dwindled even faster than the black (table 2.1).[16]

In terms of African American conditions in the 1950s, there were two flies in the ointment: unemployment and residential segregation. Starting in the mid-1950s, black unemployment grew in absolute terms relative to that of whites (fig. 2.2). A principal reason, ironically, was the movement out of the South, where black employment was high (and wages low), into northern manufacturing jobs, where the pay was much higher but job security was precarious. The employment gap grew even greater after the 1960s, but the reasons for that and the consequences are matters for chapter 3.[17]

Table 2.1 Male household heads in poverty, by race, ages 25 to 64

	1949	1959	1969
Black (%)	70.8	45.7	21.5
White (%)	31.3	12.9	6.0
Black/white ratio	2.26	3.54	3.58

Source: Ross, Danziger, and Smolensky, "Level and Trend of Poverty," 591.

Note: Income calculations include self-employment income, interest, dividends, rent, and income from government programs.

The other problem was the explosive growth in urban communities of low-income blacks. This was, of course, a "problem" only from certain perspectives. From the standpoint of the long hard climb out of virtual serfdom in the South, the urbanization and "northernization" of African Americans must be seen in a very positive light. It fostered history-making socioeconomic and civil rights advances. But violent crime is what concerns us here, and from that perspective, the growing lower-class black population in America's biggest cities proved to be a disaster. It laid the foundation for the new urban crime problem—indeed, the biggest crime problem to face Americans since the 1920s.

Only a few contemporary observers recognized the inner-city issue. One was Morton Grodzins (1917–64), longtime professor of political science at the University of Chicago. In 1958,

Figure 2.2   Unemployment, by race, 1948–60

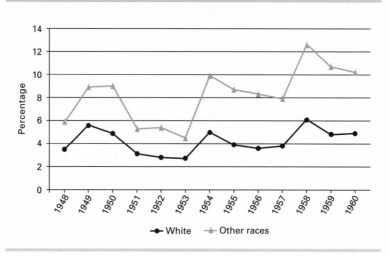

Source: U.S. Department of Commerce, Bureau of the Census, *Historical Statistics*, part I, series D 87–101, 135.

Grodzins published *The Metropolitan Area as a Racial Problem*, in which he deplored that nothing was being done to address "what is likely to be the nation's most pressing social problem," namely that "many central cities of the great metropolitan areas of the United States are fast becoming lower-class, largely Negro slums."[18] Grodzins not only nailed the demographics, he predicted most of the fallout as well. "Continued Negro migration, the comparatively greater rate of natural increase among non-whites, and the exodus of whites to the suburbs," Grodzins observed, "will dramatically raise the proportion of non-whites in central cities."[19] His demographic data, based on information from the 1940s, are updated in table 2.2, and the numbers speak for themselves.

Of course, the residential racial divide was not solely the product of black in-migration. As fast as African Americans moved to the cities, whites raced to the suburbs. In fact, as demographers later demonstrated, white migration out of the cities played a bigger role in enlarging the percentage of urban nonwhites than did black migration into the cities.[20]

It would be erroneous to explain the vast suburbanization process as solely, or even primarily, a product of antiblack attitudes, but white racial bias or fear of blacks did play a big part in the "blackening" of the central cities. Whites did not want to live in neighborhoods with blacks or, in some cases, with a certain number of blacks, which Grodzins presciently identified as the neighborhood tipping point. Even this attitude wasn't entirely based on race prejudice. As black neighborhoods spiraled downward, whites began to associate African Americans with community disorder. "These very conditions of life in the

Table 2.2 Black population changes, ten largest U.S. cities (1960 ranking), 1950–60

	1950		1960		
	Black population	% of total population	Black population	% of total population	% change 1950–60
New York	747,608	9.5	1,087,931	14.0	+45.5
Chicago	492,265	13.6	812,637	22.9	+65.1
Los Angeles	171,209	8.7	334,916	13.5	+95.6
Philadelphia	376,041	18.2	529,240	26.4	+40.7
Detroit	300,506	16.2	482,223	28.9	+60.5
Baltimore	225,099	23.7	325,589	34.7	+44.6
Houston	124,766	20.9	215,037	22.9	+72.4
Cleveland	147,847	16.2	250,818	28.6	+69.7
Washington, D.C.	280,803	35.0	411,737	53.9	+46.6
St. Louis	153,766	17.9	214,377	28.6	+39.4

Source: U.S. Census Bureau, *Historical Census Statistics on Population Totals by Race, 1790 to 1990, and by Hispanic Origin, 1970 to 1990, for Large Cities and Other Urban Places in the United States* (2005).

predominantly Negro neighborhoods," said Grodzins, "lead the larger population to resist the expansion of Negro residential areas. The racial attribute—skin color—is added to the social attributes of lower class behavior."[21]

But whether a product of racism or some other motivation, the result was the same. White urbanites tried to maintain their own racially segregated neighborhoods within cities, or they packed up and headed to the suburbs. The growing black city population, which had to find housing somewhere, kept pushing outward the boundaries of the largely monoracial black communities. Even the more successful blacks, those who had entered the ranks of the middle class, were confined to all-black (or nearly so) urban neighborhoods, as it was clear that they would not be welcome in the suburbs. A comment on this matter by the leading suburban developer speaks volumes. "If we sell one house to a Negro family," William Levitt explained, "then 90 or 95 percent of our white customers will not buy into the community. That is their attitude, not ours. . . . As a company our position is simply this: we can solve a housing problem, or we can try to solve a racial problem, but we cannot combine the two."[22] Consequently, big-city black neighborhoods kept growing in population and area, often with a middle-class black buffer zone in between the poor black and adjacent white sectors.

Grodzins foresaw many of the consequences of the growth of black urban neighborhoods.

- "Within the cities the first result is a spreading of slums." (Grodzins didn't define "slum," but he stressed dilapidated and crowded housing, lack of amenities, rowdiness, "casual and competitive sexuality," "readiness for combat," disease, crime, and family instability.[23])

- As middle-class whites move out of cities, interracial tensions will increase, because the remaining whites

will be less racially tolerant.[24] (Grodzins didn't foresee
another exacerbating factor: the antiwhite militancy
that developed among blacks in the 1960s.)

- Racial separation will create social isolation. There
  are, Grodzins observed, "Negro communities in which
  people live their whole lives without, or with minimum,
  contact with the other race." Segregation to this degree
  was more thoroughgoing than it ever had been in
  the rural South.[25] (Such isolation, we note, helped to
  perpetuate a distinctive African American lower-class
  subculture.)

- As downtown stores cater to more nonwhite and
  low-income customers, central-city department
  stores will decline, "accompanied by a general
  deterioration of the downtown area." "The slums,
  in other words, are spreading to the central business
  districts."[26]

- Corporate business offices will join the flight from the
  city. Likewise, "retail trade, the white collar shops, and
  the service industries will follow population"; that is,
  they, too, will head to the suburbs.[27]

- The municipal tax base will erode.[28]

- Blacks will try to use their numbers in the cities to
  create a political base from which they will seek to
  advance policies "for ends conceived narrowly to the
  advantage of the Negro community." Whites will resist
  black efforts to gain political power in the cities.[29]

If these predictions sound more 1960s and '70s than 1950s,
it is because Grodzins's work was ahead of its time. The key
point is that lower-class black communities in America's big
cities were expanding dramatically in the 1950s, laying the
groundwork for a massive black urban-crime problem. By 1960,

the black farm laborer had virtually disappeared, and African Americans had become more urban than whites—"a striking reversal of the historic pattern."[30]

HOUSING

The federal government tried to grapple with one urban problem—housing—as early as 1949. Seeking to address the postwar housing shortage and the growth of "slums," Congress authorized the construction of new housing, including public housing that could be set aside for the poor. It was supposed to work as follows: Congress would allocate federal funds to local redevelopment agencies, which would buy targeted tracts, demolish old buildings on those properties, and contract with developers to construct new housing, a portion of which would be dedicated to low-income occupants. "Urban renewal" became the buzzword, but implementation problems inspired ridicule.

First, government bureaucracy combined with neighborhood opposition resulted in an agonizingly slow process. Razed lots, dubbed "Hiroshima Flats," remained empty for years, and displaced residents were forced to find new accommodations. Second, developers, who made more money on high-priced housing, were reluctant to build anything that poor people could afford. The galling irony was that displaced occupants seldom could afford to move back to their old neighborhoods. Urban renewal began to be called "poor removal." Third, Congress was chary with funding. Only 325,000 out of 810,000 proposed units had been constructed by 1965. Fourth, racism reared its head. Whites tried to keep blacks out of the new developments. Failing that, construction sites were located in areas already predominantly black. Unsurprisingly, many of the housing projects (as public housing came to be called) ended up nearly all African American. That led to the fifth problem. Filled with lower-class blacks, many projects quickly succumbed to the same problems associated with poor black neighborhoods that hadn't been renewed. Violent crime was high on the list of evils as young thugs mugged and assaulted terrified occupants. By the late 1960s, the reputation of urban renewal had plummeted, and some of the projects were slated for teardown. The message should have been clear: suitable housing is a public good in and of itself, but improving the quality of housing may not reduce violent crime. Indeed, concentrating high-risk populations in housing developments, especially high-rise, high-density structures, may magnify the crime problem.[31]

THE KOREAN WAR

One event in the 1950s may have had a positive, though very short-lived, impact on violent crime: the Korean War, which lasted from 1950 to 1953. Though minimized by President Harry Truman as a "police action," the war was a full-scale, brutal military conflict that involved 5.7 million Americans, 36,574 of whom did not come home alive. When compared with World War II, however, the Korean War was a historical asterisk. Nearly three times as many American soldiers participated in the Second World War, 73 percent of whom served overseas, compared with 56 percent of the Korean War inductees. There were eleven times as many war deaths and six and a half times the number of wounded in the 1940s, and the world war cost the United States four times more to wage ($6.64 billion compared with $1.64 billion).

The war in Korea may have reduced violent crime, if only briefly, by moving young men from the streets to the barracks. The conflict began in June 1950, when Korean Communist forces from the north attacked the south (the peninsula having been divided after World War II between the Communist north and the non-Communist south). The United Nations Security Council quickly approved a military response, and although about 166,000 allied troops fought in Korea, the commanding general, Douglas MacArthur, and the vast bulk of the Korean theater forces (around 1,789,000 service people over the entire course of the war) were Americans.[32]

If we examine the increase in the size of the U.S. armed forces and annual changes in crime rates, a strong suggestion of a relationship appears, at least for 1951. Table 2.3 covers a period starting one year before the war and ending one year afterward. As is evident, in 1951, when the military force was dramatically increased by nearly 1.8 million men (only a very small number of women, mostly nurses, served in Korea), male homicide victimizations fell 7 percent. But in the very next year, the homicide rate rebounded. A similar development occurred with rates for crimes of violence known to the police. They dipped in 1951 by 3.5 percent, only to rise in 1952.

The end of the war did not produce a major demobilization, because U.S. troops remained based on the new Cold War front lines in Germany, Korea, and other strategically important locales. Perhaps that explains the lack of a demobilization homicide spike like the one that occurred at the end of World War II. There was, nonetheless, an upturn at the end of the war

Table 2.3 Military personnel during Korean War
and U.S. violent crime rates

	Military personnel on active duty	Male homicide (rate per 100k)	Violent crimes known to police (rate per 100k)
1949	1,615,360	8.7	138.4
1950	1,460,261	8.4	132.7
1951	**3,249,455**	**7.8**	**128.0**
1952	3,635,912	8.5	139.3
1953	3,555,067	8.0	145.5
1954	3,302,104	8.0	146.8

Sources: U.S. Department of Commerce, Bureau of the Census, *Historical Statistics*, part 2, series Y 904–916, 1141; National Center for Health Statistics, *Vital Statistics Rates in the United States, 1940–1960*, table 62, 373; U.S. Office of Management and Budget, *Social Indicators, 1973*, table 2/1, 64.

in violent crimes reported to the police (see table 2.3). Whether this was attributable to the war is unclear, given the lack of rapid demobilization. In sum, the Korean War mobilization appears to have produced a one-year downturn in violent crime, but any crime impact beyond that is uncertain.[33]

IMMIGRATION

Immigration to the United States picked up in the 1950s after the hiatus created by the Depression and World War II. Approximately two and a half million people legally entered this country in the 1950s, and although more than half of them were from northern and western Europe, that particular immigrant population was declining as a proportion of the total. The larger group of newcomers came from Latin America, which accounted for one of every five new entrants. From the standpoint of crime, however, European and Latino immigrants were less important than two population groups from south of the border: Mexican agricultural laborers and Puerto Rican migrants from the Caribbean, neither of which, properly speaking, were immigrants.[34]

MEXICANS

Most Mexicans entering the southwestern United States did not come to America to become American citizens: they came to work in fruit and vegetable fields and make enough money to take back to their homeland. Hundreds of thousands of Mexicans entered through regular immigration processes, but millions more came to the United States as temporary workers under the bracero program or illegally as *los mojados* (literally meaning "wets"; pejoratively, "wetbacks").

The bracero program began in 1942 after being negotiated between the governments of Mexico and the United States. It allowed each worker to enter the United States for a specific time period under a labor contract enforced (sometimes rather loosely) by agencies of the federal government. No one was thrilled with the program. Labor unions strenuously opposed it because it took jobs away from Americans and lowered wages. Growers objected to government regulations and, from their perspective, overly generous worker benefits. The *braceros* had to put up with rough, sometimes appalling, conditions in work camps, very low wages (by North American standards), and discrimination by *yanquis*. Despite it all, the farmers needed labor and the Mexicans needed work, so the program continued until 1964. Over two decades, the bracero program brought into the United States approximately four million temporary workers.

Thousands of braceros "skipped" when the terms of their contracts ran out and thereby became illegal aliens. Millions more Mexicans entered the United States with forged papers or without documentation. American immigration authorities caught about five million undocumented Mexicans during the decades of the bracero policy, many more than were admitted through the program but an unknown percentage of the actual number of illegals.

The 1952 McCarran-Walter Act made it a felony to willfully import, transport, or harbor illegal aliens, but the so-called Texas Proviso protected growers from prosecution by expressly excluding the mere employment of illegals from the definition of "harboring." The lax enforcement policy changed under the Eisenhower administration, which moved against illegal Mexicans in 1954 with a sweeping military-style campaign of raids on growers followed by mass deportations (Operation Wetback). At the same time, the administration doubled the number of braceros admitted to the United States.[35]

Very little is known with exactitude about crime by Mexicans in North America, especially during the 1950s. Judging by a few contemporaneous publications, Mexicans were perceived to be lawless, which was no doubt reinforced by the widespread unlawful entries. "In the areas where the illegal aliens were found in large numbers," one essay asserted, "crime rates skyrocketed. Lawlessness bred lawlessness."[36] The only evidence offered in support of this assertion, however, were some Texas newspaper articles.

There was at least one credible study of Mexican homicides and assaults in Houston, Texas, covering the years 1958 through 1961. It found a pattern typical of research results in subsequent decades: African Americans had the highest rates; white non-Hispanics, the lowest; and Hispanic rates were in between. A safe assumption for Houston in the late 1950s is that "Hispanic" meant Mexican, but no distinction between permanent residents of Mexican descent and temporary ones may be drawn from this study. What is clear is that during this period of low violence in the United States, when "Anglo" Houstonians had homicide offending rates in the same ballpark as state and national figures, the Mexican rates, which were in excess of 12 per 100,000, must be considered elevated (table 2.4). This conclusion is corroborated by Mexican aggravated assault rates that were 4.7 times those of Anglos.[37]

Some imprisonment figures also exist for this time period,

Table 2.4 Homicide and assault rates, Houston, Texas, by race and ethnicity, 1958–61

	Homicide (rate per 100k)		Aggravated assault (rate per 100k)	
	Offender	**Victim**	**Offender**	**Victim**
Black	31.3	32.3	497.6	513.4
Total white	5.4	5.9	65.4	71.2
Hispanic	12.9	12.1	230.4	232.0
Other white	4.7	5.6	49.5	55.7
Total	11.7	11.9	172.6	172.6

Source: Pokorny, "Human Violence," 496.

Note: "Total white" includes Hispanic and non-Hispanic whites; "Other white" includes only non-Hispanic whites; "Total" includes other and unknown race/ethnicity.

but in addition to the usual problems with inferring the incidence of crime from prison data, there are other complications. For example, figures for federal incarcerations show that huge percentages of foreign-born inmates were from Mexico: 90 percent in 1955, and 78 percent in 1960. This suggests that Mexicans were more apt than other recent immigrants to run into problems with the law. But the preponderance of these prisoners were likely to have been incarcerated for nonviolent offenses, because most crimes of violence were a matter for state, not federal, prosecution.[38]

At the state level, California has some intriguing corrections statistics, but without accurate general population data for Mexicans, we are handicapped in drawing generalizations. In 1960, men of Mexican descent were responsible for the following:

- 16.7 percent of all male incarcerations

- 16.5 percent of all murder or manslaughter prisoners

- 11.6 percent of prisoners convicted of robbery

- 19.2 percent of assault inmates

- 20.2 percent of those imprisoned for rape

- 40 percent of narcotics prisoners
  (a startlingly high figure)[39]

We cannot determine whether or not these percentages (except for drug cases) were out of proportion to the Mexican population, much less the *male* Mexican population (which may have been disproportionately high), for there are no reliable figures for the Mexican population in California prior to 1970. Even in 1970, the population figures were based on a sample of Spanish speakers, yielding an estimate for the state's Hispanic population of 13.7 percent.[40] Assuming the 1960 population percentages were below 13.7, the prison data suggest that Mexicans had disproportionately high imprisonment rates for rape, assault, homicide, and, especially, drug crimes.

We do know that Mexican lethal violence was a big problem in subsequent decades, as it had been before World War
II, but for the 1950s, the data being what they are, few other
conclusions may be drawn.

PUERTO RICANS

Puerto Ricans were the other significant migrant group in the
1950s, and they too came for the economic benefits. As American citizens, they freely traveled back and forth between the
mainland and their island, settling mainly in New York City.
The United States had acquired Puerto Rico as part of the spoils
of the 1898 Spanish-American War, and Congress granted citi-
zenship to virtually all of the islanders in 1917. After thirty-five
years under U.S. administration, the island was said to have
been "a scene of almost unrelieved misery."[41] The Great Depression had crippled the sugar crop, the main source of wealth, and
living conditions were "incredibly primitive." Sanitary facilities were rudimentary, and the ground was covered in sewage
and infested with parasites. Malnutrition stunted growth and
caused susceptibility to disease, and infant mortality and death
rates were high. Poverty was widespread, as were unemployment and underemployment, and 31 percent of the population
was illiterate.[42]

A 1917 island study by the dean of the University of Puerto
Rico devoted a chapter to crime, finding that in a one-year
period between 1915 and 1916, there were only 438 felony arrests out of a population of 1.2 million. This comes to 36.5 per
100,000 population, which is not a troubling number when one
considers that New York City's felony arrest rate for 1917 was
over nine times as great. However, 67 of the island's felonies
were homicides, which yields a rate of 5.58 per 100,000, a figure
exceeding that of the Big Apple, where the 1916 homicide rate
had been 4.4. The dean concluded that "crimes of violence are
relatively few in Porto Rico," an assertion not fully supported
by the homicide data.[43]

Puerto Rican families were big, and women married and bore children at a very young age. In the 1940s, Glazer and Moynihan reported that seven out of ten females were married before they were 21 years old. More than one-quarter of the "marriages" were not formalized, and one-third of the births were out of wedlock. Nevertheless, family units were strong, and men usually took responsibility for their children, even when they fathered them by different women. Moreover, a godparent system helped provide care for children when parental problems became overwhelming. Once on the mainland, the size of the Puerto Rican family invited poverty and welfare dependency, but its strength may have helped tamp down crime.[44]

The outflow of Puerto Ricans from the island was necessitated by high population growth and the declining agricultural economy. The great U.S. economic mobilization during World War II was the pull factor, just as it had been for African Americans leaving the South, and the booming economy sparked a *gran migración* to the mainland. Much as Italian and Jewish immigrants did half a century earlier, Puerto Ricans took up residence in New York City, the terminus for ships from the island. After the war, cheap and speedy air travel between San Juan and New York encouraged a continuous back-and-forth migration.

In 1940, there were around 70,000 Puerto Ricans on the mainland, and nearly 90 percent of them lived in New York City. By 1960, the number had grown to nearly 430,000, a 600 percent increase, and that total does not include children born in the north, of which there were many. Counting offspring, there were over 246,000 Puerto Ricans in the big city in 1950, growing to 612,574 islanders only one decade later. The proportion of Puerto Rican migrants settling in Gotham was exceptionally high in 1950, at 83 percent, but this number diminished over time, down to 70 percent in 1960, as the migrants fanned out. Still, the New York metropolitan area was home base, and many mainland Puerto Ricans styled themselves "Nuyoricans."[45]

Conditions dramatically improved on the island in the

1950s, especially after Luis Muñoz Marín, the first democrati-
cally elected governor, began attracting U.S. industry in order
to diversify the economy. (The U.S. Congress first allowed elec-
tions for the governorship in 1947, and Muñoz Marín took office in 1949.) The economic transformation, which Glazer and
Moynihan called "startling,"[46] greatly improved the Puerto Rican standard of living. The *migración* continued unabated, however, as conditions were still better in New York.

Reflecting progress on the island, the Puerto Ricans who
migrated in the 1950s were more urban, better educated, better
skilled, and generally better off than previous arrivals. Yet, compared with the rest of the people in Manhattan's melting pot,
they did not do well. Language problems, concomitant educational deficiencies, and family size were significant handicaps.
The median family income for Nuyoricans in 1960 was $3,811,
even below the figure for the city's African Americans, which
was $4,437. In 1950 New York City, Puerto Ricans had 17 percent
unemployment; for non-Hispanic whites, it was 7 percent; and
for African Americans, it was 12 percent.[47]

Figure 2.3 Migration of Puerto Ricans to and from U.S. mainland, 1920–86

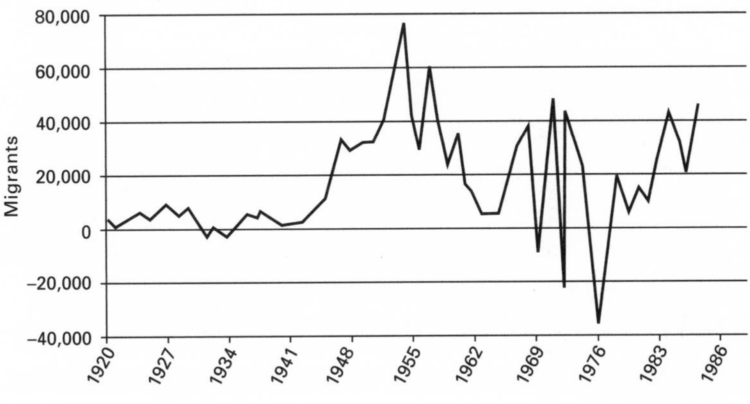

Source: Rodríguez, *Puerto Ricans,* 3.

For many of the earlier immigrants to the United States, there was behavioral continuity in terms of criminal violence between the old country and the new. Jewish migrants who came to New York City at the turn of the twentieth century were nonviolent in Europe and also in America (speaking here of average young men and not the handful of gangsters). Italian immigrants engaged in a great deal of violence in both the old and the new worlds. What about Puerto Ricans?

As discussed, around the time of World War I, homicide on the island was excessive, and evidence suggests that there were a disproportionate number of killings after the Second World War. In 1950, the homicide rate on the island hit 12.3 per 100,000, whereas the rate for the entire United States was 5.4. In 1960, the rate for Puerto Rico was sharply reduced to 6.3 per 100,000, but the rate for the United States as a whole was lower still, at 5.2.[48] It would have been helpful to know the homicide rates of mainland Puerto Ricans during the 1950s, but such data are unavailable. (As discussed in chapter 3, such figures are available for the late 1960s and early 1970s, and they show elevated homicide rates.) The likelihood is that violence among Nuyoricans did not initially develop in New York City, though it undoubtedly worsened on its mean streets.

As did earlier migrants to New York, Puerto Ricans settled in decrepit housing in Manhattan's poorest neighborhoods—East Harlem serving as the initial stopping point—and then dispersed to the Bronx, Brooklyn, and the greater metropolitan area. Slum life was what it always had been: poor, nasty, brutish, and short, but definitely not solitary. Packed into aging apartment buildings, many young Puerto Ricans quickly succumbed to the temptations of the streets: alcohol, narcotics, juvenile delinquency, and violence.

One can learn a great deal from Piri Thomas's autobiographical account, *Down These Mean Streets*, a tale of the hard life in El Barrio, also known as Spanish Harlem, in the 1940s. Thomas, a dark-skinned Puerto Rican (a significant minority of the population), ended up in prison in the 1950s and served six years for attempted armed robbery.[49] That was not, apparently, an uncommon fate for young Nuyoricans in East Harlem. Dan Wakefield's *Island in the City*, a more impersonal account of the *barrio*, described it as follows.

> By the mid-1950s, the roughly mile-square area of East Harlem was one of the world's most densely populated areas. It was estimated that nearly 300,000 people lived in that space. On a single, dark block—East 100th Street between First and Second Avenues—there were more than 4000 human beings jammed into 27 ancient tenements. It is hardly surprising that this block has come to be known by police as "the worst block in the city" from the standpoint of crime and narcotics addiction.[50]

Wakefield went on to discuss the widespread cocaine and marijuana use in East Harlem, explaining how some users moved on to heroin (decades before crack cocaine became the scourge of the city). Monsignor Joseph Fitzpatrick, the sociologist-priest who dedicated his life to the cause of Puerto Ricans, confirmed that drug abuse struck the Puerto Rican community early: "It was already widespread during the 1950s."[51] Drinking, apparently, was another social vice common to Puerto Ricans, both here and on the island. We have hard data for the early 1970s indicating serious mortality problems due to cirrhosis of the liver (as well as homicide), but we don't have comparable data for the 1950s.[52]

As far as crime goes, most of the public concern in the 1950s was centered on juvenile delinquents, and there are glimmers of data suggesting Puerto Rican overinvolvement.[53] For instance, a study of the Warwick New York State Training School for Boys, the euphemistic designation for the facility housing male delinquents, found that even in the 1940s, "the percentage of Puerto Rican inmates ... was always much higher than the share of Puerto Ricans in the New York city population."[54]

In the 1950s, when Puerto Ricans were less than 8 percent of the city's population, 20 percent of Warwick's occupants were Puerto Rican, as were 21 percent of the adolescent inmates of the Brooklyn Men's House of Detention.[55] But some scholars believe (though not with a great deal of empirical evidence) that Puerto Rican delinquency was not a major problem in the early postwar years. "During the fifties," insisted Glazer and Moynihan, "there was not an exceptionally high rate of delinquency among Puerto Rican children."[56]

One certainly gets a different impression, however, from the New York newspapers, even from the cautious *New York Times*, which presented the following.

- 1949: "Police in New York's Puerto Rican precincts encounter more violence of certain kinds, including knifings, street battles and domestic fights." But a "high police official" said that Puerto Ricans mainly committed "acts of violence against one another, not organized depredations on society as in some other slum areas."[57]

- 1956: Anthropologist Joseph Bram attributed the problems of Puerto Rican youth to cultural conflicts between the island and the mainland. His study of twenty-one boys from Puerto Rico who were in conflict with the law found an "extreme preoccupation with the concept of dignity" and a "violent reaction" to perceived infringements on that dignity. At the same conference at which Bram made his presentation, sociologist Albert K. Cohen said that the better-known theories of juvenile delinquency needed revision.[58]

- 1957: Governor Muñoz Marín, in a speech in New York City, defensively denied any link between the Puerto Rican migration and juvenile delinquency in the city. He pointed out that Puerto Ricans, who were about 6 percent of the city's population, committed roughly 6 percent of its crimes.[59]

- 1959: New York City Administrator Charles F. Preusse said in a speech at the University of Puerto Rico that the Puerto Rican delinquency rate was high, but it was not the highest in the city. He noted that Puerto Rican males, ages 16–20, were committed to correctional institutions at a rate twice that of their proportion in the general population.[60]

- 1959: Following outbreaks in which four teenagers were killed in New York City, Governor Nelson Rockefeller and Mayor Robert Wagner Jr. agreed on a program to combat juvenile delinquency, including plans to divert $2.5 million to hire additional police. Both the governor and the mayor cautioned against generalizing about the Puerto Rican community, saying that their adjustment problems were similar to those of previous immigrant groups.[61]

- 1959: Brooklyn Judge Samuel Liebowitz urged officials to discourage Caribbean migration to New York, pointing out that Puerto Ricans, who were 7 percent of the city's population, accounted for 22.3 percent of the city's delinquency cases.[62]

- 1960: A survey of a ten-block area of East Harlem found that 158 of every 1,000 children under the age of 16 "have been in trouble with the law."[63]

Even the Broadway stage reflected the perception that there was a Puerto Rican adolescent crime problem. *West Side Story*, the hit musical of 1957, updated Shakespeare's *Romeo and Juliet* by turning it into a story of lovers from two rival gangs: the "white" Jets and the Puerto Rican Sharks.

Two years later, only a few city blocks from Broadway, a real gang crime shocked even jaded New Yorkers. Two members of a Puerto Rican gang, one sporting a black cape with a red lining, went to a West Side Manhattan playground intending to battle Irish and Italian rivals. There they brutally assaulted two non-Hispanic youth who were not members of a gang. While fellow gang members held the pair down, the two Puerto Ricans stabbed them to death. The "Cape Man," as newspapers called him, 16-year-old Salvador Agron, became the youngest New Yorker ever to be sentenced to death in the electric chair.[64]

Without more systematic and comprehensive data, little more can be said about Puerto Ricans and violent crime in the 1950s. If there had been a problem, as seems likely, it worsened considerably during the great crime surge after the 1960s.

CRIME IN THE 1950s

The period immediately following the post–World War II crime spike and ending with the commencement of the great upsurge in violence in the mid-1960s had the least crime of any other comparable time span in the twentieth century. If one were to adopt as a benchmark a homicide rate of 6 per 100,000, a somewhat arbitrary number, the great crime trough may be said to have run from 1948 to 1966, a period of nineteen years (see figure 1.4).

The homicide rate for this nineteen-year period averaged 4.98 per 100,000, and between 1953 and 1963, it never exceeded 5.0 (fig. 2.4). Rates of crimes known to police (from local police records collected by the FBI) also were relatively low throughout this nineteen-year period, corroborating the homicide data (fig. 2.5).[65]

Even juvenile crime, a matter of deep concern at the time, was not quite as problematic as originally thought. "Despite inflammatory headlines and the repetition of charges about brutality," wrote one analyst, "the incidence of juvenile crime does not appear to have increased enormously during this period."[66]

Delinquency cases, most of which involved relatively insignificant matters, rose in the late 1940s and early '50s and then

Figure 2.4   Homicide victimization rates, 1948–66

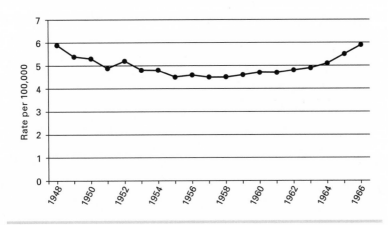

Source: U.S. Department of Justice, Bureau of Justice Statistics, "Homicide Rate Trends."

Figure 2.5   Four violent crimes known to police, rate per 100,000, 1948–66

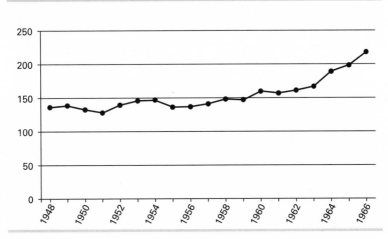

Source: U.S. Office of Management and Budget, *Social Indicators*, table 2/1, 64.

Figure 2.6 Delinquency rates, 1948–66

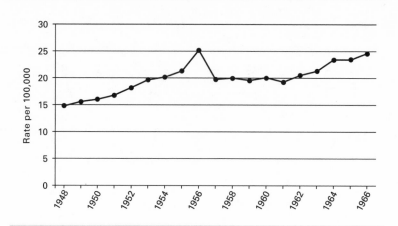

Source: U.S. Department of Commerce, Bureau of the Census, *Historical Statistics*, part 1, series H 1119–1124, 419.

Figure 2.7 Adolescent homicide rates, New York City, 1940–65

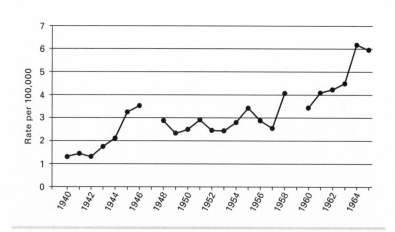

Source: Schneider, *Vampires, Dragons and Egyptian Kings*, 76.

(except for 1956, an outlier year) remained flat until the 1960s (fig. 2.6). A measure of more serious delinquencies, males committed to training schools, showed comparable development. While such commitments rose 41 percent between 1950 and 1960, the U.S. male population under the age of 18 increased nearly as much, growing by over 37 percent.[67] And in New York City, where youth gangs caused such consternation, the adolescent homicide rate remained flat from the late 1940s to the late 1950s, never exceeding 4 per 100,000 (fig. 2.7). This is not to deny that there was a youth gang problem in the Big Apple. As one authority put it, "Increasing conflict among African-American, Puerto Rican, and Euro-American gangs, and the intensifying violence associated with it, led New Yorkers to discover the gang problem."[68]

Moreover, as the decade progressed, young people became a larger portion of the crime population, while their numbers in the general population did not grow nearly as substantially. Criminologist Thorsten Sellin collected the following arrest data, showing that for violent offenses, the percentage of under-18 apprehensions grew between 1953 and 1960, while arrests of those in the 21–24 age bracket declined or held steady (table 2.5).[69]

It is also noteworthy that African American youth, at least in big cities, were disproportionately delinquent. A classic study by criminologist Marvin Wolfgang tracked a birth cohort—nearly 10,000 boys born in Philadelphia in 1945—up to their eighteenth birthdays in 1963. (Anyone older than 18 at the time of an offense would no longer be classified as a juvenile.) Wolfgang found that "race is one of the most significant variables in this analysis. Nonwhites make up 29 per cent of the birth cohort but 50.2 per cent are recorded delinquents; whites are 71 per cent of the cohort, 29 per cent of whom are delinquent." The nonwhite rate, he found, was 3 times as high as the white rate, and even more worrying, black youth committed

Table 2.5 Arrests for violent crimes, by age group, 1953 and 1960

	Percentage of total arrests					
	Under 18		18–20		21–24	
	1953	1960	1953	1960	1953	1960
Murder/manslaughter	4.1	7.7	6.9	10.6	12.6	12.6
Robbery	18.0	27.8	18.4	19.6	20.6	18.5
Aggravated assault	6.0	11.6	7.3	8.9	13.2	12.9
Rape	16.2	20.5	21.6	21.6	18.2	18.6

Source: Sellin, "Crime and Delinquency," 20.

Table 2.6 Violent crimes known to police for cities with populations of 250,000 or more and United States, 1951 and 1961

	Murder/ manslaughter (rate per 100k)	Robbery (rate per 100k)	Aggravated assault (rate per 100k)
1951			
Cities 250,000+	6.6	85.9	102.5
U.S.	5.1	46.8	68.5
Rate difference	29%	84%	50%
1961			
Cities 250,000+	7.2	152.8	168.9
U.S.	4.7	58.0	84.7
Rate difference	53%	163%	99%

Sources: Federal Bureau of Investigation, *Uniform Crime Reports for the United States and Its Possessions* (1951), table 30, 86; Federal Bureau of Investigation, *Crime in the United States, 1961,* Uniform Crime Reports, table 6, 81.

2.4 times as many UCR index offenses, the most serious crimes in the FBI's Uniform Crime Reports.[70]

Although juvenile violence was a growing concern, the two most significant developments in crime during the 1950s were big-city crime, linked to the African American migration, and the ongoing dilemma of southern violence.

URBAN CRIME

While violent crime rates remained low throughout the 1950s, the situation was ominously different in the biggest American cities. This may seem less than newsworthy to those who lived through the post-1960s era, when the words *big city* and *crime* seemed to be inextricably linked. But that link was not invariable. In the late nineteenth century, the big-city crime rate was lower than that of the countryside, and violent crime always was higher in the rural South than in the more urban Northeast. From 1900 to the late 1950s, New York City homicide rates were *lower* than those for the United States as a whole. Moreover, in the United Kingdom and Europe, some of the biggest cities had extremely low crime rates. In the 1950s, when New York City was enjoying what Americans think of as a crime honeymoon, with homicide rates around 4.0 per 100,000, the rates in London were 0.7, roughly one-sixth of Gotham's.[71]

Table 2.6 shows the difference in crime rates between the biggest urban areas and the rest of the United States at roughly the beginning and end of the 1950s. Rates for large cities were considerably higher than national rates for each offense. Moreover, the differences between the urban rates and those of the rest of the country grew greater by the early 1960s—a harbinger of developments to come.

Table 2.7 shows that, generally speaking, the more populous the municipality, the higher the crime rates. In towns with populations between 10,000 and 25,000, for example, the 1960 murder rate was only 2.4 per 100,000, just over one-third the rate of the largest cities, which was 6.8.

Table 2.7 also shows that trends in violent crime during the 1950s were mixed. Rates for murder and assault in the largest cities did *not* rise between 1950 and 1960, while robbery rates for the same municipalities climbed by one-third. This bears out the assertion that violent crime was essentially flat in the 1950s. But it also tells us something very interesting about robbery, the quintessential urban crime.

Robbery is the taking of property (theft) by force or the threat of force—a "mugging," in common parlance.[72] Such a crime usually is perpetrated by strangers; consequently, it generates great fear among urban populations. A disproportionate

Table 2.7   Offenses known to police, by size of city, 1940, 1950, and 1960

	City population					
	Over 250,000	100,000– 250,000	50,000– 100,000	25,000– 50,000	10,000– 25,000	Under 10,000
Murder and non-negligent manslaughter (rate per 100k)						
1940	6.1	6.5	5.7	3.4	3.9	4.1
1950	6.8	6.0	4.4	3.3	3.5	2.8
1960	6.8	5.6	3.3	2.9	2.4	2.7
Robbery (rate per 100k)						
1940	74.7	50.8	37.8	32.2	23.3	22.2
1950	88.0	45.0	31.1	22.6	18.3	16.8
1960	117.6	57.5	36.6	22.6	15.7	12.8
Aggravated assault (rate per 100k)						
1940	50.3	53.7	63.8	35.7	27.2	27.4
1950	180.0	68.8	73.9	51.4	35.4	30.0
1960	154.1	83.3	58.9	39.9	35.2	28.9

Source: Sellin, "Crime and Delinquency," 19.

Figure 2.8 Robbery arrests of blacks as percentage
of total U.S. robbery arrests, 1950–60

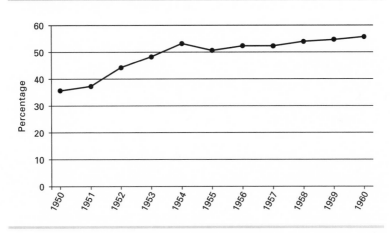

Sources: Federal Bureau of Investigation, *Uniform Crime Reports for the United States
and its Possessions* (1950), table 44, 112; Federal Bureau of Investigation, *Crime in the
United States, 1960,* Uniform Crime Reports, table 20, 95.

number of robberies, undoubtedly intraracial in the main, were
committed by lower-class African Americans. As the black migration to cities accelerated after World War II, the number
of urban robberies by blacks increased. In the large sample of
arrests compiled by the FBI in 1950, 35.7 percent of the total
robbery apprehensions were of blacks, who comprised at the
time only 10 percent of the population (fig. 2.8). By 1960, robbery arrests of blacks jumped to 55.5 percent of the total (sample
limited to cities of 2,500 or more), while the general population
was 10.5 percent African American.[73]

The increase in robbery arrests undoubtedly reflected the
enormous black migration to urban areas, where more potential
victims with more valuables and the anonymity of the big city
encouraged predators. Insufficient data exist to state with certainty that blacks were responsible for the upward trend in urban robbery, but figures show that in the 1950s, the black urban

population rose enormously, big-city robbery rates climbed, and there was growing black involvement in the offense. The connection between black urban migration and rising robbery rates is perhaps best demonstrated by a study of more than 100 cities with populations over 50,000, which found that from 1950 to 1960, each 3 percent increase in the nonwhite population correlated with 100 more robberies per 100,000 people.[74]

CRIME IN THE SOUTH

The other focal point in the 1950s, insofar as violent crime is concerned, was the South. There were high rates of violence, both black and white, below the Mason-Dixon line during the pre–World War II period. But the penchant of the South for violence and its preeminence as the most violent region in the country continued in the postwar era. Momentous changes in the region were under way, but when it came to homicide and assault, Dixie remained a sectional outlier.

The South was transformed following the Second World War from a socially isolated, agricultural, and rural backwater to a dynamic, industrial, economic growth zone. Military installations brought northerners and federal dollars. Industries took advantage of low levels of unionization, and retirees enjoyed the seductive climate. Air-conditioning made white-collar work more productive. Money poured into schools and higher education. The federal highway system and higher speed capacities for trucks and cars, along with air and rail travel, enabled goods and people to more freely flow in and out of the region. Movies and television programs disseminated nationwide brought the South into the cultural mainstream. The increased wealth raised the standard of living, and a burgeoning southern middle class reflected the changing social structure. By 1960, only 10 percent of the southern population was still working on farms, and the region had become 58 percent urban. In short, the South was becoming like the rest of America.[75]

None of this, of course, happened overnight. Indeed, the transformation of the South occurred over many decades. This may explain why the southern crime situation in the 1950s was pretty much what it had been for the first half of the twentieth century: violent crime was much higher among white southerners than among whites outside the South, and it was higher still for African Americans, whether they were in the South or had migrated to other parts of the country.

Scholars discovered the southern crime problem when historian Sheldon Hackney published his influential article "Southern Violence" in 1969.[76] In truth, they rediscovered it, since H.C. Brearley had addressed the southern crime issue in the early 1930s, as had H.V. Redfield, back in 1880.[77] Hackney framed much of his discussion around the inverse correlation between homicide and suicide, first identified by sociologist Emile Durkheim in the late nineteenth century. The correlation is intriguing, for it seems, uncannily, that population groups with high homicide rates have low suicide rates, and vice versa. As Durkheim, speaking about European countries, observed, homicide "confers a sort of immunity against suicide." In nations such as Spain, Ireland, and Italy, which have the least suicide, he found that "nowhere else is murder so common."[78]

Hackney employed a suicide-homicide ratio (SHR), utilizing the following formula: 100 × suicide rate ÷ (suicide rate + homicide rate). The closer the SHR comes to 100, the more the group engages in suicide in relation to homicide; the lower the SHR, the higher the incidence of homicide in relation to suicide. Hackney's SHRs for southerners and for the entire United States, differentiated by race, appear in table 2.8.

Among whites, Hackney concluded, "southerners show a relatively greater preference than do nonsoutherners for murder rather than suicide," and African Americans, regardless of region, "commit murder much more often than they commit suicide." Hackney continued, "High murder and low suicide rates

Table 2.8   Suicide-homicide ratios (SHRs), by race, United States and southern states, 1950, 1955, and 1960

	White		Black	
	U.S.	Southern states	U.S.	Southern states
1950	82.4	69.8	12.4	9.3
1955	88.3	73.1	15.6	9.7
1960	82.0	74.4	17.0	12.2

Source: Hackney, "Southern Violence," 908.

constitute a distinctly southern pattern of violence, one that must rank with the caste system and ahead of mint juleps in importance as a key to the meaning of being southern."[79]

Shortly after Hackney's piece was published, Raymond Gastil offered additional evidence that there was, as he put it, "a predisposition to lethal violence in Southern regional culture."[80] Criminologists have been divided ever since between those who believe that a distinctive southern culture is the crucial driver of southern violence and those who focus on the relative poverty of the southern population.[81] Chapter 5 picks up this debate, but it is noteworthy that violent crime has been inconsistently related to poverty throughout U.S. history, proving far more prevalent in some impoverished groups than in others.

Violence was a consistent feature of the South from the eighteenth century on, and this regional distinctiveness continued right through the 1950s and beyond. Murder and manslaughter known to police, as depicted in figure 2.9, were persistently higher in the southern states throughout the decade.[82] The maps do not differentiate between white and African American offenses, which, due to the extremely high black homicide rates, worsen the standing of the southern states. (Blacks were fully one-fifth of the region's residents in

Figure 2.9 State murder and manslaughter rates, in quartiles, 1950, 1955, and 1960

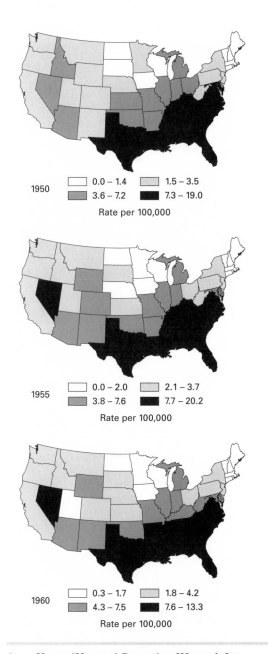

1950

☐ 0.0 – 1.4	▨ 1.5 – 3.5
▩ 3.6 – 7.2	■ 7.3 – 19.0

Rate per 100,000

1955

☐ 0.0 – 2.0	▨ 2.1 – 3.7
▩ 3.8 – 7.6	■ 7.7 – 20.2

Rate per 100,000

1960

☐ 0.3 – 1.7	▨ 1.8 – 4.2
▩ 4.3 – 7.5	■ 7.6 – 13.3

Rate per 100,000

Source: Harries, "Historical Geography of Homicide," 76.

Table 2.9 White homicide rate per 100,000, by state, 1960

State	Rate	State	Rate
Nevada	7.2	Delaware	2.3
Virginia	**6.9**	Illinois	2.3
Alaska	6.3	Kansas	2.2
South Carolina	**4.9**	Washington	2.2
New Mexico	4.8	Oregon	2.0
Arizona	4.5	Ohio	1.9
Kentucky	**4.5**	Michigan	1.8
Georgia	**4.4**	New York	1.8
Texas	**4.3**	Indiana	1.8
Wyoming	4.3	Maine	1.8
Alabama	**4.2**	South Dakota	1.7
Oklahoma	**4.0**	New Jersey	1.6
North Carolina	**3.9**	Pennsylvania	1.5
Florida	**3.8**	Wisconsin	1.3
Tennessee	**3.7**	Rhode Island	1.3
Arkansas	**3.7**	Connecticut	1.2
California	3.3	Idaho	1.1
Louisiana	**3.1**	Massachusetts	1.1
Montana	3.1	Minnesota	1.1
West Virginia	**3.1**	North Dakota	1.0
Colorado	3.0	New Hampshire	1.0
Missouri	2.8	Iowa	0.9
Mississippi	**2.5**	Nebraska	0.87
Maryland	2.5	Vermont	0
Hawaii	2.5		

Source: Gastil, "Homicide," 415.

Table 2.10 Mean assault and robbery rates, crimes known to police, South and non-South cities, 1951, 1955, and 1960

	1951	1955	1960
Assault (rate per 100k)			
South	153	158	147
Non-South	61	79	107
Robbery (rate per 100k)			
South	51	59	73
Non-South	64	75	104

Source: Jacobson, "Crime Trends in Southern and Nonsouthern Cities," 231.

the 1950s.) Still, when white rates alone are presented, as in table 2.9, the results, while improved, remain consistent with the regional violence thesis. The mean homicide rate for all states was 2.8 per 100,000, and of the twenty-one states above the mean, thirteen (62 percent) were in the South.

Despite the South's poor showing on violent crime, there was one offense in which it did not predominate: robbery. Throughout the 1950s, average assault rates were persistently and significantly higher in the South than in the rest of the country, but rates for robbery were consistently lower (table 2.10). The most likely explanation derives from the nature of the crimes and the particulars of southern culture. Overwhelmingly, assault is a crime between acquaintances (people who know one another and often are related). A rupture in the relationship—due to sexual jealousy, money matters, personal insult, or the like—frequently magnified by alcohol, triggers the violence. The southern culture of honor, a hypersensitivity to personal affront, makes such interpersonal violence more probable. As a result, crimes between acquaintances are typical of the South and have been for a long time.

Robbery, however, unlike assault, is the quintessential

impersonal crime, typically committed against strangers. It is especially common in big cities, where, if only fleetingly, strangers are likely to come into contact, and people routinely carry valuables, such as cash and jewelry. While the South certainly was urbanizing in the 1950s, the North had by far the most big cities. Thus, in the South, where the traditional southern culture of interpersonal violence prevailed, assault was more common than robbery.

When we compare robbery rates in southern and non-southern metropolitan areas, as a general rule, even the biggest cities in the South had lower robbery rates than nonsouthern

Table 2.11 Robbery rates in selected metropolitan areas, South and non-South, 1960

Southern SMSA	Population	Robbery (rate per 100k)
Atlanta	1,017,188	38.5
Baltimore	1,727,023	56.5
Birmingham	634,864	62.8
Dallas	1,083,601	57.9
Houston	1,243,158	53.7
Louisville	725,139	93.6
Memphis	627,019	16.1
Miami	935,047	168.5
Mobile	314,301	51.9
New Orleans	868,480	146.2
Richmond	408,494	62.4
Washington, D.C.	2,001,897	67.3
	Mean:	72.95

Table 2.11   *(continued)*

Nonsouthern SMSA	Population	Robbery (rate per 100k)
Boston	3,109,158	29.4
Chicago	6,220,913	237.5
Cincinnati	1,071,624	32.2
Cleveland	1,796,595	81.7
Denver	929,383	131.2
Detroit	3,762,360	130.6
Kansas City	1,039,493	55.8
Los Angeles	6,742,696	143.9
Milwaukee	1,194,290	15.5
Minneapolis	1,482,030	62.5
New York	10,694,633	64.2
Philadelphia	4,342,897	62.3
Pittsburgh	2,405,435	47.9
Saint Louis	2,060,103	152.8
San Francisco	2,783,359	102.8
Seattle	1,107,213	53.3
	Mean:	87.73

Source: Federal Bureau of Investigation, *Crime in the United States, 1960*, Uniform Crime Reports, table 4.

Note: SMSA refers to Standard Metropolitan Statistical Area, a census designation for core urban areas with a substantial population together with adjacent communities having a high degree of economic and social integration with that core.

cities (table 2.11). On average, nonsouthern robbery rates were 20 percent higher. However, when it came to murder and assault, the South contributed greatly to the 1950s nationwide crime totals.[83]

Suicide and Homicide

For over a century since Emile Durkheim first mentioned it, observers have been fascinated by the apparent inverse relationship between suicide and homicide. It remains a mystery still. Is it generally valid? And if so, why is it that population groups that murder others more kill themselves less?

One explanation, propounded by psychologist Martin Gold, originator of the suicide-murder ratio, is that corporal punishment in child rearing leads to outwardly expressed aggression, while children punished psychologically, as opposed to physically, are more apt to turn their aggression against themselves. Gold linked child-rearing practices to social class: lower-class parents seemed to favor the strap over the scolding. He thought this explained why violent crime was much more common in the lower than in the middle class.[84] What it does not explain is why violent crime rises and falls when social groups remain in the low socioeconomic stratum or why violent crime rates vary among these groups.

Gold's theory has not inspired much criminological research; nonetheless, studies suggest that the relationship cannot be dismissed out of hand. While criminologists have shown, for instance, that homicide rates are lower among poor whites than poor blacks, family researchers have found that low-income African American parents spank their toddlers significantly more frequently than low-income white parents.[85]

Subsequent research on suicide by psychiatrist Herbert Hendin has thrown cold water on the entire suicide-homicide theory.[86] His 1960s study of young African Americans aged 20 to 35 found exceptionally high suicide rates. Indeed, suicide was twice as frequent among young blacks of both sexes as among white men of the same age. The oft-observed black-white suicide differentials, it turns out, were products of a failure to take age into account. After age 45, suicide among whites was so much higher than among blacks of the same age that the total white rate rose above the total black.[87]

Both suicide and homicide, Hendin argued, are driven by impulses of extreme violence, which may be directed at another person, inward toward the seething actor himself, or, as with homicide-suicide, both. Some homicides, as criminologist Marvin Wolfgang noted, are victim-precipitated, that is, caused by the threatening behavior of the actor. A subcategory of these suicides disguised as homicides is referred to as "suicide by cop," which occurs when the actor engages in violent behavior knowing that it probably will provoke fatal retaliation by the authorities.[88]

"Suicide," Hendin wrote, "is often the outgrowth of a devastating struggle to deal with conscious rage and conscious murderous impulses." In the case of young blacks, he noted, high rates of both homicide and suicide coexist and have done so at least as far back as the 1920s. Hendin concluded, "Among young adult blacks there is a direct relation, not an inverse one, between suicide and violence. It rests on the particular black experience in our culture, an experience that generates violence within blacks and presents them with a problem of controlling it."[89]

CONCLUSION:
WHY WAS CRIME SO LOW?

The 1950s were significantly less violent than other decades of the twentieth century, especially the 1920s and the 1970s. Four explanations for the relatively low rates of violent crime follow.

1. Less Drinking and Drug Use

Numerous studies have shown that alcohol is, overwhelmingly, the substance most frequently implicated in homicidal violence. Both alcohol and narcotic drug use were low in the 1950s, and the crimes associated with intoxication and supporting an addiction likewise were reduced. Beer consumption—the poor man's indulgence—actually declined during the 1950s, and total alcohol intake held steady (table 2.12). This occurred despite the general prosperity of the period, confounding claims that boom periods (the 1920s, for instance) breed crime because they are also booze periods. It was only in the mid- to late 1960s that alcohol consumption (and crime) started to accelerate.[90]

Table 2.12 Beer and alcohol consumption in the United States, selected years

| | Beer | | |
	Gallons per capita	Absolute alcohol	Total alcohol consumed
1945	24.2	1.1	2.0
1950	24.1	1.1	2.0
1955	**22.8**	**1.0**	**1.9**
1960	**22.1**	**1.0**	**2.0**
1965	22.8	1.0	2.2
1970	25.7	1.2	2.5

Source: Levine and Reinarman, "From Prohibition to Regulation," 468.

Figure 2.10 Deaths from cirrhosis of liver, by race, age-adjusted rates, 1935–78

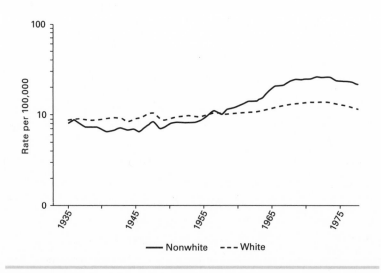

Source: Herd, "Migration," 399.

For nonwhites, judging by cirrhosis death rates in figure 2.10, alcohol intake started climbing in the late 1950s, but note that from the mid-1930s to the mid-1950s, black rates were lower than those of whites. The drinking practices of African Americans before 1960, presumably moderate, may have brought down their violent crime rates.[91]

In light of the enormous drug problem of the post-1960s period, it is enlightening to examine the drug situation in the immediately preceding decades. During World War II, supply lines, including those from Mexico, were disrupted, and opiate abuse probably hit an all-time low in the United States. Following the war, Mexico began growing poppies again, and trade routes were reestablished. Nonetheless, drug use remained low, especially among non-Hispanic whites.

It was the new arrivals in the big cities of the North, the blacks and Puerto Ricans, and the Mexican migrants on the West Coast who launched the "first wave" of heroin use.[92] Claude Brown's compelling account of growing up in Harlem in the late 1940s and early 1950s described the plague that struck his community.

> It had taken over the neighborhood, the entire community. I didn't know of one family in Harlem with three or more kids between the ages of fourteen and nineteen in which at least one of them wasn't on drugs. . . . People were more afraid than they'd ever been before. . . . People had guns in their houses because of the junkies. The junkies were committing almost all the crimes in Harlem.[93]

Data on the percentage of blacks arrested for drug violations and admitted to federal drug treatment facilities in Lexington, Kentucky, and Fort Worth, Texas, show big upticks in the 1950s (fig. 2.11). Nationwide, there were 4,262 drug arrests of African Americans in 1950, climbing to 11,816 in 1965. Figure 2.11 shows a relative decline in black arrests and admissions in the early 1960s, but this reflects growing white involvement and not greater black abstinence.

Figure 2.11   Narcotic use by African Americans, 1930–65

Blacks arrested for narcotics violations, cities with populations over 2,500
--- Blacks admitted to Lexington and Fort Worth Hospitals
Blacks living outside the South

Source: Courtwright, "Century of American Narcotic Policy," 18.

As for Hispanics, by 1966 they were more than a quarter of the addicts treated at Lexington: 13.9 percent were Puerto Rican; 12.2 percent were Mexican.[94]

The Federal Bureau of Narcotics, headed by Harry J. Anslinger, spearheaded antidrug law enforcement during the 1950s. At Anslinger's urging, Congress adopted a punitive approach, passing the Boggs Act of 1951 and the Narcotic Control Act of 1956, both of which provided lengthy mandatory sentences for possession and sale of drugs. Several states adopted baby Boggs acts, which also carried long prison sentences. Actually, Anslinger favored maximizing the punishment of possessors and sellers while simultaneously treating addicts. Such a policy made sense in the abstract, but implementation was another matter, because it was difficult to catch offenders and just as difficult to cure addicts.

While the authorities were unsuccessful in controlling heroin, sale and use was localized in a few big cities within poor black and Hispanic neighborhoods. This minimized the drug-related crime problem (cocaine was yet to burst on the scene), which was pretty much confined to those same communities. Moreover, while there is an established connection between heroin and theft, some researchers deny any link between this particular drug and crimes of violence.[95] Though we know that this story did not have a happy ending, low alcohol and opiate use in the 1950s must be counted as contributors to lower rates of violent crime.

2. The 1930s Baby Bust

Families shrank during the Depression, probably because young married couples felt that they simply couldn't afford many children. This baby bust led to fewer males of a high-crime age (roughly ages 18 to 35) in the decades that followed. For example, a man born in 1930, when the economy was in free fall, would have spent all of his young manhood, his twenties, in the decade that began with 1950.

We can see the demographics of the baby bust by considering cohorts of young males. In 1940, males between 15 and 24, age parameters adopted by the census, comprised 18 percent of the American male population. In 1950, the proportion declined to only 14.6 percent, shrinking to a century low of 13.5 percent in 1960. (In 1980, by contrast, 15- to 24-year-old males had grown to 19.5 percent of the population.) The next highest census group, the 25 to 34 cohort, made up 15.9 percent of the male population in 1940, 15.5 percent in 1950, and only 12.7 percent in 1960.[96] The birth dearth meant the decrease of a million people in the 25–34 age bracket during the 1950s.[97]

Some analysts attributed the great crime burst that began in the late 1960s to the baby boom of the immediate postwar period. The inverse is equally plausible: the baby bust of the Depression may have reduced violent crime in the 1950s simply because the young male population had shrunk. There were simply far fewer young people of the most criminogenic age group to engage in violence.

Not only were their numbers low, but the Depression cohorts had (for Americans, anyway) very low violent crime rates. Consider the homicide victimization rates of white males born between 1928 and 1932, a group reaching its maximum crime potential in the postwar period. In 1952, white males aged 20 to 24 had a homicide rate of 5.4 per 100,000. Five years later, in 1957, the same cohort, now aged 25 to 29, had a 6.0 rate. The rates were a bit higher, but still modest, for the late-Depression cohort born between 1933 and 1937. When they reached ages 20 to 24, the homicide rate for those who died in 1957 was 5.7. Five years later, in 1962, having reached ages 25 to 29, the death rate was 6.6.[98]

Table 2.13 displays homicide rates for white males aged 25 to 34 for the entire 1950s. Compare these figures with the rates for the same age and racial group in subsequent decades, including the notorious 1970s and '80s. In 1970, the rate was 12.5 per 100,000; in 1980, it was a chilling 18.5. In fact, after the 1950s, we would never again see rates this low in the twentieth century.[99]

Table 2.13 Homicide rates, white males, ages 25 to 34, 1950–54

	Rate per 100k		Rate per 100k
1950	5.4	1955	5.2
1951	5.5	1956	5.4
1952	5.6	1957	5.6
1953	5.4	1958	5.5
1954	5.4	1959	5.5

Source: National Center for Health Statistics, *Homicide in the United States 1950–1964*, table 3, 19.

To appreciate the role of the low youth population in the 1950s, I offer the following thought experiment. Imagine that during the crime-trough years, the size of the male 15–34 age group was typical of other decades in the twentieth century. Would there have been markedly higher homicide rates?

To ensure the accuracy of this analysis, start with the homicide mortality figures for 1960, a census year. In 1960, there were 2,757 deaths by homicide in this age and gender group.

The population of the group totaled 23,085,300, which was 12.9 percent of the general population of the United States. The homicide rate therefore was 11.94 per 100,000 (2,757 ÷ 23,085,300 × 100,000).

What happens when the more typical population distribution of 1970 is projected onto 1960? In 1970, males aged 15 to 34 were 14.7 percent of the entire U.S. population. Applying that same percentage, 14.7, to the 1960 general population gives us a total population of 26,360,507 for males aged 15 to 34. The 1960 homicide rate of 11.94 and the projected population of 26,360,507 yields 3,147 homicides instead of the actual 2,757, an increase of 14 percent (11.94 × 26,360,507 ÷ 100,000). In other words, homicides in 1960 were around 14 percent lower due to the reduced young male population.[100]

3. Less Black Crime

Since the late nineteenth century, African American homicide rates were consistently much higher than those of whites. They remained so in the 1950s, but that should not be taken to mean that there were no rate increases or decreases over time. When we look at black homicide rates in the years before and after the 1950s, it is evident that that decade was a far less violent period for African Americans (table 2.14).

Throughout the 1950s and into the early 1960s, African American homicide rates declined or held steady (fig. 2.12). This was true even for the segment most at risk, males between the ages of 25 and 34 (fig. 2.13). From 1950 to 1960, their homicide rates fell 18.8 percent.[101]

None of the most obvious factors

Table 2.14 Homicide rates, black males, 1940–80

	Rate per 100k
1940	54.4
1950	44.7
1960	35.0
1970	66.0
1980	65.7

Sources: National Center for Health Statistics, "Death Rates by Age, Race, and Sex"; National Center for Health Statistics, *Health, United States, 2006*, table 45, 228.

Figure 2.12 Homicide victimization rates, nonwhites, 1950–64

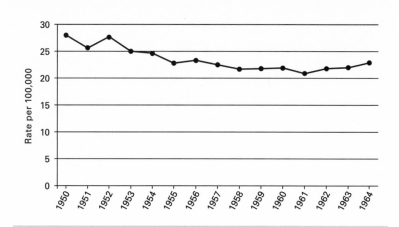

Source: National Center for Health Statistics, *Homicide 1950–1964*, table 3, 20.

Figure 2.13 Homicide victimization rates,
nonwhite males, ages 25 to 34, 1950–64

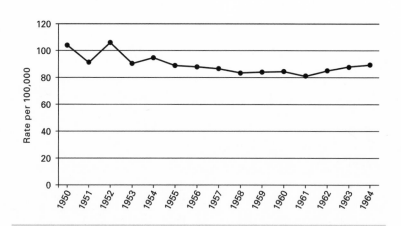

Source: National Center for Health Statistics, *Homicide*, table 3, 20.

seem to explain the drop. Take, for instance, socioeconomic progress. If economic improvement, greater social freedom, and better opportunities to advance are associated with reduced criminality, then African American crime rates *should* have declined in the 1950s. The postwar period was a time of enormous gains for blacks. However, these gains continued into the late 1960s and beyond, a period of major *increases* in black violent crime.

Demographics offers another plausible explanation, as the 1950s saw a declining young black male population. In the high-risk age bracket of 25 to 29, the drop was especially pronounced: down 5.5 percent from 1950 to 1960. However, the next highest age group, 30 to 34, saw a 10.3 percent population increase. Moreover, the young white population fell just as much as the black, if not more (a decline of 5.5 percent for white males aged 20 to 34; down 11.7 percent for the 25–29 cohort).[102] Yet, table 2.15 shows the white homicide rate essentially unchanged throughout the decade.

Low alcohol use among African Americans may have been a contributing factor, but judging by cirrhosis deaths, alcohol consumption among African Americans must have been rising sharply in the 1950s, as before decade's end, more blacks than whites succumbed to the liver disease.[103] Such a trend is difficult to square with declining murder rates. Moreover, if alcohol use was still modest in the 1950s, heroin ingestion was becoming more prevalent in poor black big-city

Table 2.15 Homicide rates by race, ages 25 to 34, 1950–59

	White (rate per 100k)	Black (rate per 100k)
1950	5.4	104.3
1951	5.5	91.5
1952	5.6	106.1
1953	5.4	90.6
1954	5.4	94.8
1955	5.2	89.1
1956	5.4	88.0
1957	5.6	86.7
1958	5.5	83.4
1959	5.5	84.2
Average	5.5	91.9

Sources: For 1950: National Center for Health Statistics, *Health, United States, 2006*, table 45, 228; for all other years: National Center for Health Statistics, *Homicide in the United States, 1950–1964*, table 3, 20.

communities. While heroin may not have increased murder rates (as would the cocaine wars in the late 1980s), it very likely was implicated in the surge in black-perpetrated robberies.

No other explanations for the black homicide decline come to mind. Given that white, but not black, rates were stable, there must have been some factor or group of factors that had a particular impact on African Americans, but what these might be remains a mystery.

Moreover, we must not overlook the fact that black homicide rates, despite the positive trend, far outstripped those of

Table 2.16   Arrests for selected offenses, by race, 1960

	White	Black
Violent crimes		
Murder/manslaughter	1,536	2,511
Robbery	10,994	14,155
Aggravated assault	15,856	26,849
Other assault	70,122	54,737
Rape	2,459	2,778
Weapons possession	14,729	17,005
Total	115,696	118,035
Nonviolent crimes		
Burglary	66,130	33,536
Larceny	129,158	65,063
Forgery	14,798	2,779
Drugs	8,506	7,570
Drunkenness	950,775	303,898
Total	1,169,367	412,846

Source: Federal Bureau of Investigation, *Crime in the United States, 1960,* Uniform Crime Reports, table 20, 95.

whites. If we compare rates for black and white males, ages 25 to 34, we see a mean differential of nearly 17 to 1 (see table 2.15).

For crimes of violence, such as murder, manslaughter, robbery, and aggravated assault, African Americans showed a disturbing preponderance. Whites were more likely to be arrested for nonviolent crimes, such as theft and drunkenness. With respect to robbery, however, African Americans were a steadily growing proportion of arrestees, from a bit over one-third in 1950 (35.7 percent) to well over one-half by decade's end (55.5 percent). Even if race bias infected arrest decisions (the police being overwhelmingly white in the 1950s), racism could not account for the enormous per capita differentials between the races or the predominance of black participation in crimes of violence (table 2.16).

Thus, the African American crime situation in the 1950s can't be said to have been auspicious, but things could always have been worse—as indeed they were at the end of the next decade. The fact is, however, black homicide rates in the 1950s probably were as low as they ever had been or ever would be in the entire twentieth century—a key reason for the relative tranquility of the period.

4. Rise of the Middle Class

America became an overwhelmingly middle-class country in the postwar era. Since the 1960s, when scholars "discovered" poverty, few academics have paid attention to the extraordinary gains made in individual income, comfort, and well-being during the 1950s.[104] These gains, however, were nothing short of spectacular, and their effect was to expand the size of the middle class, which, in the twentieth century, has always been the nonviolent class insofar as crime is concerned.

In many respects, the 1950s were the inverse of the early 1930s. The Great Depression, because of the magnitude of the downturn, expanded the size of the poverty class; the Great Boom of the 1950s reduced it. Crime in the early 1930s spiked (though not solely because of the Depression); crime in the 1950s remained flat or declined. By enlarging the size of the middle class and diminishing the number of impoverished Americans, the great postwar economic expansion reduced the size of the population most at risk for violent crime.

Economists estimate that in 1939, more than two-thirds of the American population—a staggering 68 percent—were at or below poverty standards. By 1959, that figure was nearly halved to 36 percent, a remarkable transformation. For high-crime segments of the population—males, the young, blacks, and city dwellers—the reductions in poverty, as shown in table 2.17, were nearly as impressive.[105] Thus, in only two decades, the United States had become an overwhelmingly middle-class nation, a society in which poverty itself had been transmuted from the common condition to a minority problem. The dramatic reduction in the size of the poverty class—the violent class—may have played a big part in the crime drop of the postwar period.

Table 2.17 Percentage of persons in poverty, by characteristics of household head, 1939, 1949, and 1959

	1939	1949	1959	% Change 1939–59
White men, ages 15–24	72.6	51.9	35.3	−51.4
Nonwhite men, ages 15–24	94.3	82.0	63.9	−32.2
White men, ages 25–64	63.2	45.5	25.6	−59.5
Nonwhite men, ages 25–64	90.8	75.1	52.0	−42.7
Inside SMSA	54.7	41.1	32.4	−40.8
Outside SMSA	83.4	69.3	45.2	−45.8
All persons	68.1	53.2	35.8	−47.4

Source: Ross, Danziger, and Smolensky, "Level and Trend of Poverty," 590.

Note: SMSA refers to Standard Metropolitan Statistical Area, a census designation for core urban areas with a substantial population together with adjacent communities having a high degree of economic and social integration with that core.

The reduction in crime was more than just a matter of economics. The surging economy worked synergistically with the family and suburban booms to restrain young males, the principal source of violence. David Courtwright, who chronicled the role of single young men in social disorder over the course of U.S. history, wrote the following about the postwar era.

> The postwar marriage, economic, educational, and suburban booms combined to give a record number of American men a huge emotional and financial stake in the system: wives, kids, jobs, respectability, homes, and mortgages. It was the middle-class experience mass-produced, and it exerted the same restraining influence that it had in the nineteenth century except that the number of affected men was proportionately larger.[106]

We gain perspective on the monumental changes that had taken place when we read remarks from the period by liberal economist John Kenneth Galbraith. In *The Affluent Society*, written in 1958, Galbraith stated that the economics of scarcity, applicable only a half-century earlier, must be replaced by the economics of wealth. We need not enter into the debate over economic theory, but the way Galbraith spoke about the United States of his day is revealing. After pointing out that "poverty had always been man's normal lot, and any other state was in degree unimaginable," he wrote,

> No one would wish to argue that the ideas which interpreted this world of grim scarcity would serve equally well for the contemporary United States. Poverty was the all-pervasive fact of that world. Obviously it is not of ours. One would not expect that the preoccupations of a poverty-ridden world would be relevant in one where the ordinary individual has access to amenities—foods, entertainment, personal transportation, and plumbing—in which not even the rich rejoiced a century ago.[107]

Galbraith quoted turn-of-the-century economist Alfred Marshall's comment that "the study of the causes of poverty . . . is the study of the causes of the degradation of a large part of mankind." Such a statement, Galbraith thought, was clearly inapplicable to 1950s America. "No contemporary economist," he assured us,

> would be likely to make such an observation about the United States. . . . The privation of which Marshall spoke was, going on to a century ago, the common lot at least of all who worked without special skill. As a general affliction, it was ended by increased output which, however imperfectly it may have been distributed, nevertheless accrued in substantial amount to those who worked for a living. The result was to reduce poverty from the problem of a majority to that of a minority.[108]

While it is logical to think that such a marked reduction in the size of the impoverished population must have translated into diminished violent crime, this claim must be reconciled with the fact that the percentage of the poverty class continued to decline through the 1970s—to as low as 11 percent by 1973[109]—despite enormous *increases* in violent crime. Indeed, if the size of the poor population (or its proportion of the total population) were the only, or even the principal, determinant of violent crime, crime rates would have been much higher throughout the late nineteenth and early twentieth centuries than they were in the last decades of the twentieth—which is plainly contrary to the facts.

The relationship between poverty and crime, however, is not a simple one. The size of the poverty class is but one factor influencing the volume of violent crime. Numerous other influences affect the behavior of the poor, whatever their fraction of the population. A crucial determinant is the culture of the various subgroups that comprise the low-income stratum, which includes the propensity of particular subcultures to engage in violent behavior. Nevertheless, the view here is that size also matters; a bigger poverty class, all things being equal, has the potential to produce more violent criminals than a smaller one.

In addition to size, the speed with which the ranks of the poor are enlarged or contracted also may be relevant. The marked expansion of the impoverished class in the Great Depression and its subsequent contraction during World War II each took place in just four years (1929 to 1933 and 1941 to 1945, respectively). That such enormous changes occurred in such remarkably brief time frames may well have accentuated the impact. In sum, massive and rapid expansions or contractions of the poorest segments of a population may produce crime increases or decreases, as the case may be.

On a related point, the movement of certain subcultural groups to the middle class may have contributed to a reduction in their crime levels. Those ethnic groups, such as the Irish and Italians, who had high violent crime rates in the past, seemed to have melted into the general population by the end of World War II, at least insofar as violent crime is concerned. In fact, evidence supports the idea that these immigrants were absorbed into the broader culture in the late 1930s and early 1940s, even before moving to the middle class.[110] Postwar ethnic crime data are nearly impossible to come by, but the impression is that crime rates in the 1950s for early-twentieth-century European immigrants and their progeny were a far cry from those of previous decades. No doubt, this was partly due to intermarriage and partly, in the case of the Italians, due to the aging and death of the original migrants. The Irish who arrived in the nineteenth century had long since died out, and their offspring had thoroughly assimilated.[111] We should not rule out the likelihood, however, that the decline in Euro-immigrant crime was a result of the movement of these groups into the middle class, a development that goes hand-in-hand with reductions in violence. This same positive development has been occurring in the African American community, especially since the success of the civil rights movement. However it occurs, and however long it may take, it is clear that violent subcultures can change.

◆ ◆ ◆

In 1960, Daniel Bell, one of the leading intellectuals of the postwar era, assured Americans that they were not experiencing a crime wave—it was a myth. Yes, there was racketeering, but that was just a "marginal business" activity. And there was a bit of a Negro crime problem, but this really was a class issue, implicitly resolvable, unlike a biological race issue. As for juvenile delinquency, in particular gang activity in the slums, that was "a form of social rebellion—an assertion of different values and norms." They'll probably grow out of it. The truth is, Bell assured readers, "in the *personal lives* of Americans, in the day-to-day routines of the city, there is *less* violence than a hundred or fifty or even twenty-five years ago."[112]

Bell's analysis had some merit. There *was* more violent crime in the 1850s, the early 1900s, and most certainly the 1920s than during the 1950s. Indeed, crime rates in the United States were probably lower from the late 1940s to the early 1960s than they ever had been for such a similarly protracted length of time in American history. What Bell did not know—perhaps could not know—was that he was writing at the *end* of a golden age, and America was on the cusp of one of the biggest violent crime waves of all.

CHAPTER 3

Ordeal

The Great Post-1960s Crime Rise

INTRODUCTION

No decade in the twentieth century, except perhaps the depression-wracked 1930s, seared itself into the consciousness of the nation like the 1960s. The conflicts and quarrels of that era engendered profoundly new, and often unsettling, perspectives and values that shaped the content and tone of public discourse for years afterward. From the 1970s to the 1990s, it seemed as if every public issue—from race relations to foreign relations—was thrashed out with the '60s in mind. This was due, in great measure, to the sheer intensity of the era's painful conflicts. Social lubricants wore thin, and everyone seemed angry and very close to violence. All too often, the line was crossed, and uncontrolled fury trampled civility into the dust.

Did Americans suffer through the most protracted and disturbing violent crime rise in over 100 years because they had become embittered and hostile toward one another, had their faith in authority figures shattered, or had lost all "hope of winning respect by legitimate means"? Or was it because of an increase in the number of young persons with shortened "time horizons" and a reduced "internalized commitment to self-control"?[1]

These explanations, among many, have been offered to account for the great crime rise.[2] At the end of this chapter, I discuss the three factors I believe were the most instrumental. First, however, we must examine closely the violent crime itself, separating out the other violence of the period—the ferocious protests, the horrific riots, the ideologically inspired bombings. We must scrutinize "ordinary" crime by "ordinary" people: the assaults and murders arising out of petty personal conflicts and the robberies and assaults that seemed to have little to do with the Vietnam War or racial conflict. We must ask whether these crimes—the kind that terrified Americans throughout this modern thirty years' war—were caused by America's malaise or were simply a part of it.

Before examining violent crime in detail, we turn to general history, to the bright and shining hope of the early 1960s and its shattering climax by decade's end.

THE 1960s

On January 20, 1961, millions of Americans watched on television as their youthful new president, John F. Kennedy, gave his inaugural address. In ringing words, he sought to inspire them to national service: "Ask not what your country can do for you," he beseeched, "ask what you can do for your country." And he warned foreign nations that the United States was resolute. "Let every nation know, whether it wishes us well or ill, that we shall pay any price, bear any burden, meet any hardship, support any friend, oppose any foe, to assure the survival and the success of liberty."[3]

It is telling that a president thought that the American public would be receptive to such words. They reveal the optimism and high hopes that ushered in the new decade. The nation was at peace, the Korean War and a rabid strain of domestic anticommunism having faded into the past. And the country was prosperous: six out of every ten Americans owned their own homes, and eight out of ten owned a car. Though the work week was down to forty hours, family purchasing power was 30 percent greater than it had been a decade earlier.

For African Americans, long held to the most menial jobs, income levels were rising dramatically, and the black-white income gap was narrowing. In 1940, intact black families earned a mere 42 percent of white family income; in 1960, they earned 61 percent of that income. The disparity would decline even more in the following decades. Black poverty levels were falling just as rapidly. Three-quarters of all black families were poor in

Figure 3.1   Median income of family head, by race

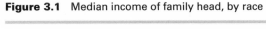

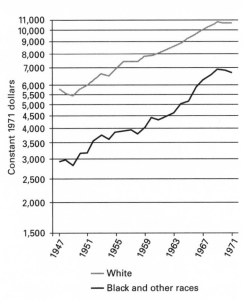

Source: U.S. Office of Management and Budget, *Social Indicators*, 153.

Figure 3.2 Individuals below low income level, by race

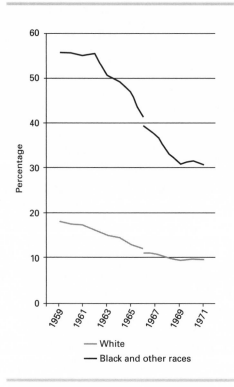

— White
— Black and other races

Source: U.S. Office of Management and Budget, *Social Indicators,* 166.

1940; this was reduced to 40 percent by 1960. A big reason for the improvement in black conditions was their continuing migration north, where salaries were much higher. By 1960, 40 percent of the African American population lived outside of the South, mainly in big cities—an extraordinary reversal of prewar demographics.[4]

The black migration to northern cities came with a huge social price tag: relocation raised violent crime levels dramatically in those urban areas. However, in 1960, few saw this as the megaproblem it would become. After all, crime figures continued to be low. Murder rates were 5.0 per 100,000, a bit less than they had been in 1950. True, robbery was up: 59.9 per 100,000, compared with 48.5 a decade earlier. Still, there was no need for panic. The big population growth was in the tranquil suburbs, and crime was an inner-city problem.

By the end of the decade, all of this optimism evaporated in a blizzard of violence and killing. Riots, crime, and disorderly protests accompanied increasingly audacious challenges to authority figures and, indeed, to authority itself. In 1968, an astonishing 81 percent of the American public told interviewers that law and order had broken down altogether in the United States.[5] By the late 1960s, presidential calls for public service would have been unimaginable. People were more apt to ask what Americans were doing *to* their country.

The social deterioration began in the second half of the decade, though the first of a series of truly shocking acts of violence—the assassination of President Kennedy—took place earlier, on November 22, 1963. Before his untimely death, Kennedy had expressed concern about juvenile delinquency and even established a Committee on Juvenile Delinquency and Youth Crime. Little came of this, even though Congress approved demonstration projects that served as forerunners of the much more elaborate and lavishly funded "war on poverty" initiated by Kennedy's successor. That advisors to Kennedy's committee considered the "disorganized slum," as they called it, principally a source of petty crime and gang fights is yet another mark of the naive optimism that began the decade.[6]

Lyndon Baines Johnson, the new president, was determined to advance Kennedy's legacy. He was a bread-and-butter FDR liberal, convinced, along with other liberals of his generation, that government could engineer socioeconomic progress. In foreign affairs, which did not especially interest him, he shared the anticommunist perspective that animated members of both political parties. Within a year and a half of taking the oath of office in 1963, Johnson led Congress in an extraordinary range of enactments the likes of which had not been seen since Roosevelt's first 100 days. He presided over an expansion of the war in Vietnam, a domestic "war" on poverty, federal aid to education, Medicare for the elderly, Medicaid for the poor, immigration reform, and two historic civil rights laws. Within five years, protest, turmoil, and violence would utterly destroy his presidency.[7]

THE GREAT FEAR

By the end of the 1960s, a great fear gripped America. It was largely a fear of crime, especially violent assaults, whose frequency had skyrocketed. Anxiety was especially pronounced in big cities, where polls indicated that one of every two people was afraid to go out alone at night. African Americans were even more frightened than whites, women were more afraid than men, and seniors were the most terrified of all. Barricaded in their apartments, some of the elderly were reported to go without meals rather than risk walking to the grocery store and back. People became reluctant to go downtown, except as work demanded it. Whites (and, where they could, middle-class African Americans) fled to the suburbs, finding jobs and entertainment outside of the central city. Tourism declined; hotels and restaurants suffered; and entertainment venues, such as theaters and concert halls, lost ticket buyers. Downtown streets emptied at night and became even more frightening. People avoided public transportation systems, which anyone, including muggers, could use. The nation's great cities—New York, Philadelphia, Chicago, and Los Angeles—were turning into centers of dread and angst.[8] A late-1960s presidential commission on the causes and prevention of violence acknowledged the problem.

> To millions of Americans few things are more pervasive, more frightening, more real today than violent crime and the fear of being assaulted, mugged, robbed, or raped. The fear of being victimized by criminal attack has touched us all in some way. People are fleeing their residences in cities to the expected safety of suburban living. Residents of many areas will not go out on the street at night. Others have added bars and extra locks to windows and doors in their homes. Bus drivers in major cities do not carry cash because incidents of robbery have been so frequent. In some areas local citizens patrol the streets at night to attain the safety they feel has not been provided.[9]

Much of the fear was focused on young black males, who committed an inordinate number of the assaults, especially in the big metropolitan areas to which they or their parents had recently migrated. But some elites—public figures, experts and academics, even the news media—were reluctant to discuss the racial dimension of the crime problem. To acknowledge the high rate of black crime, they thought, would give aid and comfort to bigotry at a time when long overdue civil rights gains finally were being realized. Some of the analysts were scared of being branded racists. Others were guilt-ridden over the long history of black oppression or were committed to a liberal ideology that deflected the race issue by treating crime as a product of discrimination, poverty, or other so-called root causes. Whatever the explanation, the result was the same—a denial of reality. At the extreme, some people even doubted that there was a crime problem. For instance, one sociologist wrote that "the euphemism 'crime in the streets' is the perpetuation of . . . [white] paranoia" grounded in the old racial canard "that blacks were out to take their lives and property."[10] Another writer, subsequently an established criminologist, thought that crime statistics were inviting too much attention to race. He called for the "elimination of racial classifications from public criminal statistical reports." After all, he pointed out, "we do not indicate the arrest rates of Baptists or Republicans."[11]

Of course, the evidence of rising crime was overwhelming. It was, in fact, as one popular account put it, "a crime wave of epic proportions."[12] What turned this wave into a tsunami were three different developments. First, the magnitude of the violence over a sustained length of time was greater than anything experienced since the late nineteenth century. Second, because the violence involved a high incidence of attacks by strangers in metropolitan areas, it put millions of people in fear and had a chilling effect on day-to-day activities in the nation's cities. Third, the wildly disproportionate black male involvement plus high rates of white victimization injected into the equation the touchy subject of race relations. The racial aspect of the problem made crime control more difficult and simultaneously made it harder to reduce race prejudice in the United States.

MEASURING CRIME

Between 1960 and 1970, rates of violent crime (essentially, murder, rape, robbery, and serious assaults) in the United States more than doubled, from 161 per 100,000 to 364. Murder rates rose 55 percent, while robbery rates climbed over 91 percent. The bulk of the increase occurred in the second half of the decade, during the time of the riots and Vietnam War protests. Whereas, between 1960 and 1964, violent crime rates averaged 168 per 100,000, never exceeding 200, between 1965 and 1969, rates never fell *below* 200, and the mean was 260. Bad as it was in the late 1960s, things grew worse with each succeeding decade. In the 1970s, the average violent crime rate rose to a shocking 452 per 100,000, only to soar still further in the 1980s, climbing another 31 percent to 594. And even that wasn't the peak; the average for the first half of the 1990s was a staggering 741 per 100,000. From 1960 to 1990, violent crime in the United States increased 353 percent. Figure 3.3 depicts the Everest-like trend over three and a half decades.

One confirmation of the upward trend is homicide mortality data—records of killings deemed by county coroners or medical examiners attributable to human agency. These data have the advantage of relying neither on public reporting of crimes (dead bodies are invariably counted, but roughly half of all nonhomicide violent crimes go unreported) nor on the effectiveness of police detection efforts. Figure 3.4 shows a homicide climb similar to that of violent crime, except with a less exaggerated peak from the late 1980s onward.[13]

Two other pieces of data are suggestive of a general crime rise, though they are less authoritative with respect to violent crime. The first indicator is property crime (burglary, larceny, and motor vehicle theft), which also spiraled upward. Property crime rates climbed 110 percent from 1960 to 1970, escalated another 48 percent in the 1970s, and didn't turn downward until the early 1980s.[14] Of course, while property crime could have

Figure 3.3 Violent crimes known to police, rate per 100,000, 1960–95

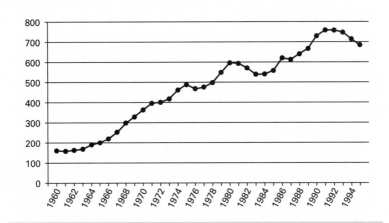

Source: Federal Bureau of Investigation, Uniform Crime Reporting Statistics, "UCR Data Online," http://www.ucrdatatool.gov/.

Figure 3.4 Homicide victimization rates, 1960–95

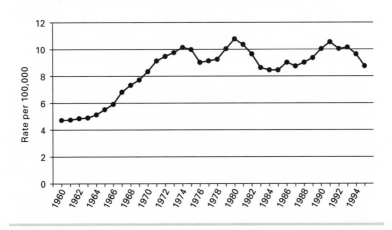

Source: U.S. Department of Justice, Bureau of Justice Statistics, "Homicide Rate Trends."

risen without an increase in violent offenses (or vice versa), surging property crime rates are indicative of the general lawlessness of the period.

GLOBAL CRIME

The second indicator of a general crime rise was the escalation in multinational lawlessness in the late 1960s and thereafter. This could mean that single-nation (U.S.-only) explanations are mistaken and that the crime rise was a respone to global developments. Francis Fukuyama pointed out that at roughly the same time violent crime rates shot up in the United States, they rose in several developed countries, including England and Wales, Sweden, Canada, Finland, and the Netherlands. (Japan, on the other hand, experienced a big crime *decline* starting in the early 1960s, and crime did not significantly increase in other developed polities in Asia, such as Korea, Hong Kong, and Singapore—though Fukuyama doesn't say why.)[15]

A systematic study of homicide in 24 industrialized countries between 1956 and 1998 by Gary LaFree and Kriss Drass seems to throw cold water on Fukuyama's assertions.[16] LaFree and Drass found that only a minority of these countries suffered rapid and sustained crime increases. Five nations (the United States, Canada, Greece, Spain, and Italy; fig. 3.5) went through late- or post-1960s crime "booms" (defined as "crime rates that increase rapidly and exhibit a positive sustained change in direction"[17]), but 19 countries did not.

Was Fukuyama wrong? Did "most of the industrialized world" *not* experience a violent crime surge? This cannot be determined from LaFree and Drass's study, as it measured only homicide, which may not be representative of trends in other violent crimes. Moreover, all but 2 (Japan and Singapore) of the 24 industrialized societies examined by LaFree and Drass experienced increased homicides, and the growth was rapid in 14 of them. They were not considered "crime boom" entities only because they did not meet the authors' statistical test for a sustained increase.[18]

Figure 3.5 Homicide victimization rates, five industrialized nations, 1956–98

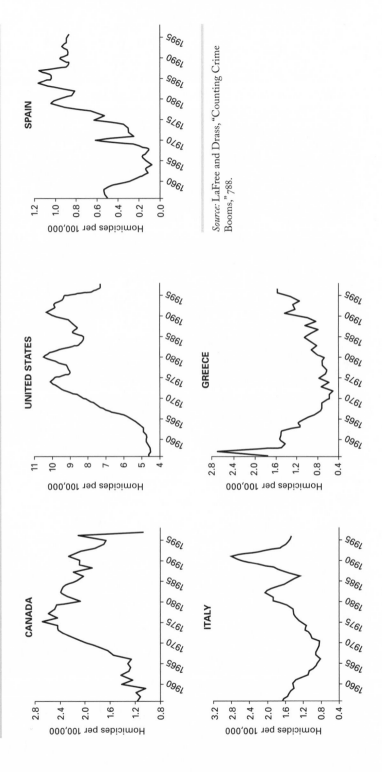

Source: LaFree and Drass, "Counting Crime Booms," 788.

It is especially interesting that the 5 crime-boom nations went through considerable social or political unrest in this period; for instance, Spain's Francisco Franco died in 1975, the same year in which Greece adopted a new constitution following the 1974 overthrow of a military junta. This tends to support Fukuyama's contention that crime and social turmoil are linked. Such a conclusion, however, would require a closer examination of conditions in each of the crime-boom countries, along with those of nonboom nations.

MAGNITUDE AND DURATION OF THE BOOM

As best we can tell—data are sketchy prior to the 1930s—the late-1960s crime rise was the biggest sustained escalation in criminal violence in the United States since the 1870s. The most accurate way to compare the 1960s with earlier eras is to examine homicide mortality rates, as we have pretty reliable data on such killings. Though much is omitted with this analysis—most obviously, other violent crimes—we at least gain a fairly trustworthy sense of the differences between crime at the beginning and end of the twentieth century.

Figure 3.6 compares the 1910–36 and 1970–95 periods. These years were selected because they were characterized by sustained periods of 8 or more homicides per 100,000 annually. (There were, however, three years in the earlier period—1910, 1918, and 1920—in which rates dipped to 7.9 and 7.8 per 100,000. Rates in the late 1960s were excluded, because, although they were rising each year, they had not quite reached 8, topping out at 7.7 in 1969.)[19]

How do the two periods compare? The early boom lasted 26 years, with a slight dip around World War I (years 9–11 on the horizontal axis of figure 3.6) and at the start of the great downturn in the last half of the 1930s. The post-1960s crime onslaught ran for a similar length of time—25 years—with a drop-off in the mid-1980s (years 14–16 in figure 3.6). Thus, the post-1960s boom, while agonizingly persistent, lasted no longer than the century's first homicide upswing.

But there was one significant difference between the two

Figure 3.6 Homicide victimization rates, 1910–36 and 1970–95

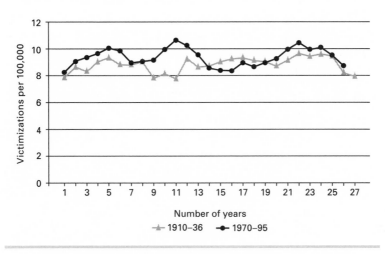

Sources: For 1910–32, Eckberg, "Estimates," 13; for 1933–95, U.S. Department of Justice, Bureau of Justice Statistics, "Homicide Rate Trends."

crime surges: the end-of-century wave was more violent. The average annual homicide rate in the earlier period was 8.89 per 100,000, but for the years 1970–95 it was 9.41, 6 percent higher. Moreover, the number of years with exceptionally high rates, here defined as 9.5 per 100,000 or higher, was considerably greater in the more recent era. There were 10 such killer years versus 4 earlier in the century. In sum, whereas the durations of the two crime upturns were roughly equal, the magnitude of the recent boom was much greater.[20]

STRANGER ASSAULT

Another distinction between the two high-crime periods renders the recent era much more socially destructive: the greater incidence of attacks, primarily robberies, by strangers. Unfortunately, lacking national data on reported crimes or arrests, we do not know with great certainty the robbery rates in the first three decades of the twentieth century, but we have reason to think they were extremely low relative to the final decades.

Robbery, which had been of little concern in the late 1800s, increased markedly as the new century began. As crime historian Roger Lane observed, despite the prevalence of handguns in the waning decades of the nineteenth century, "armed robbery was for unclear reasons virtually unknown then in the urban east."[21] This soon began to change. Jeffrey Adler's incisive work on Chicago ably documents the developments in the Windy City up to 1920. He showed that between 1890 and 1920, the population rose 146 percent and homicides increased 376 percent—but robbery-homicides jumped 1,950 percent.[22]

As disturbing as early-twentieth-century robbery growth was, it paled beside the end-of-century rates. Chicago provides proof of this, as its police department kept accurate records throughout the century, enabling us to track changes in a single jurisdiction with the same police force. From 1930 to 1970, robbery rates in Chicago rose 233 percent, and by 1980, they had climbed 285 percent (table 3.1). With 1920 as the baseline, the variance is even greater: up 325 percent by 1970 and 392 percent by 1980. Judging by Chicago's experience, robbery was much more of a threat in the post-1960s era than in earlier years.[23]

Boston is another city with credible police records affording us crime data over a long time span. Table 3.2 shows robbery arrest rates per 100,000 from the late nineteenth century to 1982. As is obvious, the rate soared, more than tripling between

Table 3.1 Robbery arrests of males, Chicago, selected years

	Arrests	Chicago population	Arrest rate (per 100k)
1920	1,231	2,701,705	45.6
1930	1,968	3,376,438	58.3
1970	6,533	3,366,957	194.0
1980	6,743	3,005,072	224.4

Sources: Willbach, "Trend of Crime in Chicago," 722; Chicago Police Department, *Chicago Police Annual Report, 1970,* 18; Chicago Police Department, *Statistical Summary, 1980,* 12.

1937–51 and 1970–71, and increasing sevenfold in the early 1980s.[24]

Comparable conclusions may be drawn from a study by James Boudouris of homicides in Detroit. From 1926 to 1929, Boudouris counted 71 homicides that involved "criminal transactions." Excluding killings that were unlikely to involve robberies or attacks on strangers, such as criminal abortions and bootlegger gang slayings, there were 17.75 incidents of this type per year, for an annual rate of 1.24 per 100,000 of Detroit's population. By contrast, from 1965 to 1968, which was only the start of the 1960s crime explosion, there were 143 such homicides, for an average of 35.75 per year and a mean annual rate of 2.45 per 100,000—a near doubling (97.6 percent rise) of the 1920s rate. In 1974, after the end date for Boudouris's study, robbery homicides in Detroit skyrocketed to a frightening 155 per year.[25]

A final piece of evidence of the rise in attacks on strangers is the proportion of prisoners convicted of robbery at various points over the course of the twentieth century. In 1904, a mere 1 percent of all state and federal commitments were for robbery. In 1910, the rate was 5 percent. By 1933, when violent crime peaked for the prewar period, the percentage rose to 12, tailing off to about 9 during the great crime dip of the 1940s and '50s. By 1970, however, 14 percent of all those sentenced to one year or more in prison were robbers, and in 1981, the figure had escalated to 18 percent.[26]

Thus, the best evidence suggests that stranger violence— robbery is perpetrated by strangers in roughly eight out of every ten cases—was a much bigger problem near the end than at the start of the twentieth century. In fact, even in the relatively short period between the late 1950s and the 1970s, there was a huge

Table 3.2 Robbery arrest rates, Boston, selected years

	Arrest rate (per 100k)
1895–1915	24
1916–1936	32
1937–1951	36
1960	55
1970–1971	119
1981–1982	258

Sources: Ferdinand, "Criminal Patterns of Boston," 93; City of Boston, *Annual Report*, 1960, 1970, 1971, 1981–82.

Table 3.3 Homicides by strangers, Atlanta, Houston, and Philadelphia, by selected dates

		Stranger homicides (%)		Stranger homicides (%)
Atlanta	1961–62	1.3	1971–72	15.0
Houston	1958–61	3.3	1979	17.6
Philadelphia	1948–52	12.4	1978	29.2

Source: Riedel, "Stranger Violence," 237.

spike in killings by strangers (table 3.3). By the late 1970s, as a big-city survey showed, around 28 percent of homicides were perpetrated by someone with whom the victim was unacquainted.[27]

It was attacks by strangers that made the late-twentieth-century crime wave so devastating. High as the murder rates were in the early decades of the century, victimization was by and large avoidable. If one didn't associate with violent young men, especially young men who drank, one faced an infinitely greater likelihood of injury or death from an errant automobile or a dangerous work site than from a criminal assault. The chances of being robbed, or, worse still, robbed and physically assaulted (or even killed), were, by conservative estimate, at least two to four times as great in the most recent crime wave.

Furthermore, the apprehension of crime, which also soared starting in the late 1960s, was almost as harmful to American society as the actuality. By 1972, four out of ten Americans were afraid to walk alone in their communities at night, and for African Americans, the poor, the elderly, and big-city dwellers, the figure was one out of two.[28]

FEARS AND REALITIES

Fear of assault was especially disastrous for big cities, where everyday activities, such as traveling to work, school, or the grocer, placed people in close proximity to strangers, sometimes scores of strangers, as on a bus or subway. While the odds of any one of these passersby mugging someone were extremely low (though they multiplied considerably in high-crime communities), the chances that an American would be violently victimized during his or her lifetime reached astronomical proportions by the mid-1980s. The likelihood of an occurrence, however, is only one of the factors affecting perceptions, as any deterrence theorist (or lottery official) will tell you. The uncertainty or unpredictability of the event, the inability to take precautions against it, and the potentially devastating consequences should it occur make all the difference.

The fear of violence after the 1960s was fully warranted. The frequency of violent confrontations between 1970 and 1990 reached the point where the word *terrifying* was not inapt. According to the National Crime Victim Survey, there were approximately 10.9 million violent crimes per year, including 1.4 million robberies. Common as automobile accidents were in the United States, one stood a much better chance of being victimized by violent crime (31 of every 1,000 adults) than of being injured in a motor vehicle (22 per 1,000).[29]

The federal Bureau of Justice Statistics once calculated, based on crime victimization rates from 1975 to 1984, the lifetime chances of being raped, robbed, or assaulted. The numbers were astounding. If crime rates remained the same (which, of course, they didn't), 83 percent of all Americans aged 12 at the time would, in their actuarial lifetimes, be victimized by an attempted or completed violent crime, and 40 percent would be injured as a result of a robbery or assault.[30]

The fear of strangers was equally justified. Nearly six out of every ten violent crimes were perpetrated by someone completely unknown to the victim or known only by sight. For robbery, the proportion of offenses perpetrated by strangers climbed as high as 84 percent. Even for aggravated assault and rape, which in the past were more likely to be committed by acquaintances of the victims, unknown assailants were responsible for a majority of the attacks.[31]

For millions of Americans, the consequences of a mugging were devastating. One-third of all violent crimes involved a weapon, and more than half of the robbers were armed with either handguns or knives. Consequently, over 2.2 million Americans *per year* suffered injuries as a result of crimes, and 350,000 of the injuries were considered serious: gunshot and knife wounds, broken bones, loss of consciousness, dislodged teeth, and internal injuries, with some requiring hospitalizations lasting two days or more. From 1973 to 1991, 36.6 million people were injured in a violent crime, and over 6 million of them suffered serious injuries.[32]

Economic losses were comparably staggering. Time lost from work due to personal victimization alone totaled an estimated $112.6 million in 1974. More comprehensive measures in 1992—including work time lost because of injuries, the need to repair or replace damaged or stolen property, and time spent as a criminal justice complainant—generated a shocking $1.4 billion figure.[33]

CITIES

The great crime wave was especially devastating in the nation's big cities, where fear of crime inhibited the movement of people that is so essential to urban life. Between 1965 and 1982, there was a 41 percent increase in the proportion of Americans expressing fear of walking about their neighborhoods (table 3.4).[34]

Popular culture reflected and exploited urban anxieties. In the 1974 film *The Taking of Pelham One Two Three*, armed hijackers seize a subway car, threatening to kill the commuters unless they are paid $1 million within an hour. That same year saw the release of the first of a series of movies entitled *Death Wish*, in which a husband hunts down the men who broke into his New York City apartment, murdered his wife, and raped his daughter. The 1981 science fiction movie *Escape from New York* portrays all of Manhattan as a giant maximum security

Table 3.4 Survey respondents reporting fear of
walking alone at night, selected years, 1965–2010

Question: "Is there any area near where you live—that is, within a mile—
where you would be afraid to walk alone at night?"

	Afraid (%)	Not afraid (%)		Afraid (%)	Not afraid (%)
1965	34	66	1994	39	60
1967	31	67	1996	39	60
1968	35	62	1997	38	61
1972	42	57	2000	34	66
1975	45	55	2001	30	69
1977	45	55	2002	35	64
1979	42	58	2003	36	64
1981	45	55	2004	32	67
1982	48	52	2005	38	62
1983	45	55	2006	37	63
1989	43	57	2007	37	62
1990	40	59	2008	37	63
1992	44	56	2009	34	66
1993	43	56	2010	37	63

Source: U.S. Department of Justice, Bureau of Justice Statistics,
"Sourcebook of Criminal Justice Statistics Online," table 2.37.2010,
http://www.albany.edu/sourcebook/pdf/t2372010.pdf.

prison, a sort of metro Devil's Island, with mined bridges and
perimeter security walls running along the shoreline to prevent
escape.[35]

Mass media, such as newspapers and television, relentlessly
broadcast crimes of violence, in both fictitious and factual por-
trayals, but researchers found that this had a variable impact
on crime perceptions and attitudes. The impact depended on

Table 3.5 Violent crimes known to police, rate per 100,000, by size of city, 1950–80

City population/year	Murder/ manslaughter	Rape	Robbery	Aggravated assault	Total violent crime	Decadal change in total rates (%)	Decadal change in robbery rates (%)
1 million +							
1950	2.6	—	63.2	52.5	358.3		
1960	6.1	20.0	133.8	198.4	1,204.8		
1970	18.4	38.5	778.0	369.9	1,204.8	+236	**+482**
1980	29.4	63.7	1,051.9	559.6	1,704.6	+42	+35
250,000 +							
1950	3.5	9.2	53.5	59.3	125.5		
1960	6.8	15.2	117.6	154.1	293.7	+134	+120
1970	17.5	39.7	589.4	333.9	980.5	+234	**+401**
1980	24.4	74.6	800.2	514.9	1,414.1	+44	+36
Under 10,000							
1950	1.6	4.4	11.3	16.6	33.9		
1960	2.7	3.3	12.8	28.9	47.7	+41	+13
1970	2.6	7.3	23.6	107.8	141.3	+196	**+84**
1980	4.5	16.5	54.9	221.6	297.5	+111	+133

Sources: Federal Bureau of Investigation, *Uniform Crime Reports for the United States and Its Possessions,* 1950 (table 3, 8); Federal Bureau of Investigation, *Crime in the United States,* Uniform Crime Reports: 1960 (table 6, 81); 1970 (table 9, 104–5); 1980 (table 14, 173–74). Data for violent crimes other than rape, 1950, cities of one million or more (except New York City, for which data are not available), calculated by author based on Federal Bureau of Investigation, *Uniform Crime Reports for the United States and Its Possessions,* 1950 (table 8, 14–15). Data for rape, 1950, cities of one million or more, are not available.

such factors as the proportion of a newspaper devoted to crime coverage and the sensational nature of the crime.[36]

While the entertainment industry sought to capitalize on the public's fears, the realities of crime provided daily reinforcement of America's angst, especially in the big metropolitan areas, where stranger crimes, robbery in particular, seemed to be out of control. In cities of a quarter million people or more, robbery reports to the police rose over 400 percent in the decade between 1960 and 1970 (table 3.5). In cities with over one million people, the increase was a stunning 482 percent. Violent crime rose everywhere in the United States, even in small cities and towns with 10,000 or fewer people, but the comparable robbery rate increase in these locales was "only" 84 percent (though it shot up another 133 percent in the decade between 1970 and 1980).

Urban murder rates also spiked in the late 1960s: compare figures from 1964 with rates from 1970 in table 3.6. By 1980, five of the biggest cities in the United States (New York, Chicago, Los Angeles, Detroit, and Philadelphia), which accounted for only 7 percent of the nation's population, generated 20 percent of U.S. homicides, which now topped 23,000 annually. (In 1960, 9,110 people were slain; 16,000 were slain in 1970.)

The association of cities with crime, especially violent crime, had by the late twentieth century hardened into dogma, though rural areas (in the South especially) in the late nineteenth and early twentieth centuries had considerably higher rates of homicide than did their urban counterparts. The big change in cities in the twentieth century was wrought largely by the entry through immigration or migration of groups that had high preexisting rates of violence. In the case of the post-1960s crime wave, African American migration to big cities and, secondarily, Mexican and Puerto Rican migrations accounted for much of the increased urban violence. Crime by non-Hispanic whites rose dramatically, too, but it was black crime in big cities that proved to be the most vexing part of the violent crime problem.

Table 3.6 Murders known to police, rate per 100,000, selected metropolitan areas, 1964, 1970, 1980, and 1990

	1964	1970	1980	1990
Atlanta	11.2	20.4	14.4	13.7
Baltimore	9.0	13.2	12.5	15.6
Chicago	7.2	12.9	14.5	15.6
Cleveland	6.4	14.5	15.9	11.3
Dallas	12.7	18.4	18.1	21.4
Detroit	5.0	14.7	16.1	16.3
Houston	11.0	16.9	27.6	21.1
Kansas City	6.2	12.6	15.0	11.4
Los Angeles	4.8	9.4	23.3	19.9
Louisville	6.3	15.0	10.4	6.9
Memphis	8.0	13.0	19.5	22.9
Miami	6.2	15.6	32.7	19.9
Newark	4.4	9.5	11.2	10.0
New Orleans	–	11.9	22.3	31.2
New York	6.1	10.5	21.0	26.9
Philadelphia	5.4	9.3	12.1	13.2
Pittsburgh	2.8	4.4	4.5	3.3
Richmond	9.5	14.9	12.4	18.7
St. Louis	7.2	14.8	15.2	12.9
San Francisco	4.3	8.3	11.7	9.2
Washington, D.C.	8.4	11.4	10.7	17.4

Sources: Federal Bureau of Investigation, *Crime in the United States*, Uniform Crime Reports: 1964 (table 4, 70ff.); 1970 (table 5, 82ff.); 1980 (table 5, 60ff.); 1990 (appendix 4, 331ff.).

Riots

In August 1965, just five days after enactment of the Voting Rights Act, the Watts section of Los Angeles erupted in violence. African American youth smashed and burned shops, stole merchandise, set buildings ablaze, and rampaged for six straight days, at the end of which 34 people had been killed, 1,032 wounded, and 3,952 arrested. It took 1,000 Los Angeles police officers, 700 sheriff's deputies, and 14,000 National Guardsmen to quell the disturbance. Property damage came to about $40 million.

The year 1965 marked the first of several long, hot summers as blacks rampaged in city after city throughout the late 1960s. Stephan and Abigail Thernstrom tallied 329 riots in 257 cities between 1964 and 1968. Economists William Collins and Robert Margo uncovered an even greater number—an astonishing 752 racial disorders from 1964 to 1971. By an objective measure of severity, 130 of the 752 riots were considered "major" and 37 were labeled "massive" in destructiveness.[37]

Even the compilation in table 3.7 is incomplete; a study of largely Hispanic disorders found 43 more riots, 12 of which were deemed major. It should be kept in mind, however, that the overwhelming majority of American cities had no disorders, and the vast majority of African Americans were not involved in any misconduct—even in riot-torn cities.[38]

The worst year for rioting was 1968, a year in which the country seemed close to coming apart at the seams. Martin Luther King Jr. was murdered on April 4, touching off a spasm of racial disturbances in 125 cities that left 46 people dead. While the King assassination was the obvious provocation for the violence that spring, there was no distinct aim or focus for most of the other disturbances. One quantitative study reported that 60 percent of the riots "had no clear-cut target or symbol."[39]

The 1960s disturbances were not like the race riots before World War II, which involved whites clashing with blacks. In the 1960s, there were few violent confrontations between mobs of whites and blacks, though whites did comprise the vast bulk of the police and armed forces sent to quell the disturbances. The 1960s eruptions were largely (though not exclusively) monoracial. Whites, however, sometimes joined in the looting, and, as noted, Hispanics engaged in several riots of their own.

While many of the disorders began with a police action, the precipitating events did not necessarily involve racial abuse or acts of gross discrimination. In fact, as was the case with Watts, the triggers scarcely seem noteworthy at all, so commonplace were they. In the most lethal of the riots, in 1967 in Detroit, where 43 people died in four nightmarish days of turmoil, the violence began with a routine police raid on a so-called blind pig, a nightclub in which liquor was served after hours in violation of state law. Subsequent charges of police brutality during the raid never were substantiated.[40]

The overwhelming majority of the rioters appeared interested only in looting to obtain free merchandise and in destroying property; there is little indication that they were intent on delivering a political message or engaging in social protest. There was massive destruction of stores (many black-owned) and widespread theft of goods, but relatively

Table 3.7 Race riots in the United States, 1964–71

	1964	1965	1966	1967	1968	1969	1970	1971	Total
Riots	11	11	53	158	289	124	68	38	752
Riot days	34	20	109	408	739	284	126	82	1,802
Deaths	2	35	11	83	66	13	13	5	228
Injuries	996	1,132	525	2,801	5,302	861	710	414	12,741
Arrests	2,917	4,219	5,107	17,011	31,680	4,730	2,027	1,408	69,099
Arson	238	3,006	812	4,627	6,041	369	283	459	15,835

Source: Collins and Margo, "The Economic Aftermath of the 1960s Riots in American Cities," table 1, 22.

few attacks on political symbols such as courthouses, city halls, or police stations. In Detroit, two-thirds of all arrests were for theft. In Newark, more than $8 million was attributable to loss of inventory due to theft and damage to stock. A quantitative study of shopkeepers in riot areas found that the rioters were selective, targeting the better-quality stores. The quality of the merchandise had more salience in explaining the choice of targets than any other factor, including retaliation for abuse by the merchant and sheer proximity to the civil disorder.[41]

This invites the question: Just what *were* the causes of the riots? Were they, as many liberal and leftist analysts thought, revolts against oppression? Given the long history of black mistreatment in the United States, such an explanation seems both plausible and satisfying. There are, however, three reasons to doubt the riots-as-revolt theory.

First of all, as already indicated, the major activity of the rioters was stealing goods; political targets seldom were the focal points of dissent.

Second, few riots occurred in the South, birthplace of Jim Crow and still home to about half the African American population. Only Tampa, Florida, had a riot that was considered major at the time. One would have expected political protest to occur where the oppression was greater. But it seems that African Americans felt less inhibited in the North, and race consciousness apparently was greater there, as well.[42]

Third, some of the worst rioting occurred in cities in which conditions for blacks were better than most and not abysmal by any measure. In Detroit and Los Angeles, for instance, blacks lived in single-family homes, not tenement slums. One year before the Watts riot, the National Urban League rated Los Angeles the best place in the United States for African Americans to reside. In Detroit, on the eve of the turmoil, median family income for nonwhites was 95 percent of white income, and nonwhite unemployment was an amazingly low 3.4 percent.[43]

THE RACE ISSUE

The violent crime wave that began in the late 1960s was a black crime phenomenon to a much greater degree than many analysts are comfortable acknowledging. African Americans comprised substantial proportions of perpetrators and victims. Nationwide, from 1976 to 1988, blacks were victims of violent crime at a rate of 42 per 1,000; for whites, the rate was 31. In over 80 percent of the single-perpetrator cases with a black victim, the offender also was black.[44]

That African Americans were disproportionately victimized is readily explained. This was mainly a matter of black-on-black crime, as whites seldom attacked blacks. Having migrated to big cities with a high degree of residential segregation, black people living in poor communities became easy targets for their more violent neighbors. No one was immune. Civil rights leader A. Philip Randolph, mugged repeatedly, was forced to move out of his Harlem apartment. Even Rosa Parks, matriarch of the civil rights movement and 81 years old at the time, was beaten and robbed in her Detroit home by a black drug addict. Jesse Jackson's famous public confession of relief at seeing a white behind him on a dark city street perfectly captured that which all Americans knew but few wished to discuss.[45]

Over a twenty-year span, from 1976 through 1995, African Americans committed a majority of the criminal homicides in the United States—53.2 percent of them, to be precise.[46] This is quite extraordinary, given that during this period, blacks comprised around 12 percent of the U.S. population. But this excessive black murder rate was not a new development. African American homicide had been exceptionally high, at least since the late 1880s. In the 1920s, black homicide rates were, on average, seven times those of whites. From 1976 through 1995, they were eight times the white rate (figure 3.7).

Criminologist Roland Chilton analyzed the role of African Americans in urban homicide in his study of forty central cities

Figure 3.7 Homicide offending rates, by race, 1976–95

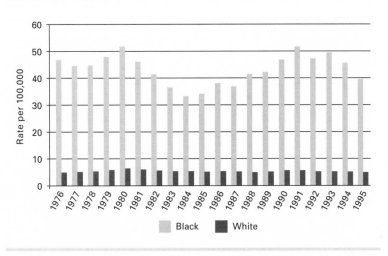

Source: U.S. Department of Justice, Bureau of Justice Statistics, "Homicide Trends in the U.S.," https://web.archive.org/web/20120808080640/http://bjs
.ojp.usdoj.gov/content/homicide/tables/oracetab.cfm.

from 1960 to 1990.[47] These cities accounted for 14 percent of the U.S. population (1990), but their residents were the source of 44 percent of all homicides known to police and the subjects of 55 percent of all homicide arrests.[48]

Homicide arrest rates for males of all races tripled during these three decades, escalating from under 20 per 100,000 in 1960 to about 60 in 1990. Rates tripled for nonwhite males as well, but these rates, which leapt from 50 to 150 per 100,000, were two and a half times higher than the all-male rate (fig. 3.8).[49] Consequently, homicide arrests of African Americans of both genders in thirty-nine of the central cities studied accounted for an extraordinary 65 to 78 percent of all homicide arrests (fig. 3.9).[50]

For the crucial decade between 1960 and 1970, Chilton found that urban homicide arrest rates doubled, from 10 to 20 per 100,000, and that nonwhite males were responsible for 77

Figure 3.8 Homicide arrest rates, thirty-nine
U.S. cities, by race and gender, 1960–90

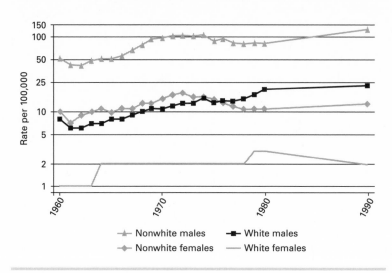

Source: Chilton, "Homicide Arrest Trends," 105.

Figure 3.9 Homicide arrests, thirty-nine U.S. cities,
percentages by race and gender, 1960–90

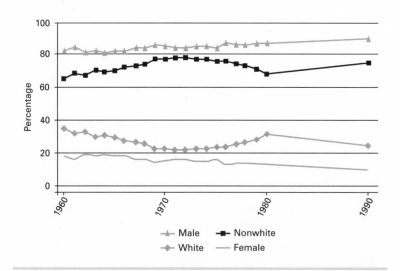

Source: Chilton, "Homicide Arrest Trends," 105.

percent of the increase. Twenty-seven percent of the nonwhite male homicide spike was attributable to a rise in the size of that population, but 73 percent was due to increases in their homicide rates.[51]

"The most salient trends in this analysis," wrote Chilton in conclusion, "are the very high rates of homicide arrests for nonwhite men. These rates are much higher than homicide arrest rates for any other segment of the population in the 1960s and 1970s. They were high in 1980 and generally higher in 1990." He added, "As uncomfortable as this information makes us, ... to avoid serious discussion of these findings and their interpretation is self-defeating."[52]

For the most part, however, criminologists were reluctant, for ideological or career-related reasons, to acknowledge the black crime problem. "Often, analysts of such issues as violent crime or teenage pregnancy deliberately make no references to race at all," sociologist William Julius Wilson, himself African American, complained, "unless perhaps to emphasize the deleterious consequences of racial discrimination or the institutionalized inequality of American society."[53]

The data on black disproportionate offending would appear to be both overwhelming and indisputable. Nevertheless, claims are sometimes made that the black crime problem is a product of "selection bias" on the part of criminal justice officials, such as overpolicing in black neighborhoods, or that it reflects incomplete or selective presentation of the data.[54] These contentions have been thoroughly reviewed by many analysts, including those whose liberal credentials are beyond reproach. These researchers concluded that the evidence of black overinvolvement in violent crime remains compelling, because that evidence is, in its essence, bias-free.[55]

A good example is the National Crime Victim Survey (NCVS), which is based solely on victimization reports by the general public. These reports are unlikely to misidentify suspected black perpetrators, because there is no incentive for the public to intentionally distort the involvement of African Americans. Moreover, because these victim data have nothing to do with the police, they are a gauge of alleged law enforcement bias.

Figures for robbery, the quintessential crime of the era, show remarkable consistency between arrests, victim reports, and, for that matter, incarcerations. In 1973, according to NCVS interviews, 67 percent of the robbery suspects were African American, whereas 63 percent of all arrested robbers were black, as were 65 percent of those imprisoned for that offense. In other words, the police arrested proportionately *fewer* blacks for robbery than were identified as assailants by robbery victims. In 1979 and 1982, as table 3.8 indicates, the correspondence between victim reports, arrests, and imprisonment was equally striking. While this consistency is more evident for robbery than for other offenses, no ready explanation for the differences between robbery and these other crimes exists.[56]

Consequently, there is no reason to doubt the general accuracy of arrest data, which show that apprehension rates of African Americans for crimes of violence between 1965 and 1990 were anywhere from about five to nine times higher than for whites (fig. 3.10).

Homicide mortality figures are another indicator of high black crime that, insofar as race bias is concerned, are considered beyond reproach. These statistics are compiled by county coroners or medical examiners whose jobs require careful and accurate descriptions of homicide victims. For the early crime spike, from 1965 to 1973, the average homicide mortality rates for nonwhite males were more than ten times those of whites (table 3.9).[57] Since it is well established that homicide is overwhelmingly intraracial, the claim that 94 percent of all black homicide victims from 1976 to 2005 were killed by other blacks is consistent with decades of prior data. Thus, the elevated homicide perpetration rates attributed to African Americans must be considered extremely reliable.

In short, substantial and credible evidence supports the idea

Table 3.8 Robbery offenders identified as black, 1973, 1979, and 1982

	Robbery offenders identified as black (%)		
	Arrest data	Victim reports	Prison data
1973	63	67	65
1979	57	60	58
1982	61	63	60

Sources: Federal Bureau of Investigation, *Crime in the United States,* Uniform Crime Reports: 1973 (table 34, 133); 1979 (table 35, 200); 1982 (table 36, 184). Langan, "Racism on Trial," 677.

Table 3.9 Homicide mortality rates, males, by race, 1965–73

	White (rate per 100k)	Nonwhite (rate per 100k)
1965	4.8	50.7
1966	4.9	54.8
1967	5.9	62.7
1968	6.5	68.9
1969	6.6	72.4
1970	7.3	72.8
1971	7.9	80.8
1972	8.2	83.1
1973	8.7	77.1
Average	6.8	69.3

Source: Klebba, "Homicide Trends," 197.

Figure 3.10 Violent crime arrest rates, by race, 1965–90

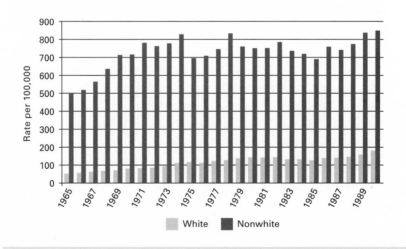

Source: Federal Bureau of Investigation, *Age-Specific Arrest Rates,* 173.

that African American offending rates are not inflated by some systematic bias in the criminal justice system. As one liberal analyst rather cautiously put it, "Invidious bias explains much less of racial disparities than does offending by black offenders."[58]

INTERRACIAL CRIME

High levels of black-on-black crime were, in fact, nothing new. Indeed, before the 1960s, the victims of black violence were overwhelmingly other African Americans. In 1920s Detroit, for instance, only 6 percent of the targets of African American killers were white. In the southern city of Birmingham, Alabama, before the Second World War, a mere 1.2 percent of all black-perpetrator homicides were interracial.[59] After the 1960s, however, though the magnitude of intraracial victimization grew with black crime rates, the new and most significant development was *white* victimization.

From the 1940s to the mid-1960s, violent crime had been relatively low in the United States. American cities were reasonably safe, and people could move about unhindered and unconcerned. Whites could enter black neighborhoods unmolested, and vice versa. Black murder rates were high, but the victims almost always were African Americans, and the locus of the crime was the black part of town, so whites were more or less indifferent to it. After the 1960s crime explosion, all of this changed. Criminals began assaulting people with impunity. Whatever compunctions criminally inclined blacks felt about attacking whites rapidly dissipated. In big cities, to which African Americans had recently migrated in vast numbers, the situation grew particularly acute. It became dangerous for whites to enter black neighborhoods, where they stood out as targets (black residents, of course, had no escape short of moving out).

The data on the interracial nature of black violent crime are incontrovertible. Murder is the easiest case to document, for the race of the victim is obvious, and the police put extra effort into detecting the perpetrators of what is considered the most serious crime. As a result, we are more certain about our facts and figures on homicide than for any other offense. The main source of the data is FBI-collected police department reports, for which additional information, such as the race of victims and perpetrators, is compiled in the FBI's Supplementary Homicide Reports (SHRs).[60]

Murders overwhelmingly are committed by intimates and acquaintances, and, as one would expect, they are predominantly intraracial. But the stranger murders (along with the much more prevalent stranger assaults and robberies) particularly paralyzed Americans with fear. From 1976 to 2005, around 14 percent of all homicides were killings by strangers, though this probably considerably underestimates the true numbers. Among these stranger homicides, nearly one in five (18.8 percent) involved a black offender and a white victim. This was many times more than the black-on-white killings in the first half of the century. By contrast, only 5 percent of the stranger killings involved whites killing blacks.[61]

The situation in big metropolitan areas was even more telling. A careful study of homicides in nine U.S. cities in 1978 showed that blacks not only committed a disproportionate number of the killings, but they also had particularly outsized involvement in killings accompanied by another felony, usually robbery. Of all the killers in these cities, 71 percent were black, 16 percent were white, and 12 percent were Hispanic. For killing-plus-felony cases, the study found that 60 percent of the white victims had been killed by blacks, as had 89 percent of the murdered African Americans. Indeed, blacks were responsible for over 72 percent of all of the homicides accompanying another felony—probably the most feared crime in America.[62]

While murder was the ultimate victimization, it wasn't the most common. Robbery with assault—mugging—took that prize. According to the National Crime Victimization Survey, during each year from 1973 to 1988 there were over 1.1 million robberies in the United States, one-third of which resulted in injuries. During the same time period, there were 4.6 million assaults annually, 36 percent of which were aggravated, that is, they involved serious injuries.[63]

Once again, though hardly ever discussed, the race factor was significant, especially in the case of robberies. In nearly six out of every ten lone-robber incidents (58 percent), the victims told interviewers that the offender was black.[64] Since victimization surveys don't rely on police actions, the chance of selection bias due to more aggressive arrests of African Americans is eliminated. As criminologist William Wilbanks discovered, when crimes of violence were involved, black offenders were more likely to target white victims. Examining crimes with black perpetrators, he found that in 1981, 64 percent of the robbery victims were white, as were 59 percent of the rape victims and 52 percent of those assaulted. To be sure, a plurality (48 percent) of white victims were robbed by other whites, not blacks (43 percent), but when analyzing crime from a race-of-offender perspective, it is noteworthy that for African Americans, whites were the preferred victims.[65]

The interracial nature of robbery was confirmed by the federal Violence Commission's 1967 survey of seventeen cities. As table 3.10 shows, 47 percent of armed robberies were commit-

Table 3.10 Percentage of interracial and intraracial robberies in seventeen cities, by race, 1967

	White victim		Black victim	
	White offender	Black offender	White offender	Black offender
Armed robbery	13.2	46.7	1.7	38.4
Unarmed robbery	17.9	43.9	1.1	37.1

Source: U.S. Office of Management and Budget, *Social Indicators, 1973*, table 2/9, 68.

ted by African Americans and victimized whites. For unarmed robberies, the black-on-white figure was 44 percent. Note the tiny percentage of white-on-black robberies.[66]

What explains high black-on-white victimization? Having migrated north to big cities, blacks found an atmosphere that combined greater freedom with greater temptation to crime. Although northern black residential communities were segregated, the rigid racial separation of virtually all public services and facilities prevalent in the South was unknown. This gave African Americans much greater mobility within the urban setting and much more contact with whites. At the same time, starting in the mid-1960s, challenging whites had become more commonplace. The civil rights movement and its radical black power offshoot prompted a new African American assertiveness, and threats of punishment for crossing racial boundaries were diminishing.

In the case of robbery, given the pecuniary motive for the crime, African American offenders may have singled out white victims because they assumed that the targets were in possession of more things worth stealing. But, of course, such an economic explanation won't wash for other crimes of violence, such as rape, assault, and murder unaccompanied by another felony. For such offenses, attacks on whites simply may have been opportunistic, a product of the presence of white people in a preponderantly black environment. Frightened and vulnerable, white targets wore virtual neon *victim* signs unmistakable to assailants. Alternatively, black-on-white crime may have been ideological—payback for the long history of racism. Interracial tensions and hostility increased sharply during this period, and antiwhite animus cannot be ruled out as a motivation for some black assaults. Nowadays we would call such offenses bias or hate crimes, although the appellation is usually associated with racially motivated crimes by whites against blacks or other minorities.

In the late 1960s, some African Americans began to defend attacks on whites as justified reprisals. Black radical Eldridge Cleaver, for instance, endorsed black-on-white rape as a kind of racial retribution.

> I became a rapist. . . . I started out by practicing on black girls in the ghetto . . . [and then] I crossed the tracks and sought out white prey. I did this consciously, deliberately, willfully, methodically. . . . Rape was an insurrectionary act. It delighted me that I was trampling upon the white man's law, upon his system of values, and that I was defiling his women—and this point, I believe, was the most satisfying to me because I was very resentful over the historical fact of how the white man has used the black woman. I felt I was getting revenge.[67]

Were poor young black males buying into a black vengeance psychology? Marvin Wolfgang, one of the leading criminologists of the era, was "increasingly convinced that among many black teen-agers and young adults there is a systematic diffusion of the *Soul on Ice* ideology that ripping off whites as a kind of compensatory behavior is acceptable, tolerated and even encouraged." Wolfgang added, "Raping white women, stealing from white commercial establishments, mugging whites in the streets and burglarizing white residential quarters are all increasingly viewed by many black juveniles especially as behavior that is Robin Hood in style and another mark of victory for the black community."[68]

Antiwhite bias also may help explain the apparent increase in viciousness among young criminals. "The most disturbing aspect of the growth in 'street crime,'" wrote Charles Silberman in the 1970s, "is the turn toward viciousness, as well as violence, on the part of many young criminals." Robbers used to push or shove in order to steal, he lamented, and now they "kill, maim, and injure without reason or remorse."[69] Could inflicting pain and punishing the victim because he's white, and not just because he's carrying valuables, have been part of the motivation? The aforementioned seventeen-city study of robberies in 1967 found that black-on-white cases were much more likely to result in injuries (table 3.11).[70]

There may be something to each of these explanations for the increase in black-on-white violence, though the matter seems never to have been thoroughly investigated (not a sur-prise, given the incendiary nature of the issue). Most likely, multiple motives were operating: pecuniary gain, racial animus, and opportunistic considerations.

Table 3.11 Victims injured in black-offender robberies in seventeen cities, by race, 1967

	Black victim (%)	White victim (%)
Armed	15	20
Unarmed	33	51

Source: Curtis, *Violence, Race, and Culture*, 91.

The important point is that interracial violence was real, not some figment of white prejudice. The fact that intraracial vio-lence was higher still does not alter this conclusion. In reality, black-on-white assaults were one of the most characteristic fea-tures of the post-1960s crime wave, and they would have major consequences for the nation.

First, they made whites more fearful of blacks, which exac-erbated racial tensions and may have slowed racial integration. As criminologists Franklin Zimring and Gordon Hawkins ob-served, "the reality of high levels of violence among African American males reinforces white fear in ways that palpably contribute to the exclusion of blacks from the social main-stream."[71] White apprehension also probably emboldened black criminals. Streetwise young muggers readily sense fear on the part of potential victims. Even police, who were in the 1960s overwhelmingly white (though this was beginning to change), seemed to be more cautious and less aggressive in high-crime black neighborhoods. After the 1960s, they arrested smaller and smaller proportions of perpetrators (as table 3.12 shows), though this may have been due to their being swamped by the massive increase in crime.[72]

Table 3.12 Percentage of reported crimes cleared by arrest

	1950	1960	1970	1980	1990
Murder	94	92	87	72	67
Rape	80	73	56	49	53
Robbery	40	39	29	24	25
Aggravated assault	77	76	65	59	57

Sources: Federal Bureau of Investigation, *Uniform Crime Reports for the United States and its Possessions,* 1950 (table 15, 49). Federal Bureau of Investigation, *Crime in the United States,* Uniform Crime Reports: 1960 (table 8, 83); 1970 (table 13, 110); 1980 (table 20, 182); 1990 (table 20, 165).

Second, racial fears related to black violent crime helped drive the great white flight to the suburbs—which effectively increased the proportion of African Americans in inner cities. In fact, working- and middle-class black families also fled to suburbia, sharpening still further the concentration of poverty in inner-city neighborhoods.[73] Black-on-white crime may have been unmentionable in polite circles, but the reality was clear to everyone. The general public—including both whites and the burgeoning black middle class—simply voted with its feet, shunning inner cities and their growing proportions of low-income African Americans.

Third, interracial crime and high violent crime in general— it wasn't all about race—fueled intensive public pressure to beef up the criminal justice system. The system had grown soft in the 1960s, catching fewer criminals and underpunishing them when they were apprehended. Starting in the 1970s, more of-fenders were incarcerated, prison sentences grew longer, parole policies were tightened, and the death penalty was reinstated. Although the U.S. Supreme Court expanded defendants' rights, thus making convictions more, rather than less, difficult, it also gave approval to plea bargaining, which made the system more efficient. Had full jury trials been required to convict, it would have been impossible for the criminal justice apparatus to cope with the massive increase in criminal prosecutions.[74]

WHITE CRIME

It wasn't only African American crime that rose dramatically during the boom years. Crime by non-Hispanic whites and Latinos also shot up significantly in the late 1960s. Worse, the high rates continued through the 1970s, and although they fell back in the 1980s, they resurged in the early 1990s. Clearly, something was affecting the United States as a whole; all segments of the population, not just African Americans, were more violent.

Determining crime rates for Hispanics is difficult at times, because some of the compilations—the FBI's Uniform Crime Reports, for instance—do not differentiate between Hispanics and whites. For nationwide data, this had little effect on non-Hispanic white totals, at least before the 1990s, as Latinos were then a small proportion of the U.S. population (6.4 percent in 1980). However, it made it difficult to determine Hispanic rates nationally; and in smaller jurisdictions, such as in the Southwest, where the size of the Latino population was significant, the lack of any distinction between whites and Hispanics rendered the undifferentiated white rates suspect. The National Crime Victimization Survey, which *did* distinguish between Hispanic and non-Hispanic whites, helped solve the problem, but the survey didn't begin until 1973, when the nation's crime rise was already well under way. Consequently, it cannot be determined if crime by Hispanics rose in the late 1960s, but it is highly unlikely that they alone were unaffected by the great crime boom.

Examining violent crime by non-Hispanic whites, it is plain that they participated fully in the crime surge. Figure 3.11 tracks homicide victimization mortality rates, which spiked at the end of the 1960s and didn't stop climbing until the 1980s. Even white females were affected. Of course, these are victimization, not offending, rates, but since 86 percent of white victims were

Figure 3.11   White homicide victimization rates, 1950–90

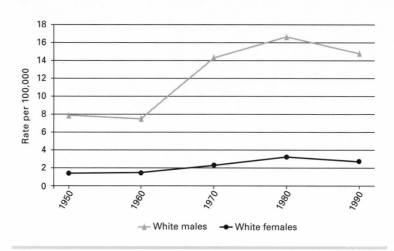

Source: National Center for Health Statistics, *Health, United States, 2006*, table 45.

Figure 3.12   White arrest rates, violent crimes, 1965–90

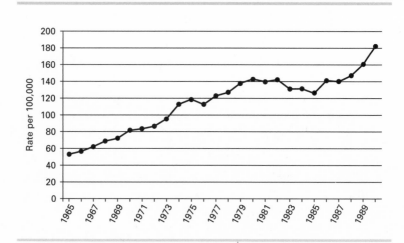

Source: Federal Bureau of Investigation, *Age-Specific Arrest Rates*, 173.

slain by other whites (1976–2005), the rates also reflect the rise in white killing, not just white deaths.[75]

Turning to arrests for all violent crimes—murder/manslaughter, robbery, rape, and aggravated assault—a mere glance at figure 3.12 says it all: white arrest rates climbed steadily but for a brief interlude in the early 1980s. Rates topped 183 arrests per 100,000 in 1990, 3.4 times the 1965 rate.[76]

Disturbing as this escalation was, there should be no illusion that the focus on black crime is misplaced. On average for 1965 through 1990, African American arrest rates were more than six times higher than those of whites (728 versus 116 per 100,000); and though blacks were only around 12 percent of the U.S. population, they still constituted 60 percent of the arrested robbers and 43 percent of the apprehended murderers (table 3.13).[77]

Nevertheless, when we compare white and black male homicide mortality rates, we see that both rose in equal proportions. The black rate, which was ten times that of whites in 1960, jumped a whopping 85 percent by 1970 (table 3.14). The white rate, though much lower, surged by an identical 85 percent over the same time period. Moreover, it rose another 44 percent in 1980, a point at which the African American rate was declining.[78]

The ascent of white crime is more puzzling than the black rise in crime. After all, far fewer whites, proportionately speaking, suffered the social and economic disadvantages of African Americans. Perhaps the best explanation for the white crime increase (and partly the black, as well) is contagion theory, in which young people, who are both especially susceptible to peer influence and more likely than their elders to engage in violence, copy one another's criminal behavior. According to contagion theory, the imitative proclivities of youth worked synergistically with the baby boom to create a crime multiplier. Once a tipping point was reached in a particular locale, crime simply exploded. (Near the end of this chapter, contagion theory is explored in greater detail.)

Table 3.13 Arrests for murder and robbery, by race, 1960–90

	Murder			Robbery		
	White	Black	Other	White	Black	Other
1960	2,084 (41.5%)	2,848 (56.7%)	94 (1.9%)	13,305 (46.6%)	14,821 (51.9%)	407 (1.4%)
1970	4,593 (38%)	7,097 (59.9%)	203 (1.7%)	24,770 (33.3%)	48,282 (64.8%)	1,432 (1.9%)
1980	9,480 (50.6%)	8,968 (47.9%)	281 (1.5%)	57,308 (41.1%)	80,494 (57.7%)	1,619 (1.2%)
1990	7,942 (43.7%)	9,952 (54.7%)	296 (1.6%)	51,229 (37.7%)	83,165 (61.2%)	1,510 (1.1%)
Total	24,099 (54.9%)	18,913 (43.1%)	874 (1.9%)	146,612 (38.8%)	226,762 (59.9%)	4,968 (1.3%)

Sources: Federal Bureau of Investigation, *Crime in the United States*, Uniform Crime Reports: 1960 (table 20, 95, table 26, 101); 1970 (table 32, 131); 1980 (table 35, 204); 1990 (table 38, 192).

Table 3.14 Age-adjusted male homicide victimization rates and percentage change from previous decade, by race, 1950–90

	Black rate (per 100k)	% change	White rate (per 100k)	% change
1950	47.0		3.8	
1960	42.3	−10	3.9	+3
1970	78.2	+85	7.2	+85
1980	69.4	−11	10.4	+44
1990	63.1	−9	8.3	−20

Source: National Center for Health Statistics, *Health, United States, 2006*, table 45.

HISPANIC CRIME

The consensus among criminologists is that violent crime rates for Hispanics were situated between higher black rates and lower rates for non-Hispanic whites.[79] The impact of their crime was felt primarily in the geographical areas in which they were residentially concentrated. During the high-crime years, people of Mexican extraction, who comprised about 60 percent of all Hispanics, principally resided in the Southwest. In 1980, 73 percent of all Mexican Americans lived in just two states, California and Texas. The other major Hispanic subgroup, Puerto Ricans (12 percent of all Hispanics), lived predominantly in the Northeast. Forty-four percent of all mainland Puerto Ricans had settled in the New York City metropolitan area, where they comprised approximately 10 percent of the total population.[80] Consequently, special attention is paid to Hispanic crime in California and New York City. In both locales, Hispanics significantly raised the crime totals, adding perhaps 30 percent to the volume of violent crime arrests.

We look first at countrywide statistics. National victimization data support the middle-position crime rate thesis, because in all but a few years, when Hispanic victimization rates

actually exceeded those of African Americans, Hispanic rates
were higher than those of non-Hispanic whites and lower than
those of blacks (fig. 3.13).[81] This outsized victimization rate indicates a disproportionately high offender rate as well, since
the pattern of intragroup criminality, prevalent with blacks and
whites, also was characteristic of Hispanics. A 1988 nationwide
survey of prosecutors' files in the biggest U.S. counties showed
that 75 percent of the Latino murder defendants were of the
same ethnicity as their victims; and 78 percent of the slain were
Hispanic when the defendants were likewise. As for the degree
of Hispanic involvement in violent crime, the same national
survey revealed that 19 percent of the killers were Hispanic,
nearly twice the general population of the sampled counties
(which were 10 percent Hispanic).[82]

Two multicity studies give additional weight to the view

Figure 3.13 Violent crime victimization rates,
ages 12 and older, by race and ethnicity, 1973–92

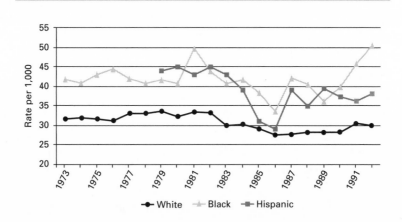

Sources: U.S. Department of Justice, Bureau of Justice Statistics: *Violent Crime,* 4;
Hispanic Victims, 2; *Criminal Victimization in the United States, 1987,* table 8, 20; *Criminal
Victimization in the United States, 1988,* table 8, 20; *Criminal Victimization in the United
States, 1989,* table 7, 6; *Criminal Victimization in the United States, 1990,* table 8, 26;
Criminal Victimization in the United States, 1991, table 7, 6; *Criminal Victimization
in the United States, 1992,* table 6, 6; *Murder in Large Urban Counties, 1988,* table 1, 2.

that Hispanic violent crime rates fell between black and white rates. The first was a nine-city 1978 study by Margaret Zahn and Philip Sagi, which determined murder rates from police and medical examiner records (see table 3.15).[83] Second was a 1980 study of 111 cities by Ramiro Martinez, which found a wide range in Latino homicide arrest rates, from 68 per 100,000 in Dallas to a mere 1.2 per 100,000 in San Francisco, with an average of 18.4. In that same year, according to the federal Bureau of Justice Statistics, the national rate for whites was 6.3 per 100,000, and for African Americans, 37.7.[84]

As for the local impact of Latino crime, separate rates for Puerto Ricans in New York and Mexicans in the Southwest point toward disturbingly high violence. One caveat is in order, however. Hispanics were a very young population. While the median age of all U.S. residents was 33 years in 1990, the median age of Mexican Americans was only 24 years. In fact, 71 percent of the Mexican American population was under 35, compared with 54 percent of the U.S. population as a whole. Given the propensity of the young to engage in violence, crime figures, to be truly meaningful, should be adjusted for age or presented within an age segment (for example, rates of Latinos and non-Latinos aged 18 to 25). As this was not always done, the value of some of the studies described below is diminished. Still, there is no gainsaying that both Puerto Rican and Mexican violence was excessive.[85]

Ira Rosenwaike did valuable work on Puerto Rican mortality, comparing two male populations aged 25 to 34 that died as a result of homicide in New York City from 1969 to 1971. The

Table 3.15 Murder offending rates in nine cities, by race, ethnicity, and gender, 1978

	Murder rate (per 100k)
Black male	72.7
Hispanic male	**42.8**
Black female	13.2
White male	10.5
Hispanic female	1.7
White female	1.2

Source: Zahn and Sagi, "Stranger Homicides," 385.

non–Puerto Rican whites had a homicide victimization rate of 19 per 100,000. The group born in Puerto Rico had a rate of 123 per 100,000, nearly six and a half times higher than the white rate.[86]

One decade later, the same researcher compared age-adjusted homicide mortality rates for non–Puerto Ricans to those of three Puerto Rican populations: those on the island, in the Big Apple, and elsewhere on the U.S. mainland. The differences were startling. Rates for both males and females combined were, compared with non–Puerto Rican whites, more than twice as high in Puerto Rico proper, four times as high on the mainland outside of New York City, and nearly eight times as high in Gotham (table 3.16). Apparently, big-city conditions encouraged considerable murderous violence among Puerto Ricans.[87] This conclusion was also reflected in a *New York Times* survey of violent crime arrests in New York City from 1970 to 1973 (table 3.17).[88]

Sociologist Andrew Karmen also confirmed the outsized Hispanic violence, finding that from 1978 to 1990, Latinos (by and large Puerto Ricans) were over one-third of the murder arrestees in New York City (table 3.18). This occurred at a time when the Hispanic population was no more than one-quarter

Table 3.16 Ratio of age-adjusted homicide victimization rates of three Puerto Rican populations to rates of whites in mainland United States, 1979–81

	Homicide rate (per 100k)			
	Puerto Ricans in Puerto Rico	Puerto Ricans in New York City	Puerto Ricans on mainland, not New York City	Whites in U.S.
Total	2.6	7.8	4.3	7.0
Male	3.1	10.5	4.9	10.9
Female	1.2	3.0	2.5	3.1

Source: Rosenwaike and Hempstead, "Mortality among Three Puerto Rican Populations," 691.

Table 3.17 Violent crime arrest rates,
New York City, by race and ethnicity, 1970–73

	Black (rate per 100k)	Hispanic (rate per 100k)	White (rate per 100k)
Murder	59	25	16
Robbery	69	18	12
Felonious assault	56	14	28
Rape	59	17	9

Source: Burnham, "3 of 5 Slain by Police," 50.

Table 3.18 Percentage of blacks, Hispanics, and non-Hispanic whites
arrested for murder, New York City, selected years, 1978–90

	Blacks (%)	Hispanics (%)	Whites (%)
1978	50	30	19
1981	51	37	11
1985	48	39	12
1990	56	36	6

Source: Karmen, *New York Murder Mystery*, 59.

of the city's total. Note that blacks and Hispanics together supplied 80 to 94 percent of the murder suspects in New York.[89]

Turning to the Southwest, where Latinos of Mexican heritage predominated, we find similar high rates of violence. As noted above, more than 60 percent of all Hispanics resided in five states of the Southwest—Arizona, California, Colorado, New Mexico, and Texas—and nearly 90 percent of the Hispanics in those five states were of Mexican origin.[90] A study of the homicide mortality rates of southwestern Latinos covering the five-year period from 1976 through 1980 found that the Latino rate was 20.5 per 100,000, whereas the Anglo rate in the

Table 3.19 Arrest rates for homicide and all violent crimes, California, by race and ethnicity, 1985

	Black (rate per 100k)	Hispanic (rate per 100k)	White (rate per 100k)
Homicide	52.3	16.3	5.8
All violent crimes	1,370.9	368.8	158.6

Sources: California State Department of Justice, Bureau of Criminal Statistics and Special Services, *Crime and Delinquency*, table 31, 135; U.S. Census Bureau, *Population Estimates by Race and Hispanic Origin*, 31, 52, 66.

same five states was 7.9. The rates for young Latino males were especially disturbing. For 15- to 19-year-olds, the figure was 52.5 per 100,000, which was even higher than the national rate for black males of the same age, 38.9. For males aged 20 to 24, the rates were an alarming 83.3 per 100,000; for Anglos, they were under 20.[91]

Data specific to Texas and California corroborate these findings. In Texas, statewide, an examination of all murders known to police found the following offense rates: for blacks, 28.5 per 100,000; for Hispanics, 12.8; and for non-Hispanic whites, 3.2.[92] Note, once again, that Hispanic rates were positioned between the white and the black rates, but at four times the white rate, they were disturbingly high. Statewide arrest rates in California in 1985 were consistent with this pattern (table 3.19).[93]

High crime by Mexicans and Mexican Americans was not a new development; it also was an issue in the 1920s and '30s. This persistence lends support to a cultural explanation for their violence.

RECAPITULATION

Before considering the causes of the crime deluge, this is an appropriate point to synthesize the material presented above.

- The crime wave that began in the middle and late 1960s was the most violent long-term spate of criminal violence since the last third of the nineteenth century, and possibly in all of American history. Between 1960 and 1990, violent crime in the United States rose an extraordinary 353 percent.

- The crime boom between 1910 and 1936 was comparable in duration to the upsurge from 1965 to 1995, but the latter was more lethal and had much higher robbery rates.

- The 1960s crime escalation began at the same time as a "youth revolution," angry and often violent protests against the Vietnam War, civil rights demonstrations, and violent disorders among African Americans in cities across the nation.

- Other industrialized nations also suffered crime booms, either in the late 1960s or during the 1970s. Four of these countries—Canada, Greece, Spain, and Italy—went through social turmoil at the same time as the United States, suggesting (though not definitively proving) a link between social unrest and criminality.

- The 1960s crime upsurge generated more fear than any previous long-term crime wave because it was distinguished by attacks by strangers, frequently committed during robberies. Crime anxiety was especially paralyzing in big cities, where muggings became a common occurrence. From 1960 to 1970, robbery rose 482 percent in cities of a million people or more and 401 percent in cities over 250,000.

- African American crime was a crucial factor in the late-1960s crime explosion, though the issue seldom was discussed forthrightly. As a result of the black urban population increase (driven by the baby boom and the Great Migration), plus escalating African American crime rates, young black males were responsible for a majority of the robberies and murders as well as other crimes of violence in the United States.

• Though the bulk of their victims were black, African Americans victimized whites at higher rates than ever before in U.S. history. This strained race relations and led to widespread public demands for more aggressive crime control measures.

• Hispanics also had very high violent crime rates, which generally fell between the rates of African Americans and non-Hispanic whites. Hispanic crime had localized impact, reflecting their residential concentration in the Southwest (primary home to Mexicans) and the New York City metropolitan area (where Puerto Ricans had settled).

• White violent crime rose substantially as well. Arrest rates of whites for violent crime were nearly four times higher in 1990 than they had been in 1965. Indeed, no segment of society seemed to be exempt from the forces—whatever they might have been—that triggered the extraordinary surge in violent crime.

WHY CRIME ROSE

There are three principal reasons for the great surge in violent crime, though the order of discussion does not necessarily indicate their order of importance. Nor are secondary causes ruled out, such as increasing drug use.

First, starting in the late 1960s, the coming of age of the baby boomers, especially the males, provided the shock troops for violence. Virtually all analyses agree on this, though there are some minor differences over the magnitude of the impact. This demographic change combined with a contagion effect through which crime reached a tipping point and then exploded. Second, the inability of the criminal justice system to cope with the sudden rush of boomer criminality created incentives for even more crime. As the chances of apprehension and incapacitation declined, crime soared. Third, and most controversially, the black migration to cities, especially the big cities of the North,

Smack

Heroin, not cocaine, was the drug of choice in the late 1960s, particularly in some of the nation's biggest cities. In 1971, New York City police made 1,100 arrests for cocaine possession, over 5,000 for marijuana, and more than 25,000 for heroin.[94] An estimated 60,000 heroin users were in the Big Apple in 1967: half of them were black; one-quarter, Puerto Rican; and one-quarter, non-Hispanic white. Parts of Central Harlem were engulfed by 200 users per 1,000 people—ten times the city average.[95]

In cities like New York, heroin use almost certainly contributed to the crime rise, but the exact amount of violence it produced is unknown. Some experts insist that evidence of "a link between heroin and violence is virtually nonexistent."[96] Others say that there may be more "psychopharmacological violence associated with heroin use than that of any other illegal drug."[97] As most addicts had expensive habits and limited means, their offenses overwhelmingly were acquisitive in nature, mainly burglary, shoplifting, and other theft crimes. However, the more violent crime of robbery almost certainly was part of the profile. A study of 239 male active heroin users in Miami found that in just one year, nearly half of them were responsible for over 3,300 robberies.[98] Other experts estimated that about one-fourth of New York City's heroin users "became involved with robbery on a regular basis, primarily to support their habits."[99]

Eric Schneider's detailed study of heroin cautiously concluded that while heroin made the crime surge "significantly worse, it was only part of the problem."[100] Cocaine, on the other hand, unquestionably fosters violence, but it did not become a big crime issue until the 1980s.

brought a culture of violence to the urban landscape. The effects of migration by a group with historically high levels of violence were compounded by the increase in young males within the African American population.

1. Demographics and Tipping Points

The one verity apparently accepted by all criminologists is that age is powerfully related to criminality. "Age is everywhere correlated with crime," flatly declared two experts, who then offered evidence from the United States and other countries for various time periods.[101] One look at figure 3.14 makes obvious the role of age in American murders during the post-1960s crime boom. As is apparent, 18- to 24-year-olds were responsible for the plurality of homicides, with the next older (25–34) and

Figure 3.14   Homicide offending rates, by age group, 1976–2005

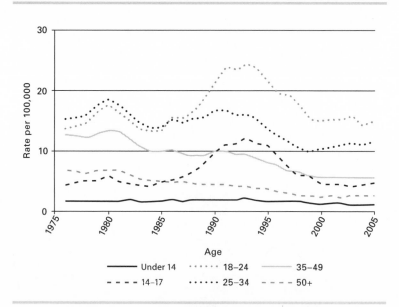

Source: U.S. Department of Justice, Bureau of Justice Statistics, "Homicide Trends in the U.S.," https://web.archive.org/web/20121103091629/http://bjs .ojp.usdoj.gov/content/homicide/teens.cfm.

younger (14–17) segments accounting for most of the remaining cases. Persons 35 and over perpetrated only 10 percent of the killings, or less.[102]

Figure 3.15 shows arrests for crimes of violence for various age groups. The disparity between the young and old is self-evident. This graph also tells us something about the predominance of young offenders in the early years of the great crime run-up. Note how in 1970 and 1980, the 15–19 group was arrested for a significantly higher proportion of violent crimes than in 1990. In fact, after controlling for other relevant factors, one study found that changes in the 15 to 29 age group from 1946 to 1984 accounted for 58 percent of the homicide rate variance.[103] This hints at the disturbing role of youth in the crime rise.

It is a safe bet that if the young population increases significantly, and especially the young male population, crime rates will rise. Thus, given a 29 percent increase in this population

Figure 3.15   Percentage of total arrests for violent crime, by age group, 1970, 1980, and 1990

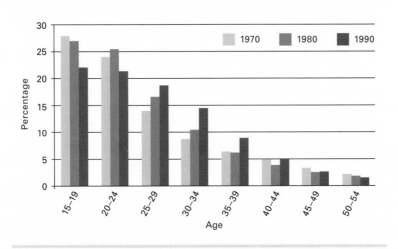

Sources: Federal Bureau of Investigation, *Crime in the United States,* Uniform Crime Reports: 1970 (table 28, 126–27); 1980 (table 32, 200–201); 1990 (table 33, 184–85).

segment in the 1960s, topped by a 43 percent rise in the following decade, the expected happened. As documented above, between 1960 and 1980, murder rates doubled, robbery rates jumped 318 percent, forcible rape rates increased 283 percent, and aggravated assault rates rose by 247 percent. It was not shocking, then, to learn that the President's Commission on Law Enforcement found that for 1960 to 1965, "40 to 50 percent of the total increase in the arrests reported by UCR could have been expected as the result of increases in population and changes in the age composition of the population."[104] Extending the commission's time frame, a criminological study likewise concluded that age composition accounted for 45 percent of the increase in crime between 1958 and 1969.[105]

But these figures were for crime in general, including property crimes. Significantly, however, when it came to *violent* crime alone, the latter study found that age distribution changes accounted for only 11 percent of the increase.[106] Here lurks a very important point. The population change, that is, the baby-boom generation's attainment of late teen age and young adulthood, most certainly augmented the volume of crime. But it was the great increase in their criminality—the massive rise in their crime rates—that made the most significant difference.

When we disaggregate homicide rates by age group, it becomes apparent that the crime rate increase from 1965 to 1970 far outstripped the increase in population. This was especially true for young killers. The 15–19 age group grew by 13.5 percent in those fateful five years, while its homicide arrest rates jumped 90 percent (table 3.20). Likewise, the 20–24 age bracket increased 25 percent, whereas its homicide rates leaped 57 percent.[107]

In short, the youth bulge played a considerable role in the violent crime rise, but it was not nearly as significant as one might think. As noted, one investigator concluded that age accounted for 11 percent of the increase from 1958 to 1969.[108] James Q. Wilson and Richard Herrnstein estimated that

Table 3.20 Percentage change in population and homicide arrest rates, by age group, for five-year intervals, 1960–75

	Ages 15–19		Ages 20–24		Ages 25–29		Ages 30–34	
	Pop.	Arrests	Pop.	Arrests	Pop.	Arrests	Pop.	Arrests
1960–65	+26.7	+1.0	+23.5	+8.4	+3.7	+9.2	−7.2	+9.0
1965–70	+13.5	+89.9	+25.1	+56.5	+21.1	+36.8	+4.2	+36.8
1970–75	+10.1	+1.9	+13.5	+7.3	+25.8	+4.8	+22.5	+1.3

Source: U.S. Census Bureau, "Population Estimates: National Estimates by Age, Sex, Race: 1900–1979 (PE-11)," http://www.census.gov/popest /data/national/asrh/pre-1980/PE-11.html.

changes in age alone explained "at least one-sixth of the increase in violent crime between 1960 and 1980," which would come to about 17 percent of the crime.[109] Economist Steven Levitt, examining the same time period, attributed 22 percent of the rise in violent crime rates to changes in age structure.[110] Thus, judging by the preceding figures for 1960 through 1980, roughly 78 to 83 percent of the violent crime surge must be accounted for by factors *other* than age. The really big change in the 1960s, in addition to the increased number of youth, was their increased propensity to commit crimes of violence. To explain this, we have to go beyond mere head counts.

A diverse array of social scientists have acknowledged the independent force of contagions, or fads, which cause behaviors to multiply rapidly as a consequence of the tendency of people, especially young people, to copy one another. As far back as 1890, French sociologist Gabriele Tarde noted "the remarkable sensitiveness of youth to the effects of imitation" and the concomitant impact on what was then increasing urban crime in France.[111] In our own time, variants of social contagion theory have been used to explain dropping out of school and teenage childbearing;[112] drug use and drinking;[113] rioting; voting; going on strike; migrating;[114] and even engaging in sexual intercourse for the first time.[115]

Nobel economist Gary Becker and co-author Kevin Murphy devoted an entire book to an economic analysis of what they called "social influences on behavior."[116] They stated that popular activities

> have interesting dynamics because a rise or fall in popularity encourages further changes in the same direction. Increased demand for an activity raises its popularity directly, and also indirectly by increasing demands of others. This dynamic process can create rapid increases and decreases in demand. . . .
>
> Teenagers may commit a lot of crimes even though the rewards are low (the price of crime is high) because their peers are committing many crimes, or they may commit few crimes even though the rewards are high because their peers are not committing many crimes.[117]

With respect to criminal activity, Edward Glaeser and associates attributed variations in crime rates across cities to a "social multiplier," that is, to decisions to engage in crime as a result of like decisions made by one's neighbors. As Glaeser observed, cities in very similar circumstances in terms of the key socioeconomic variables often have widely differing crime rates. Table 3.21 shows vividly that within the same time parameters there was considerable variance in crime rate changes from city to city (though all suffered increased rates from 1965 to 1969). Why, for instance, did violent crime in the late 1960s jump 37 percent in New York City but only 5 percent in Philadelphia? One possible explanation is that in some cities, crime "catches on" as residents copy their law-breaking neighbors, whereas in others, the contagion just doesn't get going, and rates accelerate, if at all, at a much slower pace.[118]

"Catching on" is better known as reaching the "tipping point," a term popularized by Malcolm Gladwell's book of the same name.[119] Sociologist Jonathan Crane described it as follows: "If the incidence stays below a critical point, the frequency or prevalence of the problem tends to gravitate toward some relatively low-level equilibrium. But if the incidence reaches a critical point, the process of spread will explode. In other words, an epidemic may occur, raising the incidence to an equilibrium at a much higher level."[120]

Given the sudden increase in the number of youth in the United States and their greater propensity (compared with older people) to imitate one another and to engage in violent behaviors, it seems likely that a tipping point was reached in the late 1960s, particularly in large urban areas, where violent crime surged to new and disturbing heights.[121]

Table 3.21 Violent crime rates in selected cities, average annual percentage change, 1965–69 and 1970–74

	1965–69	1970–74
New York City	37.0	4.4
Chicago	7.9	4.0
Los Angeles	10.0	0.3
Philadelphia	4.9	11.9
Detroit	25.1	1.4
Houston	16.3	−1.7
Baltimore	34.0	−1.2
Dallas	33.8	−2.0
Washington, D.C.	31.3	−7.4
Cleveland	28.6	7.7
Indianapolis	14.7	3.0
Milwaukee	22.9	18.8
San Francisco	28.3	−3.2
San Diego	15.4	13.8
San Antonio	13.0	6.0

Source: U.S. Department of Commerce, Bureau of the Census, *Statistical Abstract of the United States, 1976*, table 255, 155.

2. System Overload

As crime soared after the 1960s, the chances that offenders would be caught and punished markedly declined. If, as some economists and criminologists think, the crime drop that occurred in the mid-1990s was caused (at least in part) by higher imprisonment rates, the same incapacitative and deterrent logic would suggest that the decline in incarceration in the late 1960s and early 1970s served as a spur to violence.[122]

The root of the problem seems to have been a sheer matter

of numbers: there were just too many offenders in too short a time period for the criminal justice system to cope with them. By the late 1960s, every component of the system was under stress, from the police to the courts to the prisons. The difficulty police had in apprehending suspects has already been noted. Clearance rates (roughly the ratio of arrests to reported crimes) tumbled in the late 1960s, leaving higher numbers of offenders free to repeat their predations. Take robbery, for instance, the quintessential crime of the period (though a difficult one to solve because of the high incidence of stranger offending). In 1950 and 1960, around four in ten reported cases were cleared by police, which is not a very high rate to begin with. Even that rate declined, however, to under three in ten in 1970. And by 1980 and 1990, only one out of four robberies was solved.[123]

The problem was not with the police alone. The courts either convicted fewer defendants than they had in the early to mid-1960s or sentenced offenders to prison less often, or some combination of the above. When we examine the ratio of prison commitments to arrests for serious, mostly violent, crimes, we see a sharp drop-off starting in 1970 and no recovery until the mid-1980s (table 3.22). Moreover, in states with big crime surges, the number of people imprisoned in proportion to the general population diminished as the crime wave gathered momentum. In a sample of states, four out of five had declining imprisonment rates in 1970, despite rising violent crime rates (table 3.23).[124]

Additional evidence is provided by nationwide figures for time actually served in prison for each crime of violence. Once again, we see the relative leniency of the criminal justice system as the crime wave built up (table 3.24). In the 1950s and '60s,

Table 3.22 Ratio of adult prison commitments for serious crimes to arrests for serious crimes, per 1,000, selected years, 1960–89

1960	299
1965	261
1970	**170**
1975	185
1980	196
1985	266
1989	332

Source: U.S. Department of Justice, Bureau of Justice Statistics, *Prisoners in 1990*, table 11, 7.

robbers served a median 34 to 37 months (about three years). By the 1970s and '80s, robbery sentences were down to 25 months, just over two years in prison, and it was not until the 1990s that this number began to edge upward.[125]

Analysis by economist Morgan O. Reynolds shows the relationship between the feebleness of the criminal justice system and the surge in violence. Reynolds calculated the expected prison time for crimes of violence, which he based on "the probabilities of being apprehended, prosecuted, convicted and going to prison, and the median months served for each crime." He then plotted the expected punishment for each violent offense against the relevant crime rate (fig. 3.16). For each crime, Reynolds showed, the likely punishment nosedived from 1960 to 1970 as the crime rate soared.[126]

As the criminal justice system became increasingly dysfunctional, criminals be-

Table 3.23 Violent crimes known to police and prisoners received by state and federal prisons in five states, rate per 100,000 state population, 1960, 1970, and 1980

	Crimes	Prisoners
California		
1960	239	38
1970	**475**	**24**
1980	894	48
Illinois		
1960	365	28
1970	**468**	**22**
1980	808	56
Michigan		
1960	218	47
1970	**576**	**36**
1980	640	47
New York		
1960	126	31
1970	**685**	**23**
1980	1,030	41
Pennsylvania		
1960	99	19
1970	**220**	**22**
1980	364	24

Sources: U.S. Department of Justice, Bureau of Justice Statistics, *Historical Corrections Statistics*, table 3-10, 38; Federal Bureau of Investigation, Uniform Crime Reporting Statistics, "UCR Data Online," http://www.ucrdatatool.gov/; Federal Bureau of Investigation, *Crime in the United States, 1960*, Uniform Crime Reports, table 3, 47.

Table 3.24 Median time served in state and federal prisons
at time of first release, by offense, selected years, 1953–95

	Time served (months)			
	Murder	**Rape**	**Robbery**	**Aggravated assault**
1953	52	36	37	27
1960	52	30	34	20
1970	**42**	**35**	**30**	**18**
1980	44	33	25	17
1985	42	35	25	16
1990	70	43	30	16
1995	65	45	28	18

Source: Reynolds, "Crime and Punishment," 28.

came ever more active, which may be coincidental, of course, as the correlation between crime and punishment is not perfectly inverse. Figure 3.16 shows, for instance, that some crime rates continued to rise in the 1970s (murder, for example) and the 1980s (rape), despite more punitive sentences. Nevertheless, while the likelihood of sanctions is not the only factor affecting crime rates—far from it—strikingly, the rates started rising for all violent crimes (and, though not shown in figure 3.16, for burglary as well) at the very time the costs of wrongdoing were falling.

In sum, the available evidence indicates that the system buckled under the strain of the crime tsunami. Police couldn't cope with the greater number of offenders, courts couldn't convict or imprison as many defendants as they had earlier, and people who were convicted spent less time behind bars. As James Q. Wilson suggested, "The institutional mechanisms which could handle problems in ordinary numbers were

Figure 3.16 Four violent crimes, incidence rates and expected prison time, 1950–98

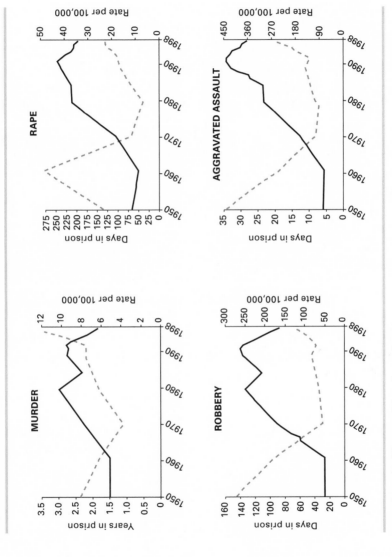

suddenly swamped, and may, in some cases, have broken down."[127] It took many years for the system to rebuild its punitive capacities, as is discussed later.

3. A Black Subculture of Violence?

While there are few doubts about the extent of African American involvement in violent crime, there is intense disagreement over the explanation for that violence. Three factors seem particularly relevant to heightened post-1960s African American violence, the first two of which are the least controversial. First is the Great Migration itself, which relocated blacks to northern cities where, compared with the rural South, informal and formal racial restraints were relaxed and more valuables were available to steal. In the 1960s alone, over 800,000 African Americans left the South for urban settings in the North and West. In the succeeding decade, another 1.5 million relocated—the biggest decadal migration of African Americans in U.S. history. The black population in the Northeast nearly doubled, rising 93 percent between 1950 and 1970. Chicago went from 23 percent African American in 1960 to 40 percent in 1980. The urbanization and northernization of African Americans provided extraordinary benefits, including significantly higher standards of living, but they also presented new opportunities for violent crime, especially robbery, which increased beyond all expectations.

The second factor was the enormous increase in black youth due to the coming of age of the baby boomers. Blacks in the 15–29 age bracket increased by 46 percent in the 1960s and another 42 percent in the 1970s.[128]

Clearly neither migration nor the youth bulge, nor both together, are sufficient to explain the extraordinarily high African American crime rates.[129] Beyond these two factors, however, consensus seems unlikely. Analysts tend to divide between economic and cultural explanations for high rates of crime among blacks. However, explanations founded simply on economic adversity, though favored by many criminologists (and liberals, generally), don't align with the historical record. African Americans have suffered adversity for most of their history, and white bigotry has been the cause of much of that suffering. However, no consistent correlation between their economic stress and violent misconduct is apparent. Measures of black economic inequality simply do not correlate with African American crime.[130] Nor does a consistent correlation between adversity and violent crime exist for other groups. In other words, the magnitude of violent crime by impoverished populations does not necessarily bear any relationship to the depths of their disadvantage. Furthermore, there is no correlation between trends in black economic conditions and black offending. Most pertinently, in the 1960s, despite enormous economic gains accompanied by marked declines in white race prejudice, black rates of violence skyrocketed.[131]

But if economic disadvantage and its deleterious side effects are not to blame, then what is? In the late 1960s, criminologist Marvin Wolfgang and psychologist Franco Ferracuti presented a new theory of crime—the subculture of violence theory.[132] This blend of psychological and sociological perspectives seemed to provide a plausible explanation for high black violence. According to this theory, in any society there may be groups with exceptionally high rates of homicide; such groups are likely to share values that support violence. "Homicide is most prevalent, or the highest rates of homicide occur, among a relatively homogeneous subcultural group in any large urban community. Similar prevalent rates can be found in some rural areas. The value system of this group, we are contending, constitutes a subculture of violence."[133]

Wolfgang and Ferracuti elucidated the meaning of "subculture." While this term ordinarily suggests "individuals sharing common values and socially interacting in some limited geographical or residential isolation," they explained that "value-sharing does not necessarily require social interaction.

Consequently a subculture may exist, widely distributed spatially and without interpersonal contact among individuals or whole groups of individuals." Delinquent gangs, spread throughout a city, fall into this category; they share, despite their isolation from one another, a "delinquent subculture."[134]

Wolfgang and Ferracuti also seem to have had racial, ethnic, and even national groups in mind, as they identified "subcultural traditions of violence" in Colombia, Sardinia, Mexico, Albania, and small Italian communities near Naples.[135] And they expressly referred to lower-class African Americans, stating that they expected to "find a large spread to the learning of, resort to, and criminal display of the violence value among minority groups such as Negroes."[136]

This theory came under heavy fire, partly because of its circular reasoning: violent behavior alone cannot prove the existence of a subculture of violence.[137] Absent independent evidence of distinctive norms that are shown to cause violence, the existence of a subculture of violence is only an inference from the violent behavior of group members. And yet the theory remains intriguing, because through the lens of modern social science, we tend to see mankind as a creature of groups—national, religious, ethnic, and racial, for example—with each group engaging in unique and significantly different types of behaviors. How can these behaviors be explained in an era that has repudiated racial or biological rationales? Only "values" or some other mental construct seem credible. Indeed, social science commonly asserts that culturally distinctive values provide meaningful explanations for all sorts of group behaviors. Some of these behaviors—saving one's earnings or seeking advanced education, for example—are considered socially beneficial, to both the specific group and society at large. Other behaviors—violent crime, obviously—are viewed in a very negative light.[138]

Reluctant as we are, for fear of stereotyping, to focus on negative group behaviors, when such behaviors have persisted over long periods of time, perhaps over multiple generations, we are presented with a prima facie (if not a conclusive) case for a causal connection between the behavior and the distinctive culture. Wolfgang and Ferracuti's theory would have been more compelling if they had stressed the importance of the historical persistence of violence by certain groups, for proof of such persistence adds credence to the claim that the behavior is supported by a particular group culture.

In the case of African Americans, compelling evidence shows persistently high rates of criminal violence since the late 1880s, and it is widely acknowledged that American blacks share a distinctive subculture. But there have been few efforts to link the two observations to show that the African American subculture, or, more narrowly, the lower-class African American subculture, is causally connected to high levels of criminal violence.

One such effort was Elijah Anderson's *Code of the Street*, a product of four years of ethnographic research in Philadelphia's inner cities.[139] The code was a set of unofficial rules of conduct for the streets of poor black neighborhoods. Its essence is a display of violence, or a predisposition to violence, designed to ward off the all too common attacks and assaults in these communities. As Anderson described it, the code hearkens back to the honor codes of Italian and Mexican immigrants and, even more pertinently, nineteenth-century white southerners.

The code was a response to the ubiquitousness of violent crime in inner cities and the need to function in an atmosphere dominated by it. "Of all the problems besetting the poor inner-city black community," Anderson wrote, "none is more pressing than that of interpersonal violence and aggression."

> This phenomenon wreaks havoc daily on the lives of community residents and increasingly spills over into downtown and residential middle-class areas. Muggings, burglaries, carjackings, and drug-related shootings, all

of which may leave their victims or innocent bystanders dead, are now common enough to concern all urban and many suburban residents.[140]

The code also was a product of the perception that law enforcement can't or won't control violent crime. "Feeling they cannot depend on the police and other civil authorities to protect them from danger," residents adhere to "a set of informal rules governing interpersonal public behavior, particularly violence. The rules prescribe both proper comportment and the proper way to respond if challenged."[141]

> By the time they are teenagers, most young people have internalized the code of the street, or at least learned to comport themselves in accordance with its rules. As we saw above, the code revolves around the presentation of self. Its basic requirement is the display of a certain predisposition to violence. A person's public bearing must send the unmistakable, if sometimes subtle, message that one is capable of violence, and possibly mayhem, when the situation requires it, that one can take care of oneself. The nature of this communication is determined largely by the demands of the circumstances but can involve facial expressions, gait, and direct talk—all geared mainly to deterring aggression.[142]

More than swagger is involved. Denizens of the black ghetto, Anderson insisted, steal from one another to obtain "trophies," objects of symbolic value—"sneakers, a pistol, even somebody else's girlfriend"—that enhance the worth of the taker. "In this often violent give-and-take, raising oneself up largely depends on putting someone else down. The level of jealousy and envy underscores the alienation that permeates the inner city. There is a general sense that very little respect is to be had, and therefore everyone competes to get what affirmation he can from what is available. The resulting craving for respect gives people thin skins and short fuses."[143]

This explains the resort to violence, sometimes lethal, that seems senseless to middle-class people as it is wildly in excess of the objective, which may be little more than obtaining an article of clothing. But for black ghetto residents, its young people particularly, "there is an especially heightened concern about being disrespected. Many inner-city young men in particular crave respect to such a degree that they will risk their lives to attain and maintain it."[144]

This obsession with respect and the readiness to resort to violence to maintain and enhance it puts one in mind of certain "honor cultures," such as that of white southerners in the nineteenth century. Thomas Sowell has argued that the similarity is not fortuitous, that African Americans adopted the southern white culture, and lower-class blacks transported some of its worst features to northern cities. "Much of the cultural pattern of Southern rednecks," Sowell wrote, "became the cultural heritage of Southern blacks, more so than survivals of African cultures, with which they had not been in contact for centuries."[145]

> Half a century after Myrdal, another study of racial attitudes noted "the intimidating ethnic style of many underclass black males," and noted that nearly half of all murder victims in America were black, and that 94 percent of them were killed by other blacks. Many of these killings were due to gang members who killed for such reasons as "Cause he look at me funny," "Cause he give me no respect," and other reasons reminiscent of the touchy pride and hair-trigger violence of rednecks and crackers in an earlier era.[146]

The *Code of the Street* offers a vivid insider look at the black subculture of violence—the very type of subculture that Wolfgang and Ferracuti postulated in their book. Anderson has, in a sense, provided the missing link—independent evidence of the distinctive norms that support and encourage violence—

that gives credence to the cultural explanation for the incredibly high levels of violence in lower-class black communities.

The work is not without its limitations: Anderson was writing about youth in the 1990s, and whether a similar code of values applies to older people in other time periods is an open question.[147] Moreover, the code does not seem to explain high black involvement with heroin and, in the 1980s, cocaine, both of which raised African American crime rates. Nor does it account for the profound *drop* in violent crime rates in the late 1990s and into the twenty-first century. But even as is, *Code of the Street* is powerful support for the subculture of violence theory. Combined with the demographic changes of the late 1960s, and the massive black migration to northern cities, the subculture of violence theory provides a credible explanation for the role of African Americans in the great rise in violent crime.[148]

♦　♦　♦

More than anything else, these three simultaneous developments—the massive growth in the young male population, the near collapse of the criminal justice system, and the urbanization and northernization of lower-class African Americans invested in a subculture of violence—set in motion a wave of violent crime without parallel in the twentieth century, perhaps unprecedented in all of American history. In many ways, this wrenching violence would define an era. That era, as chapter 4 explains, extended into the 1980s and through the first years of the 1990s, and then, as recounted in chapter 5, it ended as abruptly and unexpectedly as it had begun.

CHAPTER 4

The Violence Continues

America in the 1980s

INTRODUCTION

In 1980, nationwide homicide rates hit a postwar, and probably a twentieth-century, high of 10.2 per 100,000. The dispiriting violence that had bedeviled the United States since the late 1960s seemed never-ending. But then, suddenly, crime began to abate. Homicide rates tumbled 29 percent in four years, and the rates for all crimes of violence fell 10.5 percent during that same period.[1] Had we turned a corner? Hope barely had a chance to root when a new menace surfaced on the East and West Coasts: crack cocaine. By the second half of the decade, crack was ravaging inner cities, especially in the black and Hispanic communities. Cocaine sent crime rates right back up again (certainly for murder and very likely for robbery), banishing all thoughts of victory in the war on crime.

One event of the mid-1980s came to serve as the symbol of the entire high-crime era. The Bernhard Goetz New York subway vigilante incident pressed all the hot buttons—crime, cities, race, vengeance—all seemingly calculated to raise the mass blood pressure. When the incident occurred in 1984, violent crime in Gotham had been tapering off, but it had plateaued at such a high rate that New Yorkers scarcely had cause to feel safe. Two decades earlier, in the mid-1960s, with violence already ascending, there were about 600 murders annually in the city; in the early 1980s, there were more than double that number (fig. 4.1). Throughout the 1960s, city homicide rates averaged 8.3 per 100,000 people; from 1970 to 1985, the average was 21.5. New Yorkers had good reasons to be unimpressed by the brief progress of the early 1980s.[2]

In the 1970s and '80s, the New York subways were an especial source of dread for the otherwise intrepid urbanites, undoubtedly because of the fear of being trapped with a predator as the train hurtled between stations. The situation had grown so bad that a civilian anticrime group calling itself the Guardian Angels formed in the late 1970s. Within half a decade, the Angels had enlisted 5,000 members in its efforts to patrol the subway system.[3] A public opinion survey conducted just before the Goetz incident reported that 47 percent of the city's riders

Figure 4.1   Murders in New York City, 1955–98

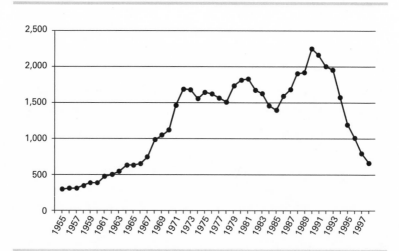

Source: Karmen, *New York Murder Mystery,* 17.

were afraid of being mugged on the subway at night, while only one in four denied that they had any qualms.

This was the context in late December 1984 when a slightly built, nerdy-looking 37-year-old white man entered a subway car and took a seat near some boisterous young black males. Bernhard Goetz had a degree in electrical engineering from New York University and ran an electronics business out of his Greenwich Village apartment. He had been mugged before, and it had been a horrifying experience. Three black teenagers tried to rob him in a subway station in 1981, pushing him into a plate-glass door and throwing him to the ground, causing knee injuries. An off-duty sanitation officer subdued one of the attackers as the other two fled. Goetz was livid when he learned that his assailant was permitted to leave the police station hours before he was released and that the young mugger was charged with nothing more than criminal mischief for ripping his jacket. (In fact, Goetz may have been mistaken about the attacker's fate. Apparently, he was convicted of criminal assault in the third degree and sentenced to six months in jail.) Goetz subsequently applied for a permit to carry a handgun. When his application was turned down, he nonetheless bought a .38-caliber revolver during a trip to Florida.[4]

As Goetz took his seat on the number 2 train, a loaded gun in his jacket, one (or possibly two) of four black youths approached him and said, "Give me five dollars." Suddenly, there was gunfire as Goetz, assuming a combat stance, shot at each of the four young men. Then, according to his subsequent confession, he went up to one of the youths, who had moved to a seat at the end of the car, and said, "You seem to be ... alright; here's another." He fired once again, this bullet severing Darrell Cabey's spinal cord, crippling him for life. Goetz ran off, rented a car, which he drove to New England, and eventually surrendered to police in Concord, New Hampshire.[5]

It seemed as if the entire city was abuzz over the episode. The *New York Post* dubbed Goetz the "subway vigilante." The voluble mayor, Ed Koch, delivered a condemnation of vigilantism. Hazel Dukes of the NAACP branded Goetz a KKK night rider. But a majority of New Yorkers, at least initially, approved of Goetz's actions, and over 70 percent of them (including 72 percent of surveyed African Americans) believed he had shot in self-defense.[6]

The Goetz case immediately became an icon of America's post-1960s crime situation: young black men confronting a frightened, angry white man in a New York City subway. As is often the case with symbols, however, the more that is known, the more ambiguous they become. Was this really an attempted robbery or just panhandling? Under New York law, a person threatened by robbery may defend himself, even with "deadly physical force." (Robbery is defined as "forcible stealing" in New York. When "aided by another person actually present," in other words, two or more robbers working together, the crime is robbery second degree.)[7]

All four of the young men—Barry Allen, Troy Canty, James Ramseur, and Cabey—had criminal records, but one expert characterized them as little more than petty thieves.[8] Ramseur and Cabey were carrying screwdrivers, apparently to break into coin boxes. They already had served short sentences for theft, and Allen had twice pled guilty to disorderly conduct, a catch-all plea for minor crimes in New York. But the young men also revealed disturbing propensities to engage in more serious misconduct. Only two months before the confrontation with Goetz, Cabey had been arrested for holding up three men with a shotgun and robbing them of cash and jewelry. When the now paralyzed Cabey appeared before a judge, these charges were dismissed, perhaps out of sympathy for the defendant's condition. Soon after the subway incident, both Allen and Ramseur committed crimes that sent them to prison. Allen served time for two robberies, for the second of which he served three and a half years. Ramseur went on to even more serious violence. He and another man raped and robbed an 18-year-old on the rooftop of a Bronx apartment building. For this, he was sentenced to eight and a half to twenty-five years.[9] In short, the conclusion that the four men were out to rob Goetz, while not beyond all doubt, certainly was consistent with their prior and subsequent behavior.

On the other hand, perhaps Goetz completely overreacted. Was he haunted by his first mugging and therefore trigger-happy? Was he a closet racist, pathologically afraid of blacks? Juries had mixed opinions. The jury that heard the criminal case against Goetz in 1987 apparently thought he acted in self-defense. They acquitted him of the most serious charges, attempted murder and first-degree assault, and convicted him only of the illegal weapon possession. But nine years later, in 1996, a Bronx civil jury found Goetz liable for damages to Cabey, who was paralyzed by Goetz's bullet. They awarded Cabey $18 million for past and future pain and suffering and $25 million in punitive damages—sums that Goetz, of course, could not pay.[10]

By the end of the 1980s, as the Goetz case receded into the background, New York and other major cities fell prey to a new peril: the terrible drug epidemic among America's youth.

CRACK

Starting in the late 1980s and continuing through the first years of the decade that followed, violent crime rates soared, fueled by a terrible cocaine epidemic among American youth. The drug-inspired violence, made all the deadlier by the use of firearms, spoiled the downward trend in crime that had begun in the early '80s.

Crack is made by cooking cocaine, baking soda, water, and other commonly available substances, such as benzocaine, to produce a rocklike material that emits vapors when heated. The name comes from the crackling noise made during the cooking process. When inhaled, crack vapors generate an instantaneous euphoria that wears off in less than ten minutes, leaving an intense craving for another "hit." Crack pellets, marketed in small glass vials, could be bought cheaply, anywhere from $2 to $20, making them popular in poor neighborhoods.

The effects on individual users and their communities were devastating. For the user, addiction was common, and the risk of serious medical problems or death was significant. The relentless need for money to feed the habit was an inducement to all sorts of theft crimes, including robberies, with the attendant risk of arrest and imprisonment. Female, and sometimes male, addicts turned to prostitution in a desperate effort to exchange sex for drugs. Crack distribution was organized by youth gangs who killed one another over turf rivalries, substantially raising homicide rates in crack-infested cities. All this crime, especially the stealing and the killing, facilitated by the widespread availability of illegal firearms, terrorized minority neighborhoods, driving out those law-abiding people who could afford to move. Adding to the blight of these communities were crack houses—often abandoned apartment buildings or other run-down structures—in which the drug was manufactured, packaged, bought, sold, and ingested. Frequently, they were the scenes of anonymous sex-for-drugs activity, a good way to contract various sexually transmitted diseases, including then-lethal HIV/AIDS.

James A. Inciardi, an expert on drugs and law enforcement, painted this disturbing picture of the user.

> Users typically smoke for as long as they have crack or the means to purchase it—money, sex, stolen goods, furniture, or other drugs. It is rare that smokers have but a single hit. More likely they spend fifty to five hundred dollars during a mission—a three- or four-day binge, smoking almost constantly, three to fifty rocks per day. During these cycles, crack users rarely eat or sleep. Once crack is tried, for many users it is not long before it becomes a daily habit. . . .

The tendency to binge on crack for days at a time, neglecting food, sleep and basic hygiene, severely compromises physical health. Thus, crack users appear emaciated most of the time. They lose interest in their physical appearance.[11]

The crack plague had major effects on violent crime and the justice system. Starting in the late 1980s, it triggered an increase in homicide and other violent offenses, such as robbery, especially in the minority neighborhoods of big cities. The crime spike reinforced long-standing public demands for a stronger criminal justice apparatus—more police, more punitive laws, longer periods of incarceration—all aimed at stemming the tide of drugs and violence. African American leaders pushed as hard as, if not harder than, whites, especially as their neighborhoods were paying the lion's share of the price.[12] The criminal justice system responded to the public's demands, dramatically increasing its capacity to punish offenders, particularly compared with its feeble efforts during the late 1960s and early 1970s.

Years later, when it became clear that the hardened system caused wildly disproportionate imprisonment of African Americans—mainly because of their high involvement with both drugs and violence—there were misgivings among black and liberal commentators and politicians, who demanded cutbacks in incarceration levels. An especially sore point was the creation of tougher federal sentencing laws for crack, as opposed to powder, cocaine. Crack, due to its low cost and rapid impact, became particularly popular with blacks and Hispanics, and they bore the brunt of the sentencing disparities. But, for the same reasons, crack was more addictive and more criminogenic than powder, so the harsher sentences were entirely rational. African American law professor Randall Kennedy argued that heavier punishment for crack was not racially discriminatory, because the burden "falls not upon blacks as a class but rather upon a subset of the black population—those in violation of the law who are apprehended."[13] Nevertheless, liberals bridled at the increase in the number of African Americans being imprisoned, and crack-to-powder sentencing differentials were reduced in 2010.[14]

Regarding the upsurge in violence, the homicide victimization figures, always the most reliable data, show a marked upturn in the late 1980s, when the crack plague was at its worst. Moreover, the upward curve for African Americans, who were more heavily involved in the crack distribution wars, was much sharper than for whites (fig. 4.2). For whites, there was a 12 percent increase from the low point in 1988 to the high point in 1991. For African Americans, the rise between the low point, 1984, and the high, 1991, was a disturbing 44 percent.[15]

Criminologist Alfred Blumstein outlined the pattern in the disastrous crack-firearm-homicide triad. He pointed to the "introduction of crack in the mid-1980s; recruitment of young minority males to sell the drugs in street markets; arming of the drug sellers with handguns for self-protection; diffusion of

Figure 4.2   Homicide victimization rates, by race, 1980–93

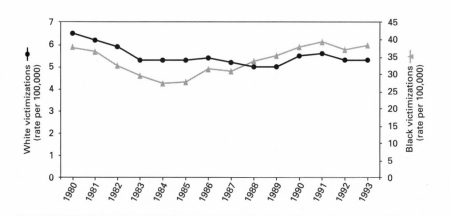

Source: U.S. Department of Justice, Bureau of Justice Statistics, *Homicide Trends in the United States, 1980–2008.*

guns to peers; irresponsible and excessively casual use of guns by young people, leading to a 'contagious' growth in homicide and possibly robbery also."[16]

Other crimes of violence, not just murder, rose as well in this same time period; for example, robbery was up 23 percent in big cities. One analysis found that after controlling for various other factors, the rate of increase in robberies in the late 1980s varied with the amount of crack use (as measured by drug arrests) and the size of the African American population. Cities with high levels of crack and a large black population had the biggest increases in robberies.[17] Another analysis concluded after various statistical controls that "the arrival of crack led to a 9% increase in murder, [and] a 19% increase in aggravated assault," the latter crime often no more than an unsuccessful attempt to kill.[18]

But crack was not increasing everyone's crime activity. Aging baby boomers were starting to retire from the violent crime business. (As discussed later, the retirement of the boomers—the most violent generation in modern American history—would turn out to be a seminal event in the great crime decline.) Someone born in the late 1940s would have been celebrating his fortieth birthday during the crack years—a senior citizen when it comes to violence. Though decreasing as a percentage of the population, younger people aged 18 to 24 were suffering from and engaging in ever more homicides. By contrast, the kill rates either were steady or falling for the 25 and older cohort. As figure 4.3 indicates, even among black males, crack mainly was devouring the young.[19]

By the end of the 1980s, the public had grown very alarmed about drugs: 87 percent of Americans polled in 1989 said it was a "very serious" problem. Twenty-seven percent identified drug abuse as the nation's most important problem, more than three times the percentage who named the economy (8 percent) and four and a half times the number most worried about crime (6 percent). Fifty-eight percent of respondents in 1989 said drugs

Figure 4.3 Black male homicide victimization rates, by age, 1980–93

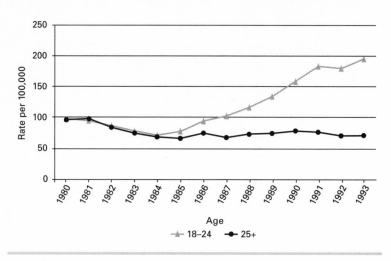

Source: U.S. Department of Justice, Bureau of Justice Statistics, *Homicide Trends in the United States, 1980–2008.*

were the main cause of crime; eight years earlier, only 13 percent blamed drugs while 37 percent thought crime mainly was due to unemployment. Despite these anxieties, the public, by 57 to 33 percent, favored drug treatment over punishment for users. (It is interesting to note, especially in light of subsequent opposition to increased imprisonment, that African Americans were more inclined toward punitiveness for drug use than whites, by 38 to 32 percent.)[20]

As the 1980s came to a close, crime continued to make Americans feel unsafe. In 1990, four out of ten declared that they were afraid to walk alone at night, a figure little changed since the early 1970s. Five times as many people were concerned with defendants being let off too easily than with violations of their rights. And well over eight out of ten thought that their local courts were not harsh enough with criminals. (This latter concern, however, was nothing new; from the nineteenth century on, Americans considered courts too soft on criminals.)

By the late 1980s, support for the death penalty was reaching a half-century high of around 80 percent.[21]

Given the striking level of public anxiety, it is not surprising that the 1980s saw an intensification of a federal "war on drugs," which included mandatory sentences for drug offenses, increased funding for state law enforcement efforts, ramped-up interdiction of imported drugs (80 percent of cocaine in the United States was believed to have come from Colombia), drug testing of prisoners and jail inmates, and domestic marijuana eradication. Stricter law enforcement efforts contributed dramatically to the increase in the number of prisoners incarcerated for drug offenses, many of whom were black or Hispanic. In figure 4.4, note the steady rise throughout the 1980s in drug offenders imprisoned. But also note that drug, violent, and property crimes as the basis for imprisonment converged in the 1990s. In other words, the drug incarceration boom was driven by the late-1980s crack epidemic. When that plague wound

Figure 4.4   Sentenced defendants admitted
to state prisons, by type of crime, 1980–97

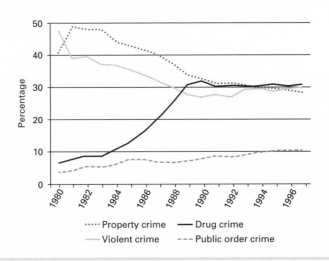

Source: U.S. Department of Justice, Bureau of Justice Statistics, *Correctional Populations*, 13.

Table 4.1 Admissions to state and federal prison, percentage black, 1975–95

	Black inmates (%)
1975	35
1980	41
1985	43
1990	51
1995	47

Sources: U.S. Department of Justice, Bureau of Justice Statistics: *Race of Prisoners*, table 2, 5; *Correctional Populations*, table 1.21, 11.

down, prison admissions for drug crimes, relative to other offenses, leveled off.[22] Since over one-quarter of all blacks sentenced to prison were convicted of drug offenses, the percentage of prisoners who were African Americans rose to 51 percent by 1990, and then began to decline (table 4.1).[23]

Notwithstanding the incarcerative impact of the war on drugs, it should be noted that in 1990, violent crimes accounted for 1.8 times as many state imprisonments of blacks as did drug offenses. Moreover, from 1990 to 1996, violent offenders were the biggest area of growth among all prisoners: violence accounted for half of the increase in black, 46 percent in white, and 54 percent in Hispanic inmates.[24]

In many respects, the war on drugs was a second front in the war on crime in the United States. Although in the mid-1990s both "wars" were won, or soon would be, criminologists remain divided over whether additional punitiveness or other factors should be credited for the victory. The other-factors camp, however, has so far been unable to agree on the causes, while the champions of punitiveness can readily document the sharp rise in imprisonment followed by an equally steep decline in crime.[25]

GUNS

Simultaneous with the crack epidemic—and intimately related to it—was an escalation in killings by handgun. Of course, gun murders are an old story in the United States. H.C. Brearley calculated that from 1920 to 1926, 71.46 percent of homicides were the result of shootings.[26] In 1993, probably the peak year for gun murders in the postwar period, the figure was actually a bit lower, at 69.6 percent. The big difference between the two high-crime eras was the age of the shooters. Levels of teenage and youth murder after the 1960s were unprecedented. Brearley, writing in 1931, observed that the ages at which the greatest number of homicides were committed were between 25 and 30. In recent decades, however, they have been between 18 and 24.[27]

It was the rise of teen killers, many of them black and nearly all of them armed, that drove up the national death toll from the late 1980s to the early 1990s. As figure 4.5 reveals, from the first half of the 1980s to the early 1990s, rates for older victims were level or declining, rates for 18- to 24-year-olds climbed 56 percent, while rates more than doubled for the 14-to-17 age group.

By the early 1990s, 90 percent of male homicide victims aged 15 to 24 died of firearm violence, and the shooting death rate for black males in this age bracket was twenty-one times

Figure 4.5 Homicide victimization rates, by age, 1980–2008

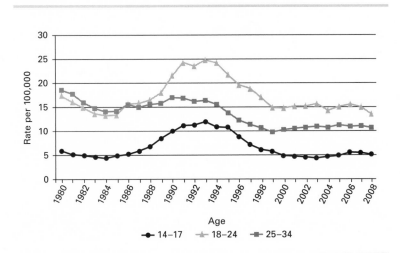

Source: U.S. Department of Justice, Bureau of Justice Statistics, *Homicide Trends in the United States, 1980–2008.*

Figure 4.6 Black male homicide victimization rates, by age, 1980–93

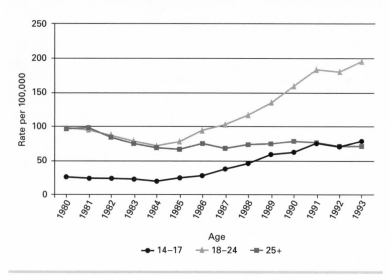

Source: U.S. Department of Justice, Bureau of Justice Statistics, *Homicide Trends in the United States, 1980–2008.*

the rate for all Americans. In a historically unusual development, black teen murder rates equaled or exceeded those of older black males. As can be seen in figure 4.6, from the mid-1980s on, teen rates rose smartly while adult rates were essentially flat.[28]

The youth killing spree declined sharply in the second half of the 1990s—a key event in the great crime fall. But even after the downturn, guns remained the means of choice for American killers, dispatching two-thirds of the homicide victims in 2010, for example.[29]

NEW IMMIGRANTS AND CRIME

Several analysts suspect that new immigrants to the United States have actually helped reduce crime rates. But it has been difficult to prove this, partly because most studies are cross-sectional and examine a brief time period, such as one year, and partly because the analyses cannot readily differentiate recent immigrants from those who have lived in the United States for many years. Moreover, few studies draw a distinction between Asian and Hispanic immigrants, to say nothing of distinguishing between various groups that comprise each of these broad categories (for example, Chinese and Vietnamese Asians). Compounding this is the unknown number of illegal immigrants, mainly Mexicans, who slip into the United States by the millions and confound efforts to accurately tally immigrant crime rates.

If we confine our examination to long-term, longitudinal studies, we find the following:

- A study of 43 cities (including the major immigrant gateways of Miami, Los Angeles, and New York) during the entire decade of the 1980s found that the bigger the fraction of immigrants, the more crime there was. But it also discerned no relationship between changes in city crime *rates* and changes in immigration.[30]

- An examination of homicides between 1980 and 2000 in San Diego, California, which experienced a dramatic increase in its foreign-born population, found that increases in the number of immigrants in the city's neighborhoods were associated with *decreased* levels of lethal violence.[31]

- Analysis of 159 U.S. cities from 1980 through 2000 found that, on average, cities that experienced increases in immigration had *diminishing* violent crime rates.[32]

- A study of robbery and homicide rates for 1990 and 2000, in 459 cities with at least 50,000 residents, found that, on the one hand, in both years, the proportion of immigrants in the population positively correlated with homicide and robbery. On the other hand, cities that experienced greater growth in immigrant populations in the 1990s tended to demonstrate sharper decreases in homicide and robbery.[33]

While the long-term (and, for that matter, the short-term) studies are contradictory, nonetheless, many criminologists conclude that immigration actually reduces crime. They call it the "immigration revitalization" perspective.[34] Note that the claim here is not that *some* immigrant groups reduce crime, but rather that the process of immigration itself, or perhaps the fact that a population group is foreign-born, seems to provide a certain level of immunity or resistance to crime.

This conclusion is premature, as even the sophisticated tools of contemporary social science have, as shown above, been unable to authoritatively conclude that recent immigration contributed to lower crime rates. Moreover, such a position is significantly at odds with the historical record. Despite the prejudice and sometimes blatant racism of the nineteenth and early twentieth centuries, the fact is that some immigrant groups—the Irish and Italians, for instance—had high rates of violent crime, whereas others—Jews and Scandinavians—did not. This pattern continues today. While most, but not all, Asian settlers have very low rates of violence when compared with native-born Americans, many of the Hispanic and Caribbean entrants do not.

The sounder position, then, is that immigration is neither anti- nor pro-crime. In and of itself, immigration is crime neutral. Everything depends on the cultural orientation toward violence of the particular incoming group, which is the product of their specific historical experiences, how their crime rates compare with prevailing rates at their destinations, and the living conditions at their place of arrival.

The failure of authorities (such as the FBI in the Uniform Crime Reports) or criminologists to differentiate the criminal activity of various contemporary immigrant groups is an

The Model Immigrant: Chinese Crime in the Twentieth Century

Chinese immigrants to America, despite their contemporary image, engaged in considerable violence in the nineteenth and early twentieth centuries, almost all of it intramural. By the 1920s, the Chinese homicide rate in San Francisco had declined dramatically, from nearly 75 per 100,000 to around 24, and by the 1930s, it stood at a modest 7 per 100,000. In Seattle, Washington, between 1928 and 1932, the male Chinese arrest rate was lower than that of whites.[35] San Francisco historian Kevin Mullen attributed the drop to the aging and dying out of tong gunmen who, because of restrictive immigration laws, could not easily be replaced. He added that while the proportion of young males in San Francisco's Chinatown in the 1930s remained as elevated as in earlier decades, the more recent Chinese immigrant came to America for education and work, not gangsterism. The new generation of Chinese immigrant was less violent, if not more law-abiding.[36]

Tong conflicts were at the root of Chinese violence, and once the tong wars abated in the 1920s, Chinese transgressions overwhelmingly were vice crimes. A study of "Oriental" crime in California found that of 65,000 Chinese arrests between 1900 and 1927, only 1 percent were offenses against the person and less than 1 percent were property crimes. Seventy-nine percent of the arrests were for such offenses as lottery playing (44 percent), gambling (23 percent), and violation of the opium and narcotic laws (12 percent).[37] Studies of Chinese crime in the Pacific Northwest found the same pattern. During the fiscal year 1935–36, at the Oakalla Prison Farm in British Columbia, a facility for short-term offenses, 24 of the 105 Chinese were received for lottery and gaming crimes and 31 for infractions of the Canadian Drug Act. And of the 179 Chinese received from 1931 to 1936 by the U.S. federal penitentiary serving the western states and Alaska, all but 10 had violated the Harrison Narcotics Act.[38]

In short, twentieth-century Chinese Americans were becoming in reality the immigrants portrayed by their idealized image. In 1946, the New York City police reported only one arrest in Chinatown—for drunkenness—and none for murder or any major crime over an astonishing eight-year period.[39]

The total number of arrests of Chinese in the United States for serious crimes was only 115 in 1940 and 136 in 1950.[40]

But even the Chinese were not completely immune to the great crime rise of the late 1960s. In 1960, 14.9 percent of the arrests of Chinese Americans were for serious offenses; by 1975, the proportion had climbed to 35.1 percent.[41] Some attributed the problem to youth gangs augmented by an influx of lower-class Chinese from Hong Kong.[42] Nonetheless, compared with crime committed by other Americans, Chinese offenses remained few. The murder/manslaughter arrest rate for Chinese Americans in 1975 was 4.1 per 100,000. For whites in that year, the rate was 3.7; for blacks, 36.6. As regards all violent crime arrests in 1975, the rates per 100,000 for whites, blacks, and Chinese Americans were 93.1, 679.9, and 52.4, respectively.[43] Nor was there any discernible increase in the number of Chinese men imprisoned in California after the 1960s (table 4.2).[44]

But by the 1980s, Chinese street gangs, strikingly similar to late-nineteenth-century tongs, reemerged with a vengeance. As one expert described them, the new tongs, like the old, were closely associated with the community gambling industry, "fiercely involved in territorial fights," and rigorously

Table 4.2 Chinese men committed to California prisons, 1945–73

	Prisoners		Prisoners		Prisoners
1945–49	60	1958	10	1967	8
1950	14	1959	6	1968	12
1951	33	1960	8	1969	8
1952	35	1961	10	1970	5
1953	27	1962	8	1971	8
1954	44	1963	8	1972	13
1955	22	1964	2	1973	11
1956	19	1965	5		
1957	23	1966	2		

Source: Takagi and Platt, "Behind the Gilded Ghetto," 12.

committed to "triad subcultural norms and values."[45] This time, gang members were young immigrants from Hong Kong, augmented by Chinese born in Vietnam.[46] New York City's Chinatown, flooded by immigrants, exploded with crime.

> For most of the 80's and 90's, shopkeepers regarded protection money as a cost of doing business in Chinatown. . . .
>
> Wherever large sums of money exchanged hands, the gangs sought a slice of the action. Counterfeit handbags did not originate with the gangs, but they soon began getting a cut. Massage parlors and prostitution rings offered another revenue stream. By the mid-80's, "China White" was added to the list. The gangs served as the final leg of a heroin distribution network that started in Thailand, Burma and Laos, the so-called Golden Triangle. In the early 90's, as much as half the heroin bought in the United States passed through Chinatown.[47]

In the mid-1980s, federal prosecutors moved in. Over the course of the next decade, using the Racketeer Influenced and Corrupt Organizations Act (RICO), they "stripped every Chinatown gang and tong of their top brass."[48] At the same time, yet another surge of Chinese immigrants, from Fujian Province, arrived, and they were more interested in school than gangs. "New blood to replenish gang ranks had become scarce. Like Italians, Jews and Irish before them, the children and grandchildren of Cantonese immigrants had set their sights beyond the street corner."[49] In 2003, the *New York Times* reported on the striking transformation. "Of all the changes that have taken place in Chinatown in the last decade, . . . none has been as dramatic, or as historic, as its disappearing gang culture."[50]

Disturbing as Chinese violent crime has been within Chinese communities, it seldom alarmed non-Chinese. Chinese gangs and tongs "neither infiltrated the American society nor victimized people who are not Chinese."[51] The average American could afford to be indifferent to Chinese crime; the average resident of America's Chinatowns could not.

The nature of Chinese crime in the United States over the course of a century has been consistent, characterized by distinctive secretive organizations, shakedowns of Chinese merchants, and a focus on organized drug, gambling, and prostitution operations within the Chinatowns of San Francisco, New York, and other cities. This pattern of Chinese crime has repeated itself with startling similarity, a consistency attributable to the unique Chinese culture and its adaptations to the American environment. As to the magnitude of Chinese crime, it has very much depended on circumstances in the United States as well as the background—law-abiding or violent—of particular Chinese immigrant cohorts. Lower-class Hong Kong Chinese brought violence and crime, but Fujian Chinese restored peace to the Chinese American community.

obstacle to meaningful analysis. Still, enough work has been done to afford a sense of the impact different groups have had on crime. Following is an examination of crime in three locations with large immigrant populations: New York City; southern California; and Miami, Florida.

NEW YORK CITY

By the late twentieth century, New York City, once again, had become a magnet for immigrants. Back in 1910, 40.8 percent of the Big Apple was foreign-born; 100 years later, 36.8 percent of the population was from other countries. Nearly three-quarters (72 percent) of the new immigrants tallied by the 2000 census had arrived in the city after 1980, at the beginning of a period that saw crime-rate instability followed by a dramatic downturn starting in the mid-1990s. Since the biggest influx of immigrants occurred in the 1990s, there was a credible belief that perhaps the newcomers were responsible for the crime decline.[52] As in the early twentieth century, however, the new arrivals' involvement with crime varied with each immigrant group.

Statewide percentages of the foreign-born in New York ranged from around 14 or 15 percent in 1985 to over 20 percent in 2007. Table 4.3 shows the growth of each of the major immigrant groups in New York City in the 1990s.

Because New York corrections authorities noted the country of birth of prisoners, the number of foreign-born in the

Table 4.3 Foreign-born population in New York City, by country of birth, 1990 and 2000

	1990		2000		Growth 1990–2000	
	Rank	No.	Rank	No.	No.	%
Total foreign-born	—	2,082,931	—	2,871,032	788,101	37.8
Dominican Republic	1	225,017	1	369,186	144,169	64.1
China	2	160,399	2	261,551	101,152	63.1
Jamaica	3	116,128	3	178,922	62,794	54.1
Guyana	6	76,150	4	130,647	54,497	71.6
Mexico	17	32,689	5	122,550	89,861	274.9
Ecuador	10	60,451	6	114,944	54,493	90.1
Haiti	7	71,892	7	95,580	23,688	32.9
Trinidad and Tobago	12	56,478	8	88,794	32,316	57.2
Colombia	8	65,731	9	84,404	18,673	28.4
Russia	—	—	10	81,408	—	—
Italy	4	98,868	11	72,481	(26,387)	−26.7
Korea	11	56,949	12	70,990	14,041	24.7
Ukraine	—	—	13	69,727	—	—
India	14	40,419	14	68,263	27,844	68.9
Poland	9	61,265	15	65,999	4,734	7.7
Philippines	16	36,463	16	49,644	13,181	36.1
Bangladesh	42	8,695	17	42,865	34,170	393.0
Pakistan	29	14,911	18	39,165	24,254	162.7
Honduras	27	17,890	19	32,358	14.468	80.9
Greece	18	31,894	20	29,805	(2,089)	−6.5

Source: New York City, Department of City Planning, Population Division, *Newest New Yorkers*, 8.
Note: The USSR was ranked fifth in 1990, with 80,815 residents. If it were a single entity in 2000, it would have ranked fourth, with approximately 164,000 persons.

Table 4.4 Foreign-born in general population and among prisoners, New York State, selected years

	% of general population	% of prisoners
1985	13.6/15.9*	7.6
1991	15.9†	12.4
2000	20.4	12.5
2007	21.6	10.4

Sources: U.S. Census Bureau, Population Division, *Historical Census Statistics on the Foreign-Born Population*, table 14; New York State Department of Correctional Services, *The Impact of Foreign-Born Inmates*, July 2008, table 1.2, 9.

  * Figures are for 1980 and 1990, respectively.

  †Figure is for 1990.

Table 4.5 Types of crimes committed by New York State prisoners, by place of birth, 1991

	Born in U.S. (%)	Foreign-born (%)
Violent felony offense	53	44
Other coercive offense	4	2
Drug offense	32	49
Property and other offenses	9	4

Source: New York State Department of Correctional Services, *The Impact of Foreign-Born Inmates*, April 1992, table 10, 16.

Table 4.6 Types of crimes committed by New York State prisoners, by Caribbean place of birth, 1991

	Dominican Republic (%)	Jamaica (%)	Colombia (%)	Cuba (%)
Violent felony offense	32	53	20	46
Other coercive offense	1	3	2	2
Drug offense	64	41	77	47
Property and other offenses	3	3	1	5

Source: New York State Department of Correctional Services, *The Impact of Foreign-Born Inmates*, April 1992, table 11, 17.

general population and their ranks among the state's prisoners can be compared (table 4.4). Aggregate figures indicate that the number of foreign-born inmates was disproportionately small, always less than their fraction of the state population.

But note the big jump in numbers between 1985 and 1991, during the crack cocaine era. The native-born prison population rose 61 percent during this six-year period, but the foreign-born inmate population positively leaped by 172 percent. A good chunk of these prisoners were from the Caribbean; indeed, natives of the Dominican Republic and Jamaica alone comprised 46 percent of the foreign inmates in 1992. Figures for 1991 show that foreign prisoners had a high participation in drug crime (much higher than had U.S.-born inmates) but a relatively lesser involvement in violent crime (table 4.5). Caribbean inmates, as shown in table 4.6, were especially likely to be serving time for drug offenses.

While Caribbeans aggravated the city's crack cocaine woes, other immigrants had a very different impact on crime. The end of the Cold War, along with the liberalization of U.S. immigration law in 1965, unleashed a whole new migrant stream from China, Russia, and the Eastern European region of the former Soviet empire. These entrants, according to Andrew Karmen, who closely examined Gotham's crime drop, had, compared with Caribbeans, low levels of criminality. Over 66,000 former Soviets relocated to New York in the early 1990s, but they supplied less than one-tenth of 1 percent of prison inmates in 1998 and had an estimated homicide victimization rate of a mere 2.5 per 100,000. The Chinese had a comparably impressive record. More than 101,000 disembarked in the 1990s, but in 1998, just 2 percent of all foreign prison inmates were from mainland China. And only 8 Chinese were murdered in 1997, for a victimization rate of approximately 3.1 per 100,000. "The relocation of these unusually law-abiding political refugees to New York," Karmen concluded, "helped to dampen the crime wave."[53]

Meanwhile, another analysis of New York City's crime decline made a different and quite telling point about the latest wave of immigrants. Franklin Zimring noted that from 1990 to 2008, the city's foreign-born Hispanics, a group with relatively high crime involvement, actually declined in population by 1.5 percent, and, even more significant, the number of Hispanics in the high-arrest age bracket of 18 to 24 diminished by 0.5 percent, while non-Hispanic foreign-born in that same age group increased their ranks by 22.3 percent. Nevertheless, Zimring concluded that immigration didn't reduce crime rates in New York, because the overall "risk profile" of the city remained about the same.[54] But a different conclusion also seems warranted: immigration helped sustain the low crime rates of the late 1990s and early 2000s, because the newest entrants were predominantly low-crime non-Hispanics rather than the high-crime Latinos who peopled the previous wave of entrants.

Figure 4.7   Gun-related homicide victimization rates, New York City, by race and ethnicity, 1990–99

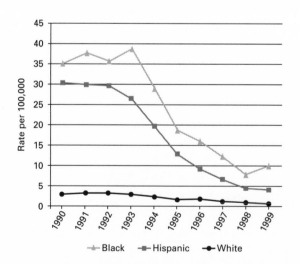

Source: Chauhan et al., "Race/Ethnic-Specific Homicide," 277.

The addition of 788,000 relatively peaceable immigrants in one decade, during which time the native population declined by 2 percent, is likely to have had a positive impact on the city's crime situation.[55]

As for Hispanic crime in New York City, independent measures showed that it was quite elevated at the start of the 1990s, but it dropped off dramatically as the great American crime decline gained steam. Nevertheless, the relative position of Hispanic violence did not change: rates remained high vis-à-vis non-Hispanic whites, but never as bad as African American rates (fig. 4.7). Whether the Hispanic rate decline was attributable to the new Hispanic arrivals or was part of the general drop-off sweeping the country remains unknown. The decline in black violence, incidentally, was probably one of the most important reasons for the city's newfound tranquility—a development apparently unrelated to the influx of law-abiding immigrants.[56]

SOUTHERN CALIFORNIA

California rivaled New York for the title Immigrant Capital of the United States. California's shared border with Mexico and the tradition of Chinese and Japanese in-migration help explain its standing. By 1995, fully one-quarter of the Golden State's population had been born in a foreign country; this figure rose to 28 percent by 2007. If one were to include the children of immigrants—and, due largely to immigrants, Latina fertility rates were among the highest in the United States—the foreign-born and their offspring comprised 38 percent of the state's population in 2007.[57] In Los Angeles County, an astonishing one-half of the population consisted of immigrants and their children under the age of 18.[58]

One analyst charted Los Angeles County's homicide trends by race/ethnicity between 1987 and 1998, revealing a pattern similar to the one we saw in New York. Rates were highest for blacks (falling precipitously after 1993), lowest for whites, and middling for Hispanics (fig. 4.8). Once again, we cannot tell whether the immigrants helped bring down the crime rates, but clearly, Latino homicide rates were elevated.[59]

A good number of California's foreign-born—an estimated 28 percent in 2007—had entered the United States illegally. Undocumented aliens comprised 8 percent of the state's total population and 10 percent of the population of Los Angeles County. Mounting public expenses associated with immigrants, and especially with illegal entrants, was a rancorous political issue that roiled the state for years. Hispanic immigrants were poor and therefore in need of various forms of public assistance. While 18 percent of native Los Angeles County households received welfare support, 41 percent of immigrant households and 48 percent of households headed by an illegal alien drew such benefits. What's more, numerous illegal immigrants were committing crimes and contributing to the state's mounting criminal justice expenses.[60]

Figure 4.8 Homicides known to police, rate per 100,000, Los Angeles County, by race and ethnicity, 1987–98

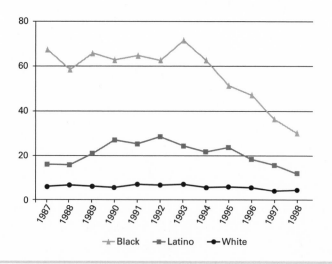

Source: Riedel, "Homicide in Los Angeles County," 55.

Public anger was channeled into Proposition 187, approved in 1994 by 59 percent of the voters. This enactment declared that illegal immigrants were causing "economic hardship" and, as a result of their criminal conduct, "personal injury and damage." Proposition 187 directed all law enforcement agents who suspect that an arrested person is in violation of immigration laws to investigate the person's immigration status and report any evidence of illegality to state and federal authorities. Since it was not authorizing stops or detentions to check immigration papers, this part of the law seems inoffensive. More controversially, however, Proposition 187 also sought to terminate welfare benefits for illegals and exclude their children from public schools. The measure was enjoined by a federal court before it could be implemented and was abandoned by the state's newly elected governor in 1999.[61]

The undocumented alien crime problem was particularly acute in California, which incarcerated an estimated 71 percent of all illegal aliens held in state prisons nationwide. A study of San Diego County reported in 1989 that illegal aliens made up 12 to 15 percent of all major felony arrests.[62] In 1994, the federal government began reimbursing states for criminal justice costs associated with illegal aliens, sums that climbed to over $1.5 billion annually in the fiscal years 2005 to 2009. The number of criminal aliens in federal prisons totaled about 55,000 in 2010, while the number in state prisons and local jails—a majority of whom were Mexican—was estimated to be 296,000 in 2009. Aside from immigration-law violations, drug offenses topped the list of their crimes. A study of seven states found that 43 percent of illegal alien prisoners were in for drug offenses, compared with 35 percent of legal alien inmates. However, undocumented offenders tended to be less violent: 28 percent of them were serving time for crimes of violence, versus 36 percent of lawful alien prisoners.[63]

Turning to the criminality of all immigrants in California, documented or not, we see relatively high violent crime

rates. In one of the few studies to convincingly examine immigrant crime in California, Susan B. Sorenson and Haikang
Shen analyzed 64,510 mortality-by-homicide cases occurring
between 1970 and 1992. Because data were coroner-generated,
independent of police or criminal courts, they were about as accurate as crime figures can be. Moreover, the records examined
by Sorenson and Shen noted whether or not the deceased had
been born here or abroad, facilitating a comparison of native
and immigrant behavior. As shown repeatedly and consistently,
victimization rates are an effective marker for group offending
because of the propensity of ethnic/racial groups to victimize
their own kind.

The results of the study were noteworthy. As figure 4.9 indicates, people born outside of the United States had higher
victimization rates over the entire twenty-two-year period.
During this time, immigrants were an estimated 17.4 percent
of California's population but were 23.3 percent of the homicide victims. For 1990 alone, bolstered by the accuracy of that
year's census data, the disproportionality widened. Immigrants

Figure 4.9   Homicide victimization rates, California residents,
ages 15–34, by domestic or foreign birth, 1970–92

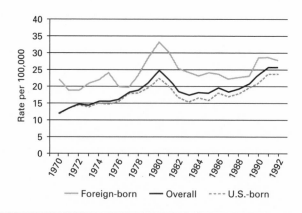

Source: Sorenson and Shen, "Homicide Risk," 98.

constituted 22.8 percent of state residents, but they were 32.8 percent of homicide victims. Among Hispanics, the foreign-born had a 24 percent greater risk than natives of being murdered.[64]

The risk of homicide victimization for foreign-born Asians, compared with Asians born in the United States, was an even greater 72 percent. Sorenson and Shen do not explain this, but I would suggest that the different ethnic/national Asian groups entering the United States during this period, such as Cambodians, Vietnamese, and Filipinos, had homicide rates substantially higher than the older stock of Chinese and Japanese Californians. By contrast, the homicide ratio of newly arrived to already present Hispanics, the aforementioned 24 percent, was not nearly as great, because rates for both groups were already fairly elevated. If different cultural propensities for violence among Asian groups explain the victimization differentials between native and foreign-born, it shows, once again, the problems created by lumping together very different populations.[65]

Rare are studies sensitive to the differences among various Hispanic and Asian communities, even though the different cultures apparently produce significantly different levels of violence. Aggregated figures show—unsurprisingly—that Asian homicide victims in California from 1991 to 1999 were disproportionately low when measured against their fraction of the population. Asians were 5.6 percent of the victims, but they were 9.6 percent of the state population according to the 1990 census.[66] By contrast, a close examination of the violence of individual Asian cultures tells a different tale. In an East Coast analysis, after controlling for poverty and other factors, Vietnamese had the highest levels of violence, Chinese and Japanese had the lowest, and Koreans had levels somewhere in between.[67] A nationwide analysis of imprisonment in 2000 found a comparable ranking. Among Asian groups, the highest percentage of incarcerated males were Laotian/Cambodian, followed by Vietnamese. Filipino and Korean levels were in the middle, and Chinese/Taiwanese and Asian Indians provided the smallest percentages of prisoners.[68]

There also have been alarming reports, but apparently no systematic studies, of ritual rape and other crimes of violence by Hmong gangs. The Hmong is a distinctive ethnic group from Southeast Asia that fled Laos for Thailand when the Communist Pathet Lao assumed power in 1975. Thousands of Hmong then resettled in the United States, mostly in California, in the late 1970s. In their culture, it seems, capturing a bride and engaging in sexual intercourse with her over her protests was acceptable behavior, leading some Hmong defendants charged with sexual assault to assert a "cultural defense" based on their home-country traditions.[69]

The preceding clearly demonstrates that the immigration revitalization hypothesis remains unproven, whereas the cultural contingency theory—that is, the notion that violent crime varies with each immigrant group, even when levels of disadvantage are comparable—seems borne out by common experience and at least some of the social science analyses.[70]

MIAMI

We close this discussion with a look at Miami, home to a very different mix of émigrés, mostly from the Caribbean: Cuba, the Dominican Republic, Puerto Rico, and Haiti. Haitians present one of the most interesting cases, as their crime rates belie their many adversities.

The year 1980 marked a dramatic and deadly change for Miami: the city began to transform from a winter haven for U.S. whites to an immigrant refuge for Caribbean peoples fleeing troubled islands. Miami had had a significant Cuban presence since the 1960s. According to the 1970 census, at least one-third of the city was Cuban-born. By 1980, Hispanics, mainly from Cuba, were a majority of the population, at 56 percent (fig. 4.10).[71]

Partly due to immigration, 1980 marked a turning point for

Figure 4.10   Demographics of Miami, Florida, 1980

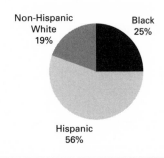

Source: U.S. Census Bureau, *Historical Census Statistics*, working paper no. 76.

violent crime in Miami. The change began, notoriously, with the *Marielito* influx. When the Cuban economy sharply declined in 1980, over 10,000 Cubans tried to leave the country, seeking asylum in the Peruvian embassy. Embarrassed by the spontaneous effort to flee the *revolución*, Fidel Castro announced that anyone wishing to leave Cuba could do so. He arranged with the U.S. government for Floridian Cubans to organize a boat lift from Mariel Harbor, whereupon Castro released 125,000 people in under six months. It was widely suspected that Fidel sought to punish the United States by dumping undesirables, whom he described as "the scum of the country." In fact, some 45 percent of the *Marielitos* had had some criminal involvement in Cuba. However, most of their misdeeds were nonviolent, and only an estimated 10 percent were thought to have been serious offenders or dangerously mentally disturbed.[72] Nevertheless, they added significantly to the violence of early 1980s Miami: 128 were arrested for murder, and 171 were themselves murder victims—all within the space of just five years, between 1980 and 1984.[73]

At roughly the same time Mariel Cubans disembarked, boatloads of desperate Haitians—60,000 between 1977 and 1981—fled from their impoverished island's latest dictatorship in dangerous makeshift vessels. One-third of those who survived the perilous journey were interned by the U.S. government, which hoped thereby to discourage a new surge of unlawful immigrants. Despite the distinct absence of any welcome from Miami's residents (unlike the case with Cubans, who benefited from a cultural affinity with the city's preexisting Cuban community), the Haitian "boat people," as they came to be known, along with middle-class Haitians from New York, created their own neighborhood, Little Haiti, in the city's northwest quadrant.[74]

To add to Miami's turbulence, in May 1980, riots erupted in black sections of the city when four white police officers were acquitted of manslaughter charges in connection with the death by clubbing of a black motorist who had fled from, and then fought with, police. National Guard units had to be called in, and after two days of violence, eighteen people were dead and hundreds were wounded. At least eight of the killings targeted whites and were especially vicious; some of the victims were doused with gasoline and set afire, and others were dragged out of their cars and beaten with concrete blocks or bricks. "Attacking and killing white people," one analysis asserted, "was the main object of the riot."[75] Rioters were less discriminating, however, in their choice of businesses to destroy, and "by the end of the disorders, commercial life in many parts of Liberty City [the largest black section of Miami] had virtually ceased to exist."[76]

The combination of disorders in the black areas of town and the Cuban Mariel influx sent Miami's crime rates soaring. Nor did it help matters that the city was fast becoming, in the words of one expert, "one of the drug import capitals of the Americas."[77] In the mid-1970s, Miami's murder rates had been high for cities of one-quarter to one-half million people—24 per 100,000 versus a U.S. average of 15 (fig. 4.11). By 1980, the 1970s were looking positively tranquil, as the city's rates spiked sharply to a shocking 66 per 100,000. These rates didn't diminish until the middle of the decade, whereupon they remained elevated but stable at an average of 35 per 100,000.[78]

Figure 4.11   Murder and manslaughter rates, Miami, Florida, 1976–2009

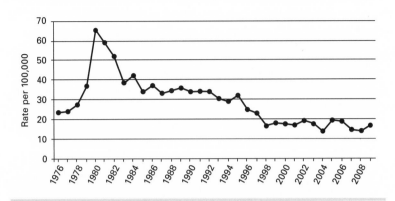

Sources: Federal Bureau of Investigation, *Crime in the United States*, Uniform
Crime Reports, 1976–1984; Federal Bureau of Investigation, Uniform Crime
Reporting Statistics, "UCR Data Online," http://www.ucrdatatool.gov/.

The *Marielito* involvement in the city's crime surge was
evident, as these Cubans provided 18 percent of the murder
victims between 1980 and 1984. Even sympathetic analysts had
to concede that the Mariels were bad news for the city.[79] "Seriously disturbed mental patients roamed the streets of Little
Havana, overwhelming the local mental health system; former
convicts survived by preying on Jewish retirees in South Miami
Beach; Mariel drug gangs peppered each other with gunfire in
any neighborhood shopping center."[80] Thanks to the labors of
Ramiro Martinez and Matthew Lee, we see graphically how
high the Mariel homicide victimization was, and we know that
high group victimization usually means high group offending
(fig. 4.12). Note the sharp drop-off in Mariel crime at the end of
the decade; this probably is explained by the one-time-only nature of their immigration and the aging out of the 1980 arrivals.

Note, too, that general Latino (as opposed to Mariel) victimization rates were extremely high, particularly at the beginning
of the 1980s, which may indicate that Hispanic immigrants were

Figure 4.12 Homicide victimization rates, U.S. cities, Miami, and Latinos in Miami, 1980–95

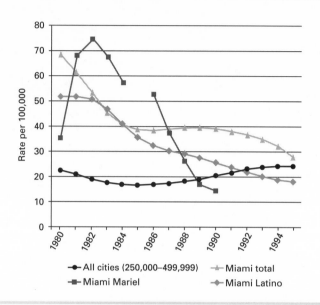

Source: Martinez and Lee, "On Immigration and Crime," 510.

contributing to the crime surge. On the other hand, the Latino rate declined at a fairly steady pace as the decade wore on, and from 1985 to 1995, as another Martinez and Lee study showed, they were a bit lower than Anglo rates (23.8 versus 26.6 per 100,000) and only a little more than one-third of African American rates (66.3 per 100,000). A calculation of homicide offender percentages was less favorable to Hispanics, however, as they contributed 38 percent of the perpetrators, whereas non-Hispanic whites were suspects in less than 5 percent of the killings.[81]

One of the most interesting immigrant case studies is that of the crime involvement, or, more accurately, noninvolvement, of Miami Haitians. These émigrés, wrote Alejandro Portes and Alex Stepick, "compared poorly with American Blacks or Mariel Cubans. On average, none had advanced beyond the fifth or sixth grade, and about four-fifths spoke little or no

English. In Haiti, about a third had been jobless (unemployed or not looking for work) before they decided to leave."[82] Once in the United States, nearly six in ten were below the poverty line, and virtually all of these immigrants were black and subject to the same levels of discrimination experienced by African Americans. Moreover, they found themselves in competition for jobs with Miami's existing black population, which created tensions between the two groups.[83]

Despite all of their adversities, Haitians had rather low crime rates. Martinez and Lee's 1985–95 study reported a homicide victimization rate of 16.7 for Haitians, which was lower than those for non-Hispanic whites and Latinos and far lower than the rate for American blacks. In fact, the Haitian crime figures may be inflated, since over 54 percent of the suspected killers of murdered Haitians were African American. In other words, the Haitian victimization rate is not an especially good

Figure 4.13 Homicide victimization rates, U.S. cities, Miami, and African Americans and Haitians in Miami, 1980–95

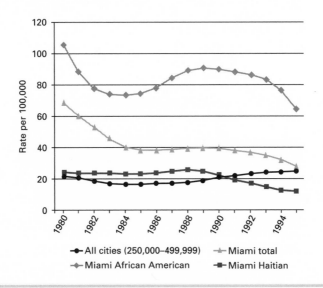

Source: Martinez and Lee, "On Immigration and Crime," 513.

indicator of Haitian offending, because, contrary to the usual situation, Haitians were the victims of an inordinate number of out-group killings. They were believed to have been only 3.5 percent of the murder suspects at a time when they were 14 percent of Miami's general population.[84]

IMMIGRANTS AND CRIME: CONCLUSIONS

Several conclusions may be drawn from the preceding survey of crime committed by the "new" immigrants. The most important is that assertions that immigration invariably reduces crime in the host country are not borne out by the evidence. Such contentions have no more support than the converse claim that immigrants inevitably raise crime rates. Evidence, both recent and historical, indicates that the crime impact of immigrants is contingent on an entering group's crime rates relative to crime rates at the destination point. Thus, while Jamaicans and Dominicans landing in New York City in the 1980s and '90s added to Gotham's crime woes, because their rates were higher than the prevailing rates in the city, the Chinese and Eastern European entrants, with their relatively low rates, had the opposite effect. Likewise, Mexicans who entered California aggravated its crime problem, whereas Asian arrivals by and large did not. And Hispanics, especially the Mariels, created more crime in Miami, while Haitians helped keep rates down.

The Haitians illustrate another point: culture trumps adversity, for both immigrants and natives, but most noticeably for immigrants. It would be hard to match Miami Haitians for hard knocks. Black, poor, uneducated, and unwelcome, they somehow managed to avoid assaulting their neighbors. Was this due to their religiosity? The strength of their families? Until scholars address these questions one must conclude only that *something* about Haitians—call it Haitian culture—enabled them to transcend economic and social disadvantage and conform to American law. Their culture, not the mere fact of immigration, immunized them against violent crime.

So, did immigration in the 1980s and '90s cause the great

crime decline? In some areas, New York City, for instance, immigrants helped sustain low crime, though they may not have actually reduced crime rates. In other places, Miami and Los Angeles, for example, immigration had the opposite effect. Nationwide, the answer must be negative. Little compelling evidence indicates that Latino immigrants were less violent than native-born Americans (referring here to Hispanics and non-Hispanic whites, not African Americans), and Latinos outnumbered all other immigrants (table 4.7). Although Asian immigrants were in the main more law-abiding than U.S. natives, sheer numbers suggest a muted impact. After all, the United States is a big country, with 248.7 million people in

Table 4.7 Legal and illegal immigration to
United States, by place of birth, 1980s and 1990s

Birthplace	1980–89	1990–99
All Latin America	4,442,000	6,467,000
Mexico	2,408,000	3,890,000
Caribbean	752,000	960,000
South America	585,000	852,000
Central America	697,000	765,000
East/Southeast Asia	1,720,000	1,922,000
Europe	538,000	1,187,000
South Asia	388,000	680,000
Middle East	398,000	324,000
Sub-Saharan Africa	155,000	349,000
Canada	90,000	184,000
Not given/Oceana	122,000	180,000
Total	7,853,000	11,293,000

Source: Camarota, *Immigrants*, 10.

Native Americans and Crime

Undoubtedly, North America's aboriginal peoples have had an enormous alcohol problem ever since the eighteenth century, when whites introduced them to liquor. The Indian arrest rate for drunkenness in 1992 was a stunning 4,700 per 100,000—nearly fifteen times the national average.[85] Do Native Americans also have a violent crime problem? The data for the late twentieth century suggest that they do and that the alcohol and violence are very much related.

- A survey of victims of domestic violence found that for all races, roughly half reported that the assailant had been drinking. For Native Americans, that figure jumped to three-quarters of all respondents.[86]

- A study of modern-day Navajo homicides found that the number of killings in which alcohol was present in the offender immediately prior to the crime was significantly higher for the Navajo (73.2 percent) than it was for either whites (39.7 percent) or African Americans (59.9 percent).[87]

- Native American murder victims were two to three times more

Figure 4.14 Violent crime arrest rates, Native Americans, whites, and blacks, 1980–2009

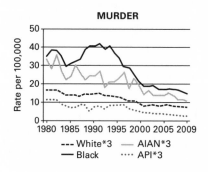

MURDER

--- White*3   — AIAN*3
— Black   ···· API*3

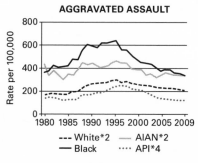

AGGRAVATED ASSAULT

--- White*2   — AIAN*2
— Black   ···· API*4

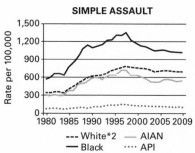

SIMPLE ASSAULT

--- White*2   — AIAN
— Black   ···· API

likely than whites or blacks to have died as a result of a brawl while under the influence of alcohol or drugs. Six percent of white and 4 percent of black murder victims died as a result of such drunken quarrels. For Indians, the rate was 13 percent.[88]

In addition to alcohol, poverty has also been significant in explaining violent crime by Indians. One-quarter of the Indian population in 1999 was below the government's poverty level—even higher than the proportion for African Americans at the time.[89]

Over the last three decades, arrest rates for Native American crimes of violence have exceeded the rates of whites in

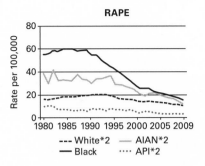

RAPE

Rate per 100,000

--- White*2   —— AIAN*2
—— Black   ···· API*2

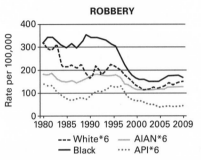

ROBBERY

Rate per 100,000

--- White*6   ⸺ AIAN*6
—— Black   ···· API*6

API = Asian/Pacific Islander
AIAN = American Indian/Alaska Native
Some data has been multiplied by a constant (e.g., *3) to make trends more visible.

Source: U.S. Department of Justice, Bureau of Justice Statistics, *Arrest in the United States*, 3–7.

three of five categories. And Indians have had the highest rates for murder, rape, and aggravated assault of any ethnic/racial group except African Americans (fig. 4.14).[90]

Still, in terms of national impact, crimes by Indians are insignificant. First of all, Native Americans are a small portion of the total U.S. population, around 1.5 percent in the 2000 census. Second, more than half of the indigenous population is concentrated in only ten states, and it is a significant minority in only three: Alaska (19 percent of the state population), Oklahoma (11 percent), and New Mexico (10 percent). Finally, nearly half of the Indian population is rural, which probably reduces their crimes against non-Indians.[91]

1990, not easily changed by an inflow amounting to 1 percent of the population.

Concededly, figures that include illegal immigrants understate the foreign influence, as they do not include children of immigrants born in the United States. However, children born here are U.S. citizens (whether or not their parents entered lawfully), and their crime rates raise a very different, and quite interesting, question, which can be called the second-generation issue. Do sons and daughters (second generation) or grandchildren (third generation) of immigrants commit more or less crime than their immigrant forebears?

REGIONAL CRIME

Persistently high rates of crime sparked by interpersonal conflict have always seemed a part of the warp and woof of southern culture. However, given the momentous changes in the southern states after World War II and the virtually complete integration of the region with the rest of the country, one might have expected a convergence of violent crime rates between the South and other sections. The evidence, though, is to the contrary. Keith Harries studied U.S. regional homicide rates over multiple decades. His maps (fig. 4.15) show that the position of the South relative to other sections of the country varied little in the postwar period, at least through the 1970s. But notice how, in 1980, the dark stain of homicide seemed to be oozing west. It isn't that the South had become less homicidal; rather, it had gained a regional competitor. We'll return momentarily to the rise of western homicide.

In the period after the 1980s, southern murder and manslaughter rates were higher than the national average straight through to 2005 (fig. 4.16). Notice, too, that the graph's line oscillations are quite similar. Rates for the South, as for the nation, declined in the early 1980s, rose sharply at the end of that decade, then slid downward during the crime decline of the twenty-first century. Apparently, whatever affected rates nationally impacted the South as well.[92]

One might think that much of the reason for the South's inordinately high violent crime rates was the significant African American population of the region. This is correct, but not the whole story. In 2000, 55 percent of the American black population resided in the South, where it comprised 19 percent of that region's residents. In that same year, over 60 percent of the homicide mortalities in the South were of African Americans, nearly all undoubtedly at the hands of fellow blacks. Moreover, the homicide victimization rate for southern blacks was five

Figure 4.15   State murder and manslaughter rates, in quartiles, 1950–80

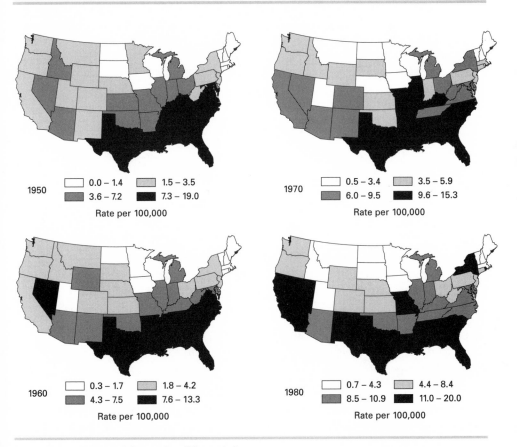

Source: Harries, "Historical Geography of Homicide," 76–77.

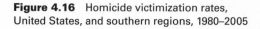

Figure 4.16 Homicide victimization rates,
United States, and southern regions, 1980–2005

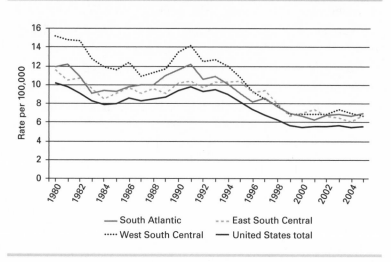

Source: U.S. Department of Justice, Bureau of Justice Statistics, *Homicide Trends*,
http://bjs.ojp.usdoj.gov/content/homicide/tables/regiontab.cfm.

times that of their white neighbors (19.54 per 100,000 versus
3.85). This racial gap held steady even during years that crime
declined. Blacks were 61 percent of the homicide victims over
the course of the eleven-year period from 1999 through 2009
(fig. 4.17).[93]

If black homicide rates were reduced to white levels, and
a big chunk of the South's killings thereby were eliminated,
the region would enjoy a less notorious standing in the murder sweepstakes. But the gains might not be as great as one
would think. While the outsized black population was a major reason for the South's unfortunate preeminence in violent
crime, white southern rates contributed mightily to that ranking. Throughout the nineteenth and twentieth centuries, white
southern violence had been much higher than that of nonsouthern whites. And in more recent years, when we compare
white homicides both in and out of the region, we see that the
old pattern persists.[94]

As mentioned earlier, after the 1970s, the western states grew increasingly homicidal, and criminologists began to claim that there was convergence between the two regions. In fact, some contended that homicide rates for whites were higher in the West than in the South, which, if true, might indicate that the southern culture of violence was indeed eroding.[95]

But it probably is true only with a big qualifier. When white Latinos and Anglos are differentiated, very different outcomes emerge for the regions. Figure 4.18 shows the South to be the most homicidal area, but it excludes Hispanic homicides, and Hispanic rates, as we know, can be quite elevated. Keeping in mind that Hispanics were twice as numerous in the West as in the South (24.3 percent of the western and 11.6 percent of the southern populations in 2000), when the term *white* includes Latinos, the West and South flip positions in the ranking of regions (fig. 4.19). This suggests that Hispanics bear some

Figure 4.17 Age-adjusted homicide mortality rates, South, by race, 1999–2009

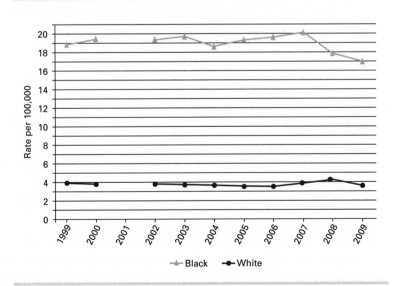

Source: National Center for Health Statistics, http://wonder.cdc.gov/ucd-icd10.html.

Figure 4.18 Age-adjusted homicide mortality rates, non-Hispanic whites, by census region, 1999–2009

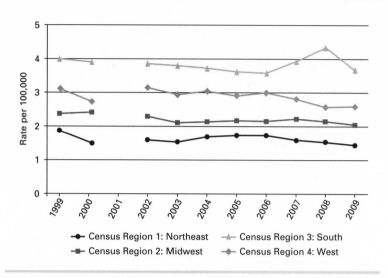

Source: National Center for Health Statistics, http://wonder.cdc.gov/ucd-icd10.html.

responsibility for the excessive murders in the West as well as for the displacement of the South as the deadliest region.[96]

Whether or not the South still is the most homicidal section of the country, the persistence of heightened rates in the region for over two centuries remains to be explained. Randolph Roth's history of homicide maintains that shortly after the American Revolution, the "slaveholding South"—as opposed to its nonslave areas—"became the first region of the United States to deviate from the long-term trend toward lower homicide rates in North America and western Europe."[97] Indeed, the roots of southern violence may run even deeper than the Revolution. Historian David Hackett Fischer traced the tradition of "retributive folk justice" (including vigilantism and blood feuds) to English-speaking people from the borders of north Britain and northern Ireland who emigrated to the Appalachian backcountry decades before the break with England.

They created, he said, "a climate of violence in the American backcountry which remained part of the culture of that region to our own time."[98]

An elegant study by psychologists Richard E. Nisbett and Dov Cohen examined the culture of honor theory as an explanation for high southern violence in the contemporary period.[99] The authors added a new twist to the account of the origins of this violence: the herding hypothesis. Like Fischer, Nisbett and Cohen also thought that there was a culture of violence in the South, especially in the more rural and isolated areas, and that this culture had its roots in the customs of seventeenth-century English borderland immigrants. Unlike Fischer, however, they placed great emphasis on violence attributed to the practice of animal herding. As they explained:

> Unlike the North, which was settled by farmers from England, Holland, and Germany, the South was settled

Figure 4.19   Age-adjusted homicide mortality rates, Hispanics and non-Hispanic whites combined, by census region, 1999–2009

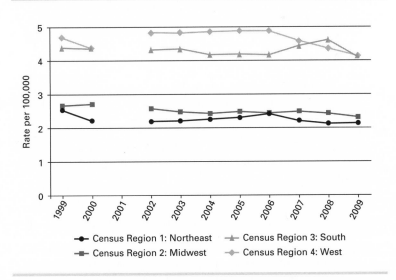

Source: National Center for Health Statistics, http://wonder.cdc.gov/ucd-icd10.html.

by herdsmen from the fringes of Britain. Herdsmen the world over tend to be capable of great aggressiveness and violence because of their vulnerability to losing their primary resources, their animals. Also, unlike the North, where population densities have been in general relatively high, the South was a low-population frontier region until well into the nineteenth century. In such regions the state often has little power to command compliance with the law, and citizens have to create their own system of order. The means for doing this is the rule of retaliation: If you cross me, I will punish you.[100]

Thus, it was an economic factor (precariousness of livelihood) and a governance issue (weak governing authority's inability to preserve order) that made the culture of honor functional for these early southerners. The link between this culture and violence and crime was described as follows:

> To maintain credible power of deterrence, the individual must project a stance of willingness to commit mayhem and to risk wounds or death for himself. Thus, he must constantly be on guard against affronts that could be construed by others as disrespect. When someone allows himself to be insulted, he risks giving the impression that he lacks the strength to protect what is his. Thus the individual must respond with violence or the threat of violence to any affront.[101]

If this tough-guy stance and hair-trigger explosiveness remind the reader of the black culture of violence discussed in chapter 3, it is not surprising. One can make a strong case that impoverished African Americans shared in the southern culture of violence and transported it to the North during their migrations. There, social isolation and discrimination perpetuated a version of this culture among lower-class blacks, accounting for the high rates of black-on-black violence. Perhaps this explains why Nisbett and Cohen found no regional differences in homicide rates among blacks:[102] they took their culture of violence with them to other regions.

As Nisbett and Cohen mainly were concerned with white southern violence, however, they focused on homicide rates among non-Hispanic whites, comparing their rates in the South to their rates in the other regions of the nation. They paid special attention to the size of cities within each region. Small cities, they argued, unlike big metropolitan areas, which are more cosmopolitan, better reflect traditional cultures. Also, they reasoned, comparing regional crime by cities avoids masking sub-state differences, which occurs when state-level measures are used. They discovered that the smaller the city, the bigger the gap between southern and nonsouthern whites. For urban places with populations under 50,000, the ratio of southern to New England rates was over 3 to 1; for cities between 50,000 and 200,000, the ratio was closer to 2 to 1; and for the biggest urban areas, the differences were negligible (fig. 4.20).[103]

Another significant finding is that murders precipitated by quarrels were much more common in the South than felony-generated killings, such as robbery-homicides. Here, too, as figure 4.21 makes evident, Nisbett and Cohen found striking differences correlated with city size.[104]

Finally, the Nisbett-Cohen study attempts to demonstrate that the herding economy of the eighteenth-century South explains intraregional homicide differences that have persisted at least into the twentieth century. They found that white male homicide offender rates were substantially higher in the hills and dry plains, where herding took place, than in the moist plains, where cotton grew and slavery flourished. Between 1976 and 1983, rates in the herding areas were 12.27 per 100,000 as compared with 4.98 in the farming areas.[105] This part of the study has been strongly challenged.

In the first place, the assertion that there was more violence in herding areas than in farming regions is contrary to Randolph Roth's insistence that the slaveholding parts of the South

Figure 4.20 White homicide offending and victimization rates, by region and city size, 1976–83

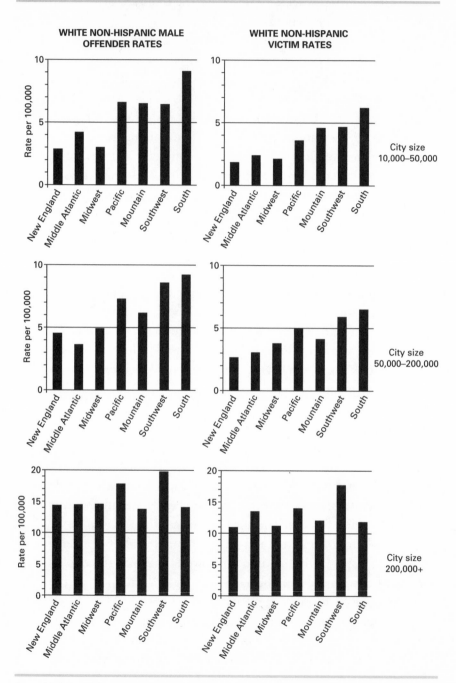

Source: Nisbett and Cohen, *Culture of Honor*, 16.

Figure 4.21   White male homicide offending rates,
by type of homicide, region, and city size

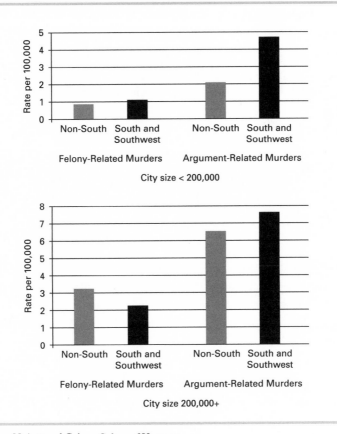

Source: Nisbett and Cohen, *Culture of Honor*, 21.

had, in the late eighteenth and early nineteenth centuries, the
highest homicide rates in the region, and, indeed, nationwide.[106]

Second, subsequent empirical tests of the herding thesis
found, contrary to Nisbett-Cohen, that once county homicide
rates were adjusted for differences in white poverty, there were
no discernible divergences in homicides between the dry plains/
hills and moist plains farming counties.[107]

Even if the herding thesis is wrong, however, the theory of
a southern culture of violence remains viable. After all, Fischer's
explanation for the historical roots of southern violence, which

did not rely on herding, has not been repudiated, and the violence of the South has persisted for over two centuries. Moreover, contemporary data continue to show that non-Hispanic southern whites have the highest rates of argument-based violent crime in the nation (compared with non-Hispanic whites of other regions). Indeed, there now is empirical evidence that both white and black southerners retain their propensities for violence, even when they migrate out of the former Confederacy.[108]

The West, due to the outsized violence of Hispanics, may soon catch up with, and even surpass, the South in violence, but that in no way diminishes the southern culture of violence thesis. It simply indicates that distinctive cultural groups with a propensity for relatively high rates of violence—certain Latinos, in this case—may impact crime rates in the region to which they migrate.

Cultures of violence may persist for decades, even centuries, and travel with their bearers. This was true, and continues to be true, for foreign migrants as well as migrating members of distinctive U.S.-born cultural groups.

♦ ♦ ♦

By the time of the civil judgment against Bernhard Goetz in 1996, New York City was a changed metropolis, and more dramatic changes were ahead. Between 1990 and 2009, homicide, robbery, and burglary in the big city would fall an astonishing 80 percent.[109] Indeed, the United States was a very different country. Violent crime by all groups, including African Americans, was on its way down nationwide. Fear of muggings and assaults had ebbed, and racial tension was starting to dissipate. In 2008, Barack Obama, the son of a black father and a white mother, was elected president of the United States. *New York Times* columnist Paul Krugman opined that Obama's candidacy would have been impossible had it not been for the decline in urban violence.[110]

Ford Motor Company bomber factory at Willow Run, Michigan, in 1942. This was the world's largest one-story war production plant. Fixtures in the background held bomber wings during assembly. Note the women workers. No one could say that crime was caused by unemployment during the 1940s, because jobs were widely available.

Men entering temporary wartime housing on Fourth Avenue, Seattle, Washington, in 1943. War production cities were unprepared for the influx of workers and their families, an apparent cause of crime in the 1940s.

Aerial view of Levittown in Nassau County, Long Island, New York, in 1951.
Whites raced to suburbs such as this, as crime was becoming a predominantly
black, inner-city problem.

[Fairchild Aerial Surveys, Benjamin and Gladys Thomas Air Photo Archives, UCLA]

DAILY NEWS

NEW YORK'S PICTURE NEWSPAPER ®

5¢

Vol. 41. No. 60   Copr 1940 News Syndicate Co. Inc.   New York 17, N.Y., Thursday, September 8, 1959*   WEATHER: Partly cloudy, showers, warm.

KILLED BECAUSE 'I FELT LIKE IT' SAYS CAPE MAN

(NEWS foto by Phil Greitzer)

Two Faces of Murder. Salvatore Agron (left), 16, self-styled "Dracula," grins at W. 47th St. station as Tony Hernandez, 17, the "Umbrella Man," looks up to his curly-haired leader. The pair were booked in Sunday's senseless Hell's Kitchen murder of two 16-year-old boys. —*Story on page 3; other pictures in centerfold*

The 1959 "Cape Man" killing of two inoffensive white youths by Hispanic gang members shocked New York. Crime would become much worse a decade later.   *[Phil Greitzer, New York Daily News]*

Soldier standing guard at the corner of 7th and N Streets, N.W., Washington, D.C. Buildings were destroyed during riots that followed the assassination of Martin Luther King Jr. on April 4, 1968. *[Warren K. Leffler, Library of Congress Prints and Photographs Division]*

National Guard personnel walking toward the crowd near Taylor Hall, at Kent State University, May 4, 1970. Escalating campus protests over the Vietnam War turned deadly, contributing to the sense that law and order had broken down completely in the United States. *[May 4 Collection, Kent State University Libraries, Special Collections and Archives]*

Homicide in a New York City food store in 1972. The clerk was shot dead for a few dollars in the till. Crime had grown more vicious in the 1970s. [Leonard Freed, Magnum Photos]

Bernhard Goetz escorted by police out of criminal court in New York City on January 16, 1985, after being arraigned for shooting young black males on the subway. Initially, New Yorkers of all races, fearful of subway muggers, were sympathetic to Goetz.

[Rene Perez, AP Photo]

A handsome Philadelphia apartment building abandoned and turned into a crack house.

[© iStock/dovate]

*Crack cocaine,
scourge of
the late 1980s.*
[Drug Enforcement
Administration]

Bryant Park, New York City, in 1983, when crime rates were high. [Bryant Park Corporation]

Bryant Park, New York City, in 2007, when crime rates were low. [Bryant Park Corporation]

CHAPTER 5

The Great Downturn

1995 to the Twenty-First Century

America woke from its crime nightmare during the last decade of the twentieth century. The cocaine war was over, muggings were on the wane, and cities were becoming as safe as they had been before the long ordeal began in the late 1960s. No one predicted the change, and no one, try as they might, could explain it. But everyone knew it was good. Urban peace was restored. People could move about without fear. They could commute to work, school, and entertainment events with little thought of assault or theft. Tourists returned; restaurants and hotels flourished. Racial tension fueled by outsized minority involvement in criminality began to ebb. An African American was elected president of the United States and reelected four years later. Some people talked of a "post-racial society."[1]

How the nation's crime situation reached this point is the subject of this chapter. It begins with the reinvigoration of the criminal justice system—police, courts, and prisons—following its near collapse in the late 1960s. It closes with an analysis of the extraordinary drop in violent crime.

CRACKDOWN

During the late 1980s and continuing through the 1990s, U.S. cities enlarged their police forces. President Bill Clinton helped boost the number of police officers with his promise to add 100,000 cops to city streets, a vow fulfilled when the Violent Crime Control and Law Enforcement Act of 1994 was passed by Congress.[2] Over the six-year period subsequent to the approval of this legislation—years of dramatic declines in crime—70,000 police officers were put to work. For cities with populations over one-quarter million, the 1990s saw the addition of 22,616 full-time sworn law enforcement personnel, a rise of 17 percent. Per capita measures show staffing gains for most municipal size categories, especially from the late 1980s on (fig. 5.1).[3]

Whether or not the increased police presence reduced

Figure 5.1 Sworn police officers, by city size, 1977–2000

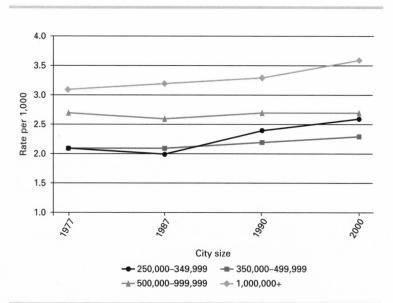

Sources: U.S. Department of Justice, Bureau of Justice Statistics: *Police Departments in Large Cities, 1990–2000* (table 2, 2); *Police Departments in Large Cities, 1987* (table 17, 7).

Table 5.1 Crimes of violence, percentage cleared by police, 1980–2005

	Murder (%)	Aggravated assault (%)	Rape (%)	Robbery (%)
1980	72	59	49	24
1985	72	62	54	25
1990	67	57	53	25
1995	65	56	51	25
2000	63	57	47	26
2005	62	55	41	25

Sources: Federal Bureau of Investigation, *Crime in the United States*, Uniform Crime Reports: 1980 (table 20, 182); 1985 (table 20, 156); 1990 (table 20, 165); 2000 (table 25, 207); 2005 (table 25), http://www2.fbi.gov/ucr/05cius/data/table_25.html.

crime is uncertain. A careful review of twenty-seven studies of the size of police forces and violent crime found no "consistent evidence that increases in police strength produce decreases in violent crime."[4] This conclusion is supported by at least one important measure of police effectiveness, the clearance rate, which is, roughly, the ratio of arrests to reported crimes. These numbers, gathered by the FBI and published in their annual Uniform Crime Reports, show little improvement over the years and actually indicate a 14 percent *decline* in solved murders (table 5.1).[5]

In cities of 100,000 people or more, the decline in clearances was precipitous (fig. 5.2). Analysts have attributed it to reductions in quarrel-based killings and increases in firearm and stranger homicides, the latter being much harder to solve. Researchers also found that police workload was not a factor. Especially intriguing is the further discovery that there was a positive correlation between drug arrests and homicide clearances, perhaps because some of the drug violators also were murderers, or because they provided information about murder suspects.[6] (Later we will consider whether drug imprisonment may have also reduced violent crime by incapacitating potential violent offenders.)

Policing is more than numbers, however, and new law enforcement strategies seem to have had a positive impact on urban life, particularly when coupled with improvements in police department organization and operation. New York City became the model for these changes, with much of the credit going to its aggressive anticrime mayor, Rudolph Giuliani (who served from 1994 to 2001), and his flamboyant police commissioner, William Bratton (1994 to 1996; reappointed in 2014). In 1994, Bratton introduced CompStat, a computerized crime-tracking innovation he combined with organizational measures to hold precinct commanders accountable for crime increases in their jurisdictions.[7] CompStat was launched along with so-called zero-tolerance policing, which included efforts to clear the streets of vagrants and loiterers (including aggressive panhandlers, addicts, and the mentally ill) who, since the 1970s, had made public places unsavory and sometimes frightening to

Figure 5.2 Proportion of cases cleared by police in cities of 100,000 population or more, 1970–2000

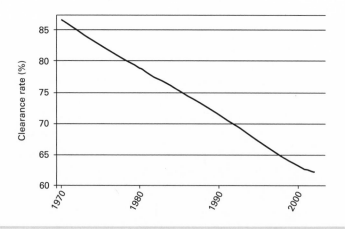

Source: Ousey and Lee, "To Know the Unknown," 142.

the middle class. Zero tolerance, in turn, is sometimes linked to "broken windows" police work, a phrase coined by James Q. Wilson and George Kelling, who urged arrests of low-level offenders as a way of stimulating and reinforcing community support for efforts to quell more serious crimes.[8]

Whether all these undertakings reduced violent crime is perhaps unprovable, but criminologist Franklin Zimring contended that at least two tactical measures by police "almost certainly reduced crime in New York City": "hot spots" enforcement, in which locations with recurring patterns of crime are assigned special patrol and long-term surveillance, and the targeting of public drug markets. The latter is credited with helping to drive down public crack cocaine dealing and its concomitant violence.[9]

Commendable as these policies were in improving urban life in the United States, the jury is still out on their effect on violent crime rates. This is because rates fell off all over the nation without any clear relationship between the enormous declines in some cities and the adoption of new policing models. In fact, many urban crime slides commenced well before 1994, when New York City pointed the way with its reforms. Without any major changes in policing, Dallas, Houston, and San Diego experienced big homicide rate drops in 1992, as did Philadelphia in 1991.[10]

SENTENCING

At the same time that policing was changing, the "get tough on crime" attitude of the 1980s and early '90s was affecting sentencing laws, the province of state legislatures and courts. State and federal governments became more punitive, establishing mandatory minimum sentences for certain offenses; providing longer sentences, especially for recidivists; and abolishing parole to prevent the early release of prisoners. These laws were especially aimed at drug law violators, criminals who used weapons, and otherwise violent criminals.

The 1994 Violent Crime Control Act (the same law that authorized 100,000 new local police officers) established truth-in-sentencing grants to encourage states to compel someone convicted of a violent crime to serve at least 85 percent of the sentence. By 1998, twenty-seven states and the District of Columbia had qualified for such grants, and other states adopted comparable laws, setting the minimum time served at various levels at or above 50 percent of the sentence.[11]

The best known of the recidivist statutes was California's "Three Strikes" law, which targeted the repeat offender. It worked as follows. If a defendant was convicted of a felony (which need not have been a crime of violence) and had one or more prior felony convictions, then, provided the earlier convictions fell within the statutory definition of "serious" or "violent" crimes, the defendant would have to receive for his latest felony conviction a much stiffer sentence than ordinarily imposed. The size of the sentence enhancement depended on the number of previous serious or violent felony convictions. If he had committed *one* such prior, his term for the new offense had to be doubled; with *two* serious or violent priors, his sentence for the third strike was mandatory life. A life-sentenced defendant would be eligible for parole, but only after a lengthy period of time as determined by legislative formula.[12]

A challenge to this law went to the U.S. Supreme Court in *Ewing v. California*. Gary Ewing's third strike was the theft of three golf clubs priced at $399 apiece, but his long criminal record, including three burglaries and a robbery at knifepoint, earned him a life sentence under the Three Strikes rule. He would be eligible for parole after twenty-five years. The Supreme Court upheld the law by a 5 to 4 vote, rejecting the claim that his punishment was cruel and unusual in violation of the Eighth Amendment. "Recidivism," wrote three of the justices in the majority, "has long been recognized as a legitimate basis for increased punishment," and given the state's interest in incapacitating repeat offenders who committed serious or violent crimes, the sentence, concluded the Court, was not cruel and unusual.[13]

The impact of various tougher sentence laws on court sentencing practices for violent crimes is shown in table 5.2, which presents the ratio of state prison sentences to arrests for such offenses. This gives us a sense of the number of people imprisoned following arrests for specific crimes. By examining these ratios over time, we get a feel for whether or not the system is getting tougher or more lenient.

Examining first the period between 1980 and 1990, it is clear that by decade's end, police had arrested more violent and weapons offenders and more than double the number of drug law violators. A major leap in drug arrests would have been expected for the late 1980s, given the crack epidemic. But prison commitments for this same period do not show a uniformly tougher system. Drug-sentencing ratios escalated fivefold, weapons-sentencing ratios tripled, but violent crime ratios present a mixed picture: they rose for rape and assault but dropped for murder and robbery.

Turning to the period between 1990 and 1996—and keeping in mind that crime had begun to decline by 1996—we see arrests for violent crimes, except assault, diminishing and drug apprehensions rising another 28 percent. But prison commitment ratios rose for violent crime (except rape) and declined for drug offenses by 25 percent.

The message is that imprisonment for drug crimes dominated the 1980s, especially the late '80s, whereas imprisonment for violent crimes grew more significant in the first half of the 1990s. Comparing 1996 and 1980, prison commitment ratios for all offenses except murder were higher. So the courts, bolstered by tougher sentencing laws, were definitely sending more people to prison for violent crimes, drug crimes, and weapons violations.

Table 5.2 Adult arrests and new court commitments to state prison, by offense, 1980, 1990, and 1996

Offense	Adult arrests			Commitments (per 1,000 arrests)		
	1980	1990	1996	1980	1990	1996
Murder	18,200	19,800	16,100	621	460	613
Rape	26,700	33,300	27,400	182	229	219
Robbery	102,200	127,400	106,700	245	233	277
Aggravated assault	236,600	410,800	445,005	45	56	62
Drug offenses	471,200	1,008,300	1,294,700	19	103	77
Weapons offenses	141,200	181,000	163,400	11	34	55

Source: U.S. Department of Justice, Bureau of Justice Statistics, *Truth in Sentencing*, 4.

IMPRISONMENT

The figures for imprisonment per capita in the United States are startling: a fairly level course ran for roughly fifty years, from 1925 to 1975, and then an enormously steep upward trajectory emerged through 2007 (fig. 5.3).[14]

One must assume the reason for this massive increase is that more people were being sent to prison than heretofore, people were imprisoned for longer periods of time, or some combination of both. Prison rates depicted in figure 5.3 are based on a yearly inventory of inmates, so the data don't tell us if longer sentences or more prison commitments account for the escalation. Some analysts say the increase was the result of longer sentences—a plausible explanation in light of the prevailing lock-'em-up sentiment. Others, however, claim it was the result of more sentences to prison, as opposed to jail or probation: offenders who might have served a brief stint in jail or might have been released on probation were spending time, though not necessarily a long time, in prison.[15]

Figure 5.3   Persons sentenced to state or federal prisons, 1925–2010

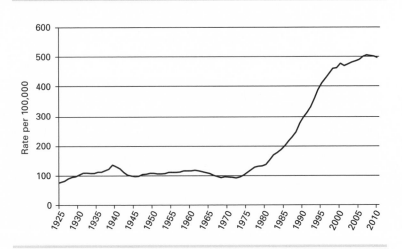

Source: U.S. Department of Justice, Bureau of Justice Statistics, "Sourcebook of Criminal Justice Statistics Online," table 6.28.2010, accessed May 2, 2012, http://www.albany.edu/sourcebook/pdf/t6282010.pdf.

Examining prison time actually served sheds light on this dispute. Few prisoners serve their full terms; they are released to parole and receive credit for time served during periods of "good behavior." Consequently, the real time spent behind bars—time served—is far less than the length of the sentence imposed. In 1996, for instance, released prisoners had served on average 44 percent of their sentences.[16]

When time served by all prisoners, regardless of offense, is broken down by length, the number of long terms in 1994 never rose above 1984 levels, and more inmates served under one year in 1994 than had a decade earlier (table 5.3). In 1994, moreover, 63 percent of all prisoners were released after serving two years or less, and 87 percent were discharged in under five years. Thus, we cannot conclude that time spent in prison grew longer.[17]

When it comes to violent crimes and drug offenses, however, the story is a bit different. By examining time served for these specific crimes, we learn that punishments did indeed grow harsher in the 1990s. There were, as table 5.4 indicates, few declines in time served after 1985 and some very sharp increases; for example, time served in 1990 was up 47 percent for murder and up 33 percent for rape.[18] (Figures for prisoners released in 2009 show further increases. For drug crimes, the mean time served was 26 months. For violent crimes, the increase was much greater: the average time in prison was 60 months.[19])

We come now to a crucial question: Was the rise in incarceration responsible for the big decline in crime? Virtually

Table 5.3 Percentage of prisoners, by length of time served, admitted 1984 and 1994

Time served	Prisoners (%)	
	1984	1994
Under 1 year	22	29
1–2 years	35	34
2–3 years	16	13
3–4 years	9	7
4–5 years	5	4
More than 5 years	13	12

Source: Raphael and Stoll, "Why Are So Many Americans in Prison?" 67.

Table 5.4 Mean time served in state prison on first release for violent and drug offenses, 1985, 1990, and 1996

	Time served (months)		
	1985	**1990**	**1996**
Violent offenses	31.7	39	39
Murder/ non-negligent manslaughter	56.5	83	84
Negligent manslaughter	28.1	31	41
Rape	41.3	55	61
Other sexual assault	27.6	30	39
Robbery	32.9	41	40
Assault	23.0	23	28
Drug offenses	14.5	14	20
Possession	12.6	12	17
Trafficking	15.6	16	22
Other drug	14.3	12	17

Sources: U.S. Department of Justice, Bureau of Justice Statistics, *Truth in Sentencing*, 8; U.S. Department of Justice, Bureau of Justice Statistics, *Sourcebook of Criminal Justice Statistics, 1990*, table 6.114, 665.

all analyses agree that harsher sentencing had some, perhaps considerable, positive impact. After all, from the standpoint of incapacitation alone (preventing additional crime by removing potential offenders from society), there would have been a protective benefit in locking up so many people who had committed multiple crimes and who would have been highly likely to engage in more had they been at large.

Strong evidence indicates that had these prisoners been unconfined, they would have committed many additional crimes. Among parolees the reoffending rate is shockingly high.

A fifteen-state sample of prisoners released in 1994 found that 30 percent of them were rearrested within six months of release, and 11 percent were reconvicted. After three years, *two-thirds* of released inmates were arrested again, 47 percent reconvicted. The latter were charged with 744,480 new crimes, over 100,000 of which were violent. Even prisoners convicted of nonviolent offenses often commit crimes of violence on release. Among released drug offenders, for example, 18.4 percent of the rearrests were for violent crimes.[20]

There can be little doubt then that incarcerating these offenders prevented thousands of new crimes. The preceding analysis doesn't address the general deterrent effect of incarceration, the tendency of punishment to discourage other would-be offenders from committing crime. Measuring deterrent effect is a tricky proposition, however, as it requires analysis capable of isolating the fear of criminal sanction from all other influences that lead people to refrain from crime, and then measuring the precise impact of that self-restraint on the incidence or rate of crime. Researchers usually sidestep the problem by using sophisticated quantitative (multiple regression) analysis that measures both incapacitative and deterrent effects without differentiating between them.

Several of these quantitative analyses of imprisonment found that the massive increase had a significant impact. One declared that the violent crime decline up to 1997 would have been 27 percent smaller had the prison buildup never occurred.[21] Another determined that the increase in incarceration over the 1990s accounted for reductions in homicide and violent crime of approximately 12 percent in each case.[22] An assessment of three decades of imprisonment in the United States maintained that there was "strong evidence of a negative relationship between prison [population] size and the crime rate." "In a phrase," the authors concluded, "more prison, less crime."[23]

While greater imprisonment helped reduce crime, it hit

black males especially hard. In 1991, 6.2 percent of the African American adult population had served time in a state or federal prison, compared with 1.1 percent of white adults. A decade later, the percentages were 8.9 for blacks and 1.4 for whites. Hispanic imprisonment rates (like crime rates) were positioned between those of non-Hispanic whites and blacks, climbing from 2.7 percent in 1991 to 4.3 percent in 2001. For black males, the situation was particularly disturbing: 16.6 percent had been imprisoned as of 2001, with projections that, if incarceration rates remained unchanged, one in three would be behind bars during their lifetimes. To put these rates in historical perspective, consider the following: in 1926, when the overwhelming majority of blacks lived in the South, with its notorious Jim Crow system, their prison rate was 106 per 100,000; in 1986, when half of the black population lived outside the South and in a far less racially biased age, the rate was over three times greater, at 342 per 100,000.[24]

Given the extraordinarily high involvement of African Americans in imprisonable misconduct—drug and violent crime, most obviously—this outcome was predictable, if unsettling. But it also must be noted that crime reductions gained in part by incarcerations positively affected African Americans and their communities much more than they did white communities. Black victimization, overwhelmingly at the hands of black offenders, was extraordinarily high. For homicide, for instance, blacks were 47 percent of all victims between 1976 and 2005, and 94 percent of those black victims were killed by other African Americans. So the crime drop unquestionably saved countless black lives and spared thousands of African Americans from nonlethal victimizations. As criminologist Franklin Zimring pithily put it, the poor and minorities "pay more," but also get more.[25]

Moreover, few serious analyses have proved that the imprisonment rate differentials between whites and blacks were due to systematic race discrimination, and in the post–civil rights era, it is highly doubtful that there was widespread intentional bias. A widely cited study by Alfred Blumstein and a follow-up article by that same author found that black imprisonment rates fairly reflected arrest rates, at least for the most serious crimes. Blumstein concluded that "the bulk of the disproportionality is a consequence of the differential involvement by blacks in the most serious kinds of crime like homicide and robbery."[26] This conclusion was buttressed by statistician Patrick Langan, who matched black prison admissions with perpetrator racial identities as reported by the National Crime Victim Survey. "In 1982," Langan wrote, "a nondiscriminatory system would have resulted in a black percentage of admissions of 44.9% while the actual percentage was 48.9%."[27]

When the length of actual periods of imprisonment by crime category are examined, the differences between the races are not disquieting. In 1982, before the crack cocaine era, the median time served by blacks for each crime category was two to three months more than time served by whites; the biggest differentials were for criminal homicides (table 5.5). At the tail end of the crack period, in 1993, blacks and whites served very similar amounts of time; the biggest difference was for rape, for which blacks served a median five months more than whites. Somewhat surprisingly, whites did slightly more time than blacks for drug crimes. It should be kept in mind that several considerations having nothing to do with race can affect the length of time a prisoner must serve. The violence of the crime committed and the inmate's prior convictions are two factors that might have resulted in longer imprisonment for African Americans.[28]

Given the lack of gross inequity in time served, the high black incarceration rates are best explained not by race bias, but by exceptionally high African American crime commission rates and the imposition of prison sentences for conduct previously punished by jail or probation. There is evidence that these

Table 5.5 Median time served in state prison, on release, for all crimes, violent crimes, and drug crimes, by race, 1982 and 1993

	Time served (months)			
	1982		1993	
	White	Black	White	Black
All offenses	15	18	12	12
All violent offenses	23	26	23	24
Murder	65	74	81	82
Manslaughter	25	31	42	46
Rape	33	38	42	47
Other sexual assault	22	24	25	24
Robbery	24	26	24	26
Assault	14	16	15	16
Drug offenses	11	13	12	11

Sources: U.S. Department of Justice, Bureau of Justice Statistics: "National Corrections Reporting Program"; *Prison Admissions and Releases,* 7.

prison sentences were sought by prosecutors because the defendants had prior convictions, probably due to earlier wars on crime and drugs.[29] In short, more blacks (and more whites) were going to prison for their crimes than ever before. Whatever the negative consequences of this, there was one overwhelmingly beneficial result: violent crime declined dramatically. To be sure, imprisonment was not the only, perhaps not even the major, reason for the decline. But its significance cannot be gainsaid.

THE CRIME WAVE RECEDES

Violent crime rates began abating in the first half of the 1980s, rebounded in the second half, and peaked in the early 1990s, after which they began plunging downward and kept on dropping right through 2013. Regarding murder, which affords the most accurate statistics, the rate essentially was cut in half—down by 53 percent from 1980 to 2010 (fig. 5.4). Most of the decline took place in the 1990s, falling 42 percent between 1990 and 2000.[30]

More encouraging still, virtually all crimes, violent and nonviolent, diminished during this period. Most significantly, the robbery scourge—the crime that frightened millions, forced the adoption of defensive lifestyles, and nearly undermined city life in late-twentieth-century America—declined just as much as murder.[31] In fact, if we rely on the National Crime Victimization Survey (thus avoiding the undercount problem arising from failures to report incidents to the police), the drop in robbery rates between 1994 and 2010 was an astonishing 70 percent (fig. 5.5). As with murder, a significant portion of the decline occurred in the 1990s: 44 percent between 1990 and 2000.[32]

In the nation's big cities, where crime was especially problematic, the declines were doubly gratifying. Table 5.6 presents

Figure 5.4 Murders and non-negligent manslaughters
known to police, rate per 100,000, 1980–2010

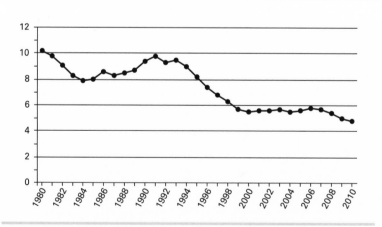

Source: Federal Bureau of Investigation, Uniform Crime Reporting Statistics, "UCR Data Online," accessed April 12, 2012, http://www.ucrdatatool.gov/.

Figure 5.5 Robbery victimization rates, 1980–2010

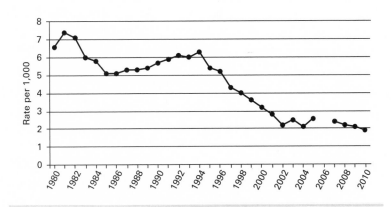

Source: U.S. Department of Justice, Bureau of Justice Statistics, National Crime Victimization Survey, https://web.archive.org/web/20100124061405/http://bjs.ojp .usdoj.gov/content/glance/tables/viortrdtab.cfm.

reported crime rates by city size for three decades. Figure 5.6 extracts only the robbery figures, vividly displaying the dramatic decline in urban dwellers' biggest nightmare. The decline in reported robberies in big cities (those with populations of one-quarter million or more) was 62 percent from 1980 to 2010. The biggest drop of all—71 percent—was in the nation's most-populated urban areas, where the robbery situation had been the worst. New York City led the pack with an eye-popping 84 percent plunge.

Generalizing on the basis of the three decades from 1960 through 1990, criminologists concluded that crime has always been worse in cities and the bigger the city, the worse the crime. However, as the late Eric Monkkonen reminded us, in the late nineteenth century, cities had *fewer* murders than did the southern countryside. Moreover, New York, the nation's biggest metropolis, had homicide rates *lower* than the national average for the first six decades of the twentieth century.[33] While cities grew remarkably safer after the mid-1990s, population size still does make a difference, as table 5.7 shows. Urban areas with

Table 5.6 Total violent crime, murder, and robbery, rate per 100,000, by size of city, 1980–2010

City population	1980			1990			2000			2010		
	Total violent crime	Murder	Robbery	Total violent crime	Murder	Robbery	Total violent crime	Murder	Robbery	Total violent crime	Murder	Robbery
1 million+	1,705	29.4	1,052	2,243	31.6	1,139	1,124	12.7	440	713	9.0	303
500,000+	1,162	20.6	638	1,320	21.9	601	1,092	14.2	400	807	10.6	289
250,000+	1,275	21.6	627	1,578	19.7	628	1,038	12.7	378	758	11.3	282

Sources: Federal Bureau of Investigation, *Crime in the United States*, Uniform Crime Reports: 1980 (table 14, 17); 1990 (table 14, 156); 2000 (table 16, 195); 2010 (table 16), accessed April 13, 2012, http://www.fbi.gov/about-us/cjis/ucr/crime-in-the-u.s/2010/crime-in-the-u.s.-2010/tables/10tbl16.xls.

Figure 5.6 Robbery rates, by city size, 1980–2010

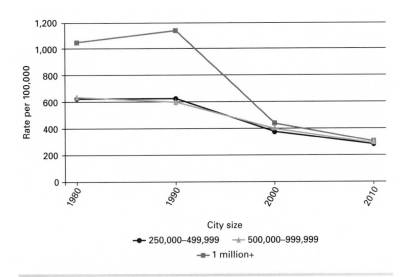

Sources: Federal Bureau of Investigation, *Crime in the United States,* Uniform Crime Reports: 1980 (table 14, 173); 1990 (table 14, 156); 2000 (table 16, 195); 2010 (table 16), accessed April 13, 2012, http://www.fbi.gov/about-us/cjis/ucr/crime-in-the-u.s/2010/crime-in-the-u.s.-2010/tables/10tbl16.xls.

Table 5.7 Murder and robbery rates, urban areas, by size of city, 2010

City population	Murder rate (per 100k)	Robbery rate (per 100k)
250,000+	10.0	294
100,000+	5.7	170
50,000+	3.9	121
25,000+	3.3	90

Sources: Federal Bureau of Investigation, *Crime in the United States,* Uniform Crime Reports: 1980 (table 14, 173); 1990 (table 14, 156); 2000 (table 16, 195); 2010 (table 16), accessed April 13, 2012, http://www.fbi.gov/about-us/ucr/crime-in-the-u.s/2010/crime-in-the-u.s.-2010/tables/10tbl16.xls.

Table 5.8 Age-adjusted homicide mortality rates, by race and ethnicity, and change in rates, by group, selected time periods

	Homicide mortality rate (per 100k)		
	Non-Hispanic whites	Hispanics	Blacks
1980	5.2	25.6	41.3
1990	4.0	16.2	36.3
2000	2.8	7.5	20.5
2002	2.8	7.6	21.6
2003	2.7	8.0	21.7
2004	2.7	7.4	20.7
2005	2.7	7.8	21.1
2006	2.7	7.6	22.4
2007	2.8	7.2	21.1
2008	2.8	6.9	19.5
2009	2.6	6.5	18.8

	Change in homicide mortality (%)		
	Whites	Hispanics	Blacks
1980–2000	−46	−71	−50
1990–2000	−30	−54	−44
1980–2009	−50	−75	−54
1990–2009	−35	−57	−46

Sources: National Center for Health Statistics, *Deaths of Hispanic Origin*, table 6, 27; National Center for Health Statistics, *Health, United States, 2011*, table 24; National Center for Health Statistics, http://wonder.cdc.gov/ucd-icd10.html.

populations of 250,000 or more continue to have higher rates of violence than cities with 100,000 or fewer residents.[34]

Perhaps the most significant development of all for the future of violent crime in the United States was the dramatic decline in crime by African Americans. From 1980 to 2009, their homicide mortality rates, the purest gauge of crime, fell by a whopping 54 percent (table 5.8). Although whites nearly matched this decline (white rates fell 50 percent), and Hispanics actually bettered it (with an extraordinary 75 percent slide), the rate drop among blacks was particularly significant for two reasons. First, African American violent crime has been persistently elevated since the late nineteenth century, and the recent change coupled with positive social gains, such as the growth of the black middle class, have kindled hope that the worst for African Americans, and indeed for all Americans, may be behind us. Second, black crime rates have been so high in absolute terms that the huge decrease takes on greater significance. Reducing black rates of 41 per 100,000 by more than half is much more significant than reducing white rates from 5 to 2.5 per 100,000, even if the percentage declines are comparable.[35]

When looking at a longer time frame, say from 1960 on, the black-white crime gap looks even more encouraging, as figures 5.7 and 5.8 show.[36] Still, hopes for a convergence between black and white rates are premature, as the racial gap for homicide remains disturbingly wide. Figures for 2012 indicate that African Americans died by homicide at a rate that was more than seven times the white rate (fig. 5.9). This is 19 percent lower than the black-white ratio had been in 1990—good progress, to be sure, but not enough to declare victory.[37]

WHY CRIME DECLINED

For those in the business of analyzing crime, the great downturn of the 1990s was a lesson in humility. None of the usual suspects seemed to account for the good news. While the economic data of the 1990s were extremely positive, and African American

Figure 5.7   Ratio of black to white arrest rates for murder, 1960–2002

Source: LaFree, O'Brien, and Baumer, "Is the Gap between
Black and White Arrest Rates Narrowing?," 188.

Figure 5.8   Ratio of black to white arrest rates for robbery, 1960–2002

Source: LaFree, O'Brien, and Baumer, "Is the Gap between
Black and White Arrest Rates Narrowing?," 188.

Figure 5.9 Ratio of black to non-Hispanic
white homicide mortality rates, 1980–2012

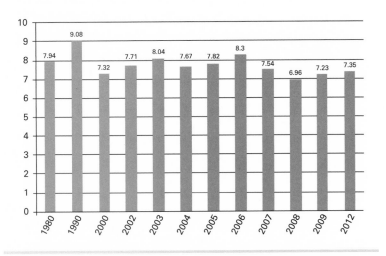

Sources: National Center for Health Statistics, *Deaths of Hispanic Origin*, table 6, 27; National Center for Health Statistics, *Health, United States, 2011*, table 24; National Center for Health Statistics, accessed June 8, 2012, http://wonder.cdc.gov/ucd-icd10.html.

conditions in particular improved greatly, there were givebacks in the new century. And when the economy tanked altogether after 2007, crime continued to fall. The new immigration, on balance, was also a wash. Hispanic immigrants probably caused more crime than not, and Asian and East European entrants were too few in number and too dispersed to significantly reduce crime rates in the vastness of the United States.

One of the few things that is unquestionably true is that the baby-boom generation—the "wild bunch" responsible for the massive escalation of violence that began in the late 1960s—began to age out of crime in the 1980s. Someone born in the peak childbirth year, 1947, would have been 33 in 1980, which is close to retirement age for violent criminals. Figures 5.10 and 5.11 show the age-25-and-over murder rate steadily declining after 1980, as a new generation took over the violent crime business.

Figure 5.10 Black male homicide offending rates, by age, 1980–2008

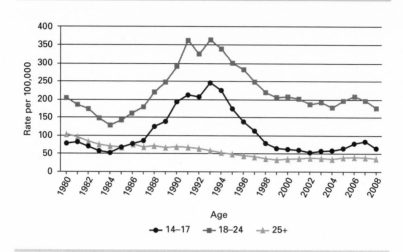

Source: U.S. Department of Justice, Bureau of Justice Statistics, *Homicide Trends in the U.S.*, accessed October 21, 2015, https://web.archive.org/web/20111219171049 /http://bjs.ojp.usdoj.gov/content/homicide/hmrt.cfm.

Figure 5.11 White male homicide offending rates, by age, 1980–2008

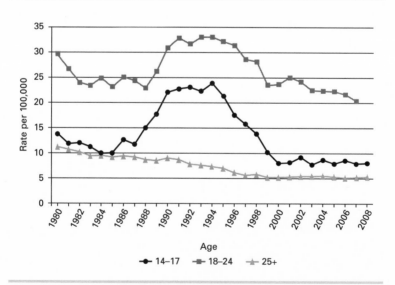

Source: U.S. Department of Justice, Bureau of Justice Statistics, *Homicide Trends in the U.S.*, accessed October 21, 2015, https://web.archive.org/web/20111219171049 /http://bjs.ojp.usdoj.gov/content/homicide/hmrt.cfm.

But note the huge homicide bulge centered around the early 1990s, as armed youth drug gangs single-handedly drove the killing rates to unprecedented peaks. This younger cohort's turn to less lethal behaviors in the second half of the decade needs explaining, and that change, of course, cannot be attributed to the aging of the boomers.[38]

Why, then, did the new post-1960s generation—the cohort born in the 1970s—become less violent after the mid-1990s? Before answering that question, the fact that the 1970s cohort was responsible for the early 1990s crime spike and (in part) the late 1990s decline must be demonstrated. In table 5.9, based on the work of criminologist Robert M. O'Brien and associates, the homicidal behavior of selected age cohorts is tracked over an extended time. The data show that the baby-boomer cohorts, born between 1945 and 1960, produced the crime tsunami of the post-1960s era while the 1970s cohorts were responsible for the 1990s upsurge and subsequent downturn.[39]

The table provides murder arrest rates by age cohort (people born in a particular five-year period) in five-year intervals from 1960 to 2005. Cohorts are numbered to facilitate tracking arrest rates over time. So, for example, the baby boomers, born between 1945 and 1960, are cohort numbers 8, 9, and 10. One can readily see that in 1975, when the great crime surge was under way, boomer cohorts occupied the high-crime age brackets of 15–19, 20–24, and 25–29. Their arrest rates were considerably higher than rates for the same age groups in 1960, which predated the crime rise. By 1995, however, the boomers were aging out, settling into the low-violence 35+ age brackets. It is clear, therefore, that the baby boomers were responsible for the high arrest rates between 1970 and 1980 and partly accountable for the declining post-1995 rates.

By the early 1990s, the period of the crime minisurge, cohorts 13 and 14, born between 1970 and 1980, had taken over violent crime. They were, if relatively briefly, even more violent than their parents. Teenage (ages 15–19) arrest rates for murder

Table 5.9 Murder arrests, rate per 100,000, by birth cohort, 1960–2005

	Age of arrestees							
	15–19	20–24	25–29	30–34	35–39	40–44	45–49	
	7	6	5	4	3	2	1	Cohort
1960	8.98	14	13.45	10.73	9.37	6.48	5.71	Rate
	8	7	6	5	4	3	2	Cohort
1965	9.07	15.18	14.69	11.7	9.76	7.41	5.56	Rate
	9	**8**	7	6	5	4	3	Cohort
1970	17.22	23.75	20.09	16	13.13	10.1	7.5	Rate
	10	**9**	**8**	7	6	5	4	Cohort
1975	17.54	25.62	21.05	15.81	12.83	10.52	7.32	Rate
	11	**10**	**9**	**8**	7	6	5	Cohort
1980	18	23.97	18.88	15.23	12.32	8.8	6.76	Rate
	12	11	**10**	**9**	**8**	7	6	Cohort
1985	16.32	21.1	16.79	12.58	9.6	7.5	5.31	Rate
	13	12	11	**10**	**9**	**8**	7	Cohort
1990	35.17	29.1	18	12.44	9.38	6.81	5.17	Rate
	14	*13*	12	11	**10**	9	**8**	Cohort
1995	35.08	31.93	16.76	10.05	7.25	5.47	3.67	Rate
	15	*14*	*13*	12	11	10	9	Cohort
2000	14.63	18.46	10.9	6.63	5.41	3.74	2.3	Rate
	16	15	*14*	*13*	12	11	10	Cohort
2005	13.87	18.7	11.85	6.8	4.69	3.69	3.09	Rate

Cohorts by birthdate

1 = 1910–15	5 = 1930–35	9 = 1950–55*	13 = 1970–75
2 = 1915–20	6 = 1935–40	10 = 1955–60*	14 = 1975–80
3 = 1920–25	7 = 1940–45	11 = 1960–65	15 = 1980–85
4 = 1925–30	8 = 1945–50*	12 = 1965–70	16 = 1985–90

* = Baby boom cohorts.

Sources: O'Brien, Stockard, and Isaacson, "Enduring Effects," 1073;
O'Brien and Stockard, "Can Cohort Replacement Explain Changes," 82.
   Note: Boldface numerals indicate baby boom cohorts; bold italic numerals indicate 1970s cohorts.

in excess of 35 per 100,000 had been unheard of before 1990. When crime fell once again, in 2000, the arrest rates of cohorts 13 and 14 declined significantly, not only below what they had been in 1990 and 1995, but also below the rates of earlier cohorts in the same age brackets. Thus, it is fair to conclude that the 1970s cohorts caused the 1990 spike and a good chunk of the 2000 decline.

Two interrelated factors were crucial in the great turn from violent crime by the 1970s cohorts. First, the cocaine epidemic ran its course, taking down with it all of the associated crimes of

The Canadian Enigma

Criminologist Franklin Zimring once astutely observed that the rise and fall of crime in Canada tracks crime patterns in the United States to a remarkable degree. Canada, like its southern neighbor, suffered a massive rise in crime in the

Figure 5.12 Homicide rates per 100,000, United States and Canada, 1960–2010

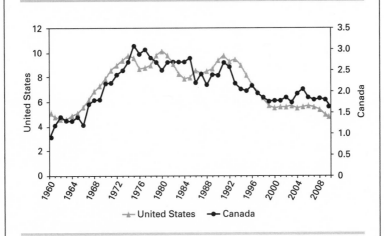

Sources: Canadian Centre for Justice Statistics, "Homicide Survey"; U.S. Department of Justice, Bureau of Justice Statistics, "Homicide Rate Trends."

1960s and enjoyed a huge decline in the 1990s (fig. 5.12). To be sure, violent crime rates have long been much higher in the United States. Homicide rates were three to four times greater, and robbery rates (before 2000) were two and a half times higher. But for homicide, rate *changes* were extraordinarily similar (table 5.10). So were the percentage declines in murder, robbery, and burglary in the 1990s.

Table 5.10 Change in crime rates, United States and Canada, 1991–99

	U.S. (%)	Canada (%)
Homicide	−42	−43
Robbery	−22	−23
Sexual assault	−23	−31
Assault	−45	−23
Burglary	−38	−35
Motor vehicle theft	−36	+3

Source: Ouimet, "Explaining the American and Canadian Crime Drop," table 1.

This suggests that forces common to both nations influenced the rise and fall of crime. What might these forces be? Intriguingly, they did *not* include a tougher criminal justice system. While the United States was hardening its system, the Canadians did business as usual. From 1991 to 1999, when crime plummeted, Canadian police personnel per capita *dropped* 11 percent, while the number of U.S. police officers rose. Nor did Canadians adopt more aggressive policing policies. Moreover, in sharp contrast to the imprisonment rate in the United States, Canada's incarceration rate *fell* 3 percent.

The most likely candidate for a common explanation is demographic. Canada had one of the biggest baby booms in the Western world, which may go a long way toward explaining its rise in crime during the 1960s. And from 1991 to 1999, both nations lost 18 percent of their respective young populations (ages 20 to 34). A Canadian analyst thought that economic gains, especially for young people, and a new ethos of moderation and self-restraint also played crucial roles in his nation's crime downturn.[40]

violence. Second, a revivified criminal justice system—more aggressive policing and increased imprisonment of offenders—removed from circulation some of the most dangerous criminals.

Abandonment of cocaine by the age cohort born after 1970 is measurable. U.S. Justice Department funding enabled researchers to track changes in offender drug use. Investigators interviewed and sampled the urine of over 13,000 persons arrested in Manhattan between 1987 and 1997, from roughly the onset to the decline of the crack epidemic. Analysts were able to determine the proportion of offenders who were using drugs and, just as significant, the types of drugs they used and the ages of the users. The heroin injectors, it turns out, were baby boomers, born between 1945 and 1954. Arrestees born between 1955 and 1969, as samples showed, had turned to crack cocaine. But among arrestees born in the 1970s—the same cohort that had driven up murder rates in the late 1980s and early 1990s—crack cocaine use fell off dramatically. Nearly half of those born before 1969 reported the use of cocaine; for those born in 1972, the figure plummeted to 20 percent. What's more, the rejection of crack stuck with subsequent adolescent cohorts. Test subjects born in 1979, who would have reached their prime years for violence in the second half of the 1990s, had less than a 5 percent usage rate.[41]

Ethnographic research confirmed the sharp curtailment of cocaine use. Richard Curtis spent ten years, from 1987 to 1997, conducting fieldwork in several Hispanic Brooklyn neighborhoods. He noted firsthand the devastation wrought by drugs, followed in the mid-1990s by what he called "an improbable transformation" motivated by fear of drugs and their consequences.

> Many youth had intimate experience with the variety of problems that afflicted their elders as an outcome of involvement with cocaine, crack, or heroin, and they made a conscious attempt to avoid similar fates. Bubbler (seventeen years old in 1996), for example, had witnessed his

mother's despair after two older, heroin-using brothers who worked for the corporate owners [i.e., drug distributors] on Fishman Street became casualties of the war on drugs and were sentenced to lengthy prison terms. Bubbler smoked only marijuana, and though he had intermittently sold crack in his middle-teens, by seventeen, he had stopped selling, moved in with his girlfriend, attended high school regularly, and sought legitimate employment. . . .

The palpable change which washed over the neighborhood beginning in 1993 was initiated and carried through by young residents who, though far from uniform in their responses to those dangers, shared a conviction that they would not succumb to the same fate that nearly erased the preceding generation.[42]

There were compelling reasons to avoid the extremely destructive consequences of the drug lifestyle—consequences that were decimating the ranks of young users and dealers and giving the rest second thoughts. Aside from the direct effects of cocaine addiction, so terribly damaging in and of itself, there were severe health risks associated with regular drug use, including physical ailments such as nose and throat disorders, acute cardiovascular or cerebrovascular emergencies (cardiac arrest or seizure), and AIDS. There was, in addition, significant risk of mental and emotional problems, ranging from irritability, restlessness, and anxiety to full-blown paranoid psychosis.[43] Health detriments were exacerbated by devastating indirect effects, such as injury or death as a result of drug gang conflicts and arrest and imprisonment if caught in the web of the criminal justice system. All of these—the addiction, disease, incarceration, and death—ultimately created a deterrent effect that led to the abandonment of hard drugs.

The extraordinarily negative effects of crack use—addiction, ill health, incarceration, and the loss of virtually all socially acceptable opportunities for self-advancement—were always present and perhaps always understood by users. But as with other risky behaviors indulged by youth, the negatives simply were ignored. So vulnerable were they to peer influences that death itself didn't seem to matter to these young "crackheads." Once crack became unacceptable to peers, however, once the whole crack subculture became socially disreputable on the streets, it was abandoned just as quickly as it had been adopted. As soon as crack fell out of favor, robbery to support habits, killing to protect distribution operations, and a plethora of violent and nonviolent offenses associated with its use also petered out.

Just as teen faddism rapidly established the crack craze in the first place (see chapter 4), the same contagion effect helped ensure its decline. While contagion analyses understandably have focused on negative social behaviors, they are just as applicable to positive behaviors. In his popular account of the fall of crime in New York City, Malcolm Gladwell explained how police policies aimed at "the little things," by which he meant low-level quality-of-life violations, can restore order in a community. Crime, he claimed, was an epidemic, but one that "can be reversed, can be tipped, by tinkering with the smallest details of the immediate environment."[44] Whether or not Gladwell was right about New York crime (which is doubtful), a copycat or bandwagon effect that can multiply the influence of positive as well as negative behaviors is completely convincing. The collapse of the crack market falls into this category.

The results (as Curtis's Brooklyn study recounted) were transformative. Neighborhoods that had been cocaine war zones, scarcely fit for law-abiding residents, saw massive declines in violence. Poor black urban areas, where cocaine gangs once flourished, became the scenes of some of the biggest declines in crime. In five New York City police precincts with populations that were over 80 percent black and suffered from high poverty, including Harlem and Brooklyn's Bedford-Stuyvesant, the murder rate dropped a remarkable 78 percent in the 1990s, even outdoing the citywide rate decline by 5 percent. These precincts had had staggering homicide rates in 1990: from two to four times the rate for the city overall.[45] Comparable results were obtained in Chicago, where seven police districts with populations over 90 percent black were responsible for 56 percent of the drop in murder and 53 percent of the decline in all violent crime from 1990 to 2000. Criminologist Wesley Skogan found that whereas fifty-two police beats, all predominantly poor African American areas, had Chicago's highest robbery rates in 1991–92, only four such areas exceeded the high robbery threshold in 2001–2002. He concluded that declining crime in black areas "largely powered the drop in violent crime in the city."[46]

The second crucial reason for the diminution of crime by the 1970s cohort was the reconstitution of the criminal justice system. When crime first shot up in the late 1960s, the system was overwhelmed. The number of arrests per reported crime went down, not up; sentencing to prison occurred less often, not more; and prison time served for serious crimes actually shortened, not lengthened. By the 1980s, however, most of the flabbiness in the system had been, or soon would be, reversed. Although police clearance rates did not improve (indeed, they stayed level or declined), the size of police forces grew and, perhaps more important, law enforcement adopted smarter tactics. Some of the new practices—CompStat and hot-spots policing, most notably—seem to have been effective. The same analysts who studied drug use in New York City wrote the following:

> In the 1990s, the number of police officers was substantially increased and the effectiveness of the NYPD was enhanced. Most important, the department has successfully achieved integrated management (via Compstat meetings) of its numerous precincts, created special squads (detectives, narcotics, gangs, vice), and employed statistical information to suppress crime and disorder

throughout the city.... In large measure, the police (and cooperating agencies) have successfully "taken back the streets" from drug dealers and other disorderly persons in the 1990s.[47]

A more recent study of crime in the Big Apple concurs. The NYPD, wrote Franklin Zimring, "placed successful emphasis on suppressing public open air drug markets. The first drug priority for policing was driving drug trade from public to private space. For a variety of reasons, this also may have reduced the risk of conflict and violence associated with contests over drug turf."[48] In other words, police antidrug tactics worked not only to drive down the public drug trade—a great good in itself— but also to bring down the killing and other violence associated with it, a wonderful collateral benefit.

As for the escalation in imprisonment, we already discussed how arrests, court commitments to prison, and time actually served in prison for drug offenses increased considerably, sometimes dramatically, in the late 1980s and early 1990s. The effect on violent crime was to drive it down anywhere from 12 to 27 percent, depending on the method used to measure the effect.[49] Incarceration for drug crimes, which, strictly speaking, are not considered crimes of violence, nevertheless contributed to the decline in violent crime, given the propensity of the cocaine offenders to engage in violence.

All told, the revitalized criminal justice system was a big gun in the crime-reduction arsenal, but its implementation was not without costs. Exceptionally high minority incarceration rates and collateral restrictions on prisoners once released, as well as huge taxpayer expenses for building and maintaining prisons and increasing the size of police departments and other justice system agencies, contributed to the high price paid for the great lockdown. But if one were to compare the toll of the enormous crime rates of the pre-1995 period—the killings, maimings, and property losses of crime victims; the negative

Abortion and Leaded Gasoline

Intellectuals abhor a vacuum. When no explanation for the decline in crime aligned with the standard socioeconomic theories, economists stepped in with elaborate quantitative analyses and bold new hypotheses.

The most famous of these studies, by John Donohue and Steven Levitt, propounded the rather startling claim that abortions, legalized in the United States in the early 1970s, drove crime down by reducing the size of the cohort that came of age, criminogenically speaking, during the mid-1990s crime decline. The crime reduction was especially impacted, Donohue and Levitt claimed, by the aborting of populations most at risk for crime.[50]

Five states, including California and New York, legalized abortions in 1970, and the Supreme Court in *Roe v. Wade*, 410 U.S. 113 (1973), declared unconstitutional the remaining state laws that outlawed the controversial procedure. As a result, the abortion rate rose 62 percent in just four years (1973–77). Nationwide, abortions reduced birth rates by an estimated 8 percent, and rates declined even more for teenagers (down 13 percent), nonwhite women (12 percent drop), and unmarried females (decline by twice the rate for married women). Arguably, these populations, or their progeny, fell into the at-risk category.[51]

As we know, the crime decrease that began in the mid-1990s was preceded by a major crime spike in the late 1980s and early 1990s. While proponents of the abortion theory emphasize its utility as an explanation for the decline, it's the upsurge that poses the biggest challenge. The combination of armed teenagers and crack cocaine drove the upswing, but the teens who were responsible for much of this violence were born when abortions were legal and increasingly common. A 15-year-old in 1990 would have been born in 1975. If the abortion theory were valid, this 1970s cohort, shorn of all those unruly unborn, would have had *lower*, not higher, crime rates. The abortion hypothesis is consistent with the great decline in crime during the mid-1990s, but it is unable to explain why, in the late 1980s and early 1990s, crime rose substantially among youth born during the legalization decade.[52]

◆   ◆   ◆

Somewhat less provocative, and therefore not as widely publicized, was the claim that reduced lead absorption, primarily from reformulated automobile gasoline, caused the great crime decline. Lead absorption has been associated with aggressive and impulsive behaviors, and at least one controlled study established a link to juvenile delinquency.[53] The federal government embarked on a major environmental campaign to reduce lead exposure in this country in the late 1960s, culminating in the landmark Clean Air Act of 1970. In 1974, the U.S. Environmental Protection Agency established a timetable for refineries to reduce lead content, and leaded gasoline was phased out in the United States starting in 1975.[54]

The results were starkly evident when the government tested for lead in the blood. Between the periods 1976–80 and 1988–91, tests for lead showed a reduction of 80 percent or more for the U.S. population as a whole. The greatest improvement, about 85 percent, occurred among young people aged 6 to 19. For African Americans, the reduction was not as great, but it still approached an impressive 75 percent.[55]

Jessica Wolpaw Reyes constructed a careful study of crime in the years 1985 to 2002, calculating the link between lead exposure (measured both as lead in gasoline and as lead in the air, but *not* blood lead levels) and crime. Startlingly, she found that "between 1992 and 2002, the phase-out of lead from gasoline was responsible for approximately a 56% decline in violent crime." Her results for murder alone were not robust, which is something of a surprise. Nevertheless, Reyes believed she had proved that individuals who were exposed to elevated levels of lead as children were more likely to commit violent crimes as adults.[56]

In this, she may be right. But the government's blood tests showed that between 1988 and 1991, lead levels fell dramatically for the age 6–19 cohort as well as for African Americans, two groups highly involved in the violent crime of those years. As crime was soaring, not declining, in 1988 through 1991, the effects were the very opposite of what we would have expected.

As with the abortion hypothesis, the leaded gasoline theory seems unable to explain why the affected populations had relatively high offending rates in the years just prior to the great crime decline.

impact on urban economies; the fear and dread, especially in big cities and in minority communities; to say nothing of the devastation of the cocaine generation—it is very unlikely that the cost of the reinvigorated system of justice would outweigh the terrible price of failing to act aggressively.[57]

To summarize, the retirement from crime of the baby boom generation was the main reason for the end of the post-1960s crime tsunami. The boomers had driven violent crime to record heights in their day, but by the 1980s, their day had passed. Their children, prey to the lure of cocaine, launched a short-term crime wave of their own. But in the face of this latest escalation, the retrenched criminal justice system responded aggressively instead of caving in as it had in the late 1960s and early '70s. The pressures of police harassment, arrests, and high rates of imprisonment, combined with the consequences of the whole grim cocaine lifestyle, set off an anticrack craze—a positive contagion—and by the mid-1990s, the short-term spike was over. The great crime tidal wave was finally receding.

CONCLUSION

Two questions naturally arise at this point. How does the great crime slide compare with earlier downturns, and how long will it last?

One criminologist, perhaps a bit carried away by the improvement, called the recent downward spiral the "largest documented crime decline of the twentieth century."[58] This is exaggerated if we measure by homicide mortality rates, the most accurate indicator. Strictly speaking, if one were to plot continuous annual decline, the eleven straight years of improvement between 1934 and 1944 are the winner (see fig. 1.4). The recent unbroken downturn, by contrast, ran seven years, between 1994 and 2000. If one were to disregard occasional aberrant upticks and look at the current long-term trend, which has continued into the new century, the earlier period still wins the laurels. From 1935 to 1964, a thirty-year interval, homicide rates averaged 5.56 per 100,000, and for twenty-one of those years, the rates were below 6.0. From 1995 to 2013, a nineteen-year run, the mean was 6.26, and in seven of the years, the rate was less than 6.0. Optimists will stress that six of the seven years with rates below 6.0 fell between 2004 and 2013.[59]

Confining our analysis to the post–World War II period, when the first decade of the twenty-first century is compared with the benchmark 1950s, the earlier decade remains the gold standard for low crime, with an average homicide mortality rate of 4.8 per 100,000, compared with the more recent decadal average of 6.0. However, rates for white males and black males were lower in 2000 and 2010 than in 1950 and 1960 (figs. 5.13 and 5.14).[60]

No one knows how long the current trend will continue. Over the course of U.S. history, the commencement of crime waves and their succeeding troughs have not been predictable. Immigration and migration of high-crime groups were, to be sure, crucial factors in escalating crime throughout the twentieth century, but no one could foresee the magnitude of the impact of these developments before crime actually rose. The same can be said for demographic changes. No one predicted that baby boomers coming of age would have launched the crime tsunami of the late 1960s. Judging by demographics alone, an uninterrupted crime trough *should* have occurred in the 1980s— but it didn't. While we can project an increase over the next decade in the size of certain at-risk groups (for example, young male African Americans), we cannot forecast their rate of criminality (fig. 5.15).[61]

If low rates continue indefinitely, we may infer that the crime tsunami was sui generis—a historical anomaly developing out of a unique combination of circumstances. If, however, crime rates start escalating, this suggests that crime follows a cyclical pattern. Crime historian Eric Monkkonen explained the violent crime cycle this way: "One might extend such [cyclical] thinking to violence control, arguing that rising violence

Figure 5.13   Age-adjusted white male homicide
mortality rates, 1950, 1960, 2000, and 2010

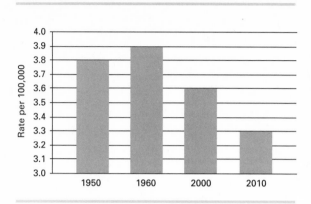

Source: National Center for Health Statistics,
Health, United States, 2013, table 34.

Figure 5.14   Age-adjusted black male homicide
mortality rates, 1950, 1960, 2000, and 2010

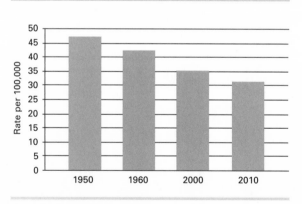

Source: National Center for Health Statistics,
Health, United States, 2013, table 34.

Figure 5.15 Projected size of black male and white male populations, ages 14–24, to 2020

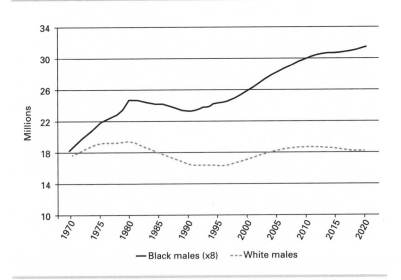

Source: Fox and Piquero, "Deadly Demographics," 350.
Note: Black male population counts multiplied by eight to aid in comparison of trendlines.

provokes a multitude of control efforts, many of which have long lags before their side effects show up in the murder rates, and that the cumulative effect ultimately drives the rates down. When the murder rate ebbs, control efforts get relaxed, thus creating the multiple conditions causing the next upswing."[62]

The best that can be said in early 2015 is that there are positive conditions suggesting that low crime will continue and some worrying indicators pointing in the opposite direction. Among the favorable factors are the following:

- The South, which has long been a high-crime region, is light-years away from being the nation's poor stepchild. The tremendous growth of the southern middle class bodes well for reduced sectional violence.

- African American violent crime rates are significantly lower than they were during the post-1960s crime

boom, and black homicide mortality rates are even
below 1950 and 1960 levels. The relocation of blacks
out of northern cities, the gentrification of black urban
neighborhoods, and the continued expansion of the
African American middle class are the most hopeful
signs in over a century of reductions in lower-class
black violent crime.

- Political pressure is mounting to gain control over
Mexican migration, both legal and illegal. Given the
high levels of Mexican violence, better border control
means improved crime control within the United
States. Of course, when the U.S. economy fails, there
is less of a need for border controls. Mexican entry
nosedived during the Great Depression of the 1930s;
and in the recent recession of 2007–2009, Mexican
inflows dropped 40 percent (compared with 2006),
largely due to a slowdown in illegal entries. As the
U.S. economy continues to improve, and especially
if the Mexican economy falters, stronger border
controls will help prevent cross-border traffic by
high-risk populations.[63]

- Asian and Eastern European immigrants, for the
most part, engage in low levels of criminality. From a
crime perspective, their continued entry is welcome.
Asian immigration to the United States is projected
to surpass Hispanic by the middle of the twenty-first
century. Asians are expected to make up 38 percent
of the foreign-born population by 2065; Hispanics, 31
percent.[64]

- From 2015 to 2020, the male population between 18 and
24 years old is expected to decline (from 4.9 percent to
4.7 percent of the total population). So no baby boom
is on the horizon. If anything, the U.S. population is
aging, and seniors don't do much violent crime. The

population aged 65 and older is projected to increase from 15 percent of the total in 2014 to 21 percent by 2030. By 2060, seniors are expected to comprise nearly one-quarter of the nation.[65]

• Improvements in policing, partly due to new technologies, along with relatively high imprisonment rates, continue to restrain the growth of crime.

These points suggest that low crime rates will last. However, there are signs that social controls on crime are weakening and will continue to do so, especially as memories of the crime tsunami fade. Fiscal pressures and liberal misgivings about aggressive crime-control policies are leading to smaller and more constrained police forces plus greater efforts to curtail imprisonment.[66] In late 2014, riots and protests over police treatment of minorities erupted, increasing the likelihood of new controls on law enforcement.[67] And in 2015, the Obama administration released more than 6,000 federal prisoners as part of an effort to undo the penalties imposed during the war on drugs.[68] We simply will have to wait to see if Monkkonen's cyclical theory or the historical anomaly explanation of violent crime is valid.

Mass Murder

All America shuddered and wept that day. On December 14, 2012, a reclusive, autistic 20-year-old man entered a small-town elementary school in Newtown, Connecticut. Armed with a semiautomatic rifle, he slaughtered 26 people, including 20 little schoolchildren, in less than five minutes.[69]

The Newtown Massacre was one of the most horrific additions to a growing list of mass murders in the United States. In terms of lives lost, however, it wasn't the worst. That dubious distinction goes to Timothy McVeigh's bombing of the federal office building in Oklahoma City on April 19, 1995—an act of domestic terrorism that annihilated 168 people.[70]

When four or more people are slain in one incident by

one or a few perpetrators, criminologists call the crime mass murder.[71] Mass murders are not new in the United States, but there appear to have been relatively few of them during the nineteenth and early twentieth centuries. As violent crime rose in the 1920s, however, mass murders escalated. In 1927, in an event as shocking as the Newtown shootings, Andrew Kehoe, the treasurer of a Michigan village school board, was so incensed over school taxes that he dynamited a public school, killing 44 people, including 38 children. After watching the explosion from his car, Kehoe blew himself up.[72]

Shocking crimes like these declined after the Great Depression and remained rare until the 1960s, when violent crime in general began to soar. The current spate of rampages may be traced back to the post-1960s high-crime era.

Three characteristics of recent mass murders are worth noting. First, the majority of the most appalling mass murders in U.S. history, measured by death toll, occurred during or just after the crime tsunami: eighteen of the twenty-one deadliest incidents in the twentieth century took place after 1966.[73] This was attributable in part to the availability of rapid-fire weapons with high-capacity ammunition clips. (Of course, the worst case remains a bombing, not a shooting.) Firearms have been easily obtainable in the United States since the Civil War, and they have been used in mass murders ever since. But the availability of guns that kill more people faster, while not a cause of mass murder, surely make such incidents deadlier.

Second, until quite recently, mass murders tracked violent crime trends. They increased and diminished as violent crime in general spiked and plummeted. A study of mass murder over the entire twentieth century found that, much like rates for all homicides, mass murder incidents were relatively low before the 1920s, skyrocketed during that high-crime decade, started falling in the late 1930s (along with ordinary violent crime), and entered a long period of decline that ended with the crime burst of the 1960s. Indeed, the correlation between mass murder and general homicide rates is fairly high ($r = 0.51$).[74] This suggests that some of the causes of conventional homicide and mass murder may be the same. It also implies that mass murders should decline as violent crime in general diminishes. This has not happened during the most recent reduction in crime rates. While the downturn in all killings in the second half of the 1990s was accompanied

Figure 5.16 Incidents of mass murder and criminal homicides in the United States, 1976–2011

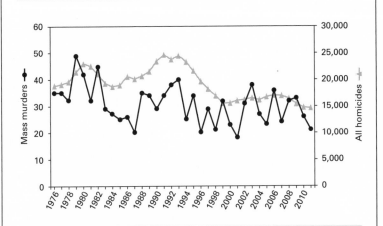

Sources: Mass murder data, including arsons that caused death, provided by Professor James Alan Fox, Northeastern University; Federal Bureau of Investigation, Uniform Crime Reporting Statistics, "UCR Data Online," accessed May 28, 2013, http://www.ucrdatatool.gov/; Federal Bureau of Investigation, *Crime in the United States, 2011*, Uniform Crime Reports, table 1.

by a decline in mass murders, the latter escalated again in the 2000s (fig. 5.16). Recent evidence suggests that the pace of public mass shootings accelerated between 2011 and 2014.[75]

Finally, just as there was a big increase in street crimes after the 1960s, such as assaults and robberies in public places, mass murders became increasingly perpetrated with other felonies. From 1900 to 1975, more than half the mass murders were household affairs, and only 15 percent were felony-related. From 1976 to 1999, by contrast, purely domestic mass murders fell to 40 percent of the total, while 25 percent were associated with other felonies—a 67 percent increase. Part of the explanation for this may be the crack epidemic, which generated large-scale robbery killings.[76]

Disturbing as mass murders are, infinitely more blood is shed by conventional killings. Over a thirty-six-year period ending in 2011, 5,528 people in the United States lost their lives to mass murder, but nearly 684,000 Americans were the victims of ordinary homicides—124 times as many deaths.[77]

History and the Study of Crime

THEORIES OF CRIME

Crime analysis is not immune to the polarization that affects all public policy debates in the United States. Just as we have clashing liberal and conservative analyses on a range of subjects, from the environment to the economy, people have sharply different perspectives on violent crime. Crime theorists tend to fall into two camps: those who favor structural analyses, which attribute crime to economic and social adversities, and those who favor cultural analyses, which relate the beliefs and values of social groups to their crime rates.

The great strength of the structural theories is that they address the seemingly universal nexus between violent crime and material deprivation. That is, they explain why virtually all violent crime is committed by the socially disadvantaged.[1] However, the structural analyses are unable to account for the differences in crime levels *among* deprived groups. Cultural theories, by contrast, provide an explanation for group differences, but lend support, if unwittingly, to stereotyping and even prejudice against cultural groups. Cultural analysis has been denounced for its racialization of crime and accused of tarnishing entire communities by rendering them "precriminal and morally suspect."[2]

In truth, the theoretical divide may not be as wide as is thought.[3] The study of crime history can, in many cases, bridge the gap between structural and cultural theories.

THE CRIME/ADVERSITY MISMATCH

Throughout American history, different social groups have engaged in different amounts of violent crime, and no consistent relationship between the extent of a group's socioeconomic disadvantage and its level of violence is evident. Impoverished Jewish, Polish, and German immigrants had relatively low crime rates, while disadvantaged Italian, Mexican, and Irish entrants committed violent crime at very high rates.[4] This crime/adversity mismatch is evident in other countries as well and is probably a global phenomenon.

In an analysis of ethnicity and crime in contemporary Great Britain, for instance, David J. Smith candidly observed that "all of the minority groups with elevated rates of crime or incarceration are socially and economically disadvantaged, but some disadvantaged ethnic minority groups do not have elevated rates of offending."[5] He noted that the homicide suspect rate in the United Kingdom was 5.4 times as high for Afro-Caribbeans and black Africans as for the general population, but it was only 2.2 times higher for Asians. This was surprising, because Smith thought that blacks were *less* disadvantaged than Asians educationally or in material well-being. They lived in less racially segregated neighborhoods, and their experience with discrimination at the hands of the justice system and the general public seemed to be no worse than that of Asians.[6]

Michael Tonry provided a second example: Moroccans and Turks in the Netherlands. Having first arrived as guest workers in the 1950s and '60s, both groups stayed on, and by the 1990s, they were "comparably disadvantaged economically and socially."[7] However, whereas crime and incarceration rates for Turks were not much above those of the native Dutch, rates for Moroccans were considerably higher. Tonry drew the following conclusion.

> Members of *some* disadvantaged minority groups in every Western country are disproportionately likely to be arrested, convicted, and imprisoned for violent, property, and drug crimes. . . .
>
> The different offending patterns and justice system experiences of members of different groups in a country are not simply the result of group differences in wealth, social status, or political power. That is why the word "some" is emphasized in the phrase "some disadvantaged minority groups" in the first sentence of this essay. Not all economically and socially disadvantaged groups are disproportionately involved in crime.[8]

CRIME AND ECONOMICS

What are the reasons for the divergence between socioeconomic disadvantage and crime? The first point to be emphasized is that *violent* crime—murder/manslaughter, aggravated assault, rape, and robbery—is not, by and large, motivated by economic issues. Murder and its junior partner, assault, are in the main precipitated by anger, sexual jealousy, perceived insults and threats, long-standing personal quarrels, and similar issues, frequently facilitated by alcohol or some other disinhibiting substance. The most important exception to the above occurs when murder and assault are used to intimidate or eliminate rivals in organized crime. While these latter crimes *are* motivated by economic interests, these interests do not reflect short-term personal economic needs but, rather, conflict over market share or the future interests of a criminal organization.

As for rape of females, one can debate whether the motivation is sexual gratification or the desire for power over women, but in neither case is the driver pecuniary or material gain.[9]

Robbery is unique among violent crimes because of the perpetrator's mixed motives: financial gain and the desire to frighten or injure the victim. Force, or threat of force, is essential to the offense, and some robbers gain satisfaction from inflicting pain or injury, especially on a social competitor, such as a member of a rival gang or competing ethnic/racial group. There are, after all, less confrontational ways than robbery to obtain valuables, such as burglary or larceny. At least some of the time, therefore, robbery, like all other violent crimes, is motivated by noneconomic considerations.

Given the overwhelmingly nonpecuniary motivation for violent crime, we would expect that its rates, as opposed to those of property crime, would not be affected by general societal economic conditions. This is borne out by the history of crime. Downturns or improvements in the national economy have had little impact on violent crime. Violent crime soared during periods of great prosperity, such as in the 1920s and the late 1960s, and declined during recessions, such as in the late 1930s and after 2007. Property crimes, by contrast, have been much more sensitive to the state of the economy, although even this relationship may be more complicated than ordinarily thought.[10]

CRIME AND SOCIAL CLASS

Even if violent crime is not influenced by general economic changes in society, there is a link between social class or socioeconomic condition and crime. Although not all disadvantaged groups commit violent crime at equally high levels, the overwhelming majority of violent crimes are committed by the poor or lower classes. This may be explained by the disinclination to violence of people in the middle and upper classes.

A relatively affluent person has powerful incentives to resolve disputes peaceably, through law and courts, rather than through the use of violence. That person's community status, job (and therefore income), domestic relationships, physical security, and health are preserved and enhanced by eschewing violence. As one analyst rather bluntly put it, "for people in economically more promising circumstances, it would literally make no sense—it would virtually be crazy—to commit robbery."[11] The poor person, by contrast, is not surrounded by this web of constraints and literally has less to lose by engaging in violence. This is all the more true when, as with so many violent criminals, the offender is young and unattached and is without steady work or has a low-paying job.[12]

Consequently, poor people are more likely to engage in violent crime, whereas the more affluent tend to commit non-violent offenses, such as fraud, embezzlement, or white-collar theft from employers. This also explains why the advance of poor groups to the middle class invariably reduces their violent crime rates.[13]

CULTURE AND VIOLENCE

While the preceding explains why poor people do more violence than the affluent, it does not explain why some disadvantaged social groups engage in more violence than others similarly situated. Cultural theories are particularly helpful in providing group-specific explanations for behaviors. A vast amount of research has been done on cultural differences and their behavioral consequences. Geert Hofstede, for instance, has developed an elaborate and empirically grounded analysis of behavioral differences related to national culture for fifty different nationalities.[14] Indeed, culture is one of the primary concepts of modern social science, serving an important analytical function in psychology, sociology, and anthropology.

Definitions of culture are myriad and often confusing, partly as a consequence of differences among academic disciplines. Hofstede provided a relatively straightforward and oft-cited version: "the collective programming of the human mind that distinguishes the members of one group or category of people from others." As he explains, these mental programs (or "software of the mind" in his memorable epigram) are unlike computer programs in that they indicate likely and predictable, but not predetermined and invariable, behaviors.[15]

Violence is one of the behaviors collectively programmed into cultural groups, but unequally distributed across them. Consequently, we see different amounts of violent behavior, including criminal misconduct, among different cultural groups. A major point of dispute is whether these behaviors are determined by the cultures themselves or whether there are deeper, underlying factors—poverty and adversity being the most commonly identified—responsible for cultural variations. Because there is no consistent correlation between the extent of a group's disadvantage and its violent behaviors, it is reasonable to conclude that culture (or subculture for groups in a large collective) is the ultimate causal factor.

Nevertheless, as has already been noted, academics are deeply reluctant to rely on cultural explanations. Crime, after all, is negative behavior, and any scholarly finding that such behavior is a group characteristic invites group stigmatization. As William Julius Wilson explained, "Many liberal scholars are reluctant to discuss or research the role that culture plays in the negative outcomes found in the inner city. It is possible that they fear being criticized for reinforcing the popular view that negative social outcomes—poverty, unemployment, drug addiction, crime—are due to the shortcomings of the people themselves."[16] Cultural explanations, it is feared, may be used to "blame the victim."

There are two responses to this charge. First, blame and responsibility are legal or ethical concepts linked to *individual* decision-making. Ultimately, choosing to engage in or refrain from crime is up to the individual, and culture does not fully explain individual choice. As Hofstede points out, "A person's behavior is only partially determined by his or her mental programs: he or she has a basic ability to deviate from them and to react in ways that are new, creative, destructive, or unexpected."[17] Consistent with this view, the law does not accept cultural defenses to criminal charges; defendants are not permitted to claim that "the culture made me do it."[18]

While this addresses the problem of reconciling individual responsibility with cultural analyses of crime, it does not fully address the issue of group stigmatization for the socially disapproved behavior of individual group members. Once again, the answer is that responsibility lies with the decision-maker, and because crime is the result of an individual and not a collective decision, there can only be individual responsibility.

This argument is logical but not wholly satisfactory. Given the appalling history of racial and ethnic prejudice and the concomitant mistreatment and abuse of minorities, distinctions between collective and individual responsibility—even if valid—are unlikely to fully ease our discomfort.

BRIDGING THE GAP, OR REAL ROOT CAUSES

Another, perhaps more convincing, argument in defense of cultural explanations looks to the origins and genesis of negative cultural characteristics. Frequently, historical circumstances for which the group cannot be held responsible shape negative cultural attributes. Take, for example, the case of African American violence, one of the most controversial issues in the study of crime and, for that reason, seldom directly discussed.

Black homicide rates have been at least seven times the rates for whites over the entire twentieth century and into the twenty-first. Can we explain this without the tinge of racism? The answer is yes, and the key is to examine African American history. To once again quote Wilson: "An adequate explanation of cultural attributes in the black community must explore the origins and changing nature of attitudes and practices going back decades, even centuries."[19] High crime may be seen as a by-product of the distinctive history of blacks in the United States.

Significant levels of black criminal violence first became manifest in the South during the final decades of the nineteenth century, a particularly painful period for African Americans. Homicide historian Randolph Roth thought that Jim Crow, the segregation system firmly established in the 1890s, so embittered African Americans that it became the central fact in the black turn to violence.

> The reversals they suffered, like the persecution and discrimination that minorities endured in the urban North and Southwest, fostered resentment and alienation, led them to divert their energies into criminal enterprises, and created a heritage of anger and violence that was passed down through successive generations. The growing homicide problem among black southerners was not caused by slavery or by the failure of Reconstruction to create a racially egalitarian society. It was caused by the hopelessness and rage that the political disaster of the 1890s and early 1900s engendered.[20]

According to Roth, the oppression suffered by African Americans in the waning decades of the nineteenth century was crucial to the onset of black violence. This adversity helped create a violent subculture, or, in Roth's words, "a heritage of anger and violence that was passed down through successive generations."[21]

However, bitterness and alienation, crucial as they were in molding black culture, would not have necessarily led to violence—especially against fellow African Americans, the victims of the overwhelming majority of black assaults. Other factors were significant in the rise of African American violent crime. These include the acceptability of interpersonal violence in the South, the milieu into which African Americans were born; the uprooting of former black slaves after emancipation and their movement to southern cities, where they entered the bottom rungs of the shattered economy; the ready availability of cheap handguns; and, finally, the social and economic turmoil of the post-Reconstruction years, the formative years of the first post-slavery generation. All of these conditions, as well as the resentment fostered by Jim Crow, created the criminal culture associated with lower-class African Americans for more than a century.

◆ ◆ ◆

The historical analysis above offers a way to break the standoff between criminologists who assert that culture is the ultimate explanatory factor for violent crime and those who adopt the structural position, for it will often be the case that a group's cultural support of violence will have historical antecedents that include social disadvantage.

Thus, cultural and structural theories may not be as far apart as is often believed. We can explain why different ethnic, religious, and racial groups behave the way they do despite the crime/adversity mismatch. To accomplish this, the history of each group's criminal behavior must be examined in order to discover the genesis of that behavior. In a great sense, that has been the mission of this book: to reveal the historical roots of violent crime committed by that national cultural group known as Americans.

Acknowledgments

I was fortunate to have the support of institutions and scholars who made my work better and my work life more manageable. I acknowledge them here with great pleasure.

In 2011, my employer, the City University of New York, granted me a research award, releasing me from one of my course obligations. I also received a Fellowship Research Grant from the Earhart Foundation: this, too, used for teaching release. Earhart came through for me a second time with support for the rights to reproduce the photographs in this book. Thanks go to Jacob Marini and Susy Mendes of John Jay College's Office of Sponsored Programs for helping me to obtain and manage the support.

I am especially grateful for the input I received from scholars who took the time to read portions of my manuscript and offer their suggestions. Without their efforts, I would have made even more mistakes than I have. Roger Lane brought to nearly the entire manuscript his wisdom and expertise as one of the foremost crime historians in the nation. It would be an understatement to say that his suggestions were tremendously helpful.

From the criminological side of academe, I received outstanding advice from my friend and longtime colleague Andrew Karmen. Andrew spent hours reading and marking up most of my chapters, and I benefited enormously from his suggestions.

I am grateful as well to Michael Pfeifer, a historian at John Jay College who gave me a young scholar's slant on my labors.

As always, I received sage counsel from my dear friend Charles "Jim" Landesman, Professor Emeritus at Hunter College, CUNY, who brought the sharp eye of an analytical philosopher to various portions of the text.

Tom Litwack, Professor Emeritus of Psychology at John Jay, tried to sensitize me to problems raised by the language I used in discussing provocative issues. I'm afraid he didn't succeed.

I also want to express my appreciation for the librarians and staff of the Lloyd Sealy Library at John Jay College, who always did their best to facilitate my research.

I gratefully acknowledge the efforts of my agent, Alexander C. Hoyt, without whose dogged determination and loyalty this book might never have been published.

Of course, no one could have been more supportive than my own personal reference librarian and cheerleader, to whom this work is dedicated.

Notes

PREFACE

1. Nese F. DeBruyne and Anne Leland, "American War and Military Operations Casualties: Lists and Statistics," *CRS Report for Congress RL32492*, Congressional Research Service, Library of Congress (Washington, DC: January 2, 2015), 2, 3, 5, 12, 17; U.S. Department of Justice, Bureau of Justice Statistics, *Highlights from 20 Years of Surveying Crime Victims: The National Crime Victimization Survey, 1973–92*, by Marianne W. Zawitz et al. (Washington, DC: GPO, 1993), 5, 16, 17, 29; U.S. Department of Justice, Bureau of Justice Statistics, *Injuries from Crime*, by Caroline Wolf Harlow (Washington, DC: GPO, 1989), 3; James Garafolo and L. Paul Sutton, *Compensating Victims of Violent Crime: Potential Costs and Coverage of a National Program* (Albany, NY: Criminal Justice Research Center, 1977), table 11, 30; U.S. Department of Justice, Bureau of Justice Statistics, *Violent Crime* (Washington, DC: GPO, 1994), 3.

2. For a discussion of the response to the rise in crime, see David Garland, *The Culture of Control: Crime and Social Order in Contemporary Society* (Chicago: University of Chicago Press, 2001). Garland contends that the rehabilitation-oriented policies prevailing during

most of the twentieth century were abandoned in favor of punitive policies supported by reactionary politicians who exploited middle-class anxieties.

3. "Crime," Gallup, http://www.gallup.com/poll/1603/crime.aspx, accessed December 12, 2014. Gallup surveys included the following question: "Is there more crime in the U.S. than there was a year ago, or less?" In February 28–March 1, 1992, 9 percent said "more" and 3 percent said "less." In October 11–14, 2001, 41 percent said "more" and 43 percent said "less." From 2005 to 2014, by contrast, public perception that crime was rising increased to 68 percent on average. However, an annual average of over 17 percent thought crime was falling, which was, in fact, consistent with data from the FBI's Uniform Crime Reports and the National Crime Victimization Survey.

4. Paul Krugman, "It's a Different Country," *New York Times*, June 9, 2008, A21.

5. Monica Davey and Julie Bosman, "Grand Jury Declines to Indict Police Officer in Ferguson Killing," *New York Times*, November 25, 2014, A1.

6. A database created by the *Washington Post* found 991 lethal shootings by police nationwide in 2015. Of the victims, 495 were white (49.9 percent), 258 were black (26 percent), and 172 were Hispanic (17.4 percent). In 79 percent of the cases, the person shot had a deadly weapon. *Washington Post*, "991 People Shot Dead by Police in 2015," accessed July 16, 2016, https://www.washingtonpost.com/graphics/national/police-shootings.

7. Manny Fernandez, Richard Pérez-Peña, and Jonah Engel Bromwich, "Five Dallas Officers Were Killed as Payback, Police Chief Says," *New York Times*, July 8, 2016, https://www.nytimes.com/2016/07/09/us/dallas-police-shooting.html; Julie Bloom, Richard Fausset, and Mike McPhate, "Baton Rouge Shooting Jolts a Nation on Edge," July 17, 2016, https://www.nytimes.com/2016/07/18/us/baton-rouge-shooting.html. That same summer, 86 percent of police in big departments told pollsters they were less willing to stop and question suspicious people as a result of high-profile incidents. Eighty-five percent said they were more reluctant to use force when it was appropriate. Rich Morin, Kim Parker, Renee Stepler, and Andrew Mercer, *Behind the Badge: Amid Protests and Calls for Reform, How Police View Their Jobs, Key Issues and Recent Fatal Encounters between Blacks and Police*, Pew Research Center, January 11, 2017, accessed

January 16, 2017, http://assets.pewresearch.org/wp-content/uploads /sites/3/2017/01/06171402/Police-Report_FINAL_web.pdf. The surveys apparently were conducted between May and August, 2016. Ibid., 91.

8. U.S. Department of Justice, Bureau of Justice Statistics, *Prisoners in 2015,* by E. Ann Carson and Elizabeth Anderson (Washington, DC: GPO, 2016), appendix table 5, 30.

9. For example, Roger Lane, *Murder in America: A History* (Columbus: Ohio State University Press, 1997); Randolph Roth, *American Homicide* (Cambridge, MA: Harvard University Press, 2009).

10. For example, Truman Capote, *In Cold Blood: A True Account of a Multiple Murder and Its Consequences* (New York: Vintage, 1965); Erik Larson, *The Devil in the White City: Murder, Magic, and Madness at the Fair That Changed America* (New York: Crown Publishers, 2003). These are vivid accounts of, respectively, the 1959 murder of a rural family and the crimes of a serial killer at the time of the Chicago World's Fair of 1893. The incidents occurred during periods when violent crime rates were relatively low, which perhaps made them all the more shocking. Capote's book is partially fictional.

11. Steven Pinker, *The Better Angels of Our Nature: Why Violence Has Declined* (New York: Viking Press, 2011).

12. For example, Jeffrey S. Adler, *First in Violence, Deepest in Dirt: Homicide in Chicago, 1875–1920* (Cambridge, MA: Harvard University Press, 2006).

13. Alfred Blumstein and Joel Wallman, eds., *The Crime Drop in America* (Cambridge: Cambridge University Press, 2000); Andrew Karmen, *New York Murder Mystery: The True Story behind the Crime Crash of the 1990s* (New York: New York University Press, 2000); Franklin E. Zimring, *The Great American Crime Decline* (New York: Oxford University Press, 2007).

14. U.S. Department of Justice, Bureau of Justice Statistics, *Rape and Sexual Assault Victimization among College-Age Females, 1995–2013,* by Sofi Sinozich and Lynn Langton (Washington, DC: GPO, 2014), 1. Females aged 18 to 24 not enrolled in post-secondary school were 1.2 times more likely to be victimized than females of the same age who were enrolled. Around 20 percent of the college victims reported incidents to the police, whereas 32 percent of the nonstudent victims reported.

CHAPTER 1. WORLD WAR II AND ITS AFTERMATH

Epigraphs: Pitirim Sorokin, *Contemporary Sociological Theories* (New York: Harper and Brothers, 1928), 341; Allan M. Winkler, *Home Front U.S.A.: America during World War II*, 2nd ed. (Wheeling, IL: Harlan Davidson, 2000), 67.

1. Anne Leland and Mari-Jana Oboroceanu, "American War and Military Operations Casualties: Lists and Statistics," *CRS Report for Congress RL 32492*, Congressional Research Service, Library of Congress (Washington, DC: February 26, 2010), 2, accessed October 21, 2015, http://fpc.state.gov/documents/organization/139347.pdf. The U.S. Civil War took more lives: 364,511 on the Union side and an estimated 164,000 to 276,000 Confederates, for a total of 528,511 to 640,511 combatants (ibid.). A recent reestimate by J. David Hacker concluded that 752,000 men died in the Civil War. Guy Gugliotta, "New Estimate Raises Civil War Death Toll," *New York Times*, April 3, 2012, D1.

2. Real GDP is in 2005 dollars. *Laborer's wages* refers to the hourly wage of unskilled labor in manufacturing, which rose from an average $0.67 per hour in 1940 to $1.06 per hour in 1945. Measuring-Worth.com, http://www.measuringworth.com, accessed May 17, 2011.

3. Winkler, *Home Front*, 47; Richard White, *"It's Your Misfortune and None of My Own": A New History of the American West* (Norman: University of Oklahoma Press, 1991), 496.

4. Dewey W. Grantham, *The South in Modern America: A Region at Odds* (New York: HarperCollins, 1994), 170.

5. Over 300,000 women served in the armed forces in World War II, but this was less than two percent of the 16 million service personnel, and women were not admitted to combat units. Winkler, *Home Front*, 57; Leland and Oboroceanu, "American War and Military Operations Casualties," 2.

6. James N. Gregory, *The Southern Diaspora: How the Great Migrations of Black and White Southerners Transformed America* (Chapel Hill: University of North Carolina Press, 2005), 117. It is noteworthy that the leading organizational advocate for African American civil rights, the NAACP, grew from 50,000 to 450,000 members during World War II. James T. Patterson, *Grand Expectations: The United States, 1945–1974* (New York: Oxford University Press, 1996), 20.

7. William E. Leuchtenburg, *Franklin D. Roosevelt and the New Deal,*

1932–1940 (New York: Harper and Row, 1963), 299–300; Winkler, *Home Front*, 1, 8, 29.

8. Winkler, *Home Front*, 9, 10, 11, 15, 16, 26. Stalin's toast was offered at the 1943 Teheran Conference during a birthday celebration for Winston Churchill. Conrad Black, *Franklin Delano Roosevelt: Champion of Freedom* (New York: PublicAffairs, 2003), 881.

9. U.S. Department of Commerce, Bureau of the Census, *Historical Statistics of the United States, Colonial Times to 1970, Bicentennial Edition,* part 1 (Washington, DC: GPO, 1975), series D 1–10, 126.

10. Winkler, *Home Front*, 19.

11. Ibid., 19–21, 25, 26, 46.

12. Ibid., 12, 42–45.

13. Ibid., 22–23.

14. Ibid., 35, 36.

15. Ibid., 38, 39, 40, 41.

16. Figures on the armed services can be found in U.S. Department of Commerce, Bureau of the Census, *Historical Statistics*, part 2, series Y 856–903, 1140. Military incarceration data are from Margaret Werner Cahalan, *Historical Corrections Statistics in the United States, 1850–1984* (Rockville, MD: Bureau of Justice Statistics, December 1986), http://www.bjs.gov/content/pub/pdf/hcsus5084.pdf., table C-6, table C-8, 227. Executions are reported at ibid., table 2-11, 23. On recent writing about U.S. war crimes, see Klaus Wiegrefe, "The Horror of D-Day: A New Openness to Discussing Allied War Crimes in WWII," *Spiegel Online*, May 4, 2010, accessed May 23, 2011, http://www.spiegel.de/international/world/0,1518,692037,00.html.

17. Winkler, *Home Front*, 56, 57, 63.

18. Gregory, *Southern Diaspora*, 32.

19. Winkler, *Home Front*, 47–48. Winkler's population figures were adjusted in accordance with U.S. Bureau of the Census, *Intercensal Estimates of the Total Resident Population of States: 1940 to 1949* (Washington, DC: GPO, 1996).

20. Gregory, *Southern Diaspora*, 101.

21. Winkler, *Home Front*, 50–51.

22. National Center for Health Statistics, *Vital Statistics Rates in the United States, 1940–1960*, by Robert D. Grove and Alice M. Hetzel (Washington, DC: GPO, 1968), table 62, 372.

23. Stephan Thernstrom and Abigail Thernstrom, *America in Black and*

White: One Nation, Indivisible (New York: Simon and Schuster, 1997), 80.

24. U.S. Census Bureau, Population Division, *Historical Census Statistics on Population Totals by Race, 1790 to 1990, and by Hispanic Origin, 1970 to 1990, for the United States, Regions, Divisions, and States by Population Division*, by Campbell Gibson and Kay Jung, working paper no. 56 (Washington, DC: GPO, 2002), table 8, A-21. Note that the black population of the United States grew by 16.9 percent in the 1940s due to natural increases (ibid.).

25. Thernstrom and Thernstrom, *America in Black and White*, 70.

26. Ibid.; Robert A. Margo, "Explaining Black-White Wage Convergence, 1940–1950," *Industrial and Labor Relations Review* 48(3) (1995): 470–73. The regional wage differential was marked for blacks and whites. Even relatively uneducated blacks in the North earned 55 percent more per year than southern blacks. Thernstrom and Thernstrom, *America in Black and White*, 79.

27. Thernstrom and Thernstrom, *America in Black and White*, 73.

28. Ibid., 74; Winkler, *Home Front*, 65–66. On Charles R. Drew's work developing blood banks, see Spencie Love, *One Blood: The Death and Resurrection of Charles R. Drew* (Chapel Hill: University of North Carolina Press, 1996).

29. John Modell, Marc Goulden, and Sigurdur Magnusson, "World War II in the Lives of Black Americans: Some Findings and an Interpretation," *Journal of American History* 76(3) (1989): 841, 842, 843, 848. Among African American businessmen, 81 percent had significant military experience (ibid., 848). It is perhaps the postwar benefits from the G.I. Bill, rather than the military experience itself, that was decisive. See Robert J. Sampson and John H. Laub, "Socioeconomic Achievement in the Life Course of Disadvantaged Men: Military Service as a Turning Point, circa 1940–1965," *American Sociological Review* 61(3) (1996): 347–67. Sampson and Laub found that "military service in the World War II era provided American men from economically disadvantaged backgrounds with an unprecedented opportunity to better their lives through on-the-job training and further education," mainly through the G.I. Bill (ibid., 364–65).

30. Exec. Order 8802, 3 C.F.R. 957 (1938–1943 Compilation), "Prohibition of Discrimination in the Defense Industry," June 25, 1941; Thernstrom and Thernstrom, *America in Black and White*, 71; Winkler, *Home Front*, 67–68.

31. Dominic J. Capeci Jr. and Martha Wilkerson, "The Detroit Riot-

ers of 1943: A Reinterpretation," *Michigan Historical Review* 16(1) (1990): 52; Grantham, *South in Modern America*, 188–89.

32. Capeci and Wilkerson, "Detroit Rioters," 52–53, 57; Kevin Boyle, "Auto Workers at War: Patriotism and Protest in the American Automobile Industry, 1939–1945," in *Autowork*, ed. Robert Ashford and Ronald Edsforth (Albany: State University of New York Press, 1995), 122.

33. Harvard Sitkoff, "Racial Militancy and Interracial Violence in the Second World War," *Journal of American History* 58(3) (1971): 671; Dominic J. Capeci Jr., *The Harlem Riot of 1943* (Philadelphia: Temple University Press, 1977). Politicians in the 1960s could have learned a lesson: liberal local administrations sympathetic to civil rights had little impact on mob violence, as Fiorello La Guardia, the mayor of New York in 1943, learned.

34. Eduardo Obregón Pagán, "Los Angeles Geopolitics and the Zoot Suit Riot, 1943," *Social Science History* 24(1) (2000): 223–56.

35. National Center for Health Statistics, *Vital Statistics*, table 63, 538.

36. FBI Uniform Crime Report data, as presented in U.S. Office of Management and Budget, *Social Indicators, 1973* (Washington, DC: GPO, 1973), table 2/1, 64.

37. U.S. Department of Commerce, Bureau of the Census, *Historical Statistics*, part 1, series D 1–10, 126.

38. Lee Kennett and James LaVerne Anderson, *The Gun in America: The Origins of a National Dilemma* (Westport, CT: Greenwood Press, 1975), 217–18, 222. The authors also pointed out that "before the war the NRA [National Rifle Association] had some 3,500 affiliated local clubs. By 1948 the number had climbed to 6,500" (ibid., 218).

39. Before the war, in 1940 and 1941, the proportion of homicides by firearms was, on average, 56.9 percent. During the war, from 1942 to 1945, the average rate was 53.2 percent. After the war, from 1946 to 1949, the rate was 56.2 percent—lower than before the conflict.

40. U.S. Department of War, *Is a Crime Wave Coming?*, by Thorsten Sellin (American Historical Association, 1946), accessed May 15, 2011, http://www.historians.org/about-aha-and-membership/aha -history-and-archives/gi-roundtable-series/pamphlets/is-a-crime -wave-coming. This pamphlet was prepared for the War Department by the American Historical Association and attributed to Sellin. A book on French juvenile delinquency in the war years states that "every European country directly involved in World War II witnessed rising juvenile crime rates," with France topping the list. Unsurpris-

ingly, the overwhelming majority of the offenses involved theft, not violence: see Sarah Fishman, *The Battle for Children: World War II, Youth Crime, and Juvenile Justice in Twentieth-Century France* (Cambridge, MA: Harvard University Press, 2002), 82.

41. Austin L. Porterfield, "A Decade of Serious Crimes in the United States: Some Trends and Hypotheses," *American Sociological Review* 13(1) (1948): 47.

42. Ibid., 47–48. Porterfield's crime indexes were constructed from data in part 1 of the FBI's Uniform Crime Reports. The offenses in part 1 were murder/manslaughter, aggravated assault, robbery, burglary, larceny, auto theft, and rape. Porterfield, "Decade of Serious Crimes," 44n1.

43. James Boudouris, "Trends in Homicide, Detroit: 1926–1968" (PhD diss., Wayne State University, 1970), table 14, 137. This source reported 125 homicides in 1943. If 34 were removed from the total, the homicide rate would be 5.4 per 100,000, a bit *below* the 1942 rate. The highest number of homicides in Detroit in the 1940s was 125. Of the 1943 homicides, 17.6 percent involved white killers of black victims, the only double-digit white-kills-black percentage in the decade. This suggests that riot deaths were counted in the homicide tally.

44. Edward Green, "Race, Social Status, and Criminal Arrest," *American Sociological Review* 35(3) (1970): 478, 480.

45. The black-to-white homicide ratio from 1925 to 1929 was 7.8, and when white rates declined more than black between 1935 and 1939, the gap jumped to 9.1.

46. Howard Harlan, "Five Hundred Homicides," *Journal of Criminal Law and Criminology* 40(6) (1950): 737.

47. See also Henry Allen Bullock, "Urban Homicide in Theory and Fact," *Journal of Criminal Law, Criminology, and Police Science* 45(5) (1955): 570. Bullock reports that in Houston, Texas, from 1945 to 1949, African Americans were 67 percent of the homicide victims and 67 percent of the assailants.

48. Arthur C. Meyers Jr., "Murder and Non-Negligent Manslaughter: A Statistical Study," *Saint Louis University Law Journal* 3 (1954–55): 32.

49. Robert C. Bensing and Oliver Schroeder Jr., *Homicide in an Urban Community* (Springfield, IL: Charles C. Thomas, 1960), 51.

50. Eric H. Monkkonen, "Homicides in New York City, 1797–1999 [and

Various Historical Comparison Sites]," study no. 3226 (Ann Arbor, MI: Inter-university Consortium for Political and Social Research, 2001); population data from U.S. Census Bureau, Population Division, *Historical Census*.

51. Boudouris, "Trends in Homicide," table 14, 137.

52. Sorokin, *Contemporary Sociological Theories*, 341–42. Sorokin (1889–1968) was professor of sociology at Harvard University (1930–55), where he founded the Department of Sociology.

53. Edwin H. Sutherland, "Crime," in *American Society in Wartime*, ed. William Fielding Ogburn (1943; repr., New York: Da Capo Press, 1972), 198. Ultimately, Sutherland concluded that the relationship between war and crime does not present "a good theoretical problem" (ibid., 197).

54. Census figures for 1860 indicate a population of white males aged 15 to 29 of 3,891,746. The estimated number of those serving on the Union side is 2,213,363. The Confederate force size is unknown, but estimates are between 850,000 and 900,000. James M. McPherson, *Battle Cry of Freedom: The Civil War Era* (New York: Oxford University Press, 2003), 306n41. This would put the total of all fighting forces at roughly 3.1 million, in which case the military would have taken approximately 80 percent of the young male population, an extraordinarily high figure. U.S. Department of Commerce, Bureau of the Census, *Historical Statistics*, part 1, series A 119–134, 16; Leland and Oboroceanu, "American War and Military Operations Casualties," 2.

55. Edith Abbott, "The Civil War and the Crime Wave of 1865–70," *Social Service Review* 1(2) (1927): 217, 219–21.

56. Randolph Roth, *American Homicide* (Cambridge, MA: Harvard University Press, 2009), 332, 334.

57. U.S. Department of Commerce, Bureau of the Census, *Historical Statistics*, part 1, series A 119–134, 15; Leland and Oboroceanu, "American War and Military Operations Casualties," 3.

58. On the link between social dissension and ordinary violent crime, Roth wrote, "Most of these [mid-nineteenth-century] murderers were unaware that their behavior had any connection with political conflict or strains on the social hierarchy. But their behavior shows the impress of broader social and political forces." Roth, *American Homicide*, 312. On New York City homicides, see Eric H. Monkkonen, *Murder in New York City* (Berkeley: University of California Press, 2001), 21.

59. Raymond Tanter, "International War and Domestic Turmoil: Some Contemporary Evidence," in *Violence in America: Historical and Comparative Perspectives*, ed. Hugh Davis Graham and Ted Robert Gurr (New York: Bantam Books, 1969), 566. Compare the views of Gary LaFree, who argued that "a crisis in institutional legitimacy" produced the crime wave of the late 1960s. Gary LaFree, *Losing Legitimacy: Street Crime and the Decline of Social Institutions in America* (Boulder, CO: Westview Press, 1998).

60. Roth, *American Homicide*, 347–48.

61. Abbott, "Civil War," 223.

62. Monkkonen, *Murder in New York City*, 18.

63. Homicide rates are from "Key Facts at a Glance: Homicide Rate Trends," Bureau of Justice Statistics, accessed October 20, 2015, https://web.archive.org/web/20121230183805/http://bjs.ojp.usdoj .gov/content/glance/tables/hmrttab.cfm#top. FBI Uniform Crime Reports data are from Office of Management and Budget, *Social Indicators*, table 2/1, 64.

64. Dane Archer and Rosemary Gartner, *Violence and Crime in Cross-National Perspective* (New Haven, CT: Yale University Press, 1984), 79–80. Crime figures on Germany are from Sellin, who reported a homicide rate of 1.56 per 100,000 in 1918 and 3.25 in 1919—a 108 percent rise. Thorsten Sellin, "Is Murder Increasing in Europe?," *Annals of the American Academy of Political and Social Science* 125 (1926): 30. Von Hentig stated that Germany lost 15.5 percent of its males aged 20 to 45 in World War I. He thought there must be a "real rise of antisocial behavior" after war to produce a crime rise in the face of such staggering losses. Hans von Hentig, *Crime: Causes and Conditions* (New York: McGraw-Hill, 1947), 349.

65. On Germany, see K.U. Mayer, "German Survivors of World War II: The Impact on the Life Course of the Collective Experience of Birth Cohorts," in *Social Structures and Human Lives: Social Change and the Life Course*, ed. Matilda White Riley, Bettina J. Huber, and Beth Hess Riley (Newbury Park, CA: Sage Publications, 1988), 229–46; Ineke Maas and Richard A. Settersten Jr., "Military Service during Wartime: Effects on Men's Occupational Trajectories and Later Economic Well-Being," *European Sociological Review* 15(2) (1999): 213–32. The G.I. Bill, officially the Servicemen's Readjustment Act of 1944 (Pub. L. No. 78-346, 58 Stat. 284m), provided support, including college or vocational education, unemployment compensation,

and home-purchase and business-startup loans, for returning World War II veterans.

66. Glen H. Elder, *Children of the Great Depression: Social Change in Life Experience* (Chicago: University of Chicago Press, 1974).

67. Sheldon Glueck and Eleanor Glueck, *Unraveling Juvenile Delinquency* (Cambridge, MA: Harvard University Press, 1950). Apparently, the Gluecks did not consider World War II or the Great Depression relevant to subsequent criminality, as they did not take into account these events in the collection, organization, or analysis of their data. John H. Laub and Robert J. Sampson, "Sheldon and Eleanor Glueck's Unraveling Juvenile Delinquency Study: The Lives of 1,000 Boston Men in the Twentieth Century," in *Looking at Lives: American Longitudinal Studies of the Twentieth Century*, ed. Erin Phelps, Frank F. Furstenburg Jr., and Anne Colby (New York: Russell Sage Foundation, 2002), 96.

68. Leana Allen Bouffard and John H. Laub, "Jail or the Army: Does Military Service Facilitate Desistance from Crime?," in *After Crime and Punishment: Pathways to Offender Reintegration*, ed. Shadd Maruna and Russ Immarigeon (Cullompton, UK: Willan Publishing, 2004), 129–51.

69. Edward S. Shattuck, "Military Service for Men with Criminal Records," *Federal Probation* 9 (1945): 12–14. It is estimated that 100,000 to 200,000 men with criminal records entered the armed forces.

70. Hans W. Mattick, "Parolees in the Army during World War II," *Federal Probation* 24 (1960): 54.

71. Robert J. Sampson and John H. Laub, *Crime in the Making: Pathways and Turning-Points through Life* (Cambridge, MA: Harvard University Press, 1993), 131; Robert J. Sampson and John H. Laub, "Life-Course Desisters? Trajectories of Crime among Delinquent Boys Followed to Age 70," *Criminology* 41(3) (2003): 301–39.

CHAPTER 2. THE GOLDEN YEARS

1. From 1950 to 1959, white homicide rates averaged 2.4 per 100,000 population; for nonwhites, the average was 24.3. National Center for Health Statistics, *Homicide in the United States, 1950–1964*, Public Health Service Publication No. 1000, series 20, no. 6 (Washington, DC: GPO, October 1967), table 3, 19, 20.

2. Additional figures flesh out the scope of the boom.

Productivity: Real GDP per capita (i.e., adjusted for inflation and population changes) climbed over 27 percent between 1947 and 1960 (http://www.measuringworth.com, accessed June 5, 2011).

Unemployment: From 1947 to 1960, the average annual unemployment rate was 4.6 percent, with a high of only 6.8 percent in the recession year of 1958 (U.S. Office of Management and Budget, *Social Indicators*, table 4/1, 135).

Home Ownership: The percentage of owner-occupied (as opposed to rented) dwellings rose from 43.6 percent in 1940 to 55 percent in 1950 and 61.9 percent in 1960 (Patterson, *Grand Expectations*, 312).

Inflation: The CPI (Consumer Price Index; standard inflation measure for the United States) rose approximately one-third between 1947 and 1960, for a modest 2.5 percent annual increase (http://www.measuringworth.com, accessed June 5, 2011).

3. U.S. Department of Commerce, Bureau of the Census, *Historical Statistics*, part 1, series G 16–30, 290. Inflation has been taken into account, as the figures are in "constant dollars." In 1947, $5,000 was the equivalent of $48,000 in 2009 purchasing power, based on the Consumer Price Index, which compares the cost of average household purchases, such as food, housing, transportation, and medical services, at different points in time (http://www.measuringworth.com, accessed July 7, 2011). Even for "unrelated individuals" (those not in families), which included more young and low-income people, the gains were impressive. Comparing incomes in 1947 and 1960 (in constant 1967 dollars), the proportion of the population in the lowest category (under $1,500) declined 16.5 percent, while the proportion of people in the middle-to-high category ($5,000–$9,999) increased 254 percent. U.S. Department of Commerce, Bureau of the Census, *Historical Statistics*, part 1, series G 16–30, 290.

4. The U.S. Census Bureau posts the following on their website:

> The Census Bureau uses a set of money income thresholds that vary by family size and composition to determine who is in poverty. If a family's total income is less than the family's threshold, then that family and every individual in it is considered in poverty. The official poverty thresholds do not vary geographically, but they are updated for inflation using Consumer Price Index (CPI-U). The official poverty definition uses money income before taxes and does not include capital gains or noncash benefits (such as public housing, Medicaid, and food

stamps). ("How the Census Bureau Measures Poverty," accessed June 5, 2011, http://www.census.gov/hhes/www/poverty/about/overview /measure.html)

Because official poverty statistics did not exist prior to 1959, economists have had to project the U.S. Census Bureau standards back in time to estimate pre-1959 poverty rates. Ross, Danziger, and Smolensky calculated that by these standards, 40.5 percent of all persons were in poverty in 1949; 22.1 percent, in 1959; and 14.4 percent, in 1969. Christine Ross, Sheldon Danziger, and Eugene Smolensky, "The Level and Trend of Poverty in the United States, 1939–1979," *Demography* 24(4) (1987): 591.

5. Patterson, *Grand Expectations*, 63.

6. U.S. Department of Commerce, Bureau of the Census, *Statistical Abstract of the United States, 1965* (Washington, DC: GPO, 1965), table 312, 227, table 313, 228. Workforce occupations in 1960 were distributed as follows: white-collar, 46.4 percent; blue-collar, 35.9 percent; service, 10.2 percent; and farm, 7.6 percent (ibid., table 312, 227).

7. Stephan Thernstrom, ed., *Harvard Encyclopedia of American Ethnic Groups* (Cambridge, MA: Harvard University Press, 1994), 559.

8. Nathan Glazer and Daniel Patrick Moynihan, *Beyond the Melting Pot: The Negroes, Puerto Ricans, Jews, Italians, and Irish of New York City* (Cambridge, MA: MIT Press, 1963), 206. Glazer and Moynihan stressed the "slow change" that characterized Italian American occupational history (ibid., 205).

9. U.S. Department of Commerce, Bureau of the Census, *Historical Statistics*, part 1, series H 492–507, 373, series H 598–601, 379, series H 700–715, 383. School expenditures per pupil are in constant 1970 dollars.

10. Patterson, *Grand Expectations*, 70–71; U.S. Department of Commerce, Bureau of the Census, *Statistical Abstract of the United States, 1969* (Washington, DC: GPO, 1969), table 825, 552.

11. Patterson, *Grand Expectations*, 72.

12. Ibid., 72–73, 333.

13. David T. Courtwright, *Violent Land: Single Men and Social Disorder from the Frontier to the Inner City* (Cambridge, MA: Harvard University Press, 1996), 37. In 1950, 78.2 percent of males aged 25–34 were married; in 1960, 81.6 percent; in 1970, 80.8 percent. U.S. Department of Commerce, Bureau of the Census, *Historical Statistics*, part 1, series A 160–171, 20–21; U.S. Census Bureau, *Demographic Trends in*

the 20th Century, by Frank Hobbs and Nicole Stoops, Census 2000 Special Reports, Series CENSR-4 (Washington, DC: GPO, 2002), table 5, A-9.

14. Patterson, *Grand Expectations*, 71.

15. Thernstrom and Thernstrom, *America in Black and White*, 81–82.

16. Ross, Danziger, and Smolensky, "Level and Trend of Poverty," 591.

17. U.S. Department of Commerce, Bureau of the Census, *Historical Statistics*, part 1, series D 87–101, 135; Robert W. Fairlie and William A. Sundstrom, "The Racial Unemployment Gap in Long-Run Perspective," *American Economic Review* 87(2) (1997): 306–10. Fairlie and Sundstrom stated that "the racial unemployment rate gap widened by 3 percentage points from 1940 to 1960. Much of this change can be attributed to regional effects. . . . Between 1940 and 1960, the percentage of the black workforce residing in the South decreased by 17.2 percentage points, compared to a slight increase for whites (1.2 percentage points). Blacks moved into regions of the country with both higher unemployment and larger racial unemployment rate gaps" (ibid., 309).

18. Morton Grodzins, *The Metropolitan Area as a Racial Problem* (Pittsburgh: University of Pittsburgh Press, 1958), 1.

19. Ibid., 2.

20. A study by Larry H. Long found that in seven out of nine major cities, from 1950 to 1960, white out-migration was the most significant factor in raising the percentage of the black population. For example, during the 1950s, the black population of Saint Louis jumped from 18 to 28.8 percent, a 60 percent increase. Long found that 21.4 percent of the gain was due to a higher rate of natural increase among nonwhites; 15.2 percent was attributable to black in-migration; and 63.4 percent was due to white out-migration. Larry H. Long, "How the Racial Composition of Cities Changes," *Land Economics* 51(3) (1975): 261.

21. Grodzins, *Metropolitan Area*, 7, 10.

22. Quoted in Patterson, *Grand Expectations*, 75.

23. Grodzins, *Metropolitan Area*, 9, 10.

24. Ibid., 11.

25. Ibid.

26. Ibid., 12.

27. Ibid., 13.

28. Ibid.

29. Ibid., 14.

30. Thernstrom and Thernstrom, *America in Black and White*, 80.

31. Patterson, *Grand Expectations*, 335–37. See also Jane Jacobs, *The Death and Life of Great American Cities* (1961; repr., New York: Random House, 1993).

32. Patterson, *Grand Expectations*, 207, 208, 215, 219, 221, 225, 227, 228, 232, 234. It is estimated that the United States furnished on behalf of the United Nations half the ground forces, 85 percent of the naval forces, and over 92 percent of the air forces in Korea. Stanley Sandler, *The Korean War: No Victors, No Vanquished* (Lexington: University Press of Kentucky, 1999), 155.

33. Military force size reported at U.S. Department of Commerce, Bureau of the Census, *Historical Statistics*, part 2, series Y 904–916, 1141. Homicide data are from National Center for Health Statistics, *Vital Statistics Rates in the United States*, table 62, 373. Rates of violent crimes known to police, drawn from the FBI's Uniform Crime Reports, are found in U.S. Office of Management and Budget, *Social Indicators*, table 2/1, 64. On women in the armed forces during the Korean War, see Linda Witt, Judith Bellafaire, Britta Granrud, and Mary Jo Binker, *"A Defense Weapon Known to Be of Value": Servicewomen of the Korean War Era* (Lebanon, NH: University Press of New England, 2005), 145. In 1952, there were 45,934 women in the armed forces. U.S. Department of Commerce, Bureau of the Census, *Statistical Abstract of the United States, 1958* (Washington, DC: GPO, 1958), table 305, 245.

34. From 1951 to 1960, 2,515,000 people emigrated to the United States, 51.8 percent of whom were from northern and western Europe or Canada. In the 1940s, the northern and western Europeans and Canadians constituted 63.8 percent of the immigrants, but by the 1980s, they were a mere 7.2 percent. Twenty-two percent of the 1950s immigrants were from Latin America. Rubén G. Rumbaut, "Origins and Destinies: Immigration to the United States Since World War II," *Sociological Forum* 9(4) (1994): 591. Mexicans entering as temporary laborers were not considered immigrants, nor were Puerto Ricans, who were and are citizens of the United States. Lawful Mexican immigrants from 1950 to 1959 numbered 273,852. U.S. Department of Commerce, Bureau of the Census, *Historical Statistics*, part 1, series C 89–119, 107.

35. Immigration and Nationality Act of 1952, Pub. L. No. 414, 182 Stat.

66 (1952); David M. Reimers, *Still the Golden Door: The Third World Comes to America* (New York: Columbia University Press, 1985), 39, 41–62. Reimers believes that the number of Mexican illegals in the 1950s was "probably not large," because Mexicans overwhelmingly engaged in seasonal agricultural work in the southwest, a somewhat limited opportunity (ibid., 62).

36. Eleanor M. Hadley, "A Critical Analysis of the Wetback Problem," *Law and Contemporary Problems* 21(2) (1956): 347.

37. Alex D. Pokorny, "Human Violence: A Comparison of Homicide, Aggravated Assault, Suicide, and Attempted Suicide," *Journal of Criminal Law, Criminology, and Police Science* 56(4) (1965): 496. Age-adjusted homicide victimization rates for 1959 to 1961 were, on average, 5.0 per 100,000 for white Texans and 2.7 for whites nationwide. "Whites" here include Mexicans. National Center for Health Statistics, *Homicide*, 14, 16. The federal government lumps Mexicans together with Cubans, Puerto Ricans, and all other South or Central Americans under the catch-alls "Hispanic" and "Latino." See U.S. Office of Management and Budget, "Revisions to the Standards for the Classification of Federal Data on Race and Ethnicity" (October 30, 1997), accessed July 15, 2011, http://www.whitehouse.gov/omb/fedreg_1997standards.

38. Twenty-eight percent of all federal prisoners in 1955 were convicted of theft offenses, the biggest category. Next came drug law violations, at 15 percent. About 5 percent were crimes of violence (murder, kidnapping, and robbery), and 6 percent were immigration offenses. U.S. Department of Justice, Bureau of Justice Statistics, *Historical Corrections Statistics*, table 6-13, 158, note j, 168.

39. California Department of Corrections, *California Prisoners, 1960* (Sacramento: California State Printing Office, [1961?]), table 13, 28.

40. U.S. Census Bureau, *Population Totals by Race*, table 19.

41. Glazer and Moynihan, *Beyond the Melting Pot*, 86.

42. Ibid., 86–87.

43. Fred K. Fleagle, *The Puerto Rican Experience* (1917; reprinted as *Social Problems in Porto Rico* [New York: Arno Press, 1975]), 84–85. New York City homicide rates from Monkkonen, "Homicides in New York City." The New York City Police Department reported 21,916 felony arrests in 1917, when the city's population was estimated at 6,504,185. This yields a rate of 337 per 100,000. Of course, when it comes to arrests, Puerto Rico and New York City are not really com-

mensurate, as the rural impoverished island probably had far fewer police per capita than the modern metropolis. Police Department, City of New York, *Annual Report 1917* (New York: Bureau of Printing, Police Department, City of New York, 1917), 19; U.S. Bureau of the Census, *Estimates of Population*, form 18 (Washington, DC: GPO, 1917), 16.

44. Glazer and Moynihan, *Beyond the Melting Pot*, 89–90.

45. Ira Rosenwaike, *Population History of New York City* (Syracuse, NY: Syracuse University Press, 1972), 121, 138. Rosenwaike calculated birth and fertility rates for Puerto Ricans in New York City, which remained elevated throughout the 1950s (ibid., 152).

46. Glazer and Moynihan, *Beyond the Melting Pot*, 91.

47. Ibid., 91, 95, 96, 116–17.

48. In 1950, there were 271 homicides in Puerto Rico, which had a population of 2,210,703. U.S. Department of Health, Education, and Welfare, *Vital Statistics of the United States, 1950*, vol. 1 (Washington, DC: GPO, 1953), table 11.16, 328. In 1960, there were 147 homicides among a population of 2,349,544. U.S. Department of Health, Education, and Welfare, *Vital Statistics of the United States, 1960*, vol. 2, Mortality (Washington, DC: GPO, 1963), table 10-4, table 10-7. Puerto Rican population figures are from U.S. Department of Commerce, Bureau of the Census, *Statistical Abstract of the United States, 1970* (Washington, DC: GPO, 1970), sec. 1, Population, no. 10, 11.

49. Piri Thomas, *Down These Mean Streets* (1967; repr., New York: Random House, 1997). Around one-fifth of the Puerto Ricans in New York in the 1930s were listed by the census as "Negro." Glazer and Moynihan, *Beyond the Melting Pot*, 92. Writing in the late 1950s, Oscar Handlin claimed that 75 percent of Puerto Ricans on the island were white, which approximates the 68 percent in Dean Fleagle's older account. Oscar Handlin, *The Newcomers: Negroes and Puerto Ricans in a Changing Metropolis* (Cambridge, MA: Harvard University Press, 1959), 59; Fleagle, *Puerto Rican Experience*, 3. In any event, Puerto Ricans are a mixed-race people who had, certainly compared to the mainland United States, few "color problems."

50. Dan Wakefield, *Island in the City: Puerto Ricans in New York* (New York: Citadel Press, 1959), 235.

51. Ibid., 105; Joseph P. Fitzpatrick, *The Stranger Is Our Own: Reflections on the Journey of Puerto Rican Migrants* (Kansas City, MO: Sheed and Ward, 1996), 44–45.

52. The homicide rate in 1969–71 for New Yorkers born in Puerto Rico, ages 25 to 34, was 123 per 100,000; for white New York residents in the same age category, but not born on the island, the rate was 19 per 100,000. For the same populations, the ratio of cirrhosis death rates was 3.63 for the island-born to 1.0 for mainlanders. Ira Rosenwaike, "Mortality among the Puerto Rican Born in New York City," *Social Science Quarterly* 64 (1983): 380. Alcoholism was said to be "a serious problem" on the island as well. The data show a significant increase in liquor consumption and cirrhosis deaths between 1961–62 and 1970–71. Nelson A. Fernández, "Nutrition in Puerto Rico," *Cancer Research* 35 (1975): 3288, 3289.

53. Puerto Ricans also were instrumental in two sensational adult crimes. On November 1, 1950, two Puerto Ricans seeking independence for the island attempted to assassinate President Harry S. Truman, who was residing at Blair House. One of the terrorists and a White House police officer were killed, but the president was unharmed. The second assailant was caught, tried, and sentenced to death, which Truman commuted to a life term. In 1979, President Jimmy Carter further commuted his sentence to time served.

    On March 1, 1954, some three years after the attack on Truman, four Puerto Rican nationalists traveled from New York to Washington, D.C., entered the gallery of the U.S. House of Representatives, and fired weapons at the congressmen, wounding five. They quickly were apprehended, convicted, and sentenced to long prison terms. These sentences also were commuted in 1979 by President Carter. David McCullough, *Truman* (New York: Simon and Schuster, 1992), 810–13; "Puerto Ricans Get Maximum Terms," *New York Times*, July 9, 1954, 1; Martin Tolchin, "President to Free 4 Puerto Ricans in Washington Shootings of 1950's," *New York Times*, September 7, 1979, A1.

54. Erwin Schepses, "Puerto Rican Delinquent Boys in New York City," *Social Service Review* 23(1) (1949): 52.

55. Jason Barnosky, "The Violent Years: Responses to Juvenile Crime in the 1950s," *Polity* 38(3) (2006): 318. The 1960 census counted 613,000 Puerto Ricans in New York City, which was 7.9 percent of a total population of 7,781,984. Glazer and Moynihan, *Beyond the Melting Pot*, 94.

56. Glazer and Moynihan, *Beyond the Melting Pot*, 122. Glazer and Moynihan relate how Puerto Ricans, along with Chinese and Japanese, were brought to Hawaii in the 1930s to work on the planta-

tions, and how the Chinese and Japanese moved rapidly into cities and high-paying jobs, while the Puerto Ricans fell into dependency. They had the highest rates of juvenile delinquency and the highest proportion of families on relief (ibid., 90). Even decades later, a study found that the delinquency rate was high among Hawaiians and Puerto Ricans and low among Japanese and Chinese. "The Puerto Ricans produce approximately twice as many alleged delinquents as might be expected by chance." Harwin L. Voss, "Ethnic Differentials in Delinquency in Honolulu," *Journal of Criminal Law, Criminology, and Police Science* 54(3) (1963): 324.

57. Charles Grutzner, "City Puerto Ricans Found Ill-Housed," *New York Times*, October 4, 1949.

58. "Youth Study Cites Cultural Factor," *New York Times*, March 17, 1956. It should be noted that Albert K. Cohen, the sociologist mentioned in the 1956 *New York Times* article, produced a well-known book on delinquency in which he contended that gangs adhere to a "delinquent subculture" which "takes its norms from the larger culture but turns them upside down." Albert K. Cohen, *Delinquent Boys: The Culture of the Gang* (New York: Free Press, 1955), 28.

59. Wayne Phillips, "Munoz in Defense of Puerto Ricans," *New York Times*, October 8, 1957.

60. "Crime Data Cited on Puerto Ricans," *New York Times*, October 11, 1959.

61. Milton Bracker, "Governor, Mayor Agree on Policy to Combat Gangs," *New York Times*, September 5, 1959.

62. Peter Kihss, "Liebowitz Urges Cut in Migration to Combat Crime," *New York Times*, September 25, 1959.

63. Richard Eder, "Night Cloaks Crime in City's Toughest Block," *New York Times*, July 25, 1960.

64. Agron was not executed. Following a campaign by Eleanor Roosevelt and other prominent persons, Nelson Rockefeller, the governor of New York, commuted his sentence to life in prison. He was paroled in 1979 after serving twenty years and died in 1986 at the age of 43. Robert D. McFadden, "State to Free the 'Capeman,' Street-Gang Leader Who Killed 2 in 1959," *New York Times*, September 22, 1979, 25; Owen Moritz, "Salvador Agron 'Cape Man,'" *New York Daily News*, September 5, 2009.

65. U.S. Department of Justice, Bureau of Justice Statistics, "Homicide Rate Trends"; U.S. Office of Management and Budget, *Social Indica-*

tors, table 2.1, 64. The four violent crimes are murder and nonnegligent manslaughter (which are combined), forcible rape, robbery, and aggravated assault.

66. James Gilbert, *A Cycle of Outrage: America's Reaction to the Juvenile Delinquent in the 1950s* (New York: Oxford University Press, 1986), 66. Gilbert concluded that there probably was an increase in juvenile crime and in attention paid to crime, that law enforcement agencies were asserting more control over young people, and that changes in the behavior of youth were "susceptible to interpretation as criminal" (ibid., 71).

67. U.S. Department of Commerce, Bureau of the Census, *Historical Statistics*, part 1, series H 1125–1134, H 1119–1124, 419; U.S. Census Bureau, *Demographic Trends*, table 5, part C, A-9.

68. Eric C. Schneider, *Vampires, Dragons, and Egyptian Kings: Youth Gangs in Postwar New York* (Princeton: Princeton University Press, 1999), 76, 77.

69. Thorsten Sellin, "Crime and Delinquency in the United States: An Over-All View," *Annals of the American Academy of Political and Social Science* 339 (1962): 20. Between 1950 and 1960, the population under 18 years old grew by 15.5 percent. U.S. Census Bureau, *Demographic Trends*, table 5, part C, A-10. Between 1953 and 1960, the increase in arrests for violent crimes committed by people under the age of 18 was as follows: murder/manslaughter, 88 percent; robbery, 54 percent; aggravated assault, 93 percent; and rape, 27 percent.

70. Marvin E. Wolfgang, "Crime in a Birth Cohort," *Proceedings of the American Philosophical Society* 117(5) (1973): 404, 405, 406. Wolfgang also found that 18 percent of the delinquents were recidivists and they were responsible for about two-thirds of all violent crimes. Ten percent of the black delinquents and 3 percent of the white were chronic offenders (ibid., 407–8). In 1960, the seven index crimes were murder and nonnegligent manslaughter, forcible rape, robbery, aggravated assault, burglary, larceny $50 and over, and auto theft. Federal Bureau of Investigation, *Crime in the United States, 1960*, Uniform Crime Reports (Washington, DC: GPO, 1960), 32.

71. Monkkonen, *Murder in New York City*, 9; Ted Robert Gurr, "Historical Trends in Violent Crime: A Critical Review of the Evidence," *Crime and Justice* 3 (1981): 311.

72. The word *mugging*, defined as "attacking with intent to rob," has been traced back to 1864. It derives from *mug*, or "face," and began

in 1818 as a boxing term with the connotation of striking someone in the face. Robert K. Barnhart, ed., *Chambers Dictionary of Etymology* (New York: W.W. Wilson, 1988).

73. Federal Bureau of Investigation, *Uniform Crime Reports for the United States and Its Possessions* (Washington, DC: GPO, 1950), table 44, 112; Federal Bureau of Investigation, *Crime in the United States, 1960*, Uniform Crime Reports, table 20, 95; U.S. Census Bureau, *Demographic Trends*, table 8, part G, A-26.

74. Allen E. Liska and Paul E. Bellair, "Violent-Crime Rates and Racial Composition: Covergence over Time," *American Journal of Sociology* 101(3) (1995): 595. The Liska and Bellair study held constant numerous economic, population, and family structure variables.

75. Grantham, *South in Modern America*, 192–95.

76. Sheldon Hackney, "Southern Violence," *American Historical Review* 74(3) (1969): 906–25.

77. H.C. Brearley, *Homicide in the United States* (1932; repr., Montclair, NJ: Patterson Smith, 1969), 19–23; H.V. Redfield, *Homicide, North and South* (Philadelphia: J.B. Lippincott, 1880).

78. Emile Durkheim, *Suicide: A Study in Sociology* (1897; repr., trans. John A. Spaulding and George Simpson [Glencoe, IL: Free Press, 1951]), 317. However, it may be that Catholic countries such as Spain, Ireland, and Italy undercounted (and continue to undercount) suicide, which is a religious taboo.

79. Hackney, "Southern Violence," 908.

80. Raymond Gastil, "Homicide and a Regional Culture of Violence," *American Sociological Review* 36(3) (1971): 412. Gastil's work is perhaps best known for his Index of Southernness, a rating assigned to each state based on the degree of southern influence therein. Gastil's multiple regression analysis found that the r for the Index of Southernness was 0.72, higher than any other factor of the ten correlated with state homicide rates for whites. Next highest was 0.60, for the percent of population ages 20–34. "Outside of the centers of Southern and Northern society," he concluded, "state homicide rates grade into one another in rough approximation to the extent to which Southerners have moved into mixed states" (ibid., 422, 425).

81. For an overview of the "structural" (as the economic explanation is sometimes referred to) versus cultural debate in the sociological literature, see Patricia L. McCall, Kenneth C. Land, and Lawrence E. Cohen, "Violent Criminal Behavior: Is There a General and Con-

tinuing Influence of the South?," *Social Science Research* 21(3) (1992): 286–310. The issue is discussed in the concluding chapter.

82. Keith D. Harries, "The Historical Geography of Homicide in the U.S., 1935–1980," *Geoforum* 16(1) (1985): 76. According to Harries, these maps represent state-based "homicide" rates, but as his source is the Uniform Crime Reports, the rates are of murders and nonnegligent manslaughters known to police departments, not homicide mortality rates (ibid.).

83. Federal Bureau of Investigation, *Crime in the United States, 1960*, Uniform Crime Reports, table 4. If we exclude the outliers, Chicago and Miami, the robbery rate for the South is 64.26 and for the non-South, 77.74; the difference is still 20.2 percent.

84. Martin Gold, "Suicide, Homicide, and the Socialization of Aggression," *American Journal of Sociology* 63(6) (1958): 651–61. See also Andrew F. Henry and James F. Short Jr., *Suicide and Homicide: Some Economic, Sociological, and Psychological Aspects of Aggression* (Glencoe, IL: Free Press, 1954). Henry and Short hypothesized that suicide and homicide are acts of aggression arising out of frustration. The more an individual is externally restrained, they reasoned, the more frustrated he will be and the more likely it is that he will engage in aggression against others. Higher-status individuals, being less externally restrained than lower-status people, are, according to their analysis, more likely to prefer suicide to homicide. As Gold pointed out, however, "it is debatable that members of higher-status categories are less restrained externally than their lower-status counterparts." "External restraints on behavior are exerted [*sic*] not only by persons but also by norms—norms which may apply more stringently to persons in higher-status positions." Gold, "Suicide," 652. Psychiatrist Herbert Hendin, who questions Henry and Short's work, points out that suicide, unlike homicide, occurs across the socioeconomic spectrum. Herbert Hendin, *Suicide in America* (New York: W. W. Norton, 1995), 108.

85. Recent family research confirms that low-income African American parents of toddlers spank more frequently than low-income white parents, while findings on the spanking of Latino toddlers have been inconsistent. Lisa J. Berlin et al., "Correlates and Consequences of Spanking and Verbal Punishment for Low-Income White, African American, and Mexican American Toddlers," *Child Development* 80(5) (2009): 1404.

86. Hendin, *Suicide in America*, 108–18.

87. Ibid., 110; Herbert Hendin, "Black Suicide," *Archives of General Psychiatry* 21(4) (1969): 407–22.

88. Marvin E. Wolfgang, "Suicide by Means of Victim-Precipitated Homicide," *Journal of Clinical and Experimental Psychopathology and Quarterly Review of Psychiatry and Neurology* 20 (1959): 335–49. Wolfgang found that approximately one out of four homicides were victim-precipitated, meaning that the party killed had been the first to engage in or threaten violence.

89. Hendin, *Suicide in America*, 110–11, 116.

90. Harry G. Levine and Craig Reinarman, "From Prohibition to Regulation: Lessons from Alcohol Policy for Drug Policy," *Milbank Quarterly* 69(3) (1991): 468; Robert Nash Parker and Kathleen Auerhahn, "Alcohol, Drugs, and Violence," *Annual Review of Sociology* 24 (1998): 294.

91. Denise Herd, "Migration, Cultural Transformation and the Rise of Black Liver Cirrhosis Mortality," *British Journal of Addiction* 80 (1985): 399. Black alcohol intake increased during the migration to northern cities, probably because black income (and, therefore, money to spend on drink) was greater in the North, and inhibitions on drinking, which were stronger in the South, had been left behind.

92. Eric C. Schneider, *Smack: Heroin and the American City* (Philadelphia: University of Pennsylvania Press, 2008), xiv.

93. Claude Brown, *Manchild in the Promised Land* (1965; repr., New York: Simon and Schuster, 1999), 180.

94. David T. Courtwright, "A Century of American Narcotic Policy," in *Treating Drug Problems*, vol. 2, ed. Dean R. Gerstein and Henrick J. Harwood (Washington, DC: National Academy Press, 1992), 17, 18.

95. Parker and Auerhahn, "Alcohol, Drugs, and Violence," 295.

96. U.S. Census Bureau, *Demographic Trends*, appendix table 5, A-10.

97. Mitra Toossi, "A Century of Change: The U.S. Labor Force, 1950–2050," *Monthly Labor Review* 16 (2002): 17, accessed October 14, 2011, http://www.bls.gov/opub/mlr/2002/05/art2full.pdf.

98. A. Joan Klebba, "Homicide Trends in the United States, 1900–74," *Public Health Reports* 90(3) (1975): 200.

99. National Center for Health Statistics, *Health, United States, 2006* (Hyattsville, MD: GPO, 2006), table 45, 227; National Center for Health Statistics, *Homicide*, table 3, 19.

100. U.S. Department of Health, Education, and Welfare, *Vital Statistics of the United States, 1960*, part A, table 5-11, 5-188; U.S. Department of Health, Education, and Welfare, *Vital Statistics of the United States,*

1950, table 57, 452; U.S. Census Bureau, *Demographic Trends*, appendix table 5, A-9. Using different measures, Theodore Ferdinand found that between 1950 and 1965, 11.6 percent of the increase in arrests for FBI index crimes was solely attributable to changes in age structure. Changes in violent crimes due to population shifts were 5.5 percent for murder; 47.1 percent for rape; 13.4 percent for robbery; and 9.2 percent for aggravated assault. Theodore N. Ferdinand, "Demographic Shifts and Criminality: An Inquiry," *British Journal of Criminology* 10 (1970): 174. In 1967, the President's Commission on Law Enforcement found that nearly half of the increase in arrests in the early 1960s was attributable to population changes. "Commission studies based on 1960 arrest rates indicate that between 1960 and 1965 about 40 to 50 percent of the total increase in the arrests reported by UCR could have been expected as the result of increases in population and changes in the age composition of the population." U.S. Commission on Law Enforcement and Administration of Justice, *The Challenge of Crime in a Free Society* (Washington, DC: GPO, 1967), 28.

101. National Center for Health Statistics, *Homicide*, table 3, 20.

102. U.S. Department of Commerce, Bureau of the Census, *Historical Statistics*, part 1, series A 119–134, 17.

103. Between 1950 and 1973, cirrhosis mortality increased over 200 percent for nonwhites of both sexes, but only increased 66 and 50 percent for white males and females, respectively. Herd, "Migration," 399.

104. On the rediscovery of poverty, see James T. Patterson, *America's Struggle against Poverty in the Twentieth Century* (1981; repr., Cambridge, MA: Harvard University Press, 2000), 97ff.

105. Ross, Danziger, and Smolensky, "Level and Trend of Poverty," 590.

106. Courtwright, *Violent Land*, 211–12.

107. John Kenneth Galbraith, *The Affluent Society* (New York: Houghton Mifflin, 1958), 14.

108. Ibid., 250–51.

109. Robert D. Plotnick et al., "The Twentieth Century Record of Inequality and Poverty in the United States," discussion paper no. 1166-98 (Madison, WI: Institute for Research on Poverty, July 1998): appendix D, 57, accessed August 13, 2011, http://irp.wisc.edu /publications/dps/pdfs/dp116698.pdf.

110. A multigenerational study of poor communities in Cambridge and

Somerville, Massachusetts, between 1935 and 1945, found the following percentages of all criminal convictions attributable to violent crimes: immigrant fathers, 10.9 percent; native-born fathers, 14.7 percent; sons of immigrants, 11.6 percent; and sons of native-born, 13.5 percent. Joan McCord, "Ethnicity, Acculturation, and Opportunities: A Study of Two Generations," in *Ethnicity, Race, and Crime*, ed. Darnell F. Hawkins (Albany: State University of New York Press, 1995), 75.

111. Glazer and Moynihan, discussing New York City in 1963, commented in passing that the Irish "have in significant numbers joined the middle and upper classes" (*Beyond the Melting Pot*, 274). They also gave the percentages of the New York City population in 1900 and 1960 for the various European immigrant groups, though they called the 1960 percentages "a guess" (ibid., 8, 318).

Foreign white stock, by country, as percentage of New York City population, 1900 and 1960

	1900 (%)	1960 (%)
England, Scotland, Wales	5	2
Germany	22	4
Ireland	20	4
Russia	7	7
Poland	—	5
Italy	6	11

Source: Glazer and Moynihan, *Beyond the Melting Pot*, 318.

Figures include foreign-born and native whites of foreign or mixed parentage. Note that Russians and Poles in New York City were largely Jews. The low figure for Italians in 1900 reflects the fact that most southern Italians entered the United States after 1900. In 1920, Italians comprised 14 percent of the city.

112. Daniel Bell, *The End of Ideology: On the Exhaustion of Political Ideas in the Fifties* (New York: Collier Books, 1961), 156, 159, 170, 171.

CHAPTER 3. ORDEAL

Epigraphs: National Commission on the Causes and Prevention of Violence, *To Establish Justice, To Insure Domestic Tranquility* (Washington, DC: GPO, 1969), 18; Mary A. Johnson, "Crime: New Frontier; Jesse Jackson Calls It Top Civil-Rights Issue," *Chicago Sun-Times*, November 29, 1993, 4.

1. Randolph Roth contended that homicide booms, including that of the late 1960s, "occur whenever a state loses legitimacy, fellow feeling diminishes, and men lose hope of winning respect by legitimate means" (*American Homicide*, 455). For similar views, see Gary LaFree, *Losing Legitimacy*. LaFree stressed the loss of legitimacy by economic institutions (ibid., 115), but this is difficult to reconcile with the economic boom occurring at the time. The youth population/time horizons argument was made by James Q. Wilson and Richard J. Herrnstein in *Crime and Human Nature* (New York: Free Press, 1985), 422, 437.

2. Analysts have offered intriguing explanations for the crime rise. Edward Banfield stressed the lack of self-control of the lower classes. Edward C. Banfield, *The Unheavenly City Revisited* (1968; repr., Boston: Little, Brown, 1974), 192. Psychologist Steven Pinker attributed it to a "decivilizing mindset" that encouraged susceptible individuals and subcultures to actual violence (*Better Angels*, 113–14). Robert Putnam linked crime to a loss of social capital. Robert D. Putnam, *Bowling Alone: The Collapse and Revival of American Community* (New York: Simon and Schuster, 2000), 308.

3. John F. Kennedy, "Inaugural Address," January 20, 1961, American Presidency Project (Gerhard Peters and John T. Woolley), http://www.presidency.ucsb.edu/ws/?pid=8032.

4. Patterson, *Grand Expectations*, 312, 316, 321, 458; James P. Smith and Finis R. Welch, *Closing the Gap: Forty Years of Economic Progress for Blacks* (Santa Monica, CA: Rand Corp., 1986), 104; U.S. Census Bureau, *Historical Census Statistics on Population Totals by Race, 1790 to 1990, and by Hispanic Origin, 1970 to 1990, for the United States, Regions, Divisions, and States*, by Campbell Gibson and Kay Jung, working paper no. 56 (Washington, DC: GPO, 2002), table 1, 4. The proportion of poor *individuals* (as opposed to poor *families*) was 55.9 percent for nonwhites in 1960 and 17.8 percent for whites. The census at this point did not differentiate African Americans and other nonwhites.

5. Thernstrom and Thernstrom, *America in Black and White*, 176.
6. Juvenile Delinquency and Youth Offenses Control Act of 1961, Pub. L. No. 87-274, 75 Stat. 572 (Sept. 22, 1961); Peter Marris and Martin Rein, *Dilemmas of Social Reform: Poverty and Community Action in the United States* (1967; repr., Piscataway, NJ: Transaction Publishers, 2009), 19, 21, 134, 143. The committee's reformist bent was in keeping with the widely held view of the 1960s that enhancing legitimate opportunities among the poor would reduce crime. The committee's most influential consultants were the well-known criminologists Lloyd Ohlin and Richard Cloward, whose book *Delinquency and Opportunity* had just been published. Ohlin and Cloward adopted Robert Merton's social strain theory, contending that juvenile gangs were formed in lower-class communities to achieve through illegitimate means the success that was unattainable through legitimate channels. Their unique contribution was to identify three different types of gangs: one devoted to theft and extortion, another to violence (against other gangs), and a third to drug consumption. Whether these distinctions were accurate in their day is debatable; they hardly seem applicable to the urban environment at the end of the decade. Even less relevant to the late 1960s is Cloward and Ohlin's benign description of adult crime in the city "slums."

> The disorganized slum, populated in part by failures in the conventional world, also contains the outcasts of the criminal world. This is not to say that crime is nonexistent in such areas, but what crime there is tends to be individualistic, unorganized, petty, poorly paid, and unprotected. This is the haunt of the small-time thief, the grifter, the pimp, the jackroller, the unsophisticated "con" man, the pickpocket who is all thumbs, and others who cannot graduate beyond "heisting" candy stores or busting gas stations.

Moreover, they predicted that "violence will diminish in Negro neighborhoods" as blacks gain control over illegal sources of wealth in their communities and increase their political power. Richard A. Cloward and Lloyd C. Ohlin, *Delinquency and Opportunity: A Theory of Delinquent Gangs* (New York: Free Press, 1960), 173, 202.
7. Patterson, *Grand Expectations*, 524–25, 530, 600, 602.
8. Charles E. Silberman, *Criminal Violence, Criminal Justice* (New York: Random House, 1978), 3.
9. Donald J. Mulvihill, Melvin M. Tumin, and Lynn A. Curtis, *Crimes*

of Violence, staff report from Task Force on Individual Acts of Violence to National Commission on the Causes and Prevention of Violence, vol. 11 (Washington, DC: GPO, 1969), xxv. The Commission on the Causes and Prevention of Violence, created by President Johnson's Executive Order 11412, June 10, 1968, was headed by Milton S. Eisenhower, brother of the former president. Leading scholars served on or advised its numerous task forces. The heads of the Task Force on Individual Acts of Violence acknowledged special debts to Marvin E. Wolfgang and James Short Jr., well-known criminologists of the period.

10. John A. Davis, "Blacks, Crime, and American Culture," *Annals of the American Academy of Political and Social Science* 423 (1976): 89.

11. Gilbert Geis, "Statistics Concerning Race and Crime," *Crime & Delinquency* 11(2) (1965): 149. See also Harold E. Pepinsky, "The Growth of Crime in the United States," *Annals of the American Academy of Political and Social Science* 423 (1976): 23–30, in which Pepinsky asserts that crime growth is merely a byproduct of new crime measurement technologies. Liberal discomfort with the realities of crime continues. A scholar recently claimed that there had been no great crime rise in the late 1960s and any subsequent increase in crime was due to over-imprisonment. "Not only were Americans less likely to be murdered in the 1960s than they had been in earlier decades," asserted Heather Ann Thompson, "but they were also more likely to be murdered *after* the nation began funding a more punitive law-and-order state. By creating urban crises and by undercutting gains made by the American working class," Thompson concluded, "mass incarceration had created a greater crime problem in America. Prisons not only impoverished people, leading them to commit more crimes of necessity, but they also made people more violent and antisocial." Heather Ann Thompson, "Why Mass Incarceration Matters: Rethinking Crisis, Decline, and Transformation in Postwar American History," *Journal of American History* 97(3) (2010): 728.

12. Silberman, *Criminal Violence*, 3.

13. It is estimated that approximately 51 percent of violent victimizations and 64 percent of property victimizations are not reported to the police. U.S. Department of Justice, Bureau of Justice Statistics. *Crime and Victimization in the Three Largest Metropolitan Areas, 1980–98*, by Janet L. Lauritsen and Robin J. Schaum (Washington, DC: GPO, 2005), 1; "Key Facts at a Glance: Homicide Rate Trends,"

Bureau of Justice Statistics, accessed December, 2, 2011, https://web
.archive.org/web/20121230183805/http://bjs.ojp.usdoj.gov/content
/glance/tables/hmrttab.cfm#topaccessed December, 2, 2011, http://
bjs.ojp.usdoj.gov/content/glance/tables/hmrttab.cfm#top.

14. Federal Bureau of Investigation, "Uniform Crime Reporting Statistics," accessed December 2, 2011, http://www.ucrdatatool.gov/.

15. Francis Fukuyama, *The Great Disruption: Human Nature and the Reconstitution of Social Order* (New York: Free Press, 1999), 4–6, 31, 79, 280.

16. Gary LaFree and Kriss A. Drass, "Counting Crime Booms among Nations: Evidence for Homicide Victimization Rates, 1956 to 1998," *Criminology* 40(4) (2002): 769–800.

17. Ibid., 792–93.

18. Ibid., 782. Measuring homicide alone enabled LaFree and Drass to avoid definitional inconsistencies between countries and therefore provided greater cross-national accuracy.

19. The pre-1933 data used here were statistically adjusted by Douglas Lee Eckberg, whose work is commonly accepted by crime historians. Douglas Lee Eckberg, "Estimates of Early Twentieth-Century U.S. Homicide Rates: An Econometric Forecasting Approach," *Demography* 32(1) (1995): 13.

20. Crime historian Roger Lane has suggested that the earlier homicide rate may have been elevated by inferior medical care, and that improved response to trauma (including faster and better emergency care) may have reduced rates in the post-1960s period (Roger Lane, private communication to author, March 5, 2012). If true, then homicide rates may mask the greater assaultive violence of the recent crime boom.

21. Roger Lane, *Roots of Violence in Black Philadelphia, 1860–1900* (Cambridge, MA: Harvard University Press, 1986), 103.

22. Adler, *First in Violence*, 269.

23. Robbery arrest totals for 1920 and 1930 are for males, aged 16 or over, as derived from Harry Willbach, "The Trend of Crime in Chicago," *American Institute of Criminal Law & Criminology* 31 (1940–41): 722. Rates for 1970 and 1980 are posted online. Chicago Police Department, *Chicago Police Annual Report, 1970*, 18, accessed December 5, 2011, https://portal.chicagopolice.org/portal/page/portal/ClearPath/News/Statistical%20Reports/Annual%20Reports/1970_AR.pdf; Chicago Police Department, *Statistical Summary, 1980: Chicago*

Police Department, 12, accessed December 5, 2011, https://portal.chi
cagopolice.org/portal/page/portal/ClearPath/News/Statistical%
20Reports/Annual%20Reports/1980_AR.pdf.

24. Rates from 1895 to 1951 are annual averages derived from graphic
representations in Theodore N. Ferdinand, "The Criminal Patterns
of Boston Since 1849," *American Journal of Sociology* 73(1) (1967): 93.
Rates for 1960, 1970–71, and 1981–82 are based on Boston Police reports of the number of arrests. For 1970–71 and 1981–82, the year-long
periods ran from July 1 to June 30. City of Boston, *Annual Report of
the Police Commissioner for the City of Boston,* accessed December 8,
2011, http://www.bpl.org/online/govdocs/bpd_reports.htm#1961.

25. James Boudouris, "A Classification of Homicides," *Criminology* 11
(1973–74): 536. Boudouris utilized twenty-five subcategories for
criminal transaction homicides, mostly differentiated by the location of the assault; for example, street, home garage, bar, and saloon.
I excluded the following subcategories: citizen, unknown; criminal
abortion; gang war, extortion, riot snipers, miscellaneous; for insurance; public police officer. Populations were averages for each four-
year period using annual estimates based on constant change over
the intercensal period. Thus, Detroit's population from 1926 to 1929
averaged 1,424,913. For 1965 to 1968, the annual population average
was 1,455,950. The 1974 robbery-homicide figure is from Franklin
Zimring, "Determinants of the Death Rate from Robbery: A Detroit Time Study," *Journal of Legal Studies* 6(2) (1977): 318.

26. U.S. Department of Commerce and Labor, Bureau of the Census,
Prisoners and Juvenile Delinquents in Institutions, 1904 (Washington,
DC: GPO, 1907), table xiv, 31; U.S. Department of Justice, Bureau
of Justice Statistics, *Historical Corrections Statistics,* table 3-17, 45.
Robbers are difficult to apprehend, in large measure because they
are strangers to the victim. It is possible that over the course of the
twentieth century, police improved their capacity to arrest robbers,
but robbery clearances declined after the 1960s. It is also possible
that over the century, courts convicted a bigger percentage of accused robbers or judges sentenced more of them to prison terms. I
am not aware of any evidence for these propositions.

27. Marc Riedel, "Stranger Violence: Perspectives, Issues, and Problems," *Journal of Criminal Law and Criminology* 78(2) (1987): 237.
Riedel derived these data from Robert S. Munford et al., "Homicide Trends in Atlanta," *Criminology* 14(2) (1976): 213–32; Alex D.
Pokorny, "A Comparison of Homicides in Two Cities," *Journal of*

Criminal Law, Criminology, and Police Science 56(4) (1965): 479–87; and Henry P. Lundsgaarde, *Murder in Space City: A Cultural Analysis of Houston Homicide Patterns* (New York: Oxford University Press, 1977). A nine-city survey conducted by Zahn and Sagi in 1978 found the following figures: family homicide, 18 percent; acquaintance homicide, 54 percent; stranger homicide with another felony, 16 percent; and stranger homicide with no other felony, 12 percent. Margaret A. Zahn and Philip C. Sagi, "Stranger Homicides in Nine American Cities," *Journal of Criminal Law and Criminology* 78(2) (1987): 383.

28. The Gallup survey included the following question: "Is there any area around here—that is, within a mile—where you would be afraid to walk alone at night?" In 1965, 34 percent of the respondents said yes, and in 1972, positive responses rose to 41 percent. Group responses in the affirmative in 1972 were as follows: blacks, 49 percent; residents of cities over 1 million, 53 percent; aged 50 and over, 49 percent; income under $3,000 per year, 58 percent. Hazel Erskine, "The Polls: Fear of Violence and Crime," *Public Opinion Quarterly* 38(1) (1974): 137, 138, 140, 141.

29. Violent crime victimization estimates were calculated from National Crime Victimization Survey (NCVS) data for 1975, 1980, 1985, and 1990 at http://bjs.ojp.usdoj.gov/content/glance/tables/viortrdtab .cfm, accessed December 13, 2011. The automobile injury data apparently are based on incidents in 1991. U.S. Department of Justice, Bureau of Justice Statistics, *Highlights from 20 Years of Surveying Crime Victims: The National Crime Victimization Survey, 1973–92*, by Marianne W. Zawitz et al. (Washington, DC: GPO, 1993), 6, 46.

30. U.S. Department of Justice, Bureau of Justice Statistics, *Lifetime Likelihood of Victimization*, by Herbert Koppel (Washington, DC: GPO, 1987), 2. Calculations were based on the average annual victimization rates for robbery and assault from 1975 to 1984 and for rape from 1973 to 1982, which were held constant for the estimated life spans. A lifetime was taken to start at age 12. As persons aged and their projected life spans grew shorter, the likelihood of victimization perforce would be reduced. Thus, 72 percent of people aged 20 were likely to be victimized in their lifetimes. For 30-year-olds, the figure dropped to 53 percent; for 40-year-olds, 36 percent (ibid., 3).

31. From 1982 to 1984, 57 percent of all violent crimes were by strangers, rising to 59 percent in 1991. From 1982 to 1984, strangers committed 77 percent of all robberies, 56 percent of aggravated assaults, and 55 percent of rapes. U.S. Department of Justice, Bureau of Justice

Statistics, *Violent Crime by Strangers and Nonstrangers,* by Anita D. Timrots and Michael R. Rand (Washington, DC: GPO, 1987), 2; U.S. Department of Justice, Bureau of Justice Statistics, *Highlights from 20 Years,* 24.

32. U.S. Department of Justice, Bureau of Justice Statistics, *Highlights from 20 Years,* 5, 16, 17, 29; U.S. Department of Justice, Bureau of Justice Statistics, *Injuries from Crime,* by Caroline Wolf Harlow (Washington, DC: GPO, 1989), 3. Thirty-two percent of all violent crimes involved weapons, including 92 percent of aggravated assaults, 55 percent of robberies, and 20 percent of rapes. Forty percent of the armed robbers used handguns, and 26 percent of them used knives. The time frame for these data appears to be 1979 to 1987. For data on injuries, the time period was 1979 to 1986, during which a yearly average of 2,210,760 persons were injured in criminal assaults. Time was lost from work in approximately 9 percent of violent victimizations, and in 54 percent of the cases, the lost time was between one and five days.

33. James Garafolo and L. Paul Sutton, *Compensating Victims of Violent Crime: Potential Costs and Coverage of a National Program* (Albany, NY: Criminal Justice Research Center, 1977), table 11, 30; U.S. Department of Justice, Bureau of Justice Statistics, *Violent Crime* (Washington, DC: GPO, 1994), 3.

34. U.S. Department of Justice, Bureau of Justice Statistics, "Sourcebook of Criminal Justice Statistics Online," table 2.37.2010, accessed December 24, 2011, http://www.albany.edu/sourcebook/pdf/t2372010 .pdf.

35. Examples of crime films with "desperate ghettos ruled by ruthless street gangs" include *New Jack City* (1991), *Colors* (1988), *Fresh* (1995), *Menace II Society* (1993), *Predator II* (1992), *Sugar Hill* (1993), and several Stephen Segal pictures. Movies with "graffiti-covered . . . violent, out of control urban schools" include *Lean on Me* (1988), *Dangerous Minds* (1996), *The Substitute* (1996), and *187* (1997). *Trespass* (1992), *Falling Down* (1993), and *Judgment Night* (1993) featured "middle-class white guys" lost in and fighting their way out of "inner-city neighborhoods infested with drugs and gun-toting criminals." Film titles and descriptions are from Steve Macek, "Places of Horror: Fincher's 'Seven' and Fear of the City in Recent Hollywood Film," *College Literature* 26(1) (1999): 81.

36. For an overview of research on the mass media's effects, see Linda

Heath and Kevin Gilbert, "Mass Media and Fear of Crime," *American Behavioral Scientist* 39 (1996): 379–86.

37. William J. Collins and Robert A. Margo, "The Economic Aftermath of the 1960s Riots in American Cities: Evidence from Property Values," Vanderbilt University and NBER, May 2004, table 1, 22, accessed November 13, 2011, http://aeaweb.org/annual_mtg_papers /2005/0109_1015_0203.pdf; Thernstrom and Thernstrom, *America in Black and White*, 159.

38. Gregg Lee Carter, "Hispanic Rioting during the Civil Rights Era," *Sociological Forum* 7(2) (1992): 306, 307. Carter used the following severity scale, first developed by Seymour Spilerman. See Seymour Spilerman, "Structural Characteristics of Cities and the Severity of Racial Disorders," *American Sociological Review* 41(5) (1976): 7744.

    0 Low intensity—rock and bottle throwing, some fighting, and little property damage. Crowd size <125; arrests <15; injuries <8.

    1 Rock and bottle throwing, fighting, looting, serious property damage, and some arson. Crowd size 75–250; arrests 10–30; injuries 5–15.

    2 Substantial violence, looting, arson, and property destruction. Crowd size 200–500; arrests 25–75; injuries 10–40.

    3 High intensity—major violence, bloodshed, and destruction. Crowd size >400; arrests >65; injuries >35.

    A study of 673 cities with populations over 25,000 found that from 1961 to 1968, 75 percent of them had no disorders. Seymour Spilerman, "The Causes of Racial Disturbances: A Comparison of Alternative Explanations," *American Sociological Review* 35(4) (1970): 631. Sidney Fine estimated riot participation in Watts and Newark at 15 percent of the black population; in Detroit, 11 percent. Sidney Fine, *Violence in the Model City: The Cavanagh Administration, Race Relations, and the Detroit Riot of 1967* (Ann Arbor: University of Michigan Press, 1989), 343.

39. Michael Newton and Judy Ann Newton, *Racial and Religious Violence in America: A Chronology* (New York: Garland, 1991), 515; Susan Olzak and Suzanne Shanahan, "Deprivation and Race Riots: An Extension of Spilerman's Analysis," *Social Forces* 74(3) (1996): 942.

40. Fine, *Violence in the Model City*, 155–60, 299.

41. Ibid., 249; National Advisory Commission on Civil Disorders, *Re-*

port of the National Advisory Commission on Civil Disorders (New York: Bantam Books, 1968), 115n16; Richard A. Berk and Howard E. Aldrich, "Patterns of Vandalism During Civil Disorders as an Indicator of Selection of Targets," *American Sociological Review* 37(5) (1972): 533–47.

42. Thernstrom and Thernstrom, *America in Black and White*, 164.

43. Fine, *Violence in the Model City*, 71.

44. U.S. Department of Justice, Bureau of Justice Statistics, *Criminal Victimization in the United States: 1973–88 Trends* (Washington, DC: GPO, 1991), table 4, 13; U.S. Department of Justice, Bureau of Justice Statistics, *Report to the Nation on Crime and Justice*, 2nd ed. (Washington, DC: GPO, 1988), 33.

45. Silberman, *Criminal Violence*, 160; Johnson, "Crime," 4; James Bennet, "Sadness and Anger After a Legend Is Mugged," *New York Times*, September 1, 1994, A16.

46. U.S. Department of Justice, Bureau of Justice Statistics, "Homicide Trends in the United States," by James Alan Fox and Marianne W. Zawitz (Washington, DC: GPO, 2010), http://www.bjs.gov/content/pub/pdf/htius.pdf.

47. Roland Chilton, "Homicide Arrest Trends and the Impact of Demographic Changes on a Set of U.S. Central Cities," in *Trends, Risks, and Interventions in Lethal Violence: Proceedings of the Third Annual Spring Symposium of the Homicide Research Working Group*, ed. Carolyn Block and Richard Block (Washington, DC: GPO, 1995), 99–113. The forty central cities studied were Atlanta, Baltimore, Birmingham, Boston, Buffalo, Chicago, Cleveland, Columbus, Dallas, Denver, Detroit, El Paso, Fort Worth, Houston, Indianapolis, Jersey City, Long Beach, Los Angeles, Louisville, Memphis, Miami, Milwaukee, Newark, New Orleans, New York City, Oakland, Oklahoma City, Omaha, Philadelphia, Phoenix, Pittsburgh, Portland, Rochester, Saint Louis, Saint Paul, San Antonio, San Francisco, Toledo, Wichita, and Washington, D.C. Some of Chilton's analysis covered thirty-nine instead of forty cities because New York City did not provide arrest data by race until 1977.

48. Ibid., 99.

49. Ibid., 104.

50. Ibid.

51. Ibid., 104, 106, 107.

52. Ibid., 111.

53. William Julius Wilson, *The Truly Disadvantaged: The Inner City, the*

Underclass, and Public Policy (Chicago: University of Chicago Press, 1987), 149. As for the disinclination of criminologists to address the race/crime nexus, Michael Tonry attributed this to "fierce attacks on [Daniel Patrick] Moynihan," fears of "perpetuating negative stereotypes of blacks," and a desire "to avoid being labeled a racist." Michael Tonry, *Malign Neglect: Race, Crime, and Punishment in America* (New York: Oxford University Press, 1995), viii.

54. An example of selection bias would be police policies that focus on misconduct that is believed to be more common among African Americans, such as, in the 1980s, the use of crack cocaine. See, for example, Tonry, *Malign Neglect.* More recently, New York Police Department pedestrian stop-and-frisk policies came under fire for unselectively targeting young men in black communities. However, directing more police patrols to African American neighborhoods, whether to control cocaine use or frisk for weapons, is unlikely to increase reports to the police of serious violent crimes, such as murder, assault, rape, and robbery, nor is it apt to significantly alter arrest rates for such offenses. Consequently, such policies, whatever their flaws, are unlikely to bias the selection of African Americans for prosecution for violent crimes.

55. Bias charges are thoroughly reviewed in Samuel Walker, Cassia Spohn, and Miriam DeLone, *The Color of Justice: Race, Ethnicity, and Crime in America,* 3rd ed. (Belmont, CA: Wadsworth, 2004); and William Wilbanks, *The Myth of a Racist Criminal Justice System* (Monterey, CA: Brooks/Cole, 1987), 57–83. Bias charges were refuted in Alfred Blumstein, "On the Racial Disproportionality of United States' Prison Populations," *Journal of Criminal Law and Criminology* 72(3) (1982): 1259–81; Patrick A. Langan, "Racism on Trial: New Evidence to Explain the Racial Composition of Prisons in the United States," *Journal of Criminal Law and Criminology* 76(3) (1985): 666–83; Tonry, *Malign Neglect,* 50–79; and Wilbanks, *Myth of a Racist Criminal Justice System.*

56. See Langan, "Racism on Trial," 677. Langan chose the years 1973, 1979, and 1982 because prisoner survey data were available for those years. There was much greater variance in the data for rape and assault than for robbery, but the reasons for this difference are unclear.

57. Klebba, "Homicide Trends in the United States." The mortality rates are age-adjusted.

58. Tonry, *Malign Neglect,* 50.

59. Detroit figures for 1926 to 1929 were extrapolated from James Bou-

douris, "Trends in Homicide," table 15, 138. Birmingham data are from Howard Harlan, "Five Hundred Homicides," 737, 745.

60. The Supplementary Homicide Reports are part of the FBI's Uniform Crime Reporting (UCR) program developed from monthly submissions to the FBI by police departments nationwide. The submissions on homicide incidents include details on location as well as victim and offender characteristics, such as the race of the parties.

61. "Homicide Trends in the U.S.," Bureau of Justice Statistics, accessed October 15, 2015, https://web.archive.org/web/20111219171049/http://bjs.ojp.usdoj.gov/content/homicide/hmrt.cfm. In over one-third of the homicides, the offender-victim relationship was not known, but it is unlikely that the principals in these cases had a preexisting relationship that the investigators simply did not know about. Consequently, most of these cases probably were stranger killings, which means that stranger homicides actually constituted well over 14 percent of the total. A study of homicides in nine U.S. cities in 1978 confirms this. This study found that 29 percent of the killings were committed by strangers, with 18 percent unknown. Zahn and Sagi, "Stranger Homicides," 383. The analysts found 1,748 homicides total, including 399 stranger cases. Subtracting from the total 260 cases with unknown relationships, 36 cases with all data missing from the files, and 70 police killings leaves 1,382 cases ($399 \div 1,382 = 28.87$ percent).

62. Zahn and Sagi, "Stranger Homicides," 387–88. The nine cities studied were Philadelphia and Newark in the Northeast; Chicago and Saint Louis in the Midwest; Memphis and Dallas in the South; and Oakland, San Jose, and an unnamed city (at the request of the police chief) in the West.

63. U.S. Department of Justice, Bureau of Justice Statistics, *Criminal Victimization in the United States*, table 10, 20, table 17, 31.

64. U.S. Department of Justice, Bureau of Justice Statistics, *Highlights from 20 Years*, 23.

65. William Wilbanks, "Is Violent Crime Intraracial?," *Crime & Delinquency* 31(1) (1985): 121, 122.

66. U.S. Office of Management and Budget, *Social Indicators 1973*, table 2/9, 68. The data source was Mulvihill et al., *Crimes of Violence*.

67. Eldridge Cleaver, *Soul on Ice* (1968; repr., New York: Dell, 1991), 33.

68. Quoted in Banfield, *Unheavenly City*, 195. In a similar vein, Charles Silberman wrote this in the late 1970s: "After 350 years of fearing

whites, black Americans have discovered that the fear runs the other way, that whites are intimidated by their very presence. . . . The taboo against expression of anti-white anger is breaking down, and 350 years of festering hatred has come spilling out" (*Criminal Violence*, 153).

69. Silberman, *Criminal Violence*, 4, 5.

70. Lynn A. Curtis, *Violence, Race, and Culture* (Lexington, MA: D.C. Heath, 1975), 91.

71. Franklin E. Zimring and Gordon Hawkins, *Crime Is Not the Problem: Lethal Violence in America* (New York: Oxford University Press, 1997), 86.

72. From 1950 to 1970, murder and manslaughter clearances were separately reported in the Uniform Crime Reports; table 3.12 presents only murder arrests. In 1980 and 1990, arrests for both offenses were combined.

73. William H. Frey, "Central City White Flight: Racial and Nonracial Causes," *American Sociological Review* 44(3): (1979) 425–48; William Julius Wilson, "Another Look at *The Truly Disadvantaged*," *Political Science Quarterly* 106(4) (1991–92): 641.

74. Led by Chief Justice Earl Warren, the Supreme Court ordered the exclusion from criminal trials of evidence of guilt improperly obtained: Mapp v. Ohio, 367 U.S. 643 (1961) (physical evidence obtained in violation of the Fourth Amendment); Miranda v. Arizona, 384 U.S. 436 (1966) (incriminating statements obtained without a reading of rights warnings). The Court also established the right of every defendant to an attorney, publicly funded if the accused was impoverished: Gideon v. Wainwright, 372 U.S. 335 (1963) (felony defendants); Argersinger v. Hamlin, 407 U.S. 25 (1972) (misdemeanants). These decisions tilted the system in favor of criminal defendants. But at the same time, the Court (in Santobello v. New York, 404 U.S. 257 [1971]) approved plea bargaining. In nine out of ten convictions in the United States, pleas of guilty accompanied by a waiver of defendant's trial rights supplanted the full criminal trial. U.S. Department of Justice, Bureau of Justice Statistics, *Felony Case Processing in State Courts, 1986*, by Carla K. Gaskins (Washington, DC: GPO, 1990), 1. In addition, the Court upheld the constitutionality of capital punishment in Gregg v. Georgia, 428 U.S. 153 (1976).

75. National Center for Health Statistics, *Health, United States, 2006*, table 45. Homicide rates are age-adjusted. U.S. Department of Justice,

Bureau of Justice Statistics, "Homicide Trends," accessed October 21, 2015, https://web.archive.org/web/20111219171049/http://bjs.ojp.usdoj.gov/content/homicide/hmrt.cf.

76. Federal Bureau of Investigation, *Age-Specific Arrest Rates and Race-Specific Arrest Rates for Selected Offenses, 1965–1992* (Washington, DC: GPO, 1993), 173.

77. Ibid.; Federal Bureau of Investigation, *Crime in the United States, 1960*, Uniform Crime Reports, table 20, 95, table 26, 101; Federal Bureau of Investigation, *Crime in the United States, 1970*, Uniform Crime Reports, table 32, 131; Federal Bureau of Investigation, *Crime in the United States, 1980*, Uniform Crime Reports, table 35, 204; Federal Bureau of Investigation, *Crime in the United States, 1990*, Uniform Crime Reports, table 38, 192.

78. National Center for Health Statistics, *Health, United States, 2006*, table 45.

79. For the sake of brevity, I refer to non-Hispanic whites simply as "whites" and non-Hispanic blacks as "blacks."

80. U.S. Census Bureau, *We, the American Hispanics* (Washington, DC: GPO, 1993), 3, 4; U.S. Census Bureau, *Population Estimates by Race and Hispanic Origin for States, Metropolitan Areas, and Selected Counties: 1980 to 1985*, by David L. Word, Current Population Reports, P-25, no. 1040 (Washington, DC: GPO, 1989), 65–79; Frank D. Bean and Marta Tienda, *The Hispanic Population of the United States* (New York: Russell Sage Foundation, 1987), 175.

81. U.S. Department of Justice, Bureau of Justice Statistics, *Violent Crime*, 4; U.S. Department of Justice, Bureau of Justice Statistics, *Hispanic Victims*, by Lisa D. Bastian (Washington, DC: GPO, 1990), 2; U.S. Department of Justice, Bureau of Justice Statistics, *Criminal Victimization in the United States, 1987* (Washington, DC: GPO, 1989), table 8, 20; U.S. Department of Justice, Bureau of Justice Statistics, *Criminal Victimization in the United States, 1988* (Washington, DC: GPO, 1989), table 8, 20; U.S. Department of Justice, Bureau of Justice Statistics, *Criminal Victimization in the United States, 1989* (Washington, DC: GPO, 1990), table 7, 6; U.S. Department of Justice, Bureau of Justice Statistics, *Criminal Victimization in the United States, 1990* (Washington, DC: GPO, 1992), table 8, 26; U.S. Department of Justice, Bureau of Justice Statistics, *Criminal Victimization in the United States, 1991* (1992), table 7, 6; U.S. Department of Justice, Bureau of Justice Statistics, *Criminal Victimization in the*

United States, 1992 (Washington, DC: GPO, 1993), table 6, 6; U.S. Department of Justice, Bureau of Justice Statistics, *Murder in Large Urban Counties, 1988* (Washington, DC: GPO, 1993), table 1, 2.

82. U.S. Department of Justice, Bureau of Justice Statistics, *Murder in Large Urban Counties, 1988*, table 3, 3. There also is statewide and city-level evidence of the intra-ethnic nature of Hispanic crime. In Chicago, from 1965 to 1981, for example, 83 percent of the killers of Latinos shared the same ethnicity. Carolyn R. Block, "Race/Ethnicity and Patterns of Chicago Homicide 1965 to 1981," *Crime & Delinquency* 31(1) (1985): 113. In the state of Texas, between 1980 and 1983, if the killer was Hispanic, 86 percent of the victims were, too. Salvador F. Rodriguez, "Patterns of Homicide in Texas: A Descriptive Analysis of Racial/Ethnic Involvement by Crime-Specific Categories" (PhD diss., University of Texas, Austin, 1990), 19, 20. Ramiro Martinez reports additional findings of high intra-ethnic rates for Hispanic murders in Miami, Florida, at 85 percent, and in New York City, at 78 percent. Ramiro Martinez Jr., "Latinos and Lethal Violence: The Impact of Poverty and Inequality," *Social Problems* 43(2) (1996): 134n4.

83. Zahn and Sagi, "Stranger Homicides," 385.

84. Martinez, "Latinos and Lethal Violence," 139; U.S. Department of Justice, Bureau of Justice Statistics, "Homicide Trends," accessed October 21, 2015, https://web.archive.org/web/20111219171049/http://bjs.ojp.usdoj.gov/content/homicide/hmrt.cf. The rate for whites in the Bureau of Justice Statistics analysis was inflated somewhat by the inclusion of white Hispanics.

85. U.S. Census Bureau, *We, the American Hispanics*, 4.

86. Rosenwaike, "Mortality among the Puerto Rican Born," 380.

87. Ira Rosenwaike and Katherine Hempstead, "Mortality among Three Puerto Rican Populations: Residents of Puerto Rico and Migrants in New York City and in the Balance of the United States, 1979–81," *International Migration Review* 24(4) (1990): 691. Note that the figures in the first three columns of table 3.16 are *ratios*, not rates; they indicate the relationship between the various Puerto Rican homicide rates and the rates of non–Puerto Rican whites, the latter of which appear in the far-right column.

88. David Burnham, "3 of 5 Slain by Police Here Are Black, Same as the Arrest Rate," *New York Times*, August 26, 1973, 50.

89. Karmen, *New York Murder Mystery*, 59. Puerto Ricans have been a

significant, though declining, share of New York City's Hispanic population. In the early 1970s, when the *New York Times* survey was conducted, two out of three Hispanics were Puerto Ricans. For Karmen's analysis, the proportion of Puerto Ricans would have been 50 to 60 percent. Carmen Teresa Whalen and Víctor Vázquez-Hernández, eds., *The Puerto Rican Diaspora: Historical Perspectives* (Philadelphia: Temple University Press, 2005), 3; Laird W. Bergad, *The Latino Population of New York City, 1990–2010* (Center for Latin American, Caribbean & Latino Studies, November 2011), accessed January 2, 2012, http://clacls.gc.cuny.edu/files/2013/10/The-Latino-Population-of-New-York-City-1990-2010.pdf, 4, 5; U.S. Census Bureau, *Historical Census Statistics on Population Totals by Race, 1790 to 1990, and by Hispanic Origin, 1970 to 1990, for Large Cities and Other Urban Places in the United States,* by Campbell Gibson and Kay Jung, working paper no. 76 (Washington, DC: GPO, 2005), table 33.

90. U.S. Census Bureau, *Population Estimate,* 31, 52, 66.

91. Jack C. Smith, James A. Mercy, and Mark L. Rosenberg, "Suicide and Homicide among Hispanics in the Southwest," *Public Health Reports* 101(3) (1986): 266, 267, 269.

92. Rodriguez, "Patterns of Homicide," 19, 20.

93. California State Department of Justice, Bureau of Criminal Statistics and Special Services, *Crime and Delinquency in California, 1985* (Sacramento, CA: 1986), table 31, 135.

94. Gerald T. McLaughlin, "Cocaine: The History and Regulation of a Dangerous Drug," *Cornell Law Review* 58 (1972–73): 538n9.

95. Schneider, *Smack,* 121.

96. Parker and Auerhahn, "Alcohol, Drugs, and Violence," 295.

97. James A. Inciardi, *The War on Drugs III: The Continuing Saga of the Mysteries and Miseries of Intoxication, Addiction, Crime, and Public Policy* (Boston: Allyn and Bacon, 2002), 192.

98. James A. Inciardi, "Heroin Use and Street Crime," *Crime & Delinquency* 25 (1979): 342.

99. Bruce D. Johnson, Andrew Golub, and Eloise Dunlap, "The Rise and Decline of Hard Drugs, Drug Markets, and Violence in Inner-City New York," in *The Crime Drop in America,* ed. Alfred Blumstein and Joel Wallman (Cambridge: Cambridge University Press, 2000), 173.

100. Schneider, *Smack,* 116.

101. Travis Hirschi and Michael Gottfredson, "Age and the Explanation of Crime," *American Journal of Sociology* 89(3) (1983): 581. The age ef-

fect may not be as universal as these authors suggest. In Japan and Scotland, for example, another study found "no evidence that the proportion of young males in the population affects the homicide rate." But these analysts do not dispute the effect of age on rates in the United States. Rosemary Gartner and Robert Nash Parker, "Cross-National Evidence on Homicide and the Age Structure of the Population," *Social Forces* 69(2) (1990): 363.

102. "Homicide Trends in the U.S.," Bureau of Justice Statistics, accessed January 18, 2012, https://web.archive.org/web/20111219171049/http://bjs.ojp.usdoj.gov/content/homicide/hmrt.cfm.

103. Lawrence E. Cohen and Kenneth C. Land, "Age Structure and Crime: Symmetry versus Asymmetry and the Projection of Crime Rates through the 1990s," *American Sociological Review* 52(2) (1987): 180.

104. President's Commission on Law Enforcement and Administration of Justice, *The Challenge of Crime in a Free Society* (Washington, DC: GPO, 1967), 28.

105. Charles F. Wellford, "Age Composition and the Increase in Recorded Crime," *Criminology* 11 (1973): 63.

106. Ibid., 65, 66 (my calculation).

107. Homicide rates for age groups are from Robert M. O'Brien, Jean Stockard, and Lynne Isaacson, "The Enduring Effects of Cohort Characteristics on Age-Specific Homicide Rates, 1960–1995," *American Journal of Sociology* 104(4) (1999): 1073.

108. Wellford, "Age Composition," 65, 66.

109. Wilson and Herrnstein, *Crime and Human Nature*, 426.

110. Steven D. Levitt, "The Limited Role of Changing Age Structure in Explaining Aggregate Crime Rates," *Criminology* 37(3) (1999): 589.

111. Gabriel Tarde, *Penal Philosophy*, trans. Rapelje Howell (1890; repr., London: William Heinemann, 1912), 356.

112. Jonathan Crane, "The Epidemic Theory of Ghettos and Neighborhood Effects on Dropping Out and Teenage Childbearing," *American Journal of Sociology* 96(5) (1991): 1226–59.

113. Denise B. Kandel, "Drug and Drinking Behavior among Youth," *Annual Review of Sociology* 6 (1980): 235–85.

114. Mark Granovetter, "Threshold Models of Collective Behavior," *American Journal of Sociology* 83(6) (1978): 1420–43.

115. David C. Rowe and Joseph L. Rodgers, "An 'Epidemic' Model of Adolescent Sexual Intercourse: Applications to National Survey Data," *Journal of Biosocial Science* 23 (1991): 211–19.

116. Gary S. Becker and Kevin M. Murphy, *Social Economics: Market Be-*

havior in a Social Environment (Cambridge, MA: Harvard University Press, 2000), 5.

117. Ibid., 133, 136.

118. Edward L. Glaeser, Bruce Sacerdote, and Jose A. Scheinkman, "Crime and Social Interactions," *Quarterly Journal of Economics* III (1996): 507–48. Contagion theory does not preclude other explanations for city differentials. For instance, one group of analysts found that the size of a city, the extent of its social disintegration, and the level of social deprivation correlated with very high or very low UCR Index crime rates in three decennial census time periods, 1960, 1970, and 1980. Kenneth C. Land, Patricia L. McCall, and Lawrence E. Cohen, "Characteristics of U.S. Cities with Extreme (High or Low) Crime Rates: Results of Discriminant Analyses of 1960, 1970, and 1980 Data," *Social Indicators Research* 24(3) (1991): 209–31. "Those cities with extremely high (low) crime rates," this study found, "tend to be the largest (smallest), most (least) socially disintegrated, and most (least) deprived" (ibid., 228).

119. Malcolm Gladwell, *The Tipping Point: How Little Things Can Make a Big Difference* (Boston: Little, Brown, 2000).

120. Crane, "Epidemic Theory," 1227.

121. Cf. James Q. Wilson, who wrote, "There is, perhaps, a 'critical mass' of young persons such that, when that number is reached, or when an increase in that mass is sudden and large, a self-sustaining chain reaction is set off that creates an explosive increase in the amount of crime, addiction, and welfare dependancy." James Q. Wilson, *Thinking about Crime* (1975; repr., New York: Basic Books, 1983), 24.

122. For an argument that an increase in the prison population was the most significant factor in the crime decline of the 1990s, see Steven D. Levitt, "Understanding Why Crime Fell in the 1990's: Four Factors that Explain the Decline and Six that Do Not," *Journal of Economic Perspectives* 18(1) (2004): 163–90. As for the suggestion that the same imprisonment theory should apply to the late-1960s crime upswing, see William J. Stuntz, *The Collapse of American Criminal Justice* (Cambridge, MA: Harvard University Press, 2011), 28. "Proof is impossible," wrote Stuntz, "but the low and falling prison populations of the 1960s and early 1970s probably contributed to rising levels of serious crime during those years" (ibid., 252).

123. Federal Bureau of Investigation, *Uniform Crime Reports for the United States and Its Possessions* (1950), table 15, 49; Federal Bureau

of Investigation, *Crime in the United States, 1960*, Uniform Crime
Reports, table 8, 83; Federal Bureau of Investigation, *Crime in the
United States, 1970*, Uniform Crime Reports, table 13, 110; Federal
Bureau of Investigation, *Crime in the United States, 1980*, Uniform
Crime Reports, table 20, 182; Federal Bureau of Investigation, *Crime
in the United States, 1990*, Uniform Crime Reports, table 20, 165.
Clearance rates are a measure of police effectiveness. If one were
to look at all occurrences, even those not reported to the police, the
rate for crimes solved would be much lower. The National Crime
Victimization Survey, which began in 1973, found in that year an
estimated 1,107,800 robberies, whereas the UCR reported 384,220
robberies known to police, which is 34.7 percent of the survey total.
There were 127,530 robbery arrests in 1973, which was 33.2 percent of
reported robberies, but only 11.5 percent of the crime survey total.
Thus, roughly one out of nine robberies resulted in an arrest. Of
course, the police can't be faulted for failing to solve crimes that are
never reported. Federal Bureau of Investigation, *Crime in the United
States, 1973*, Uniform Crime Reports (Washington, DC: GPO, 1973),
table 24, 121.

124. U.S. Department of Justice, Bureau of Justice Statistics, *Prisoners
in 1990* (Washington, DC: GPO, 1991), table 11, 7. "Serious crimes"
was defined as murder/manslaughter, rape, robbery, aggravated assault, and burglary (ibid.). U.S. Department of Justice, Bureau of
Justice Statistics, *Historical Corrections Statistics*, table 3-10, 38; Federal Bureau of Investigation, "Uniform Crime Reporting Statistics,"
accessed January 6, 2012, http://www.ucrdatatool.gov/index.cfm;
Federal Bureau of Investigation, *Crime in the United States, 1960*,
Uniform Crime Reports, table 3, 47.

125. Morgan O. Reynolds, "Crime and Punishment in America," National Center for Policy Analysis, policy report no. 193 (June 1995),
table A-5, 28, accessed January 6, 2012, http://www.ncpa.org/pdfs
/st193.pdf; Isaac Ehrlich, "Crime, Punishment, and the Market for
Offenses," *The Journal of Economic Perspectives* 10(1) (1996): 45. Median time served for all felons released from state prison, regardless
of crime, was twenty-one months in 1940, 1951, and 1960, sinking to
fourteen months in 1974, and climbing back to nineteen months in
the late 1970s. Patrick A. Langan, "America's Soaring Prison Population," *Science* 251(5001) (1991): table 1, 1570.

126. Reynolds, "Crime and Punishment," 3, 5, 6. Reynolds calculated the

expected prison time by dividing the number of prison commitments for each crime by the number of crimes reported to police
and then multiplying the result by the median time served. For example, for murder in 1960, there were 3,720 prison commitments and
9,140 reported crimes, for a ratio of 0.407. The median time served
for murder in 1960 was 52 months, or 4.33 years (0.407 × 4.33 = 1.76
years). In 1970, this figure fell to 1.1 years (4,999 ÷ 15,810 × 3.5).

127. Wilson, *Thinking about Crime*, 24–25.

128. U.S. Census Bureau, *Demographic Trends*, appendix table 11, A-36;
Gregory, *The Southern Diaspora*, 330.

129. Black migration alone cannot explain high crime. For one thing,
blacks generally improved their socioeconomic status by migrating.
Moreover, not all migrating (or immigrating) groups evince high
crime rates. Eastern European Jews, for example, and (as far as we
know) white southern U.S. migrants did not contribute to higher
crime rates at their destination points. And, perhaps most important, black crime was elevated in the South as well as the North.
With regard to demographics, the increase in baby boomers of high-
crime age is insufficient to explain the crime increase.

130. Miles D. Harer and Darrell Steffensmeier, "The Differing Effects of
Economic Inequality on Black and White Rates of Violence," *Social
Forces* 70 (1992): 1035–54.

131. This isn't to say that poor people don't commit more violent crime
than the affluent. They do, for reasons discussed in the concluding
chapter.

132. Marvin Wolfgang and Franco Ferracuti, *The Subculture of Violence:
Towards an Integrated Theory in Criminology* (London: Tavistock
Publications, 1967).

133. Ibid., 152.

134. Ibid., 102.

135. Ibid., 153, 272.

136. Ibid., 264.

137. For a discussion of the empirical shortcomings of the subculture
of violence theory, see Howard S. Erlanger, "The Empirical Status
of the Subculture of Violence Thesis," *Social Problems* 22(2) (1974):
280–92.

138. Thomas Sowell has argued that much more attention should be
given to the contribution of various cultures to societies and to human history than to the impact of society on members of a particular
group. In *Race and Culture*, Sowell undertook to show some of the

ways in which group "cultures or 'human capital' have affected the advancement of particular groups, the societies of which they were a part, and ultimately the human race." Thomas Sowell, *Race and Culture: A World View* (New York: Basic Books, 1994), xii. For a lively popular treatment of the role of culture and cultural persistence in shaping behavior—including criminal behavior related to the southern culture of honor—see Malcolm Gladwell, *Outliers: The Story of Success* (New York: Little, Brown, 2008), 161–77.

139. Elijah Anderson, *Code of the Street: Decency, Violence, and the Moral Life of the Inner City* (New York: W.W. Norton, 1999). Anderson's research apparently was conducted in the 1990s. Consequently, some of his discussion, especially about crack cocaine, is not applicable to the early years of the great crime rise of the late 1960s. But his main point about the way the code of the street operated certainly has a ring of authenticity to it and seems appropriate to the entire high-crime era, and probably to earlier periods as well. Compare the comment of Butterfield, who wrote of black violence in the late nineteenth century:

> All this violence was not simply pathology. It grew out of the old white southern code of honor, an extreme sensitivity to insult and the opinion of others. . . . Pud [a nineteenth-century black man], slightly changing the white man's terminology, spoke of his reputation and demanded respect, rather than using the word "honor." . . . Over the years, "respect" was a word more and more African-Americans would use. (Fox Butterfield, *All God's Children: The Bosket Family and the American Tradition of Violence* [New York: Alfred A. Knopf, 1995], 63)

140. Anderson, *Code of the Street*, 32.

141. Ibid., 33.

142. Ibid., 72–73.

143. Ibid., 75.

144. Ibid., 76.

145. Thomas Sowell, *Black Rednecks and White Liberals* (San Francisco: Encounter Books, 2006), 27.

146. Ibid., 30. The Myrdal reference is to Gunnar Myrdal, *An American Dilemma: The Negro Problem and Modern Democracy*, 2 vols. (1944; repr., New Brunswick, NJ: Transaction Publishers, 1996). The other study referred to by Sowell was Dinesh D'Souza, *The End of Racism: Principles for a Multicultural Society* (New York: Free Press, 1995).

147. According to an ethnographic study made during the 1980s, a simi-

lar code of violence prevailed in East Harlem's Puerto Rican barrio. As one of the crack dealers interviewed by the author insisted: "You gotta be a little wild in the streets.... [Y]ou can't let people push you around, because when the other guys see that, they want to do the same thing too. You get that reputation, like, 'That nigga's soft.'" Philippe Bourgois, *In Search of Respect: Selling Crack in El Barrio* (1996; repr., Cambridge: Cambridge University Press, 2003), 25. Alice Goffman, one of Anderson's students, did her own ethnographic study of life in a poor black Philadelphia neighborhood in the mid-2000s. Alice Goffman, *On the Run: Fugitive Life in an American City* (Chicago: University of Chicago Press, 2014). While Goffman emphasized the impact of the criminal justice system on the residents' lives, the steady drumbeat of violent crime by the young men in the study was a telling backdrop. She did not offer an explanation for the high levels of black lower-class violence which, judging by her account, continued to be significant even in the twenty-first century.

148. Compare James W. Clarke, "Black-on-Black Violence," *Society* 33(5) (1996): 49:

> It was under these circumstances in the 1960s that a swollen generation of black "baby boomers" came of age as teenagers and were socialized into this subculture of violence. It is a subculture in which, for generations, white law and its white enforcers have been viewed, correctly, with distrust. It is also a subculture in which male honor and respect continue to rest on evidence of one's physical courage and sexual prowess, just as they did in the last century. What has changed in the last thirty years is only the rapid growth in the number of young black males who share these self-destructive values and the young women who are frequently their victims.

CHAPTER 4. THE VIOLENCE CONTINUES

1. Federal Bureau of Investigation, "Uniform Crime Reporting Statistics," accessed December 25, 2012, http://www.ucrdatatool.gov/. Murders and nonnegligent manslaughters known to police went from 10.2 per 100,000 in 1980 to 7.9 in 1984. Violent crime rates fell from 596.6 per 100,000 to 538.9.

2. Karmen, *New York Murder Mystery*, 17; Monkkonen, "Homicides in New York City."

3. In terms of the likelihood of victimization, subway crime, which was estimated at less than 3 percent of the city's total, was less of a threat

than the public thought. Moreover, the likelihood of being trapped with an assailant on a train was not as great as the odds of an assault on a train platform or stairway. Dennis Jay Kenney, "Crime on the Subways: Measuring the Effectiveness of the Guardian Angels," *Justice Quarterly* 3(4) (1986): 482, 485, 487; Dennis Jay Kenney, *Crime, Fear, and the New York City Subways: The Role of Citizen Action* (New York: Praeger, 1987).

4. Richard Stengel, Marcia Gauger, and Barry Kalb, "A Troubled and Troubling Life," *Time*, April 8, 1985; Myra Friedman and Michael Daly, "My Neighbor Bernie Goetz," *New York Magazine*, February 18, 1985; George P. Fletcher, *A Crime of Self-Defense: Bernhard Goetz and the Law on Trial* (Chicago: University of Chicago Press, 1988), 12, 12n33.

5. Fletcher, *A Crime of Self-Defense*, 1, 2.

6. Ibid., 2, 4; Lillian B. Rubin, *Quiet Rage: Bernie Goetz in a Time of Madness* (Berkeley: University of California Press, 1986), 197.

7. New York Penal Law, §160.10 (1). New York Penal Law, §35.15, states that a person may not use deadly physical force upon another person unless "he reasonably believes that such other person is committing or attempting to commit a . . . robbery."

8. Fletcher, *Crime of Self-Defense*, 3.

9. Ibid., 2, 3; Todd S. Purdum, "2 of Those Shot by Goetz Face New Jail Terms," *New York Times*, April 9, 1986; "Where Are Other 3 Now? In and Out of Jail," *New York Daily News*, April 24, 1996.

10. Fletcher, *Crime of Self-Defense*, 198; Adam Nossiter, "Bronx Jury Orders Goetz to Pay Man He Paralyzed $43 Million," *New York Times*, April 24, 1996, A1.

11. Inciardi, *The War on Drugs III*, 149, 151, 152, 153, 154, 156, 162.

12. On the support of the Congressional Black Caucus in 1986 for harsher anticrack penalties, see John J. DiIulio Jr., "My Black Crime Problem, and Ours," *City Journal* (Spring 1996), http://www.city-journal.org/html/6_2_my_black.html. Black leaders had strongly supported aggressive law enforcement at least since the late 1960s, including New York's harsh Rockefeller drug laws, the model for subsequent drug policies. Michael Javen Fortner, *Black Silent Majority: The Rockefeller Drug Laws and the Politics of Punishment* (Cambridge, MA: Harvard University Press, 2015).

13. Randall Kennedy, "The State, Criminal Law, and Racial Discrimination: A Comment," *Harvard Law Review* 107(6) (1994): 1269. Re-

garding the "additional complications with crack use" as compared
with powder cocaine, see Inciardi, *The War on Drugs III*, 161–62.

14. The Anti-Drug Abuse Act of 1986, Pub. L. No. 99-570, 100 Stat.
3207 (1986), provided equivalent sentences for significantly different
amounts of powder and crack cocaine. A first-time trafficker in possession of 5 grams of crack faced a minimum five-year mandatory
sentence. The same trafficker had to be in possession of 500 grams of
powder to be eligible for that level of sentence. Only thirteen states
established any sentencing differentials between powder and crack,
and Iowa alone adopted (and then repealed) the 100-to-1 federal
differential (i.e., the same sentence for a hundred times more powder than crack). U.S. Sentencing Commission, *Cocaine and Federal
Sentencing Policy*, Report to the Congress (May 2007), 2–3, 98, http://
www.ussc.gov/Legislative_and_Public_Affairs/Congressional_Tes
timony_and_Reports/Drug_Topics/200705_RtC_Cocaine_Sen
tencing_Policy.pdf. The Fair Sentencing Act of 2010, Pub. L. No.
111-220, 124 Stat. 2372 (2010), raised to 28 grams the amount of crack
cocaine needed for a five-year mandatory minimum prison sentence
for trafficking and eliminated the five-year mandatory minimum for
first-time simple possession.

15. U.S. Department of Justice, Bureau of Justice Statistics, *Homicide
Trends in the United States, 1980–2008*, by Alexia Cooper and Erica L. Smith (Washington, DC: GPO, 2011), http://bjs.ojp.usdoj
.gov/content/pub/pdf/htus8008.pdf, accessed April 14, 2012.

16. Alfred Blumstein, "Disaggregating the Violence Trends," in *The
Crime Drop in America*, ed. Alfred Blumstein and Joel Wallman
(Cambridge: Cambridge University Press, 2000), 39. Support for
Blumstein's assessment came from Daniel Cork, in "Examining
Space-Time Interaction in City-Level Homicide Data: Crack Markets and the Diffusion of Guns among Youth," *Journal of Quantitative Criminology* 15(4) (1999): 379–406. Cork found in 149 U.S. cities
"a sudden increase in juvenile gun homicide within 2 years of a similar, sharp increase in crack arrests among juveniles" (ibid., 403).

17. Eric Baumer et al., "The Influence of Crack Cocaine on Robbery,
Burglary, and Homicide Rates: A Cross-City, Longitudinal Analysis," *Journal of Research in Crime and Delinquency* 35(3) (1998): 318, 334.

18. Jeff Grogger and Michael Willis, "The Emergence of Crack Cocaine
and the Rise in Urban Crime Rates," *Review of Economics and Statistics* 82(4) (2000): 526. There was disagreement on the impact of

crack on some offenses. Baumer et al. believed that crack reduced burglaries as robbery provided the quicker and easier path to drug money. Grogger and Willis found that burglary rose by 6.3 percent and found increases in larceny and auto theft as well.

19. U.S. Department of Justice, Bureau of Justice Statistics, *Homicide Trends in the United States, 1980–2008*, accessed April 14, 2012; James Alan Fox, "Demographics and U.S. Homicide," in *The Crime Drop in America*, ed. Alfred Blumstein and Joel Wallman (Cambridge: Cambridge University Press, 2000), 293–94.

20. U.S. Department of Justice, Bureau of Justice Statistics, *Sourcebook of Criminal Justice Statistics, 1990*, ed. Kathleen Maguire and Timothy J. Flanagan (Washington, DC: GPO, 1991), table 2.3, 154–55, table 2.26, 174, table 2.92, 232, table 2.94, 233. These are Gallup poll figures, except for table 2.92, which was based on a Harris poll.

21. Ibid., figure 2.1, 199, table 2.37, 184, table 2.43, 191, table 2.44, 192–93. All data were provided by Gallup, except for table 2.44, which was based on a Roper survey.

22. Office of National Drug Control Policy, *National Drug Control Strategy* (Washington, DC: GPO, 1989), 16, 62–63; U.S. Department of Justice, Bureau of Justice Statistics, *Correctional Populations in the United States, 1997* (Washington, DC: GPO, 2000), 13.

23. In 1980, 25.4 percent of all blacks in state prison had been sentenced for drug offenses; in 1996, this figure rose only slightly, to 27.2 percent. U.S. Department of Justice, Bureau of Justice Statistics, *Prisoners in 1997*, by Darrell K. Gilliard and Allen J. Beck (Washington, DC: GPO, 1998), table 16, 12; U.S. Department of Justice, Bureau of Justice Statistics, *Race of Prisoners Admitted to State and Federal Institutions, 1926–86*, by Patrick A. Langan (Washington, DC: GPO, 1991), table 2, 5; U.S. Department of Justice, Bureau of Justice Statistics, *Correctional Populations*, table 1.21, 11.

24. U.S. Department of Justice, Bureau of Justice Statistics, *Prisoners in 1997*, table 16, 12.

25. As criminologist Zimring conceded, "Fifteen years after the decline began, there is little consensus among experts about what changes in circumstances produced the crime decline or what is likely to happen next." Zimring, *Great American Crime Decline*, v.

26. Brearley, *Homicide in the United States*, 68.

27. Ibid., 78. Brearley cited Edwin Sutherland, the dean of American criminologists, as the source of his information on the age of mur-

derers. Federal Bureau of Investigation, *Crime in the United States, 1993,* Uniform Crime Reports (Washington, DC: GPO, 1993), table 2.11, 18.

28. U.S. Bureau of Justice Statistics, "Homicide Trends in the United States," accessed June 10, 2012; Garen Wintemute, "Guns and Gun Violence," in *The Crime Drop in America,* ed. Alfred Blumstein and Joel Wallman (Cambridge: Cambridge University Press, 2000), 48.

29. In 2010, 67.5 percent of all murders were committed using firearms. Federal Bureau of Investigation, *Crime in the United States, 2010,* Uniform Crime Reports, "Expanded Homicide Data Table 7," accessed June 16, 2012, http://www.fbi.gov/about-us/cjis/ucr/crime-in -the-u.s/2010/crime-in-the-u.s.-2010/tables/10shrtbl07.xls.

30. Kristin F. Butcher and Anne Morrison Piehl, "Cross-City Evidence on the Relationship between Immigration and Crime," *Journal of Policy Analysis and Management* 17(3) (1998): 457–93. The additional crime produced by immigrants could have been offset by various crime-reducing factors.

31. Ramiro Martinez Jr., Jacob I. Stowall, and Matthew T. Lee, "Immigration and Crime in an Era of Transformation: A Longitudinal Analysis of Homicides in San Diego Neighborhoods, 1980–2000," *Criminology* 48(3) (2010): 797–829.

32. Graham C. Ousey and Charis E. Kubrin, "Exploring the Connection between Immigration and Violent Crime Rates in U.S. Cities, 1980–2000," *Social Problems* 56(3) (2009): 447–73.

33. Tim Wadsworth, "Is Immigration Responsible for the Crime Drop? An Assessment of the Influence of Immigration on Changes in Violent Crime between 1990 and 2000," *Social Science Quarterly* 91(2) (2010): 531–53.

34. Martinez, Stowall, and Lee, "Immigration and Crime," 799. See Eyal Press, "Do Immigrants Make Us Safer?," *New York Times Magazine,* December 3, 2006, 20, 22–24, discussing the views of criminologists Robert J. Sampson and Ramiro Martinez Jr.

35. A study of 1,944 Japanese, Chinese, and Filipino male arrests in Seattle for the five-year period between 1928 and 1932 found that 9.6 percent of Chinese males aged 15 and over were arrested annually, while for white males of the same age, the figure was 11.1 percent. Norman S. Hayner, "Social Factors in Oriental Crime," *American Journal of Sociology* 43(6) (1938): 909.

36. Kevin J. Mullen, *Dangerous Strangers: Minority Newcomers and*

Criminal Violence in the Urban West, 1850–2000 (New York: Palgrave Macmillan, 2005), 78–79. These early-twentieth-century Chinese immigrants came to be known as "paper sons," owing to a common practice calculated to evade immigration restrictions. Chinese males in the United States would return to China and reenter the United States with a family, consisting of a wife and "sons" who were not their biological children.

37. Walter G. Beach, *Oriental Crime in California* (1932; repr., New York: AMS Press, 1971), 55, 57, 60.

38. Hayner, "Social Factors," 913.

39. Patricia Page, "Chinatown: Not East, Not West," *New York Times Magazine*, December 15, 1946, 24.

40. Chang Pao-Min, "Health and Crime among Chinese-Americans: Recent Trends," *Phylon* 42(4) (1981): 363n21.

41. Ibid., 365.

42. Walter Miller, "The Rumble This Time," *Psychology Today* 10 (1977): 56, as reported in Paul Takagi and Tony Platt, "Behind the Gilded Ghetto: An Analysis of Race, Class, and Crime in Chinatown," *Crime and Social Justice* 9 (1978): 19.

43. "Violent crime" encompasses murder and nonnegligent manslaughter, robbery, aggravated assault, and rape. Calculations are based on revised 1970 U.S. census population figures for whites (178,098,000) and African Americans (22,581,000) and on 1970 U.S. census population figures for Chinese (435,062). U.S. Department of Commerce, Bureau of the Census, *Statistical Abstract of the United States, 1974* (Washington, DC: GPO, 1974), table 25, 26, table 33, 30. Arrest data are from Federal Bureau of Investigation, *Crime in the United States, 1975*, Uniform Crime Reports (Washington, DC: GPO, 1975), table 39, 192.

44. Takagi and Platt, "Behind the Gilded Ghetto," 12. Since these were prison commitments, as opposed to arrests or jail commitments, one may assume that the offenses were of a more serious nature. These data say nothing about juvenile delinquency or minor crime by adults.

45. Ko-lin Chin, *Chinese Subculture and Criminality* (Westport, CT: Greenwood Press, 1990), 67.

46. Ibid., 121.

47. Denny Lee, "Years of the Dragons," *New York Times*, May 11, 2003, sec. 14, 1.

48. Ibid.

49. Ibid.

50. Ibid.

51. Chin, *Chinese Subculture*, 145.

52. Around 43 percent of the immigrants to New York City between 1980 and 2000 arrived during the 1990s. New York City, Department of City Planning, Population Division, *The Newest New Yorkers 2000: Immigrant New York in the New Millennium*, briefing booklet (October 2004), 5, 8, accessed May 29, 2012, http://www.nyc.gov/html/dcp/pdf/census/nny_briefing_booklet.pdf.

53. Karmen, *New York Murder Mystery*, 223–24. I calculated the Chinese victimization rate by dividing the 8 homicides reported by Karmen for 1997 into the 2000 population of Chinese in New York City (261,555) as reported in New York City, Department of City Planning, Population Division, *Newest New Yorkers*, 8.

54. Franklin E. Zimring, *The City That Became Safe: New York's Lessons for Urban Crime and Its Control* (New York: Oxford University Press, 2012), 62–64. Zimring said that "the increase in low-risk Asian populations is good crime news, but their foreign-born status doesn't make a big dent in city crime because native-born Asian populations aren't high crime risks either" (ibid., 64). Zimring is correct to point out that immigration qua immigration should not be credited with reducing Asian crime involvement. He also may be correct to conclude that the city's mix of high- and low-crime populations remained about the same, and therefore immigration did not reduce crime rates. Nevertheless, the increase in Asian and other low-crime groups, such as Eastern Europeans, along with the decrease in high-crime Hispanic groups, helped sustain the crime drop by maintaining the proportion of the city's law-abiding population. Had more violent groups immigrated to New York, that surely would have had a negative impact on the crime situation.

55. New York City, Department of City Planning, Population Division, *Newest New Yorkers*, 5.

56. Preeti Chauhan et al., "Race/Ethnic-Specific Homicide Rates in New York City: Evaluating the Impact of Broken Windows Policing and Crack Cocaine Markets," *Homicide Studies* 15(3) (2011): 277. This study examined homicides in police precincts differentiated by the predominant racial or ethnic characteristics of the precinct populations. In the 1990s, there was a fair amount of black in-migration

to the city from Africa and Guyana, as well as from the Caribbean. The 2000 census estimated the Africa-born population of the state of New York at 3.0 percent, but in 2000, Africans were only 1.2 percent of the state's foreign-born prison inmates. U.S. Census Bureau, *The Foreign-Born Population: 2000*, by Nolan Malone, Kaari F. Baluja, Joseph M. Costanzo, and Cynthia J. Davis, Census 2000 Brief, C2KBR-34 (Washington, DC: GPO, 2003), table 4,7, http://www.census.gov/prod/2003pubs/c2kbr-34.pdf; New York City, Department of City Planning, *Newest New Yorkers*, 6; New York Department of Correctional Services, *The Impact of Foreign-Born Inmates on the New York State Department of Correctional Services* (January 2001), table 5.2. While the African population overwhelmingly was black, it was culturally distinct from African Americans and probably had little impact on crime by native blacks. It would, of course, be analytically unsound to examine all black crime rates together without regard to the cultural differences, and the same point is applicable to the culturally distinctive Latino and Asian groups.

57. Steven A. Camarota, *Immigrants in the United States, 2007: A Profile of America's Foreign-Born Population* (Washington, DC: Center for Immigration Studies, 2007), 6, 8, http://www.cis.org/articles/2007/back1007.pdf.

58. Hans P. Johnson, "Birth Rates in California," *California Counts* 9(2) (November 2007), 8, Public Policy Institute of California, http://www.ppic.org/content/pubs/cacounts/CC_1107HJCC.pdf. From 1982 to 2004, U.S.-born Latina birth rates were just above two children per woman, whereas foreign-born Latina rates were between three and four children each. In the early 1990s, the foreign-born Latina rate exceeded four children per woman (ibid., 8–9).

59. Marc Riedel, "Homicide in Los Angeles County: A Study of Latino Victimization," in *Violent Crime: Assessing Race and Ethnic Differences*, ed. Darnell F. Hawkins (New York: Cambridge University Press, 2003), 55. But see Martinez, Stowall, and Lee, "Immigration and Crime," which found that in San Diego, increases over time in the size of the neighborhood foreign-born population led to decreases in levels of lethal violence.

60. Camarota, *Immigrants*, 27, 31, 36.

61. Proposition 187 was supported by roughly 66 percent of Anglo voters, opposed by over 70 percent of Hispanic voters, and rejected by a bare majority of blacks and Asians who cast ballots. Robin Dale

Jacobson, *The New Nativism: Proposition 187 and the Debate over Immigration* (Minneapolis: University of Minnesota Press, 2008), xix. A federal court enjoined Proposition 187 on the legal theory of federal preemption, stating that "the authority to regulate immigration belongs exclusively to the federal government and state agencies are not permitted to assume that authority." League of United Latin American Citizens v. Wilson, 908 F. Supp. 755 (C.D. Cal. 1995). Republican Governor Pete Wilson (1991–99) had been a vigorous supporter of Proposition 187, but in 1999, his successor, Democratic Governor Gray Davis, terminated appeals designed to overturn the district court ruling.

62. Susan Pennell, Christine Curtis, and Jeff Tayman, *The Impact of Illegal Immigration on the Criminal Justice System* (San Diego, CA: San Diego Association of Governments, 1989), 3, 6.

63. Rebecca L. Clark and Scott A. Anderson, *Illegal Aliens in Federal, State, and Local Criminal Justice Systems* (Washington, DC: Urban Institute, June 30, 1999), 2, 6, 72, https://www.ncjrs.gov/pdffiles1/nij/grants/181049.pdf; U.S. Government Accountability Office, *Criminal Alien Statistics: Information on Incarcerations, Arrests, and Costs*, GAO-11-187 (2011), http://www.gao.gov/new.items/d111187.pdf. Federal distributions to the states for criminal justice expenses from illegal aliens were provided by the Violent Crime Control and Law Enforcement Act of 1994, Pub. L. No. 103-322, 108 Stat. 1796 (1994), which is implemented by the State Criminal Alien Assistance Program (SCAAP). The number of aliens (not necessarily undocumented) who have been removed from the United States because of the commission of a crime increased substantially between 2001, when 71,079 people were deported, and 2011, when that figure rose to 216,698. Of the latter, 1,119 had committed murder, 5,848 were guilty of sex crimes, and 44,653 had drug law violations ("FY 2014 ICE Immigration Removals," U.S. Immigration and Customs Enforcement, accessed May 21, 2012, http://www.ice.gov/removal-statistics/).

64. Susan B. Sorenson and Haikang Shen, "Homicide Risk among Immigrants in California, 1970 through 1992," *American Journal of Public Health* 86(1) (1996): 97–100. These results come with a caution. Although the census purports to count all residents, whether illegal or lawful, there probably was an undercount of illegal aliens, who had little incentive to cooperate with government employees. If, as a result, the Hispanic population was really much larger than believed, the victimization rates reported here may be inflated. Both

contrary and confirming outcomes were reported in Karl Eschbach et al., "Mortality of Foreign-Born and US-Born Hispanic Adults at Younger Ages: A Reexamination of Recent Patterns," *American Journal of Public Health* 97(7) (2007): 1297–1304. These analysts found that among male Hispanics in California, ages 15–44, for 1999–2001, the foreign-born had *lower* homicide rates than U.S.-born (2.81 per 100,000 versus 4.76). But these findings were contrary to their Texas figures for the same period (3.13 for foreign-born; 2.72 for U.S.-born).

65. Sorenson and Shen, "Homicide Risk," 99. Another distortion produced by conjoining different cultural groups was created by the study's consolidation of Asian rates with those of "others," where the latter included American Indians. The probable effect of including Indians, known for their high homicide rates, was to reduce the foreign-to-native homicide ratio, since Indians would not be counted among the foreign-born, and their homicides would be added to the U.S.-born total.

66. Bohsiu Wu, "Homicide Victimization in California: An Asian and Non-Asian Comparison," *Violence and Victims* 23(6) (2008): 748.

67. Richard D. Alba, John R. Logan, and Paul E. Bellair, "Living with Crime: The Implications of Racial/Ethnic Differences in Suburban Location," *Social Forces* 73(2) (1994): 395–434.

68. Rubén G. Rumbaut et al., "Immigration and Incarceration," in *Immigration and Crime: Race, Ethnicity, and Violence*, ed. Ramiro Martinez Jr. and Abel Valenzuela Jr. (New York: New York University Press, 2006), 71. For a plea to go beyond "pan-ethnic categories" when studying immigrant crime, see Stephanie M. DiPietro and Robert J. Bursik Jr., "Studies of the New Immigration: The Dangers of Pan-Ethnic Classifications," *Annals of the American Academy of Political and Social Science* 641(1) (2012): 247–67.

69. Richard Straka, "The Violence of Hmong Gangs and the Crime of Rape," *FBI Law Enforcement Bulletin* 72(2) (2003): 12–16; Alice J. Gallin, "The Cultural Defense: Undermining the Policies against Domestic Violence," *Boston College Law Review* 35(3) (1994): 723–45.

70. There certainly is room for further study on this issue. Sorenson and Shen were criticized for failing to take account of differences in socioeconomic and demographic characteristics. When such factors were included, a nationwide mortality study covering the period from 1979 to 1989 found no difference in homicide risk between immigrant and U.S.-born men. This suggests that immigrants neither

worsen nor improve crime rates. Interestingly, the same study, with the same controls, found a 229 percent higher risk of death by homicide among Hispanics than non-Hispanic whites—but without regard to whether the birthplace was foreign or domestic. Gopal K. Singh and Mohammad Siahpush, "All-Cause and Cause-Specific Mortality of Immigrants and Native Born in the United States," *American Journal of Public Health* 91(3) (2001): 396.

71. John L. Martin, Leon F. Bouvier, and William Leonard, *Shaping Florida: The Effects of Immigration, 1970–2020* (Washington, DC: Center for Immigration Studies, December 1995), http://www.cis .org/FloridaImmigrants19702020; U.S. Census Bureau, *Historical Census Statistics on Population Totals by Race, 1790 to 1990, and by Hispanic Origin, 1970 to 1990, for Large Cities and Other Urban Places in the United States*, by Campbell Gibson and Kay Jung, working paper no. 76 (Washington, DC: GPO, 2005).

72. Alejandro Portes and Alex Stepick, *City on the Edge: The Transformation of Miami* (Berkeley: University of California Press, 1993), 20, 21, 22.

73. Ramiro Martinez, "Homicide among the 1980 Mariel Refugees in Miami: Victims and Offenders," *Hispanic Journal of Behavioral Sciences* 19(2) (1997): 112.

74. Portes and Stepick, *City on the Edge*, 51, 54, 55, 56.

75. Bruce Porter and Marvin Dunn, *The Miami Riot of 1980: Crossing the Bounds* (Lexington, MA: D.C. Heath, 1984), xiii, 176.

76. Portes and Stepick, *City on the Edge*, 47–49.

77. James A. Inciardi and Anne E. Pottieger, "Drug Use and Street Crime in Miami: An (Almost) Twenty-Year Retrospective," in *The American Drug Scene*, ed. James A. Inciardi and Karen McElrath (Los Angeles: Roxbury, 2004), 363; Raymond A. Mohl, "Changing Economic Patterns in the Miami Metropolitan Area, 1940–1980," *Tequesta* 1(42) (1982): 69–70. Mohl did Inciardi one better, declaring that "Miami in the 1980s is the undisputed drug capital of the world" (ibid., 69).

78. Miami's homicide rates were reported in the FBI's annual Uniform Crime Reports (UCRs) for 1976–84. Before 1976, the UCR folded Miami's rates into those of Dade County. For data from 1985 to 2010, the UCR Data Online Tool was used (http://www.ucrdatatool.gov/, accessed June 1, 2012). Murder rates for cities comparable in size to Miami (250,000 to 500,000 population) averaged 14.8 per 100,000

in 1976. Federal Bureau of Investigation, *Crime in the United States, 1976*, Uniform Crime Reports (Washington, DC: GPO, 1976), table 14, 153.

79. The 18 percent figure for Mariel Cubans was based on Ramiro Martinez's tally of 171 Mariel victimizations for the years 1980 to 1984, divided into the UCR count for Miami murders, which totaled 934 in that same time period (Martinez, "Homicide among the 1980 Mariel Refugees," 112).

80. Portes and Stepick, *City on the Edge*, 59.

81. Ramiro Martinez and Matthew T. Lee, "Immigration and the Ethnic Distribution of Homicide in Miami, 1985–1995," *Homicide Studies* 2(3) (1998): 297. This study reported 1,221 offenders for whom race/ethnicity was known. The racial/ethnic distribution was 56 Anglo (4.6 percent), 657 African American (53.8 percent), 465 Latino (38.1 percent), and 43 Haitian (3.5 percent). The discrepancy between the low Hispanic victimization rates relative to Anglos and the relatively high Hispanic offender rates seems to be that there were outsized white victimizations at the hands of African Americans—a startling 50.6 percent of the victim total!

82. Portes and Stepick, *City on the Edge*, 56.

83. Ibid., 57, 189–90.

84. Martinez and Lee, "Immigration and Ethnic Distribution," 297. Of 1,221 homicide offenders for whom the race/ethnicity was known, 43 (3.5 percent) were Haitian. Problems with the Haitian general population count create doubt about the trustworthiness of the crime rates. The 1990 census reported only 18,035 Haitians in the city of Miami, not including the rest of Dade County (Martin, Bouvier, and Leonard, *Shaping Florida*). But this is believed to be a serious undercount, partly due to noncooperation with census takers, which, in turn, was related to the high number of illegal Haitian immigrants. Martinez and Lee adopted a "conservative" figure of 49,511 for the Haitian population, which they said was 14 percent of the city's population ("Immigration and Ethnic Distribution," 296n4). If 14 percent is accurate, then Haitian victimization (6.3 percent of all murder victims) and offending (4.6 percent of murder suspects where race/ethnicity was known) indicate a low involvement with violent crime. If the census count of 18,035 were accurate, then Haitians would have been 5 percent of the Miami city population (358,548), which would align fairly closely with their victimization

and offending percentages. In sum, whether one uses the official count or the Martinez-and-Lee population estimates, Haitians had a low rate of violent crime involvement.

85. David Lester, *Crime and the Native American* (Springfield, IL: Charles C. Thomas, 1999), 27.

86. U.S. Department of Justice, Bureau of Justice Statistics, *American Indians and Crime*, by Lawrence A. Greenfeld and Steven K. Smith (Washington, DC: GPO, 1999), 10.

87. Jerrold E. Levy and Stephen J. Kunitz, "Indian Reservations, Anomie, and Social Pathologies," *Southwestern Journal of Anthropology* 27(2) (1971): 107.

88. U.S. Department of Justice, Bureau of Justice Statistics, *American Indians*, 21.

89. The percentage in poverty of American Indians and Alaska natives combined was 25.7. U.S. Census Bureau, *We the People: American Indians and Alaska Natives in the United States*, by Stella U. Ogunwole (Washington, DC: GPO, 2006), 12. Among blacks in 1999, 23.6 percent were below the poverty line. U.S. Census Bureau, *Income, Poverty, and Health Insurance Coverage in the United States: 2010*, by Carmen DeNavas-Walt, Bernadette D. Proctor, and Jessica C. Smith, Current Population Reports, P60-239 (Washington, DC: GPO, 2011), table A-2.

90. U.S. Department of Justice, Bureau of Justice Statistics, *Arrest in the United States, 1980–2009*, by Howard N. Snyder (Washington, DC: GPO, 2011), 3–7. The white category apparently included Hispanics, which inflated the rates.

91. As of the 2000 census, the Indian and Alaskan native population, along with mixed Indian/Alaskans and people of other races, totaled 4,119,301, or 1.5 percent of the entire U.S. population, which was 281,412,906. U.S. Census Bureau, *The American Indian and Alaskan Native Population: 2000*, by Stella U. Ogunwole, Census 2000 Brief, C2KBR/01-15 (Washington, DC: GPO, 2002), 3, 4, http://www.census.gov/prod/2002pubs/c2kbr01-15.pdf; U.S. Department of Justice, Bureau of Justice Statistics, *American Indians*, 1, 4, 16; U.S. Department of Agriculture, "Minority Counties are Geographically Clustered," by Douglas E. Bowers and Peggy Cook, *Rural Conditions and Trends* 9(2) (1999): 14–19, accessed June 7, 2012, http://webarchives.cdlib.org/sw1bc3ts3z/http://ers.usda.gov/Publications/RCAT/RCAT92/.

92. Rates in figure 4.16 are from the FBI's "Supplementary Homicide Reports, 1980–2005," as reported by the Bureau of Justice Statistics, https://web.archive.org/web/20111219171049/http://bjs.ojp.usdoj .gov/content/homicide/hmrt.cfm. The figure shows three regions: South Atlantic—Delaware, District of Columbia, Florida, Georgia, Maryland, North Carolina, South Carolina, Virginia, and West Virginia; East South Central—Alabama, Kentucky, Mississippi, and Tennessee; and West South Central—Arkansas, Louisiana, Oklahoma, and Texas.

93. Figures are derived from mortality data, not police records, as the former facilitate disaggregation by race and region. Centers for Disease Control and Prevention, National Center for Health Statistics, accessed June 8, 2012, http://wonder.cdc.gov/ucd-icd10.html. The homicide mortality figures cover an eleven-year time frame, but exclude one year, 2001, because the data set included deaths due to the attack on the World Trade Center, which killed nearly 3,000 people.

94. If black rates had been the same as white rates (one-fifth of actual), total black homicides from 1999 to 2009 would have been reduced by 32,770, which would have brought the total homicide count for whites and blacks to 34,066. This yields a rate of 3.83 per 100,000, roughly half of the actual rate, which is 7.51. Centers for Disease Control and Prevention, National Center for Health Statistics, 95, accessed June 8, 2012, http://wonder.cdc.gov/ucd-icd10.html.

95. See Gregory S. Kowalski and Thomas A. Petee, "Sunbelt Effects on Homicide Rates," *Sociology and Social Research* 75(2) (1991): 75, which finds regional convergence based on the average of homicides in 3,133 counties between 1979 and 1982. Patrick W. O'Carroll and James A. Mercy, "Regional Variation in Homicide Rates: Why Is the West So Violent?," *Violence and Victims* 4(1) (1989): 17–25, finds that rates, based on state mortality data for 1980, were higher in the West for whites, blacks, and "others." Karen F. Parker and Matthew V. Pruitt, "How the West Was One: Explaining the Similarities in Race-Specific Homicide Rates in the West and South," *Social Forces* 78(4) (2000): 1483–1508, finds that for cities in 1990, after controlling for structural conditions, southern residence has a statistically significant, positive effect on the white homicide rate, but no significant effect on black rates.

96. U.S. Census Bureau, *The Hispanic Population, 2000*, by Betsy Guzmán, Census 2000 Brief, C2KBR/01-3 (Washington, DC: GPO, 2001),

2–3; Centers for Disease Control and Prevention, National Center for Health Statistics, accessed June 8, 2012, http://wonder.cdc.gov /ucd-icd10.html.

97. Roth, *American Homicide*, 183.

98. David Hackett Fischer, *Albion's Seed: Four British Folkways in America* (New York: Oxford University Press, 1989), 6, 766–70.

99. Richard E. Nisbett and Dov Cohen, *Culture of Honor: The Psychology of Violence in the South* (Boulder, CO: Westview Press, 1996).

100. Ibid., xv.

101. Ibid.

102. Ibid., 17.

103. Ibid., 16, 17.

104. Ibid., 21.

105. Ibid., 18.

106. In the Ozark and Appalachian highlands, where there were few slaves, Roth found low homicide rates. In slave areas after 1800, rates ranged from 8 to 28 per 100,000. "After the Revolution," Roth concluded, "homicide rates were thus most strongly linked to the presence or absence of slavery" (*American Homicide*, 180). Roth did find extraordinarily high homicide rates on the Kentucky-Tennessee border—600 per 100,000—which lends support to the claim that herding regions were very violent. But these rates occurred during the Civil War, and political feuds were the principal driver (ibid., 336).

107. Rebekah Chu, Craig Rivera, and Colin Loftin, "Herding and Homicide: An Examination of the Nisbett-Reaves Hypothesis," *Social Forces* 78(3) (2000): 971–87. A study of 163 to 184 nations found little relationship between cattle, goat, sheep, and pig herding and homicide. Irshad Altheimer, "Herding and Homicide Across Nations," *Homicide Studies* 17(1) (2013): 27–58. It is strange that the leading book on the relationship between eighteenth-century migrants and southern culture, the highly regarded work of David Hackett Fischer, makes scant reference to herding and does not attribute to it any of the cultural significance claimed by Nisbett and Cohen (Fischer, *Albion's Seed*, 741–43).

108. Matthew R. Lee, Shaun A. Thomas, and Graham C. Ousey, "Southern Culture and Homicide: Examining the Cracker Culture/Black Rednecks Thesis," *Deviant Behavior* 31(1): 60–96 (2009). This study found that a "southern culture index" had "a robust and highly significant positive effect on black homicide in southern as well as non-

southern counties" (ibid., 84). The index was based on the proportion of the county population that was born in the South, descended from early Scots-Irish ancestry, and evangelical Christian. The culture index also was found to be positively related to *white* argument-based homicide rates, a result corroborated in Matthew R. Lee et al., "Revisiting the Southern Culture of Violence," *Sociological Quarterly* 48(2): 253–75 (2007).

109. Zimring, *City That Became Safe*, x.

110. Krugman, "It's a Different Country," A21.

CHAPTER 5. THE GREAT DOWNTURN

Epigraph: Wendy Ruderman, "414 Homicides a Record Low for New York," *New York Times*, December 29, 2012, A1.

1. It wasn't just talk. Rates of racial or ethnic intermarriage in the United States more than doubled between 1980 (6.7 percent) and 2008 (14.6 percent). Jeffrey S. Passel, Wendy Wang, and Paul Taylor, *Marrying Out: One-in-Seven New U.S. Marriages Is Interracial or Interethnic,* Pew Research Center, June 4, 2010, ii, accessed June 7, 2013, http://www.pewsocialtrends.org/files/2010/10/755-marrying-out.pdf.

2. The Violent Crime Control and Law Enforcement Act of 1994, Pub. L. No. 103-322, 108 Stat. 1796 (1994), signed by President Clinton, provided grants for 100,000 new police officers, $9.7 billion for prisons, and $6.1 billion for prevention programs.

3. U.S. Department of Justice, Bureau of Justice Statistics, *Police Departments in Large Cities, 1990–2000,* by Brian A. Reaves and Matthew J. Hickman (Washington, DC: GPO, 2002), table 2, 2; U.S. Department of Justice, Bureau of Justice Statistics, *Police Departments in Large Cities, 1987,* by Brian A. Reaves (Washington, DC: GPO, 1989), table 17, 7. It took five years to hire the 100,000 officers; by 2000, 70,000 additional police actually were working. U.S. Department of Justice, Office of Community Oriented Policing Services, *Attorney General's Report to Congress,* 2000, 4, accessed April 28, 2012, http://www.cops.usdoj.gov/pdf/e12990066_f.pdf. This is considerably more than the 22,616 indicated by the Bureau of Justice Statistics report; presumably the discrepancy is due to the application of the Violent Crime Control Act to police departments of any size, whereas the report covered only sixty-two departments in cities with populations of 250,000 or more.

4. John E. Eck and Edward R. Maguire, "Have Changes in Policing Reduced Violent Crime? An Assessment of the Evidence," in *The Crime Drop in America*, ed. Alfred Blumstein and Joel Wallman (Cambridge: Cambridge University Press, 2000), 217.

5. Federal Bureau of Investigation, *Crime in the United States, 1980*, table 20, 182; Federal Bureau of Investigation, *Crime in the United States, 1985*, Uniform Crime Reports (Washington, DC: GPO, 1985), table 20, 156; Federal Bureau of Investigation, *Crime in the United States, 1990*, table 20, 165; Federal Bureau of Investigation, *Crime in the United States, 2000*, Uniform Crime Reports (Washington, DC: GPO, 2001), table 25, 207, http://www.fbi.gov/about-us/cjis/ucr/crime-in-the-u.s/2000/toc00.pdf; Federal Bureau of Investigation, *Crime in the United States, 2005*, Uniform Crime Reports (Washington, DC: GPO, 2006), table 25, accessed April 27, 2012, http://www2.fbi.gov/ucr/05cius/data/table_25.html.

6. Graham C. Ousey and Matthew R. Lee, "To Know the Unknown: The Decline in Homicide Clearance Rates, 1980–2000," *Criminal Justice Review* 35(2) (2010): 141–58.

7. Eli B. Silverman, *NYPD Battles Crime: Innovative Strategies in Policing* (Boston: Northeastern University Press, 1999), 100–105. In 2014, New York City Mayor Bill de Blasio reappointed Bratton to serve as police commissioner.

8. James Q. Wilson and George L. Kelling, "Broken Windows," *Atlantic Monthly*, March 1982, 29–38.

9. Zimring, *City That Became Safe*, 142.

10. Eck and Maguire, "Changes in Policing," 234. Zimring's conclusion that the NYPD drove down New York City's crime over and above the national reductions was based on "a process of elimination"; that is, his ruling out alternative explanations. He admits to being unable to explain 60 percent of the city's robbery rate drop and 85 percent of its murder decline (Zimring, *City That Became Safe*, 131, 154). For another effort to explain the crime decline in the Big Apple by a process of elimination, this one more skeptical about the effectiveness of police strategies, see Karmen, *New York Murder Mystery*. Steven Levitt claimed that nationwide, "the increase in police between 1991 and 2001 can account for a crime reduction of 5–6 percent across the board" ("Understanding Why Crime Fell," 177).

11. U.S. Department of Justice, Bureau of Justice Statistics, *Truth in Sentencing in State Prisons*, by Paula M. Ditton and Doris James Wilson (Washington, DC: GPO, 1999), 2–3.

12. For a detailed description and critique of California's law, see Franklin E. Zimring, Gordon Hawkins, and Sam Kamin, *Punishment and Democracy: Three Strikes and You're Out in California* (New York: Oxford University Press, 2001). A thoughtful critical review of this book may be found in Gary LaFree, "Too Much Democracy or Too Much Crime? Lessons from California's Three-Strikes Law," *Law & Social Inquiry* 27(4) (2002): 875–902.

13. Ewing v. California, 538 U.S. 11 (2003). In *Lockyer v. Andrade* (538 U.S. 63 [2003]), decided the same day as *Ewing*, the court upheld, 5–4, two consecutive terms of 25 years to life for the theft of $150 worth of videotapes from two different stores. Andrade, a longtime heroin addict, had a lengthy history of criminal convictions, including residential burglary and transportation of marijuana (two federal convictions), as well as a parole violation for escaping from federal prison. In November 2012, California's electorate approved by a two-to-one margin Proposition 36, which modified the three-strikes law so as to bar 25-to-life sentences for offenders whose third strikes were relatively minor. Jack Leonard and Maura Dolan, "Softer 3-Strikes Law Has Defense Lawyers Preparing Case Reviews," *Los Angeles Times*, November 8, 2012, AA-1.

14. U.S. Department of Justice, Bureau of Justice Statistics, "Sourcebook of Criminal Justice Statistics Online," table 6.28.2010, accessed May 2, 2012, http://www.albany.edu/sourcebook/pdf/t6282010.pdf.

15. Blumstein and Beck contended that increased prison commitments accounted for 41.5 percent of the growth in prison population between 1980 and 1996, while 57.7 of the increase was due to longer sentences. Alfred Blumstein and Allen J. Beck, "Population Growth in U.S. Prisons, 1980–1996," *Crime & Justice* 26 (1999): 43. Patrick Langan thought that higher imprisonment rates (more prison sentences for every 100 arrests) explained 51 percent of the increase between 1974 and 1986 ("America's Soaring Prison Population," 1572).

16. U.S. Department of Justice, Bureau of Justice Statistics, *Truth in Sentencing*, 1.

17. Steven Raphael and Michael A. Stoll, "Why Are So Many Americans in Prison?," discussion paper no. 1328-07 (Madison, WI: Institute for Research on Poverty, May 2007), 67, accessed May 10, 2012, http://www.irp.wisc.edu/publications/dps/pdfs/dp132807.pdf. John Pfaff stated that "the primary engine driving prison growth—at least over the past ten to fifteen years—has been changes in admissions, not time served." He added that courts were imposing prison sen-

tences on "those who otherwise would not have gone to prison for short terms." John F. Pfaff, "The Myths and Realities of Correctional Severity: Evidence from the National Corrections Reporting Program on Sentencing Practices," *American Law and Economics Review* 13 (2011): 519.

18. U.S. Department of Justice, Bureau of Justice Statistics, *Truth in Sentencing*, 8; U.S. Department of Justice, Bureau of Justice Statistics, *Sourcebook of Criminal Justice Statistics, 1990*, table 6.114, 665. Figures for the "first release" of a prisoner do not take account of parole violations, which, during this period, became an increasingly important factor in incarcerations. In 1985, 23 percent of all state prison admissions were for parole violations; by 1997, the figure was 35 percent, which is a 52 percent increase. U.S. Department of Justice, Bureau of Justice Statistics, *Truth in Sentencing*, 4.

19. Pew Center on the States, *Time Served: The High Cost, Low Return of Longer Prison Terms*, June 2012, 3, accessed June 29, 2012, http://www .pewtrusts.org/~/media/legacy/uploadedfiles/wwwpewtrustsorg /reports/sentencing_and_corrections/PrisonTimeServedpdf.pdf. It is not clear that the Pew report was using the same measure for time served as the U.S. Bureau of Justice Statistics.

20. University at Albany, Hindelang Criminal Justice Research Center, *Sourcebook of Criminal Justice Statistics, 2003*, table 6.48, 513, http:// www.albany.edu/sourcebook/pdf/t648.pdf; U.S. Department of Justice, Bureau of Justice Statistics, *Probation and Parole in the United States, 2005*, by Lauren E. Glaze and Thomas P. Bonczar (Washington, DC: GPO, 2007), table 3, 6. For 1995, 2000, and 2005, an average of 60.3 percent of adults whose sentence of probation was terminated were successful completers (ibid.). U.S. Department of Justice, Bureau of Justice Statistics, *Recidivism of Prisoners Released in 1994*, by Patrick A. Langan and David J. Levin (Washington, DC: GPO, 2002), 3, 4, 9.

21. William Spelman, "The Limited Importance of Prison Expansion," in *The Crime Drop in America*, ed. Alfred Blumstein and Joel Wallman (Cambridge: Cambridge University Press, 2000), 123.

22. Levitt, "Understanding Why Crime Fell," 178–79.

23. Bert Useem and Anne Morrison Piehl, *Prison State: The Challenge of Mass Incarceration* (New York: Cambridge University Press, 2008), 80.

24. U.S. Department of Justice, Bureau of Justice Statistics, *Prevalence*

of Imprisonment in the U.S. Population, 1974–2001, by Thomas P. Bonczar (Washington, DC: GPO, 2003), 1, 5; U.S. Department of Justice,
Bureau of Justice Statistics, *Race of Prisoners*, 7. Leasing of prisoners
had ended by 1926, so there was no financial incentive for the southern states to sentence blacks to prison. Moreover, given the region's
lack of resources at the time, the expense of long-term incarceration was a disincentive to imprisonment. Nevertheless, the South
imposed longer terms than the North, for whites as well as blacks.

25. Zimring, *City That Became Safe*, 205. One could, of course, expand
Zimring's offhand cost-benefit analysis by considering issues such as
reduced fear of crime; economic benefits of crime reduction to African American communities; high costs of incarceration to the states;
and collateral consequences of felony conviction to ex-offenders, including the loss of voting rights and eligibility for certain jobs. For
a polemical attack on these collateral consequences, see Michelle
Alexander, *The New Jim Crow: Mass Incarceration in the Age of Colorblindness* (New York: The New Press, 2010). Some analysts even
claim that the increases in incarceration of persons concentrated in
poor neighborhoods added to the social and economic adversity of
these areas and reduced community "social controls" over crime. See,
for example, James P. Lynch and William J. Sabol, "Effects of Incarceration on Informal Social Control in Communities," in *Imprisoning America: The Social Effects of Mass Incarceration*, ed. Mary Pattillo,
David Weiman, and Bruce Western (New York: Russell Sage Foundation, 2004), 135–64; Jeffrey Fagan, Valerie West, and Jan Holland,
"Reciprocal Effects of Crime and Incarceration in New York City
Neighborhoods," *Fordham Urban Law Journal* 30 (2003): 1551–1602.

26. Alfred Blumstein, "Racial Disproportionality of U.S. Prison Populations Revisited," *University of Colorado Law Review* 64 (1993): 759;
Blumstein, "On the Racial Disproportionality of United States' Prison Populations," 1259–81.

27. Langan, "Racism on Trial," 682. For an overview of the issue, see
Walker, Spohn, and DeLone, *Color of Justice*, 5th ed. (Belmont, CA:
Wadsworth, 2012), 423–26.

28. See data under 1993 in U.S. Department of Justice, Bureau of Justice
Statistics, "National Corrections Reporting Program: Time Served in
State Prison, by Offense, Release Type, Sex, and Race," accessed May
1, 2012, http://bjs.ojp.usdoj.gov/index.cfm?ty=pbdetail&iid=2045;
U.S. Department of Justice, Bureau of Justice Statistics, *Prison*

Admissions and Releases, 1982, by Stephanie Minor-Harper and Lawrence A. Greenfeld (Washington, DC: GPO, 1985), 7. Other nonracial factors that could affect time served include prison rule infractions, previous misconduct on release to probation or parole, and information contained in the presentence investigation report. Regarding the significance of the latter, see Joan Petersilia, "Racial Disparities in the Criminal Justice System: A Summary," *Crime & Delinquency* 31(1) (1985): 29–30.

29. John Pfaff has demonstrated that the ratio of felony filings to arrests has risen steadily from 1994 to 2008 (data from thirty-four states), while the ratio of prison admissions to felony filings has remained flat. He suggests that the rise in felony filings, essentially a product of prosecutorial decision making, was due to an increasing number of defendants with prior convictions. These prior convictions were, in turn, a product of the wars on drugs and crime during the crime wave from the late 1960s to the early 1990s. John Pfaff, "Prison Growth: An Empirical Assessment," *Fordham Lawyer* (Fall 2012), 7–8.

30. Federal Bureau of Investigation, Uniform Crime Reporting Statistics, "UCR Data Online," accessed December 23, 2014, http://www.ucrdatatool.gov/. The decline was not unbroken, as there were slight upticks in 2005, 2006, and 2012.

31. One might say that robbery is a bit too narrow to describe the source of public fear, as robbery is defined in the criminal codes as theft plus force or threat. To put a finer point on the matter, the public was afraid of attempted and completed robbery as well as violent assault, commonly characterized as "mugging," which has been defined as "an assault upon a person especially with the intent to rob." *The American Heritage Dictionary of the English Language*, 4th ed. (New York: Houghton Mifflin, 2006).

32. "Key Facts at a Glance: National Crime Victimization Survey Violent Crime Trends, 1973–2008," Bureau of Justice Statistics, accessed May 1, 2012, https://web.archive.org/web/20100124061405/http://bjs.ojp.usdoj.gov/content/glance/tables/viortrdtab.cfm. The gap in the trend line in figure 5.5 is for 2006, for which data were not reported by the Bureau of Justice Statistics because of methodological changes that made it incompatible with data from other years. All violent crime measured by the victim survey—rape, robbery, and aggravated and simple assault—declined in the aggregate by 71

percent from 1994 to 2010. Property crime rates, as measured by offenses reported to police, declined 45 percent from 1980 to 2010. The FBI defines serious property crimes as burglary, larceny, and motor vehicle theft. Federal Bureau of Investigation, Uniform Crime Reporting Statistics, "UCR Data Online," accessed April 12, 2012, http://www.ucrdatatool.gov/.

33. Monkkonen, *Murder in New York City*, 9.

34. Federal Bureau of Investigation, *Crime in the United States, 1980*, table 5, 76; Federal Bureau of Investigation, *Crime in the United States, 2010*, table 8, http://www.fbi.gov/about-us/cjis/ucr/crime-in -the-u.s/2010/crime-in-the-u.s.-2010/tables/table-8/10tbl08ny.xls. New York City had a major impact on the crime figures for the group of cities with populations in excess of one million, as there were only eight such cities in 1990, and New York alone counted for 37 percent of the aggregate population. The eight cities were New York, Los Angeles, Chicago, Houston, Philadelphia, San Diego, Dallas, and Detroit. Zimring contended that "the declines in New York City were the chief cause of the high declines in auto theft and homicide in the Northeast" (*Great American Crime Decline*, 14).

35. Black rates went from 41.3 per 100,000 in 1980 to 18.8 in 2009, a decline of 54 percent. For the same period, white rates fell 50 percent, from 5.2 per 100,000 to 2.6. Data from 1980 were based on a fifteen-state survey conducted from 1979 to 1981. National Center for Health Statistics, *Deaths of Hispanic Origin, 15 Reporting States, 1979–81*, series 20, no. 18 (Hyattsville, MD: National Center for Health Statistics, 1990), table 6, 27, http://www.cdc.gov/nchs/data/series/sr_20 /sr20_018.pdf. All other data were from National Center for Health Statistics, *Health, United States, 2011: With Special Feature on Socioeconomic Status and Health* (Hyattsville, MD: National Center for Health Statistics, 2012), table 24; U.S. Department of Health and Human Services, Centers for Disease Control and Prevention, "Underlying Cause of Death, 1999–2010," accessed June 8, 2012, http:// wonder.cdc.gov/ucd-icd10.html.

36. Gary LaFree, Robert M. O'Brien, and Eric Baumer, "Is the Gap between Black and White Arrest Rates Narrowing? National Trends for Personal Contact Crimes, 1960 to 2002," in *The Many Colors of Crime: Inequalities of Race, Ethnicity, and Crime in America*, ed. Ruth D. Peterson, Lauren J. Krivo, and John Hagan (New York: New York University Press, 2006), 188. A cautionary note: figures

5.7 and 5.8, drawn from Uniform Crime Reports data, combine Hispanic and white arrests, thereby inflating the white total and making the black-white ratio appear more favorable to blacks. This problem, noted by Steffensmeier et al., appears to have been especially significant beginning in the late 1980s, perhaps because of the increase at that time of the U.S. Hispanic population. Darrell Steffensmeier et al., "Reassessing Trends in Black Violent Crime, 1980–2008: Sorting Out the 'Hispanic Effect' in UCR Arrests, NCVS Offenders Estimates, and U.S. Prisoner Counts," *Criminology* 49(1) (2011): 225–26. This study found little overall change in the race-violence relationship between 1980 and 2008.

37. National Center for Health Statistics, *Deaths of Hispanic Origin*, table 6, 27. All other data were from National Center for Health Statistics, *Health, United States, 2011*, table 24; National Center for Health Statistics, "About Underlying Cause of Death," http://wonder.cdc.gov/ucd-icd10.html.

38. Rates are from the FBI's Supplementary Homicide Reports, 1980–2005, as reported in Bureau of Justice Statistics, "Homicide Trends in the U.S.," accessed June 19, 2012, https://web.archive.org/web/20111219171049/http://bjs.ojp.usdoj.gov/content/homicide/hmrt.cfm. *The Wild Bunch* (1969) is a movie about, appropriately enough, an aging outlaw gang looking to make one last big heist in the Southwest of 1913, a locale that had changed significantly since its Wild West past.

39. Table 5.9 is a combination and modification of tables from the following: O'Brien, Stockard, and Isaacson, "The Enduring Effects of Cohort Characteristics"; Robert M. O'Brien and Jean Stockard, "Can Cohort Replacement Explain Changes in the Relationship between Age and Homicide Offending?," *Journal of Quantitative Criminology* 25(1) (2009): 82. Age cohorts overlap because the exact birth year is not reported by the Uniform Crime Reports. Consequently, a 29-year-old arrested in 1970 could have been born in 1940 or 1941, and a 25-year-old could have been born in 1944 or 1945.

40. Zimring, *Great American Crime Decline*, 108, 121, 123, 125; Canadian Centre for Justice Statistics, "Homicide Survey," Statistics Canada, accessed April 16, 2012, http://www5.statcan.gc.ca/cansim/; Marc Ouimet, "Explaining the American and Canadian Crime Drop in the 1990's," *Champ pénal/Penal Field*, 1 (2004), accessed April 16, 2012, http://champpenal.revues.org/448#text. The U.S./Canada rob-

bery ratio, by my calculations, was 2.5 to 1 before 2000 and 1.5 to 1 afterward. The U.S. crime decline, in other words, created greater convergence in the rates of the two countries.

41. Johnson, Golub, and Dunlap, "Rise and Decline of Hard Drugs," 167–69.

42. Richard Curtis, "The Improbable Transformation of Inner-City Neighborhoods: Crime, Violence, Drugs, and Youth in the 1990s," *Journal of Criminal Law and Criminology* 88(4) (1998): 1259, 1263.

43. For a brief summary, see U.S. Department of Health and Human Services, National Institute on Drug Abuse, "DrugFacts: Cocaine," accessed June 22, 2012, http://www.drugabuse.gov/publications /drugfacts/cocaine.

44. Gladwell, *The Tipping Point*, 146. Positive as it was for the urban environment, the suppression of these low-level public disorders has never convincingly been shown to reduce murders, robberies, or any serious crime. It is not clear why the perpetrators of serious crime would be impacted by the suppression of low-level offenses.

45. Barry Latzer, "The Great Black Hope," *Claremont Review of Books* 9(1) (2008–2009): 34.

46. Wesley G. Skogan, *Police and Community in Chicago: A Tale of Three Cities* (New York: Oxford University Press, 2006), 242, 244.

47. Johnson, Golub, and Dunlap, "Rise and Decline of Hard Drugs," 188. For an analysis of the NYPD's tactics, see Silverman, *NYPD Battles Crime*.

48. Zimring, *City That Became Safe*, 99.

49. Spelman, "Limited Importance," 123; Levitt, "Understanding Why Crime Fell," 178–79. See also Useem and Piehl, *Prison State*.

50. The original abortion/crime analysis was in John J. Donohue III and Steven D. Levitt, "The Impact of Legalized Abortion on Crime," *Quarterly Journal of Economics* 116(2) (2001): 379–420. However, the issue gained its greatest publicity from Steven D. Levitt and Stephen J. Dubner, *Freakonomics: A Rogue Economist Explores the Hidden Side of Everything* (New York: William Morrow, 2006). Subsequently, researchers found serious methodological errors that substantially undermined Donohue and Levitt's hypothesis. Christopher L. Foote and Christopher F. Goetz, "The Impact of Legalized Abortion on Crime: Comment," *Quarterly Journal of Economics* 123(1) (2008): 407–23; Ted Joyce, "A Simple Test of Abortion and Crime," *Review of Economics and Statistics* 91(1) (2009): 112–23.

51. Phillip B. Levine et al., "Roe v. Wade and American Fertility," NBER Working Paper No. 5615 (June 1996), 2, http://www.nber .org/papers/w5615.pdf?new_window=1, 2; "Induced Abortion in the United States," Guttmacher Institute, July 2014, accessed October 15, 2015, http://www.guttmacher.org/pubs/fb_induced_abortion.html.

52. For further detail and additional proof, see Philip J. Cook and John H. Laub, "After the Epidemic: Recent Trends in Youth Violence in the United States," NBER Working Paper No. 8571 (October 2001), http://www.nber.org/papers/w8571.pdf?new_window=1.

53. H.L. Needleman et al., "Bone Lead Levels in Adjudicated Delinquents. A Case Control Study," *Neurotoxicology and Teratology* 24 (2003): 711–17.

54. Clean Air Act, 42 U.S.C. §7401 et seq. (1970); Jessica Wolpaw Reyes, "Environmental Policy as Social Policy? The Impact of Childhood Lead Exposure on Crime," NBER Working Paper No. 13097 (May 2007), 51, 3–4, http://www.nber.org/papers/w13097.pdf.

55. James L. Pirkle et al., "The Decline in Blood Lead Levels in the United States: The National Health and Nutrition Examination Surveys (NHANES)," *Journal of the American Medical Association* 272(4) (1994): 287.

56. Reyes, "Environmental Policy," 2.

57. The estimated lifetime costs for all intentional injuries in the United States between 1987 and 1990 totaled a staggering $178 billion. In 1987 alone, physical injury as a result of rape, robbery, assault, murder, and arson caused about $10 billion in potential health-related costs, $23 billion in lost productivity, and almost $145 billion in reduced quality of life. Among survivors with physical injury, rapes cost $60,000; robberies, $25,000; assaults, $22,000; and arson, $50,000. Murders cost almost $2.4 million each. Ted R. Miller, Mark A. Rossman, and Shelli B. Rossman, "Victim Costs of Violent Crime and Resulting Injuries," *Health Affairs* 12(4) (1993): 186.

58. Zimring, *City That Became Safe*, ix.

59. Homicide mortality rates for 1933 to 2006 are from "Homicide Trends in the U.S.," Bureau of Justice Statistics, accessed June 26, 2012, https://web.archive.org/web/20111219171049/http://bjs.ojp.us doj.gov/content/homicide/hmrt.cfm.

60. National Center for Health Statistics, *Health, United States, 2013: With Special Feature on Prescription Drugs* (Hyattsville, MD: National Center for Health Statistics, 2014), table 34. The white rates

for 1950 and 1960 include Hispanics, whereas the white rates in 2000 and 2009 do not. However, the proportion of whites who were Hispanic in the earlier period was too small to have a significant impact on white rates.

61. James Alan Fox and Alex R. Piquero, "Deadly Demographics: Population Characteristics and Forecasting Homicide Trends," *Crime & Delinquency* 49(3) (2003): 350.

62. Monkkonen, *Murder in New York City*, 22–23.

63. Michael Fix et al., *Migration and the Global Recession* (Washington, DC: Migration Policy Institute, September 2009), 3, http://www.migrationpolicy.org/pubs/mpi-bbcreport-sept09.pdf.

64. However, even in 2065, Hispanics will comprise a bigger proportion of the total U.S. population. Pew Research Center, *Modern Immigration Wave Brings 59 Million to U.S., Driving Population Growth and Change Through 2065*, September 28, 2015, 10, accessed January 16, 2017, http://www.pewhispanic.org/files/2015/09/2015-09-28_modern-immigration-wave_REPORT.pdf.

65. U.S. Census Bureau, *Projections of the Size and Composition of the U.S. Population: 2014 to 2060*, by Sandra L. Colby and Jennifer M. Ortman, Current Population Reports, P25-1143 (Washington, DC: GPO, 2015), 4.

66. Between 2000 and 2011, police officers per capita in cities with populations of one million or more fell back to 3.2 per 1,000, which is the same as the 1987 rate. In cities with over one-half million people, the rate fell to 2.5 per 1,000, which is 0.1 below the 1987 figure. Federal Bureau of Investigation, *Crime in the United States, 2011*, Uniform Crime Reports, release date September 2012, table 74, http://www.fbi.gov/about-us/cjis/ucr/crime-in-the-u.s/2011/crime-in-the-u.s.-2011/tables/table_74_full-time_law_enforcement_employees_by_population_group_percent_male_and_female_2011.xls. Between 2000 and 2010, per capita spending on the correctional population by states and private management declined by 7 percent. U.S. Department of Justice, Bureau of Justice Statistics, *State Corrections Expenditures, FY 1982–2010*, by Tracey Kyckelhahn (Washington, DC: GPO, 2012), table 2, 4.

67. For a brief discussion of proposed police reforms following the riots and protests that occurred after police-minority incidents in Ferguson, Missouri, and Staten Island, New York, see Drake Bennett, "Building a Better Police Department," *Bloomberg Businessweek*, De-

cember 11, 2014, http://www.businessweek.com/articles/2014-12-11/from-ferguson-to-new-york-building-a-better-police-department.

68. Erik Eckholm, "Thousands Start Life Anew with Early Prison Releases," *New York Times*, November 2, 2015, A10.

69. James Barron, "Gunman Massacres 20 Children at School in Connecticut; 28 Dead, Including Killer," *New York Times*, December 15, 2012, A1; N.R. Kleinfield, Ray Rivera, and Serge F. Kovaleski, "Newtown Killer's Obsessions, in Chilling Detail," *New York Times*, March 29, 2013, A1.

70. McVeigh, who was driven by contempt for the federal government, was executed on June 11, 2001. Christopher S. Wren, "McVeigh Is Executed for Oklahoma City Bombing," *New York Times*, June 11, 2001, http://www.nytimes.com/2001/06/11/national/11CND-EXECUTE.html.

71. Mass murders are sometimes distinguished from serial murders, because the latter involve separate events. Some analysts further differentiate spree killers from serial killers, because the spree murderer (but not the serial) apparently cools off between victimizations. For a discussion evincing considerable skepticism about the utility of the latter distinction, see James Alan Fox and Jack Levin, *Extreme Killing: Understanding Serial and Mass Murder*, 2nd ed. (Los Angeles: Sage Publications, 2012), 19–21. As for the number of actors required for a mass murder, Grant Duwe's definition excluded "collective violence," but otherwise was imprecise. Grant Duwe, "The Patterns and Prevalence of Mass Murder in Twentieth-Century America," *Justice Quarterly* 21(4) (2004): 734. Fox and Levin limited mass murders to killings committed by "one or a few assailants" (*Extreme Killing*, 136).

72. "Maniac Blows Up School, Kills 42, Mostly Children; Had Protested High Taxes," *New York Times*, May 19, 1927; Arnie Bernstein, *Bath Massacre: America's First School Bombing* (Ann Arbor: University of Michigan Press, 2009). A nonsystematic examination of *New York Times* articles from the nineteenth century uncovered only a small number of mass murders, for example, "Family of Five Murdered. J.H. Tettaton Under Arrest for Killing His Stepmother and Her Four Children in Missouri," *New York Times*, April 27, 1899. A large proportion of mass murders, like this Missouri killing, were and are familial, but homicide historian Roth stated that "marital murders remained relatively rare among European Americans and African Americans through the nineteenth century" (*American Homicide*, 254).

73. Roth, *American Homicide*, 230. Duwe found that of the twenty-five deadliest murders in his twentieth-century study, fourteen occurred between 1980 and 1999 ("Patterns and Prevalence," 752).

74. Duwe, "Patterns and Prevalence," 741.

75. A study of shootings in public places with four or more victims urelated to the shooter found that an incident occurred every 200 days in the 29-year period from 1982 to September 5, 2011, but increased to every 64 days from September 6, 2011, to October 15, 2014. Amy P. Cohen, Deborah Azrael, and Matthew Miller, "Rate of Mass Shootings Has Tripled Since 2011, Harvard Research Shows," *Mother Jones*, October 15, 2014, http://www.motherjones.com/print/261796.

76. Duwe, "Patterns and Prevalence," 749.

77. Mass murder victimizations subtracted from total homicide victimizations, 1976 to 2011, yields 683,932 conventional homicides. Dividing this figure by the 5,528 mass murders produces 123.7. Professor James Alan Fox cautions that some of the arson killings may not have been intentional murders, but they were prosecuted under the felony-murder rule (e-mail to author, May 30, 2013).

CONCLUSION. HISTORY AND THE STUDY OF CRIME

1. As I explain in my forthcoming analysis of prewar crime, this statement was not entirely true in nineteenth-century America, as the upper classes in the South engaged in considerable violence, with duels serving as a prominent example. In contemporary society, however, there are compelling reasons for the middle and upper classes to refrain from violence.

2. For a thoughtful discussion of the racialization problem, see Jeanette Covington, "Racial Classification in Criminology: The Reproduction of Racialized Crime," *Sociological Forum* 10(4) (1995): 547–68.

3. Recently, criminologists have recognized that structural explanations for violent crime are insufficient, and they are offering "structural-cultural" perspectives instead. After determining that higher rates of black, as opposed to Latino, violent crime could not be explained by structural differences alone, three analysts writing jointly concluded, "Our findings are consistent with structural-cultural approaches, . . . which suggest that it may be beneficial to move beyond 'structure only' perspectives and shift toward approaches that can account for the intersecting influences of both structural conditions *as well as* variations in culture and norms shaping race/ethnicity effects on crime." Ben Feldmeyer, Darrell Steffensmeier, and Jeffery

T. Ulmer, "Racial/Ethnic Composition and Violence: Size-of-Place Variations in Percent Black and Percent Latino Effects on Violence Rates," *Sociological Forum* 28(4) (2013): 838.

4. This is yet another matter discussed in detail in my forthcoming analysis of crime before World War II.

5. David J. Smith, "Ethnic Differences in Intergenerational Crime Patterns," *Crime and Justice* 32 (2005): 60.

6. Ibid., 75–76, 83–84. The homicide rates presented by Smith were for a three-year period ending 1999–2000.

7. Michael Tonry, ed., *Ethnicity, Crime, and Immigration: Comparative and Cross-National Perspectives* (Chicago: University of Chicago Press, 1997), 2.

8. Ibid., 1.

9. See, for example, Irina Anderson and Victoria Swainson, "Perceived Motivation for Rape: Gender Differences in Beliefs about Female and Male Rape," *Current Research in Social Psychology* 6, no. 8 (2001), accessed July 23, 2012, http://www.uiowa.edu/crisp/files/crisp/files/6.8.pdf.

10. See David Cantor and Kenneth C. Land, "Unemployment and Crime Rates in the Post–World War II United States: A Theoretical and Empirical Analysis," *American Sociological Review* 50(3) (1985): 317–32. Cantor and Land found, for the 1946–82 period, evidence of a significant positive partial effect of unemployment on crimes that contain a property component (robbery, burglary, and larceny), but no measurable economic-hardship influence on the purely violent crimes. They pointed out that in light of routine activity theory, the property-crime effects of unemployment were complicated by the extent to which dwellings and valuables might be guarded by people who were out of work. In other words, unemployment may increase motivations to steal, but it may also make it more difficult to steal by increasing the availability of guardians for valuables (ibid., 319, 320, 329). Regarding routine activity theory, see Marcus Felson and Lawrence E. Cohen, "Human Ecology and Crime: A Routine Activity Approach," *Human Ecology* 8 (1980): 389–406.

11. Jack Katz, *Seductions of Crime: Moral and Sensual Attractions in Doing Evil* (New York: Basic Books, 1988), 316.

12. Cf. Mark Cooney's argument that "the protection of the law allows high-status people to abjure lethal conflict," whereas low-status groups "can or will not depend on law" and instead develop a code

that encourages violent self-help. Mark Cooney, "The Decline of Elite Homicide," *Criminology* 35(3) (1997): 394–95, 397.

13. How to achieve group social advance is, in many respects, at the heart of the conflict between liberals (or progressives) and conservatives. The former generally favor governmental redistribution of wealth to the disadvantaged, whereas conservatives favor opportunities to advance without active governmental involvement or through governmental promotion of business.

14. Geert Hofstede, *Culture's Consequences: Comparing Values, Behaviors, Institutions, and Organizations Across Nations* (Thousand Oaks, CA: Sage Publications, 2001). Hofstede's behavioral analysis is wide-ranging and not limited to violence or violent crime. For a popular account of cultural influences on behavior, see Gladwell, *Outliers.*

15. Geert Hofstede, Gert Jan Hofstede, and Michael Minkov, *Cultures and Organizations: Software of the Mind* (New York: McGraw-Hill, 2010), 5, 6.

16. William Julius Wilson, "Being Poor, Black, and American: The Impact of Political, Economic, and Cultural Forces," *American Educator* 35(1) (2011): 22.

17. Hofstede, Hofstede, and Minkov, *Cultures and Organizations,* 5.

18. See chapter 4 for a discussion of Hmong immigrants who unsuccessfully asserted a cultural defense to rape charges when they captured brides and forced sex upon them as they had done traditionally in Laos.

19. Wilson, "Being Poor, Black, and American," 22.

20. Roth, *American Homicide,* 434.

21. Ibid.

Bibliography

Abbott, Edith. "The Civil War and the Crime Wave of 1865–70." *Social Service Review* 1(2): 1927.

Adler, Jeffrey S. *First in Violence, Deepest in Dirt: Homicide in Chicago, 1875–1920*. Cambridge, MA: Harvard University Press, 2006.

Aebi, Marcelo F., and Antonia Linde. "Is There a Crime Drop in Western Europe?" *European Journal on Criminal Policy and Research* 16 (2010): 251–77.

Alba, Richard D., John R. Logan, and Paul E. Bellair. "Living with Crime: The Implications of Racial/Ethnic Differences in Suburban Location." *Social Forces* 73 (1994): 395–434.

Alexander, Michelle. *The New Jim Crow: Mass Incarceration in the Age of Colorblindness*. New York: The New Press, 2010.

Altheimer, Irshad. "Herding and Homicide Across Nations." *Homicide Studies* 17 (2013): 27–58.

Alvarez, Lizette, and Timothy Williams. "Documents Tell Zimmerman's Side in Martin Case." *New York Times*, June 21, 2012.

The American Heritage Dictionary of the English Language. 4th ed. New York: Houghton Mifflin, 2006.

Anderson, Elijah. *Code of the Street: Decency, Violence, and the Moral Life of the Inner City*. New York: W.W. Norton, 1999.

Anderson, Irina, and Victoria Swainson. "Perceived Motivation for Rape: Gender Differences in Beliefs about Female and Male Rape." *Current Research in Social Psychology* 6 (2001). Accessed July 23, 2012. http://www.uiowa.edu/crisp/files/crisp/files/6.8.pdf.

Appy, Christian G. *Working-Class War: American Combat Soldiers and Vietnam.* Chapel Hill: University of North Carolina Press, 1993.

Archer, Dane, and Rosemary Gartner. *Violence and Crime in Cross-National Perspective.* New Haven, CT: Yale University Press, 1984.

Banfield, Edward C. *The Unheavenly City Revisited.* Boston: Little, Brown, 1974. First published in 1968.

Barnhart, Robert K., ed. *Chambers Dictionary of Etymology.* New York: W.W. Wilson, 1988.

Barnosky, Jason. "The Violent Years: Responses to Juvenile Crime in the 1950s." *Polity* 38 (2006): 314–44.

Barron, James. "Gunman Massacres 20 Children at School in Connecticut; 28 Dead, Including Killer." *New York Times,* December 15, 2012.

Baum, Matthew A., and Samuel Kernell. "Economic Class and Popular Support for Franklin Roosevelt in War and Peace." *Public Opinion Quarterly* 65 (2001): 198–229.

Baumer, Eric, Janet L. Lauritsen, Richard Rosenfeld, and Richard Wright. "The Influence of Crack Cocaine on Robbery, Burglary, and Homicide Rates: A Cross-City, Longitudinal Analysis." *Journal of Research in Crime and Delinquency* 35 (1998): 316–40.

Beach, Walter G. *Oriental Crime in California.* New York: AMS Press, 1971. First published in 1932.

Bean, Frank D., and Marta Tienda. *The Hispanic Population of the United States.* New York: Russell Sage Foundation, 1987.

Becker, Gary S., and Kevin M. Murphy. *Social Economics: Market Behavior in a Social Environment.* Cambridge, MA: Harvard University Press, 2000.

Bell, Daniel. *The End of Ideology: On the Exhaustion of Political Ideas in the Fifties.* New York: Collier Books, 1961.

Bennet, James. "Sadness and Anger After a Legend Is Mugged." *New York Times,* September 1, 1994.

Bennett, Drake. "Building a Better Police Department." *Bloomberg Businessweek,* December 11, 2014. Accessed January 3, 2015. http://www.businessweek.com/articles/2014-12-11/from-ferguson-to-new-york-building-a-better-police-department.

Bensing, Robert C., and Oliver Schroeder Jr. *Homicide in an Urban Community.* Springfield, IL: Charles C. Thomas, 1960.

Bergad, Laird W. *The Latino Population of New York City, 1990–2010.* Center for Latin American, Caribbean & Latino Studies, November 2011. Accessed January 2, 2012. http://clacls.gc.cuny.edu/files/2013/10 /The-Latino-Population-of-New-York-City-1990-2010.pdf.

Berk, Richard A., and Howard E. Aldrich. "Patterns of Vandalism during Civil Disorders as an Indicator of Selection of Targets." *American Sociological Review* 37 (1972): 533–47.

Berlin, Lisa J., Jean M. Ispa, Mark A. Fine, Patrick S. Malone, Jeanne Brooks-Gunn, and Christy Brady-Smith. "Correlates and Consequences of Spanking and Verbal Punishment for Low-Income White, African American, and Mexican American Toddlers." *Child Development* 80 (2009): 1403–20.

Bernstein, Arnie. *Bath Massacre: America's First School Bombing.* Ann Arbor: University of Michigan Press, 2009.

Black, Conrad. *Franklin Delano Roosevelt: Champion of Freedom.* New York: PublicAffairs, 2003.

Blau, Judith R., and Peter M. Blau. "The Cost of Inequality: Metropolitan Structure and Violent Crime." *American Sociological Review* 47 (1982): 114–29.

———. "Metropolitan Structure and Violent Crime." *American Sociological Review* 47 (1982): 114–29.

Block, Carolyn R. "Race/Ethnicity and Patterns of Chicago Homicide 1965 to 1981." *Crime & Delinquency* 31 (1985): 104–16.

Bloom, Julie, Richard Fausset, and Mike McPhate. "Baton Rouge Shooting Jolts a Nation on Edge." *New York Times*, July 17, 2016. https:// www.nytimes.com/2016/07/18/us/baton-rouge-shooting.html.

Blumstein, Alfred. "Disaggregating the Violence Trends." In *The Crime Drop in America*, edited by Alfred Blumstein and Joel Wallman, 13–44. Cambridge: Cambridge University Press, 2000.

———. "On the Racial Disproportionality of United States' Prison Populations." *Journal of Criminal Law and Criminology* 72 (1982): 1259–81.

———. "Racial Disproportionality of U.S. Prison Populations Revisited." *University of Colorado Law Review* 64 (1993): 743–60.

Blumstein, Alfred, and Allen J. Beck. "Population Growth in U.S. Prisons, 1980–1996." *Crime & Justice* 26 (1999): 17–61.

Blumstein, Alfred, and Joel Wallman, eds. *The Crime Drop in America.* Cambridge: Cambridge University Press, 2000.

Boudouris, James. "A Classification of Homicides." *Criminology* 11 (1973–74): 525–40.

———. "Trends in Homicide, Detroit: 1926–1968." PhD diss., Wayne State University, 1970.

Bouffard, Leana Allen, and John H. Laub. "Jail or the Army: Does Military Service Facilitate Desistance from Crime?" In *After Crime and Punishment: Pathways to Offender Reintegration*, edited by Shadd Maruna and Russ Immarigeon, 129–51. Cullompton, UK: Willan, 2004.

Bourgois, Philippe. *In Search of Respect: Selling Crack in El Barrio*. Cambridge: Cambridge University Press, 2003. First published in 1996.

Boyle, Kevin. "Auto Workers at War: Patriotism and Protest in the American Automobile Industry, 1939–1945." In *Autowork*, edited by Robert Ashford and Ronald Edsforth, 99–126. Albany: State University of New York Press, 1995.

Bracker, Milton. "Governor, Mayor Agree on Policy to Combat Gangs." *New York Times*, September 5, 1959.

Branch, Taylor. *At Canaan's Edge: America in the King Years 1965–68*. New York: Simon and Schuster, 2006.

Brearley, H.C. *Homicide in the United States*. Montclair, NJ: Patterson Smith, 1969. First published in 1932.

Brown, Claude. *Manchild in the Promised Land*. New York: Simon and Schuster, 1999. First published in 1965.

Bullock, Henry Allen. "Urban Homicide in Theory and Fact." *Journal of Criminal Law, Criminology, and Police Science* 45 (1955): 565–75.

Burnham, David. "3 of 5 Slain by Police Here Are Black, Same as the Arrest Rate." *New York Times*, August 26, 1973.

Butcher, Kristin F., and Anne Morrison Piehl. "Cross-City Evidence on the Relationship between Immigration and Crime." *Journal of Policy Analysis and Management* 17 (1998): 457–93.

Butterfield, Fox. *All God's Children: The Bosket Family and the American Tradition of Violence*. New York: Alfred A. Knopf, 1995.

Cahalan, Margaret Werner. *Historical Corrections Statistics in the United States, 1850–1984*. Rockville, MD: Bureau of Justice Statistics, December 1986. http://www.bjs.gov/content/pub/pdf/hcsus5084.pdf.

California Department of Corrections. *California Prisoners, 1960*. Sacramento: California State Printing Office, [1961?].

California State Department of Justice, Bureau of Criminal Statistics and Special Services. *Crime and Delinquency in California, 1985*. Sacramento, CA: 1986.

Camarota, Steven A. *Immigrants in the United States, 2007: A Profile of*

America's Foreign-Born Population. Washington, DC: Center for Immigration Studies (November 2007). http://www.cis.org/articles /2007/back1007.pdf.

Campbell, Angus, and Howard Schuman. *Racial Attitudes in Fifteen American Cities*. Ann Arbor, MI: Survey Research Center, Institute for Social Research, University of Michigan, 1968.

Canadian Centre for Justice Statistics. "Homicide Survey." Statistics Canada. Accessed April 16, 2012. http://www5.statcan.gc.ca/cansim/.

Cantor, David, and Lawrence E. Cohen. "Comparing Measures of Homicide Trends: Methodological and Substantive Differences in the Vital Statistics and Uniform Crime Report Time Series (1933–1975)." *Social Science Research* 9 (1980): 121–45.

Cantor, David, and Kenneth C. Land. "Unemployment and Crime Rates in the Post–World War II United States: A Theoretical and Empirical Analysis." *American Sociological Review* 50 (1985): 317–32.

Capeci, Dominic J., Jr. *The Harlem Riot of 1943*. Philadelphia: Temple University Press, 1977.

Capeci, Dominic J., Jr., and Martha Wilkerson. "The Detroit Rioters of 1943: A Reinterpretation." *Michigan Historical Review* 16 (1990): 49–72.

Capote, Truman. *In Cold Blood: A True Account of a Multiple Murder and Its Consequences*. New York: Vintage, 1965.

Carson, Jamie L., and Benjamin A. Kleinerman. "A Switch in Time Saves Nine: Institutions, Strategic Actors, and FDR's Court-Packing Plan." *Public Choice* 113 (2002): 301–24.

Carter, Gregg Lee. "Hispanic Rioting during the Civil Rights Era." *Sociological Forum* 7 (1992): 301–22.

Chauhan, Preeti, Magdalena Cerdá, Steven F. Messner, Melissa Tracy, Kenneth Tardiff, and Sandro Galea. "Race/Ethnic-Specific Homicide Rates in New York City: Evaluating the Impact of Broken Windows Policing and Crack Cocaine Markets." *Homicide Studies* 15 (2011): 268–90.

Chernick, Howard, and Cordelia Reimers. "Welfare Reform and New York City's Low-Income Population." *Economic Policy Review* 7 (2001): 83–97.

Chicago Police Department. *Chicago Police Annual Report, 1970*. Accessed December 5, 2011. https://portal.chicagopolice.org/portal /page/portal/ClearPath/News/Statistical%20Reports/Annual%20 Reports/1970_AR.pdf.

————. *Statistical Summary, 1980.* Accessed December 5, 2011. https://
portal.chicagopolice.org/portal/page/portal/ClearPath/News/Sta
tistical%20Reports/Annual%20Reports/1980_AR.pdf.

Child Trends, DataBank. "Family Structure: Indicators on Children and
Youth." (2015): appendix 1, 9. http://www.childtrends.org/wp-con
tent/uploads/2015/03/59_Family_Structure.pdf.

Chilton, Roland. "Homicide Arrest Trends and the Impact of Demo-
graphic Changes on a Set of U.S. Central Cities." In *Trends, Risks,
and Interventions in Lethal Violence: Proceedings of the Third Annual
Spring Symposium of the Homicide Research Working Group,* edited by
Carolyn Block and Richard Block, 99–113. Washington, DC: U.S.
Government Printing Office, 1995.

Chin, Ko-lin. *Chinese Subculture and Criminality.* Westport, CT: Greenwood Press, 1990.

Chiricos, Theodore G. "Rates of Crime and Unemployment: An Analysis
of Aggregate Research Evidence." *Social Problems* 34 (1987): 187–212.

Chu, Rebekah, Craig Rivera, and Colin Loftin. "Herding and Homicide:
An Examination of the Nisbett-Reaves Hypothesis." *Social Forces* 78
(2000): 971–87.

City of Boston. *Boston Police Department, 1981–1982 Annual Report.* Accessed December 16, 2012. http://archive.org/stream/annualreport
ofpo8182bost#page/no/mode/1up.

————. *Fifty-Fifth Annual Report of the Police Commissioner for the City of
Boston for the Year Ending November 30, 1960.* Accessed December 8,
2011. http://archive.org/stream/annualreportofpo1960bost#page/n2
/mode/1up.

————. *Sixty-Fifth Annual Report of the Police Commissioner for the City
of Boston for the Year Ending December 31, 1970.* Accessed December
16, 2012. http://archive.org/stream/annualreportofpo1970bost#page
/n6/mode/1up.

————. *Sixty-Sixth Annual Report of the Police Commissioner for the City
of Boston for the Year Ending December 31, 1971.* Accessed December
16, 2012. http://archive.org/stream/annualreportofpo1971bost#page
/n7/mode/2up.

Clark, Rebecca L., and Scott A. Anderson. *Illegal Aliens in Federal,
State, and Local Criminal Justice Systems.* Washington, DC: The
Urban Institute, June 30, 1999. https://www.ncjrs.gov/pdffiles1/nij
/grants/181049.pdf.

Clarke, James W. "Black-on-Black Violence." *Society* 33 (1996): 46–50.

Cleaver, Eldridge. *Soul on Ice*. New York: Dell, 1991. First published in 1968.

Cloward, Richard A., and Lloyd C. Ohlin. *Delinquency and Opportunity: A Theory of Delinquent Gangs*. New York: Free Press, 1960.

Cogan, John. "The Decline in Black Teenage Employment: 1950–70." *American Economic Review* 72 (1982): 621–38.

Cohen, Albert K. *Delinquent Boys: The Culture of the Gang*. New York: Free Press, 1955.

Cohen, Amy P., Deborah Azrael, and Matthew Miller. "Rate of Mass Shootings Has Tripled Since 2011, Harvard Research Shows." *Mother Jones*, October 15, 2014. http://www.motherjones.com/print /261796.

Cohen, Lawrence E., and Kenneth C. Land. "Age Structure and Crime: Symmetry versus Asymmetry and the Projection of Crime Rates through the 1990s." *American Sociological Review* 52 (1987): 170–83.

Collins, William J., and Robert A. Margo. "The Economic Aftermath of the 1960s Riots in American Cities: Evidence from Property Values." Vanderbilt University and NBER, May 2004. Accessed November 13, 2011. http://aeaweb.org/annual_mtg_papers/2005/0109_1015_0203 .pdf.

Condran, John G. "Changes in White Attitudes toward Blacks: 1963–1977." *Public Opinion Quarterly* 43 (1979): 463–76.

Cook, Philip J., and John H. Laub. "After the Epidemic: Recent Trends in Youth Violence in the United States." NBER Working Paper No. 8571, October 2001. http://www.nber.org/papers/w8571.pdf?new _window=1.

Cooney, Mark. "The Decline of Elite Homicide." *Criminology* 35 (1997): 381–407.

Cork, Daniel. "Examining Space-Time Interaction in City-Level Homicide Data: Crack Markets and the Diffusion of Guns among Youth." *Journal of Quantitative Criminology* 15 (1999): 379–406.

Courtwright, David T. "A Century of American Narcotic Policy." In *Treating Drug Problems*, vol. 2, edited by Dean R. Gerstein and Henrick J. Harwood, 1–62. Washington, DC: National Academy Press, 1992.

———. *Violent Land: Single Men and Social Disorder from the Frontier to the Inner City*. Cambridge, MA: Harvard University Press, 1996.

Covington, Jeanette. "Racial Classification in Criminology: The Reproduction of Racialized Crime." *Sociological Forum* 10 (1995): 547–68.

Crane, Jonathan. "The Epidemic Theory of Ghettos and Neighborhood Effects on Dropping Out and Teenage Childbearing." *American Journal of Sociology* 96 (1991): 1226–59.

Curtis, Lynn A. *Violence, Race, and Culture*. Lexington, MA: D.C. Heath, 1975.

Curtis, Richard. "The Improbable Transformation of Inner-City Neighborhoods: Crime, Violence, Drugs, and Youth in the 1990s." *Journal of Criminal Law and Criminology* 88 (1998): 1233–76.

Davey, Monica, and Julie Bosman. "Grand Jury Declines to Indict Police Officer in Ferguson Killing." *New York Times*, November 25, 2014, A1.

Davis, John A. "Blacks, Crime, and American Culture." *Annals of the American Academy of Political and Social Science* 423 (1976): 89–98.

DeBruyne, Nese F., and Anne Leland. "American War and Military Operations Casualties: Lists and Statistics." *CRS Report for Congress RL32492*. Congressional Research Service, Library of Congress, Washington, DC (January 2, 2015).

DiIulio, John J., Jr. "My Black Crime Problem, and Ours." *City Journal* (Spring 1996). http://www.city-journal.org/html/6_2_my_black.html.

DiPietro, Stephanie M., and Robert J. Bursik Jr. "Studies of the New Immigration: The Dangers of Pan-Ethnic Classifications." *Annals of the American Academy of Political and Social Science* 641 (2012): 247–67.

Donohue, John J., III, and Steven D. Levitt. "The Impact of Legalized Abortion on Crime." *Quarterly Journal of Economics* 116 (2001): 379–420.

D'Souza, Dinesh. *The End of Racism: Principles for a Multicultural Society*. New York: Free Press, 1995.

Duany, Jorge. "The Census Undercount, the Underground Economy, and Undocumented Migration: The Case of Dominicans in Santurce, Puerto Rico." Ethnographic Evaluation of the 1990 Decennial Census Report No. 17, 1992. Accessed December 23, 2012. http://www.census.gov/srd/papers/pdf/ev92-17.pdf.

Durkheim, Emile. *Suicide: A Study in Sociology*. Translated by John A. Spaulding and George Simpson. Glencoe, IL: Free Press, 1951. First published in 1897.

Duwe, Grant. "The Patterns and Prevalence of Mass Murder in Twentieth-Century America." *Justice Quarterly* 21 (2004): 729–61.

Eck, John E., and Edward R. Maguire. "Have Changes in Policing Reduced Violent Crime? An Assessment of the Evidence." In *The Crime Drop in America*, edited by Alfred Blumstein and Joel Wallman, 207–65. Cambridge: Cambridge University Press, 2000.

Eckberg, Douglas Lee. "Estimates of Early Twentieth-Century U.S. Homicide Rates: An Econometric Forecasting Approach." *Demography* 32 (1995): 1–16.

Eckholm, Erik. "Thousands Start Life Anew with Early Prison Releases." *New York Times*, November 2, 2015, A10.

Eder, Richard. "Night Cloaks Crime in City's Toughest Block." *New York Times*, July 25, 1960.

Ehrlich, Isaac. "Crime, Punishment, and the Market for Offenses." *The Journal of Economic Perspectives* 10 (1996): 43–67.

Elder, Glen H. *Children of the Great Depression: Social Change in Life Experience*. Chicago: University of Chicago Press, 1974.

Erlanger, Howard S. "The Empirical Status of the Subculture of Violence Thesis." *Social Problems* 22 (1974): 280–92.

Erskine, Hazel. "The Polls: Fear of Violence and Crime." *Public Opinion Quarterly* 38 (1974): 131–45.

Eschbach, Karl, Jim P. Stimpson, Yong-Fang Kuo, and James S. Goodwin. "Mortality of Foreign-Born and US-Born Hispanic Adults at Younger Ages: A Reexamination of Recent Patterns." *American Journal of Public Health* 97 (2007): 1297–1304.

Exec. Order 8802, 3 C.F.R. 957 (1938–43 Compilation). "Prohibition of Discrimination in the Defense Industry." June 25, 1941.

Fagan, Jeffrey, Valerie West, and Jan Holland. "Reciprocal Effects of Crime and Incarceration in New York City Neighborhoods." *Fordham Urban Law Journal* 30 (2003): 1551–1602.

Fairlie, Robert W., and William A. Sundstrom. "The Racial Unemployment Gap in Long-Run Perspective." *American Economic Review* 87 (1997): 306–10.

Farley, Reynolds. "The Waning of American Apartheid?" *Contexts* 10 (2011): 36–43.

Federal Bureau of Investigation. *Age-Specific Arrest Rates and Race-Specific Arrest Rates for Selected Offenses, 1965–1992*. Washington, DC: Government Printing Office, 1993.

———. *Crime in the United States*. Uniform Crime Reports. Washington, DC: Government Printing Office, 1940–1993.

———. *Crime in the United States, 2000*. Uniform Crime Reports. Re-

lease date October 22, 2001. http://www.fbi.gov/about-us/cjis/ucr
/crime-in-the-u.s/2000/toc00.pdf.

———. *Crime in the United States, 2005.* Uniform Crime Reports. Release date September 2006. http://www2.fbi.gov/ucr/05cius/.

———. *Crime in the United States, 2007.* Uniform Crime Reports. Release date September 2008. http://www2.fbi.gov/ucr/cius2007
/index.html.

———. *Crime in the United States, 2010.* Uniform Crime Reports. Release date September 2011. http://www.fbi.gov/about-us/cjis/ucr
/crime-in-the-u.s/2010/crime-in-the-u.s.-2010.

———. *Crime in the United States, 2011.* Uniform Crime Reports. Release date September 2012. http://www.fbi.gov/about-us/cjis/ucr
/crime-in-the-u.s/2011/crime-in-the-u.s.-2011.

———. *Preliminary Annual Uniform Crime Report, January–December,
2011.* Accessed June 29, 2012. http://www.fbi.gov/about-us/cjis/ucr
/crime-in-the-u.s/2011/preliminary-annual-ucr-jan-dec-2011/data
-tables/table-3.

———. *Uniform Crime Reports for the United States and Its Possessions.*
Washington, DC: Government Printing Office, 1950.

———. *Uniform Crime Reports for the United States and Its Possessions.*
Washington, DC: Government Printing Office, 1951.

Federal Security Agency, U.S. Public Health Service: *Vital Statistics of the
United States 1943,* Part 1. Washington, DC: Government Printing
Office, 1945.

Feldmeyer, Ben, Darrell Steffensmeier, and Jeffery T. Ulmer. "Racial/
Ethnic Composition and Violence: Size☒of☒Place Variations in Percent Black and Percent Latino Effects on Violence Rates." *Sociological Forum* 28, no. 4 (2013): 811–41.

Felson, Marcus, and Lawrence E. Cohen. "Human Ecology and Crime:
A Routine Activity Approach." *Human Ecology* 8 (1980): 389–406.

Ferdinand, Theodore N. "The Criminal Patterns of Boston Since 1849."
American Journal of Sociology 73 (1967): 84–99.

———. "Demographic Shifts and Criminality: An Inquiry." *British
Journal of Criminology* 10 (1970): 169–75.

Fernandez, Manny, Richard Pérez-Peña, and Jonah Engel Bromwich.
"Five Dallas Officers Were Killed as Payback, Police Chief Says."
New York Times, July 8, 2016. https://www.nytimes.com/2016/07/09
/us/dallas-police-shooting.html.

Fernández, Nelson A. "Nutrition in Puerto Rico." *Cancer Research* 35 (1975): 3272–91.

Feyrer, James, Bruce Sacerdote, Ariel Dora Stern, Albert Saiz, and William C. Strange. "Did the Rust Belt Become Shiny? A Study of Cities and Counties That Lost Steel and Auto Jobs in the 1980s." In *Brookings-Wharton Papers on Urban Affairs 2007*, edited by Gary Burtless and Janet Rothenberg Pack. Washington, DC: Brookings Institution Press, 2007.

Fine, Sidney. *Violence in the Model City: The Cavanagh Administration, Race Relations, and the Detroit Riot of 1967.* Ann Arbor: University of Michigan Press, 1989.

Fischer, David Hackett. *Albion's Seed: Four British Folkways in America.* New York: Oxford University Press, 1989.

Fischer, Hannah, Kim Klarman, and Mari-Jana Oboroceanu. "American War and Military Operations Casualties: Lists and Statistics." *CRS Report for Congress RL32492.* Congressional Research Service, Library of Congress, Washington, DC (May 14, 2008).

Fishman, Sarah. *The Battle for Children: World War II, Youth Crime, and Juvenile Justice in Twentieth-Century France.* Cambridge, MA: Harvard University Press, 2002.

Fitzpatrick, Joseph P. *The Stranger Is Our Own: Reflections on the Journey of Puerto Rican Migrants.* Kansas City, MO: Sheed and Ward, 1996.

Fix, Michael, Demetrios G. Papademetriou, Jeanne Batalova, Aaron Terrazas, Serena Yi-Ying Lin, and Michelle Mittelstadt. *Migration and the Global Recession.* Washington, DC: Migration Policy Institute, September 2009. http://www.migrationpolicy.org/pubs/mpi-bbc report-sept09.pdf.

Fleagle, Fred K. *The Puerto Rican Experience.* Reprinted as *Social Problems in Porto Rico.* New York: Arno Press, 1975. First published in 1917.

Fletcher, George P. *A Crime of Self-Defense: Bernhard Goetz and the Law on Trial.* Chicago: University of Chicago Press, 1988.

Foote, Christopher L., and Christopher F. Goetz. "The Impact of Legalized Abortion on Crime: Comment." *Quarterly Journal of Economics* 123 (2008): 407–23.

Fortner, Michael Javen. *Black Silent Majority: The Rockefeller Drug Laws and the Politics of Punishment.* Cambridge, MA: Harvard University Press, 2015.

Fox, James Alan. "Demographics and U.S. Homicide." In *The Crime Drop in America*, edited by Alfred Blumstein and Joel Wallman, 288–317. Cambridge: Cambridge University Press, 2000.

———. *Trends in Juvenile Violence: A Report to the United States Attorney General on Current and Future Rates of Juvenile Offending*. Washington, DC: Bureau of Justice Statistics, March 1996.

Fox, James Alan, and Jack Levin. *Extreme Killing: Understanding Serial and Mass Murder*. 2nd ed. Los Angeles: Sage Publications, 2012.

Fox, James Alan, and Alex R. Piquero. "Deadly Demographics: Population Characteristics and Forecasting Homicide Trends." *Crime & Delinquency* 49 (2003): 339–59.

Frey, William H. "Central City White Flight: Racial and Nonracial Causes." *American Sociological Review* 44 (1979): 425–48.

———. "The New Great Migration: Black Americans' Return to the South, 1965–2000." In *Redefining Urban and Suburban America: Evidence from Census 2000*, vol. 2, edited by Alan Berube, Bruce Katz, and Robert E. Lang, 87–110. Washington, DC: Brookings Institution Press, 2005.

Friedman, Myra, and Michael Daly. "My Neighbor Bernie Goetz." *New York Magazine*, February 18, 1985.

Fukuyama, Francis. *The Great Disruption: Human Nature and the Reconstitution of Social Order*. New York: Free Press, 1999.

Galbraith, John Kenneth. *The Affluent Society*. New York: Houghton Mifflin, 1958.

Galea, Sandro, Adam Karpati, and Bruce Kennedy. "Social Capital and Violence in the United States, 1974–1993." *Social Science and Medicine* 55 (2002): 1373–83.

Gallin, Alice J. "The Cultural Defense: Undermining the Policies against Domestic Violence." *Boston College Law Review* 35 (1994): 723–45.

Garafolo, James, and L. Paul Sutton. *Compensating Victims of Violent Crime: Potential Costs and Coverage of a National Program*. Albany, NY: Criminal Justice Research Center, 1977.

Garland, David. *The Culture of Control: Crime and Social Order in Contemporary Society*. Chicago: University of Chicago Press, 2001.

Gartner, Rosemary, and Robert Nash Parker. "Cross-National Evidence on Homicide and the Age Structure of the Population." *Social Forces* 69 (1990): 351–71.

Gastil, Raymond. "Homicide and a Regional Culture of Violence." *American Sociological Review* 36 (1971): 412–27.

Geis, Gilbert. "Statistics Concerning Race and Crime." *Crime & Delinquency* 11 (1965): 142–50.

Gilbert, James. *A Cycle of Outrage: America's Reaction to the Juvenile Delinquent in the 1950s.* New York: Oxford University Press, 1986.

Gladwell, Malcolm. *Outliers: The Story of Success.* New York: Little, Brown, 2008.

———. *The Tipping Point: How Little Things Can Make a Big Difference.* Boston: Little, Brown, 2000.

Glaeser, Edward L., Bruce Sacerdote, and Jose A. Scheinkman. "Crime and Social Interactions." *Quarterly Journal of Economics* 111 (1996): 507–48.

Glazer, Nathan, and Daniel Patrick Moynihan. *Beyond the Melting Pot: The Negroes, Puerto Ricans, Jews, Italians, and Irish of New York City.* Cambridge, MA: MIT Press, 1963.

Glueck, Sheldon, and Eleanor Glueck. *Unraveling Juvenile Delinquency.* Cambridge, MA: Harvard University Press, 1950.

Goertzel, Ted. "Econometric Modeling as Junk Science." *The Skeptical Inquirer* 26 (2002): 19–23.

Goffman, Alice. *On the Run: Fugitive Life in an American City.* Chicago: University of Chicago Press, 2014.

Gold, Martin. "Suicide, Homicide, and the Socialization of Aggression." *American Journal of Sociology* 63 (1958): 651–61.

Gottfredson, Michael R., and Travis Hirschi. *A General Theory of Crime.* Stanford, CA: Stanford University Press, 1990.

Governor's Commission on the Los Angeles Riots. *Violence in the City—An End or a Beginning?* 1965. Accessed November 12, 2011. http://www.usc.edu/libraries/archives/cityinstress/mccone/contents.html.

Granovetter, Mark. "Threshold Models of Collective Behavior." *The American Journal of Sociology* 83 (1978): 1420–43.

Grantham, Dewey W. *The South in Modern America: A Region at Odds.* New York: HarperCollins, 1994.

Green, Edward. "Race, Social Status, and Criminal Arrest." *American Sociological Review* 35 (1970): 476–90.

Greene, Judith A. "Zero Tolerance: A Case Study of Police Policies and Practices in New York City." *Crime & Delinquency* 45 (1999): 171–87.

Gregory, James N. *The Southern Diaspora: How the Great Migrations of*

Black and White Southerners Transformed America. Chapel Hill: University of North Carolina Press, 2005.

Grimshaw, Allen D. "Lawlessness and Violence in America and Their Special Manifestations in Changing Negro-White Relationships." *Journal of Negro History* 44 (1959): 52–72.

Grodzins, Morton. *The Metropolitan Area as a Racial Problem.* Pittsburgh: University of Pittsburgh Press, 1958.

Grogger, Jeff, and Michael Willis. "The Emergence of Crack Cocaine and the Rise in Urban Crime Rates." *Review of Economics and Statistics* 82 (2000): 519–29.

Grusky, David B., Bruce Western, and Christopher Wimer, eds. *The Great Recession.* New York: Russell Sage Foundation, 2011.

Grutzner, Charles. "City Puerto Ricans Found Ill-Housed." *New York Times,* October 4, 1949.

Gugliotta, Guy. "New Estimate Raises Civil War Death Toll." *New York Times,* April 3, 2012.

Gurr, Ted Robert. "Historical Trends in Violent Crime: A Critical Review of the Evidence." *Crime and Justice* 3 (1981): 295–353.

Guttmacher Institute. "Induced Abortion in the United States." July 2014. Accessed October 15, 2015. http://www.guttmacher.org/pubs /fb_induced_abortion.html.

Hackney, Sheldon. "Southern Violence." *American Historical Review* 74 (1969): 906–25.

Hadley, Eleanor M. "A Critical Analysis of the Wetback Problem." *Law and Contemporary Problems* 21 (1956): 334–57.

Hagan, John. *Northern Passage: American Vietnam War Resisters in Canada.* Cambridge, MA: Harvard University Press, 2001.

Handlin, Oscar. *The Newcomers: Negroes and Puerto Ricans in a Changing Metropolis.* Cambridge, MA: Harvard University Press, 1959.

Harer, Miles D., and Darrell Steffensmeier. "The Differing Effects of Economic Inequality on Black and White Rates of Violence." *Social Forces* 70 (1992): 1035–54.

Harlan, Howard. "Five Hundred Homicides." *Journal of Criminal Law and Criminology* 40 (1950): 736–52.

Harries, Keith D. "The Historical Geography of Homicide in the U.S., 1935–1980." *Geoforum* 16 (1985): 73–83.

Harrington, Michael. *The Other America.* New York: Scribner, 1997. First published in 1962.

Hayner, Norman S. "Social Factors in Oriental Crime." *American Journal of Sociology* 43 (1938): 908–19.

Heath, Linda, and Kevin Gilbert. "Mass Media and Fear of Crime." *American Behavioral Scientist* 39 (1996): 379–86.

Heim, Carol E. "Structural Changes: Regional and Urban." In *The Twentieth Century*, vol. 3 of *The Cambridge Economic History of the United States*, edited by Stanley L. Engerman and Robert E. Gallman, 93–190. Cambridge: Cambridge University Press, 2000.

Helmer, John. *Drugs and Minority Oppression.* New York: Seabury Press, 1975.

Hendin, Herbert. "Black Suicide." *Archives of General Psychiatry* 21(4) (1969): 407–22.

———. *Suicide in America.* New York: W.W. Norton, 1995.

Henry, Andrew F., and James F. Short Jr. *Suicide and Homicide: Some Economic, Sociological, and Psychological Aspects of Aggression.* Glencoe, IL: Free Press, 1954.

Herd, Denise. "Migration, Cultural Transformation and the Rise of Black Liver Cirrhosis Mortality." *British Journal of Addiction* 80 (1985): 397–410.

Hirschi, Travis, and Michael Gottfredson. "Age and the Explanation of Crime." *American Journal of Sociology* 89 (1983): 552–84.

Hofstede, Geert. *Culture's Consequences: Comparing Values, Behaviors, Institutions, and Organizations Across Nations.* Thousand Oaks, CA: Sage Publications, 2001.

Hofstede, Geert, Gert Jan Hofstede, and Michael Minkov. *Cultures and Organizations: Software of the Mind.* New York: McGraw-Hill, 2010.

Inciardi, James A. "Heroin Use and Street Crime." *Crime & Delinquency* 25 (1979): 335–46.

———. *The War on Drugs III: The Continuing Saga of the Mysteries and Miseries of Intoxication, Addiction, Crime, and Public Policy.* Boston: Allyn and Bacon, 2002.

Inciardi, James A., and Anne E. Pottieger. "Drug Use and Street Crime in Miami: An (Almost) Twenty-Year Retrospective." In *The American Drug Scene*, 4th ed., edited by James A. Inciardi and Karen McElrath, 361–83. Los Angeles: Roxbury, 2004.

"Induced Abortion in the United States." Guttmacher Institute, 2011. Accessed June 27, 2012. http://www.guttmacher.org/pubs/fb_in duced_abortion.html.

Jacobs, Jane. *The Death and Life of Great American Cities*. New York: Random House, 1993. First published in 1961.

Jacobson, Alvin L. "Crime Trends in Southern and Nonsouthern Cities: A Twenty-Year Perspective." *Social Forces* 54(1) (1975): 226–42.

Jacobson, Robin Dale. *The New Nativism: Proposition 187 and the Debate over Immigration*. Minneapolis: University of Minnesota Press, 2008.

Jargowsky, Paul A. *Stunning Progress, Hidden Problems: The Dramatic Decline of Concentrated Poverty in the 1990s*. Washington, DC: The Brookings Institution, May 2003. Accessed March 24, 2012. http://www.brookings.edu/reports/2003/05demographics_jargowsky.aspx.

Johnson, Bruce D., Andrew Golub, and Eloise Dunlap. "The Rise and Decline of Hard Drugs, Drug Markets, and Violence in Inner-City New York." In *The Crime Drop in America*, edited by Alfred Blumstein and Joel Wallman, 164–206. Cambridge: Cambridge University Press, 2000.

Johnson, David R. *American Law Enforcement: A History*. St. Louis: Forum Press, 1981.

Johnson, Hans P. "Birth Rates in California." *California Counts* 9 (November 2007). San Francisco Public Policy Institute of California. http://www.ppic.org/content/pubs/cacounts/CC_1107HJCC.pdf.

Johnson, Lyndon B. Commencement address at Howard University, June 4, 1965. Accessed August 30, 2011. http://www.lbjlib.utexas.edu /johnson/archives.hom/speeches.hom/650604.asp.

Johnson, Mary A. "Crime: New Frontier; Jesse Jackson Calls It Top Civil-Rights Issue." *Chicago Sun-Times*, November 29, 1993.

Joyce, Ted. "A Simple Test of Abortion and Crime." *Review of Economics and Statistics* 91 (2009): 112–23.

Kandel, Denise B. "Drug and Drinking Behavior among Youth." *Annual Review of Sociology* 6 (1980): 235–85.

Karmen, Andrew. *New York Murder Mystery: The True Story behind the Crime Crash of the 1990s*. New York: New York University Press, 2000.

Kasarda, John D. "Industrial Restructuring and the Changing Location of Jobs." In *Economic Trends*, vol. 1 of *State of the Union: America in the 1990s*, edited by Reynolds Farley. New York: Russell Sage Foundation, 1995.

———. "Inner-City Concentrated Poverty and Neighborhood Distress: 1970 to 1990." *Housing Policy Debate* 4 (1993): 253–302.

Katz, Jack. *Seductions of Crime: Moral and Sensual Attractions in Doing Evil.* New York: Basic Books, 1988.

Kennedy, John F. "Inaugural Address." January 20, 1961. American Presidency Project (Gerhard Peters and John T. Woolley). http://www.presidency.ucsb.edu/ws/?pid=8032.

———. *Profiles in Courage.* New York: Black Dog and Leventhal, 1984. First published in 1955.

Kennedy, Randall. "The State, Criminal Law, and Racial Discrimination: A Comment." *Harvard Law Review* 107 (1994): 1255–78.

Kennett, Lee, and James LaVerne Anderson. *The Gun in America: The Origins of a National Dilemma.* Westport, CT: Greenwood Press, 1975.

Kenney, Dennis Jay. *Crime, Fear, and the New York City Subways: The Role of Citizen Action.* New York: Praeger, 1987.

———. "Crime on the Subways: Measuring the Effectiveness of the Guardian Angels." *Justice Quarterly* 3 (1986): 481–96.

Kihss, Peter. "Liebowitz Urges Cut in Migration to Combat Crime." *New York Times,* September 25, 1959.

Klebba, A. Joan. "Homicide Trends in the United States, 1900–74." *Public Health Reports* 90 (1975): 195–204.

Kleinfield, N.R., Ray Rivera, and Serge F. Kovaleski. "Newtown Killer's Obsessions, in Chilling Detail." *New York Times,* March 29, 2013.

Kowalski, Gregory S., and Thomas A. Petee. "Sunbelt Effects on Homicide Rates." *Sociology and Social Research* 75 (1991): 73–79.

Krugman, Paul. "It's a Different Country." *New York Times,* June 9, 2008.

LaFree, Gary. *Losing Legitimacy: Street Crime and the Decline of Social Institutions in America.* Boulder, CO: Westview Press, 1998.

———. "Too Much Democracy or Too Much Crime? Lessons from California's Three-Strikes Law." *Law & Social Inquiry* 27 (2002): 875–902.

LaFree, Gary, and Kriss A. Drass. "Counting Crime Booms among Nations: Evidence for Homicide Victimization Rates, 1956 to 1998." *Criminology* 40 (2002): 769–800.

———. "The Effect of Changes in Intraracial Income Inequality and Educational Attainment on Changes in Arrest Rates for African Americans and Whites, 1957 to 1990." *American Sociological Review* 61 (1996): 614–34.

LaFree, Gary, Robert M. O'Brien, and Eric Baumer. "Is the Gap between Black and White Arrest Rates Narrowing? National Trends for Personal Contact Crimes, 1960 to 2002." In *The Many Colors of Crime: Inequalities of Race, Ethnicity, and Crime in America*, edited by Ruth D. Peterson, Lauren J. Krivo, and John Hagan, 179–98. New York: New York University Press, 2006.

Land, Kenneth C., Patricia L. McCall, and Lawrence E. Cohen. "Characteristics of U.S. Cities with Extreme (High or Low) Crime Rates: Results of Discriminant Analyses of 1960, 1970, and 1980 Data." *Social Indicators Research* 24 (1991): 209–31.

Lane, Roger. *Murder in America: A History*. Columbus: Ohio State University Press, 1997.

———. *Roots of Violence in Black Philadelphia, 1860–1900*. Cambridge, MA: Harvard University Press, 1986.

Langan, Patrick A. "America's Soaring Prison Population." *Science* 251 (1991): 1568–73.

———. "Racism on Trial: New Evidence to Explain the Racial Composition of Prisons in the United States." *Journal of Criminal Law and Criminology* 76 (1985): 666–83.

Larson, Erik. *The Devil in the White City: Murder, Magic, and Madness at the Fair That Changed America*. New York: Crown Publishers, 2003.

Latzer, Barry. "The Great Black Hope." *Claremont Review of Books* 9 (2008–2009): 32–36.

Laub, John H., and Robert J. Sampson. "Sheldon and Eleanor Glueck's Unraveling Juvenile Delinquency Study: The Lives of 1,000 Boston Men in the Twentieth Century." In *Looking at Lives: American Longitudinal Studies of the Twentieth Century*, edited by Erin Phelps, Frank F. Furstenburg Jr., and Anne Colby, 87–115. New York: Russell Sage Foundation, 2002.

Lee, Denny. "Years of the Dragons." *New York Times*, May 11, 2003.

Lee, Matthew R., William B. Bankston, Timothy C. Hayes, and Shaun A. Thomas. "Revisiting the Southern Culture of Violence." *Sociological Quarterly* 48 (2007): 253–75.

Lee, Matthew R., Shaun A. Thomas, and Graham C. Ousey. "Southern Culture and Homicide: Examining the Cracker Culture/Black Rednecks Thesis." *Deviant Behavior* 31 (2009): 60–96.

Leigh, Wilhelmina A., and Danielle Huff. *African Americans and Home-ownership: Separate and Unequal, 1940 to 2006*. Washington, DC: Joint Center for Political and Economic Studies (2007). Accessed March 23, 2012. http://www.northstarnews.com/userimages/refer

ences/African%20Americans%20and%20Home%20Ownership
.Brief_Joint%20Center%20for%20Political%20Studies.pdf.

Leland, Anne, and Mari-Jana Oboroceanu. "American War and Military Operations Casualties: Lists and Statistics." *CRS Report for Congress RL 32492.* Congressional Research Service, Library of Congress. Washington, DC (February 26, 2010). http://fpc.state.gov/docu ments/organization/139347.pdf.

Leonard, Jack, and Maura Dolan. "Softer 3-Strikes Law Has Defense Lawyers Preparing Case Reviews." *Los Angeles Times,* November 8, 2012.

Lester, David. *Crime and the Native American.* Springfield, IL: Charles C. Thomas, 1999.

Leuchtenburg, William E. *Franklin D. Roosevelt and the New Deal, 1932–1940.* New York: Harper and Row, 1963.

Levine, Harry G., and Craig Reinarman. "From Prohibition to Regulation: Lessons from Alcohol Policy for Drug Policy." *Milbank Quarterly* 69 (1991): 461–94.

Levine, Phillip B., Douglas Staiger, Thomas J. Kane, and David J. Zimmerman. "Roe v. Wade and American Fertility." NBER Working Paper No. 5615, June 1996. http://www.nber.org/papers/w5615 .pdf?new_window=1.

Levitt, Steven D. "The Limited Role of Changing Age Structure in Explaining Aggregate Crime Rates." *Criminology* 37 (1999): 581–97.

———. "Understanding Why Crime Fell in the 1990's: Four Factors That Explain the Decline and Six That Do Not." *Journal of Economic Perspectives* 18 (2004): 163–90.

Levitt, Steven D., and Stephen J. Dubner. *Freakonomics: A Rogue Economist Explores the Hidden Side of Everything.* New York: William Morrow, 2006.

Levy, Jerrold E., and Stephen J. Kunitz. "Indian Reservations, Anomie, and Social Pathologies." *Southwestern Journal of Anthropology* 27 (1971): 97–128.

Liska, Allen E., and Paul E. Bellair. "Violent-Crime Rates and Racial Composition: Convergence over Time." *American Journal of Sociology* 101 (1995): 578–610.

Long, Larry H. "How the Racial Composition of Cities Changes." *Land Economics* 51 (1975): 258–67.

Love, Spencie. *One Blood: The Death and Resurrection of Charles R. Drew.* Chapel Hill: University of North Carolina Press, 1996.

Lunch, William L., and Peter W. Sperlich. "American Public Opinion and the War in Vietnam." *Western Political Quarterly* 32 (1979): 21–44.

Lundsgaarde, Henry P. *Murder in Space City: A Cultural Analysis of Houston Homicide Patterns*. New York: Oxford University Press, 1977.

Lynch, James P., and William J. Sabol. "Effects of Incarceration on Informal Social Control in Communities." In *Imprisoning America: The Social Effects of Mass Incarceration*, edited by Mary Pattillo, David Weiman, and Bruce Western, 135–64. New York: Russell Sage Foundation, 2004.

Maas, Ineke, and Richard A. Settersten Jr. "Military Service during Wartime: Effects on Men's Occupational Trajectories and Later Economic Well-Being." *European Sociological Review* 15 (1999): 213–32.

Macek, Steve. "Places of Horror: Fincher's 'Seven' and Fear of the City in Recent Hollywood Film." *College Literature* 26 (1999): 80–97.

Margo, Robert A. "Explaining Black-White Wage Convergence, 1940–1950." *Industrial and Labor Relations Review* 48 (1995): 470–81.

Marris, Peter, and Martin Rein. *Dilemmas of Social Reform: Poverty and Community Action in the United States*. Piscataway, NJ: Transaction Publishers, 2009. First published in 1967.

Martin, John L., Leon F. Bouvier, and William Leonard. *Shaping Florida: The Effects of Immigration, 1970–2020*. Washington, DC: Center for Immigration Studies, December 1995. http://www.cis.org/Florida Immigrants19702020.

Martin, Philip, and Elizabeth Midgley. *Immigration: Shaping and Reshaping America*. Population Bulletin 61, no. 4. Washington, DC: Population Reference Bureau, 2006.

Martinez, Luis, and Amy Bingham. "U.S. Veterans: By the Numbers." ABC News, November 11, 2011. Accessed March 15, 2012. http://abc news.go.com/Politics/us-veterans-numbers/story?id=14928136#.

Martinez, Ramiro, Jr. "Homicide among the 1980 Mariel Refugees in Miami: Victims and Offenders." *Hispanic Journal of Behavioral Sciences* 19 (1997): 107–22.

———. "Latinos and Lethal Violence: The Impact of Poverty and Inequality." *Social Problems* 43 (1996): 131–46.

Martinez, Ramiro, Jr., and Matthew T. Lee. "Immigration and the Ethnic Distribution of Homicide in Miami, 1985–1995." *Homicide Studies* 2 (1998): 291–304.

———. "On Immigration and Crime." In *The Nature of Crime: Continuity and Change*, vol. 1 of *Criminal Justice 2000*, edited by Gary LaFree,

485–524. National Institute of Justice, 2000. https://www.ncjrs.gov /criminal_justice2000/vol_1/02j.pdf.

Martinez, Ramiro, Jr., Jacob I. Stowall, and Matthew T. Lee. "Immigration and Crime in an Era of Transformation: A Longitudinal Analysis of Homicides in San Diego Neighborhoods, 1980–2000." *Criminology* 48 (2010): 797–829.

Massey, Douglas S., and Nancy A. Denton. *American Apartheid: Segregation and the Making of the Underclass.* Cambridge, MA: Harvard University Press, 1993.

Mattick, Hans W. "Parolees in the Army during World War II." *Federal Probation* 24 (1960): 49–55.

Mayer, K.U. "German Survivors of World War II: The Impact on the Life Course of the Collective Experience of Birth Cohorts." In *Social Structures and Human Lives: Social Change and the Life Course,* edited by Matilda White Riley, Bettina J. Huber, and Beth Hess Riley, 229–46. Newbury Park, CA: Sage Publications, 1988.

McCall, Patricia L., Kenneth C. Land, and Lawrence E. Cohen. "Violent Criminal Behavior: Is There a General and Continuing Influence of the South?" *Social Science Research* 21 (1992): 286–310.

McClellan, Chandler, and Erdal Tekin. "Stand Your Ground Laws and Homicides." Discussion paper 6705. Institute for the Study of Labor, 2012. Accessed August 28, 2012. ftp://ftp.iza.org/RePEc/Discussion paper/dp6705.pdf.

McCord, Joan. "Ethnicity, Acculturation, and Opportunities: A Study of Two Generations." In *Ethnicity, Race, and Crime,* edited by Darnell F. Hawkins, 69–81. Albany: State University of New York Press, 1995.

McCullough, David. *Truman.* New York: Simon and Schuster, 1992.

McDonald, Michael P., and Samuel L. Popkin. "The Myth of the Vanishing Voter." *American Political Science Review* 95 (2001): 963–74.

McFadden, Robert D. "State to Free the 'Capeman,' Street-Gang Leader Who Killed 2 in 1959." *New York Times,* September 22, 1979.

McLaughlin, Gerald T. "Cocaine: The History and Regulation of a Dangerous Drug." *Cornell Law Review* 58 (1972–73): 537–73.

McPherson, James M. *Battle Cry of Freedom: The Civil War Era.* New York: Oxford University Press, 2003.

Merton, Robert K. "Social Structure and Anomie." *American Sociological Review* 3 (1938): 672–82.

Messner, Steven F., Eric P. Baumer, and Richard Rosenfeld. "Dimensions of Social Capital and Rates of Criminal Homicide." *American Sociological Review* 69 (2004): 882–903.

Messner, Steven F., and Richard Rosenfeld. *Crime and the American Dream.* 3rd ed. Belmont, CA: Wadsworth, 2001.

Meyers, Arthur C., Jr. "Murder and Non-Negligent Manslaughter: A Statistical Study." *Saint Louis University Law Journal* 3 (1954–55): 18–34.

Miller, Ted R., Mark A. Rossman, and Shelli B. Rossman. "Victim Costs of Violent Crime and Resulting Injuries." *Health Affairs* 12 (1993): 186–97.

Miller, Walter. "The Rumble This Time." *Psychology Today* 10 (1977): 52–59.

Modell, John, Marc Goulden, and Sigurdur Magnusson. "World War II in the Lives of Black Americans: Some Findings and an Interpretation." *Journal of American History* 76 (1989): 838–48.

Mohl, Raymond A. "Changing Economic Patterns in the Miami Metropolitan Area, 1940–1980." *Tequesta* 1 (1982): 63–73.

Monkkonen, Eric H. "Homicide in Los Angeles, 1830–2003." Columbus, OH: Historical Violence Database, Criminal Justice Research Center, Ohio State University. http://cjrc.osu.edu/researchprojects/hvd/usa/la/.2005.

———. "Homicides in New York City, 1797–1999 [and Various Historical Comparison Sites]." Study no. 3226. Ann Arbor, MI: Interuniversity Consortium for Political and Social Research, November 2001.

———. *Murder in New York City.* Berkeley: University of California Press, 2001.

Morin, Rich, Kim Parker, Renee Stepler, and Andrew Mercer. *Behind the Badge: Amid Protests and Calls for Reform, How Police View Their Jobs, Key Issues and Recent Fatal Encounters between Blacks and Police.* Pew Research Center, January 11, 2017. Accessed January 16, 2017. http://assets.pewresearch.org/wp-content/uploads/sites/3/2017/01/06171402/Police-Report_FINAL_web.pdf.

Moritz, Owen. "Salvador Agron 'Cape Man.'" *New York Daily News,* September 5, 2009.

Moynihan, Daniel Patrick. "Defining Deviancy Down." *The American Scholar* 62 (1993): 17–30.

Mullen, Kevin J. *Dangerous Strangers: Minority Newcomers and Criminal Violence in the Urban West, 1850–2000.* New York: Palgrave Macmillan, 2005.

Mulvihill, Donald J., Melvin M. Tumin, and Lynn A. Curtis. *Crimes of Violence*, staff report from Task Force on Individual Acts of Violence to National Commission on the Causes and Prevention of Violence, vol. 11. Washington, DC: Government Printing Office, 1969.

Munford, Robert S., Ross S. Kazer, Roger A. Feldman, and Robert R. Stivers. "Homicide Trends in Atlanta." *Criminology* 14 (1976): 213–32.

Murray, Charles. *Losing Ground: American Social Policy, 1950–1980*. New York: Basic Books, 1984.

Myrdal, Gunnar. *An American Dilemma: The Negro Problem and Modern Democracy*. 2 vols. New Brunswick, NJ: Transaction Publishers, 1996. First published in 1944.

National Advisory Commission on Civil Disorders. *Report of the National Advisory Commission on Civil Disorders*. New York: Bantam Books, 1968.

National Center for Health Statistics. "Death Rates by Age, Race, and Sex, United States, 1900–1953: Selected Causes." 1956. Accessed November 1, 2012. http://www.cdc.gov/nchs/data/dvs/mx194049.pdf.

———. *Deaths: Preliminary Data for 2009*. By Kenneth D. Kochanek, Jiaquan Xu, Sherry L. Murphy, Arialdi M. Miniño, and Hsiang-Ching Kung. National Vital Statistics Reports, vol. 59, no. 4. Hyattsville, MD: National Center for Health Statistics, 2011.

———. *Deaths of Hispanic Origin, 15 Reporting States, 1979–81*. Vital and Health Statistics, series 20, no. 18. Hyattsville, MD: National Center for Health Statistics, December 1990. http://www.cdc.gov/nchs/data/series/sr_20/sr20_018.pdf.

———. *Health, United States, 2006*. Hyattsville, MD: Government Printing Office, 2006.

———. *Health, United States, 2011: With Special Feature on Socioeconomic Status and Health*. Hyattsville, MD: Government Printing Office, 2012.

———. *Health, United States, 2013: With Special Feature on Prescription Drugs*. Hyattsville, MD: Government Printing Office, 2014.

———. *Homicide in the United States, 1950–1964*. Public Health Service Publication No. 1000, series 20, no. 6. Washington, DC: Government Printing Office, October 1967.

———. *Vital Statistics Rates in the United States, 1940–1960*. By Robert D. Grove and Alice M. Hetzel. Washington, DC: Government Printing Office, 1968.

National Commission on the Causes and Prevention of Violence. *To

Establish Justice, To Insure Domestic Tranquility. Washington, DC: Government Printing Office, 1969.

Needleman, H.L., C. McFarland, R.B. Ness, S.E. Fienberg, and M.J. Tobin. "Bone Lead Levels in Adjudicated Delinquents: A Case Control Study." *Neurotoxicology and Teratology* 24 (2003): 711–17.

Neumayer, Eric. "Inequality and Violent Crime: Evidence from Data on Robbery and Violent Theft." *Journal of Peace Research* 42 (2005): 101–12.

Newport, Frank. "Americans Have Become More Negative on Impact of Immigrants." Gallup News Service. .July 20, 2012. http://www .gallup.com/poll/28132/americans-become-more-negative-impact -immigrants.aspx.

Newton, Michael, and Judy Ann Newton. *Racial and Religious Violence in America: A Chronology.* New York: Garland, 1991.

New York City, Department of City Planning, Population Division. *The Newest New Yorkers 2000: Immigrant New York in the New Millennium.* Briefing booklet. October 2004. http://www.nyc.gov/html /dcp/pdf/census/nny_briefing_booklet.pdf.

New York City, Department of Health and Mental Hygiene, Office of Chief Medical Examiner. "Update on the Results of DNA Testing of Remains Recovered at the World Trade Center Site and Surrounding Area." February 1, 2009. Accessed June 12, 2012. http:// www.nyc.gov/html/ocme/downloads/pdf/public_affairs_ocme_pr _february_2009.pdf.

New York Daily News. "Where Are Other 3 Now? In and Out of Jail." April 24, 1996.

New York State Department of Correctional Services. *The Impact of Foreign-Born Inmates on the New York State Department of Correctional Services.* By David D. Clark. April 1992.

———. *The Impact of Foreign-Born Inmates on the New York State Department of Correctional Services.* By David D. Clark. July 2008. http:// www.doccs.ny.gov/Research/Reports/2008/Impact_of_Foreign -Born_Inmates_2008.pdf.

New York Times. "Crime Data Cited on Puerto Ricans." October 11, 1959.

———. "Family of Five Murdered. J.H. Tettaton Under Arrest for Killing His Stepmother and Her Four Children in Missouri." April 27, 1899.

———. "Maniac Blows Up School, Kills 42, Mostly Children; Had Protested High Taxes." May 19, 1927.

———. "Puerto Ricans Get Maximum Terms." July 9, 1954.

————. "Youth Study Cites Cultural Factor." March 17, 1956.

Nisbett, Richard E., and Dov Cohen. *Culture of Honor: The Psychology of Violence in the South.* Boulder, CO: Westview Press, 1996.

Nossiter, Adam. "Bronx Jury Orders Goetz to Pay Man He Paralyzed $43 Million." *New York Times*, April 24, 1996.

O'Brien, Robert M., and Jean Stockard. "Can Cohort Replacement Explain Changes in the Relationship between Age and Homicide Offending?" *Journal of Quantitative Criminology* 25 (2009): 79–101.

O'Brien, Robert M., Jean Stockard, and Lynne Isaacson. "The Enduring Effects of Cohort Characteristics on Age-Specific Homicide Rates, 1960–1995." *American Journal of Sociology* 104 (1999): 1061–95.

O'Carroll, Patrick W., and James A. Mercy. "Regional Variation in Homicide Rates: Why Is the West So Violent?" *Violence and Victims* 4 (1989): 17–25.

Office of National Drug Control Policy. *National Drug Control Strategy.* Washington, DC: Government Printing Office, 1989.

Oliver, William M., and James F. Hilgenberg. *A History of Crime and Criminal Justice in America.* 2nd ed. Durham, NC: Carolina Academic Press, 2010.

Olzak, Susan, and Suzanne Shanahan. "Deprivation and Race Riots: An Extension of Spilerman's Analysis." *Social Forces* 74 (1996): 931–61.

Ouimet, Marc. "Explaining the American and Canadian Crime Drop in the 1990's." *Champ pénal/Penal Field* 1 (2004). Accessed April 16, 2012. http://champpenal.revues.org/448#text.

Ousey, Graham C., and Charis E. Kubrin. "Exploring the Connection between Immigration and Violent Crime Rates in U.S. Cities, 1980–2000." *Social Problems* 56 (2009): 447–73.

Ousey, Graham C., and Matthew R. Lee. "To Know the Unknown: The Decline in Homicide Clearance Rates, 1980–2000." *Criminal Justice Review* 35 (2010): 141–58.

Pagán, Eduardo Obregón. "Los Angeles Geopolitics and the Zoot Suit Riot, 1943." *Social Science History* 24 (2000): 223–56.

Page, Patricia. "Chinatown: Not East, Not West." *New York Times Magazine*, December 15, 1946.

Pao-Min, Chang. "Health and Crime among Chinese-Americans: Recent Trends." *Phylon* 42 (1981): 356–68.

Parker, Karen F. *Unequal Crime Decline: Theorizing Race, Urban Inequality, and Criminal Violence.* New York: New York University Press, 2008.

Parker, Karen F., and Matthew V. Pruitt. "How the West Was One: Explaining the Similarities in Race-Specific Homicide Rates in the West and South." *Social Forces* 78 (2000): 1483–1508.

Parker, Robert Nash. *Alcohol and Homicide: A Deadly Combination of Two American Traditions.* Albany: State University of New York Press, 1995.

Parker, Robert Nash, and Kathleen Auerhahn. "Alcohol, Drugs, and Violence." *Annual Review of Sociology* 24 (1998): 291–311.

Passel, Jeffrey S. *The Size and Characteristics of the Unauthorized Migrant Population in the U.S.* Washington, DC: Pew Hispanic Center, March 7, 2006. http://www.pewhispanic.org/files/reports/61.pdf.

Passel, Jeffrey S., Wendy Wang, and Paul Taylor. *Marrying Out: One-in-Seven New U.S. Marriages Is Interracial or Interethnic.* Pew Research Center, June 4, 2010. Accessed June 7, 2013. http://www.pewsocial trends.org/files/2010/10/755-marrying-out.pdf.

Patterson, James T. *America's Struggle against Poverty in the Twentieth Century.* Cambridge, MA: Harvard University Press, 2000. First published in 1981.

———. *Grand Expectations: The United States, 1945–1974.* New York: Oxford University Press, 1996.

Pennell, Susan, Christine Curtis, and Jeff Tayman. *The Impact of Illegal Immigration on the Criminal Justice System.* San Diego, CA: San Diego Association of Governments, 1989.

Pepinsky, Harold E. "The Growth of Crime in the United States." *Annals of the American Academy of Political and Social Science* 423 (1976): 23–30.

Petersilia, Joan. "Racial Disparities in the Criminal Justice System: A Summary." *Crime & Delinquency* 31 (1985): 15–34.

Pew Center on the States. *Time Served: The High Cost, Low Return of Longer Prison Terms.* June 2012. Accessed June 29, 2012. http://www .pewtrusts.org/~/media/legacy/uploadedfiles/wwwpewtrustsorg/re ports/sentencing_and_corrections/PrisonTimeServedpdf.pdf.

Pew Research Center. *Modern Immigration Wave Brings 59 Million to U.S., Driving Population Growth and Change Through 2065.* September 28, 2015. Accessed January 16, 2017. http://www.pewhispanic.org/files /2015/09/2015-09-28_modern-immigration-wave_REPORT.pdf.

Pfaff, John F. "The Myths and Realities of Correctional Severity: Evidence from the National Corrections Reporting Program on Sentencing Practices." *American Law and Economics Review* 13 (2011): 491–527.

———. "Prison Growth: An Empirical Assessment." *Fordham Lawyer* (Fall 2012), 6–9.

Phillips, Wayne. "Munoz in Defense of Puerto Ricans." *New York Times*, October 8, 1957.

Pinker, Steven. *The Better Angels of Our Nature: Why Violence Has Declined.* New York: Viking Press, 2011.

Pirkle, James L., Debra J. Brody, Elaine W. Gunter, Rachel A. Kramer, Daniel C. Paschal, Katherine M. Flegal, and Thomas D. Matte. "The Decline in Blood Lead Levels in the United States: The National Health and Nutrition Examination Surveys (NHANES)." *Journal of the American Medical Association* 272 (1994): 284–91.

Plotnick, Robert D., Eugene Smolensky, Eirik Evenhouse, and Siobhan Reilly. "The Twentieth Century Record of Inequality and Poverty in the United States." Discussion paper no. 1166-98. Madison, WI: Institute for Research on Poverty, July 1998. Accessed August 13, 2011. http://irp.wisc.edu/publications/dps/pdfs/dp116698.pdf.

Pokorny, Alex D. "A Comparison of Homicides in Two Cities." *Journal of Criminal Law, Criminology, and Police Science* 56 (1965): 479–87.

———. "Human Violence: A Comparison of Homicide, Aggravated Assault, Suicide, and Attempted Suicide." *Journal of Criminal Law, Criminology, and Police Science* 56 (1965): 488–97.

Police Department, City of New York. *Annual Report 1917.* New York: Bureau of Printing, Police Department, City of New York, 1917.

Porter, Bruce, and Marvin Dunn. *The Miami Riot of 1980: Crossing the Bounds.* Lexington, MA: D.C. Heath, 1984.

Porterfield, Austin L. "A Decade of Serious Crimes in the United States: Some Trends and Hypotheses." *American Sociological Review* 13 (1948): 44–54.

Portes, Alejandro, and Alex Stepick. *City on the Edge: The Transformation of Miami.* Berkeley: University of California Press, 1993.

President's Commission on Law Enforcement and Administration of Justice. *The Challenge of Crime in a Free Society.* Washington, DC: Government Printing Office, 1967.

Press, Eyal. "Do Immigrants Make Us Safer?" *New York Times Magazine*, December 3, 2006.

Purdum, Todd S. "2 of Those Shot by Goetz Face New Jail Terms." *New York Times*, April 9, 1986.

Putnam, Robert D. *Bowling Alone: The Collapse and Revival of American Community.* New York: Simon and Schuster, 2000.

Raphael, Steven, and Michael A. Stoll. "Why Are So Many Americans in Prison?" Discussion paper no. 1328-07. Madison, WI: Institute for Research on Poverty, May 2007. http://www.irp.wisc.edu/publica tions/dps/pdfs/dp132807.pdf.

Redfield, H. V. *Homicide, North and South*. Philadelphia: J. B. Lippincott, 1880.

Reimers, David M. *Still the Golden Door: The Third World Comes to America*. New York: Columbia University Press, 1985.

Reyes, Jessica Wolpaw. "Environmental Policy as Social Policy? The Impact of Childhood Lead Exposure on Crime." NBER Working Paper No. 13097, May 2007. http://www.nber.org/papers/w13097.pdf.

Reynolds, Morgan O. "Crime and Punishment in America." Policy report no. 193. National Center for Policy Analysis, June 1995. Accessed January 6, 2012. http://www.ncpa.org/pdfs/st193.pdf.

Ricketts, Erol, and Isabel Sawhill. "Defining and Measuring the Underclass." *Journal of Policy Analysis and Management* 7 (1988): 316–25.

Riedel, Marc. "Homicide in Los Angeles County: A Study of Latino Victimization." In *Violent Crime: Assessing Race and Ethnic Differences*, edited by Darnell F. Hawkins, 44–66. New York: Cambridge University Press, 2003.

———. "Stranger Violence: Perspectives, Issues, and Problems." *Journal of Criminal Law and Criminology* 78 (1987): 223–58.

Rodríguez, Clara E. *Puerto Ricans: Immigrants and Migrants*. Americans All. Accessed July 18, 2011. https://americansall.org/sites/default /files/resources/pdf/ethnic-and-cultural/9.9_Puerto_Ricans_Immi grants_and_Migrants.pdf.

Rodriguez, Salvador F. "Patterns of Homicide in Texas: A Descriptive Analysis of Racial/Ethnic Involvement by Crime-Specific Categories." PhD diss., University of Texas, Austin, 1990.

Rosenwaike, Ira. "Mortality among the Puerto Rican Born in New York City." *Social Science Quarterly* 64 (1983): 375–85.

———. *Population History of New York City*. Syracuse, NY: Syracuse University Press, 1972.

Rosenwaike, Ira, and Katherine Hempstead. "Mortality among Three Puerto Rican Populations: Residents of Puerto Rico and Migrants in New York City and in the Balance of the United States, 1979–81." *International Migration Review* 24 (1990): 684–702.

Ross, Christine, Sheldon Danziger, and Eugene Smolensky. "The Level and Trend of Poverty in the United States, 1939–1979." *Demography* 24 (1987): 587–600.

Roth, Randolph. *American Homicide*. Cambridge, MA: Harvard University Press, 2009.

Roth, Randolph, Michael D. Maltz, and Douglas L. Eckberg. "Homicide Rates in the Old West." *Western Historical Quarterly* 42 (2011): 173–95.

Rowe, David C., and Joseph L. Rodgers. "An 'Epidemic' Model of Adolescent Sexual Intercourse: Applications to National Survey Data." *Journal of Biosocial Science* 23 (1991): 211–19.

Rubin, Lillian B. *Quiet Rage: Bernie Goetz in a Time of Madness*. Berkeley: University of California Press, 1986.

Ruderman, Wendy. "414 Homicides a Record Low for New York." *New York Times*, December 29, 2012.

Rumbaut, Rubén G. "Origins and Destinies: Immigration to the United States Since World War II." *Sociological Forum* 9 (1994): 583–621.

Rumbaut, Rubén G., Roberto G. Gonzales, Golnaz Komaie, Charlie V. Morgan, and Rosaura Tafoya-Estrada. "Immigration and Incarceration." In *Immigration and Crime: Race, Ethnicity, and Violence*, edited by Ramiro Martinez Jr. and Abel Valenzuela Jr., 64–89. New York: New York University Press, 2006.

Sampson, Robert J., and John H. Laub. *Crime in the Making: Pathways and Turning-Points through Life*. Cambridge, MA: Harvard University Press, 1993.

———. "Life-Course Desisters? Trajectories of Crime among Delinquent Boys Followed to Age 70." *Criminology* 41 (2003): 301–39.

———. "Socioeconomic Achievement in the Life Course of Disadvantaged Men: Military Service as a Turning Point, circa 1940–1965." *American Sociological Review* 61 (1996): 347–67.

———. "Urban Poverty and the Family Context of Delinquency: A New Look at Structure and Process in a Classic Study." *Child Development* 65 (1994): 523–40.

Sandler, Stanley. *The Korean War: No Victors, No Vanquished*. Lexington: University Press of Kentucky, 1999.

Schepses, Erwin. "Puerto Rican Delinquent Boys in New York City." *Social Service Review* 23 (1949): 51–61.

Schlesinger, Arthur M., Jr. *The Age of Roosevelt: The Coming of the New Deal*. New York: Houghton Mifflin, 1958.

Schneider, Eric C. *Smack: Heroin and the American City*. Philadelphia: University of Pennsylvania Press, 2008.

———. *Vampires, Dragons, and Egyptian Kings: Youth Gangs in Postwar New York*. Princeton: Princeton University Press, 1999.

Sears, David O., and John B. McConahay. *The Politics of Violence: The New*

Urban Blacks and the Watts Riot. Boston, MA: Houghton Mifflin, 1973.

Sellin, Thorsten. "Crime and Delinquency in the United States: An Over-All View." *Annals of the American Academy of Political and Social Science* 339 (1962): 11–23.

———. "Is Murder Increasing in Europe?" *Annals of the American Academy of Political and Social Science* 125 (1926): 29–34.

Shattuck, Edward S. "Military Service for Men with Criminal Records." *Federal Probation* 9 (1945): 12–14.

Silberman, Charles E. *Criminal Violence, Criminal Justice*. New York: Random House, 1978.

Silverman, Eli B. *NYPD Battles Crime: Innovative Strategies in Policing*. Boston, MA: Northeastern University Press, 1999.

Singh, Gopal K., and Mohammad Siahpush. "All-Cause and Cause-Specific Mortality of Immigrants and Native Born in the United States." *American Journal of Public Health* 91 (2001): 392–99.

Sitkoff, Harvard. "Racial Militancy and Interracial Violence in the Second World War." *Journal of American History* 58 (1971): 661–81.

Skogan, Wesley G. *Police and Community in Chicago: A Tale of Three Cities*. New York: Oxford University Press, 2006.

Smith, David J. "Ethnic Differences in Intergenerational Crime Patterns." *Crime and Justice* 32 (2005): 59–129.

Smith, Jack C., James A. Mercy, and Mark L. Rosenberg. "Suicide and Homicide among Hispanics in the Southwest." *Public Health Reports* 101 (1986): 265–70.

Smith, James P., and Finis R. Welch. *Closing the Gap: Forty Years of Economic Progress for Blacks*. Santa Monica, CA: Rand Corp., 1986.

Smolensky, Eugene, and Robert Plotnick. "Inequality and Poverty in the United States: 1900 to 1990." Discussion paper no. 998-93. Madison, WI: Institute for Research on Poverty, 1992. Accessed December 14, 2012. http://www.irp.wisc.edu/publications/dps/pdfs/dp99893.pdf.

Sorenson, Susan B., and Haikang Shen. "Homicide Risk among Immigrants in California, 1970 through 1992." *American Journal of Public Health* 86 (1996): 97–100.

Sorokin, Pitirim. *Contemporary Sociological Theories*. New York: Harper and Brothers, 1928.

Sowell, Thomas. *Black Rednecks and White Liberals*. San Francisco: Encounter Books, 2005.

————. *Race and Culture: A World View.* New York: Basic Books, 1994.

Spelman, William. "The Limited Importance of Prison Expansion." In *The Crime Drop in America*, edited by Alfred Blumstein and Joel Wallman, 97–129. Cambridge: Cambridge University Press, 2000.

Spilerman, Seymour. "The Causes of Racial Disturbances: A Comparison of Alternative Explanations." *American Sociological Review* 35 (1970): 627–49.

————. "Structural Characteristics of Cities and the Severity of Racial Disorders." *American Sociological Review* 41 (1976): 771–93.

Steffensmeier, Darrell, Ben Feldmeyer, Casey T. Harris, and Jeffery T. Ulmer. "Reassessing Trends in Black Violent Crime, 1980–2008: Sorting Out the 'Hispanic Effect' in UCR Arrests, NCVS Offenders Estimates, and U.S. Prisoner Counts." *Criminology* 49 (2011): 197–251.

Stengel, Richard, Marcia Gauger, and Barry Kalb. "A Troubled and Troubling Life." *Time*, April 8, 1985, 35.

Straka, Richard. "The Violence of Hmong Gangs and the Crime of Rape." *FBI Law Enforcement Bulletin* 72 (2003): 12–16.

Stuntz, William J. *The Collapse of American Criminal Justice.* Cambridge, MA: Harvard University Press, 2011.

Sugrue, Thomas J. *The Origins of the Urban Crisis: Race and Inequality in Postwar Detroit.* Princeton: Princeton University Press, 1996.

Sutherland, Edwin H. "Crime." In *American Society in Wartime*, edited by William Fielding Ogburn. New York: Da Capo Press, 1972. First published in 1943.

Sutherland, Edwin H., and Donald R. Cressey. *Criminology.* 8th ed. Philadelphia: J.B. Lippincott, 1970.

Takagi, Paul, and Tony Platt. "Behind the Gilded Ghetto: An Analysis of Race, Class, and Crime in Chinatown." *Crime and Social Justice* 9 (1978): 2–25.

Tanter, Raymond. "International War and Domestic Turmoil: Some Contemporary Evidence." In *Violence in America: Historical and Comparative Perspectives*, edited by Hugh Davis Graham and Ted Robert Gurr, 550–69. New York: Bantam Books, 1969.

Tarde, Gabriel. *Penal Philosophy.* Translated by Rapelje Howell. London: William Heinemann, 1912. First published in 1890.

Thernstrom, Stephan, ed. *Harvard Encyclopedia of American Ethnic Groups.* Cambridge, MA: Harvard University Press, 1994. First published in 1980.

Thernstrom, Stephan, and Abigail Thernstrom. *America in Black and White: One Nation, Indivisible*. New York: Simon and Schuster, 1997.

Thomas, Piri. *Down These Mean Streets*. New York: Random House, 1997. First published in 1967.

Thompson, Heather Ann. "Why Mass Incarceration Matters: Rethinking Crisis, Decline, and Transformation in Postwar American History." *Journal of American History*, 97 (2010): 703–34.

Tolchin, Martin. "President to Free 4 Puerto Ricans in Washington Shootings of 1950's." *New York Times*, September 7, 1979.

Tomlinson, T.M. "The Development of a Riot Ideology among Urban Negroes." *American Behavioral Scientist* 11 (1968): 27–31.

Tonry, Michael, ed. *Ethnicity, Crime, and Immigration: Comparative and Cross-National Perspectives*. Chicago: University of Chicago Press, 1997.

———. *Malign Neglect: Race, Crime, and Punishment in America*. New York: Oxford University Press, 1995.

Toossi, Mitra. "A Century of Change: The U.S. Labor Force, 1950–2050." *Monthly Labor Review* 16 (2002): 15–28.

University at Albany, Hindelang Criminal Justice Research Center. *Sourcebook of Criminal Justice Statistics, 2003*. Table 6.48. http://www.albany.edu/sourcebook/pdf/t648.pdf.

U.S. Army Center of Military History. "Afghanistan and Iraq in a Decade." August 25, 2011. Accessed March 14, 2012. http://www.army.mil/article/64302/Afghanistan_and_Iraq_in_a_decade/.

U.S. Bureau of the Census. "Current Population Survey, Annual Social and Economic Supplements." Accessed November 6, 2011. https://www.census.gov/hhes/www/poverty/publications/pubs-cps.html.

———. *Measuring 50 Years of Economic Change Using the March Current Population Survey*. Current Population Reports, P60-203. Washington, DC: Government Printing Office, 1998.

U.S. Census Bureau. *Age and Sex Composition: 2010*. By Lindsay M. Howden and Julie A. Meyer. 2010 Census Briefs, C2010BR-03. May 2011. http://www.census.gov/prod/cen2010/briefs/c2010br-03.pdf.

———. *The American Indian and Alaskan Native Population: 2000*. By Stella U. Ogunwole. Census 2000 Brief, C2KBR/01-15. Washington, DC: Government Printing Office, 2002. http://www.census.gov/prod/2002pubs/c2kbr01-15.pdf.

———. "America's Families and Living Arrangements: 2012." Accessed

November 20, 2012. http://www.census.gov/hhes/families/data/cps 2012.html.

———. *The Black Population: 2000.* By Jesse McKinnon. Census 2000 Brief, C2KBR/01-5. Washington, DC: Government Printing Office, 2001. www.census.gov/prod/2001pubs/c2kbr01-5.pdf.

———. "Census Regions and Divisions of the United States." Accessed October 7, 2012. http://www2.census.gov/geo/pdfs/maps-data/maps /reference/us_regdiv.pdf.

———. *The Changing Shape of the Nation's Income Distribution, 1947–1998.* Current Population Reports, P60-204. Washington, DC: Government Printing Office, 2000.

———. *Demographic Trends in the 20th Century.* By Frank Hobbs and Nicole Stoops. Census 2000 Special Reports, Series CENSR-4. Washington, DC: Government Printing Office, 2002.

———. *The Foreign-Born Population: 2000.* By Nolan Malone, Kaari F. Baluja, Joseph M. Costanzo, and Cynthia J. Davis. Census 2000 Brief, C2KBR-34. Washington, DC: Government Printing Office, 2003. http://www.census.gov/prod/2003pubs/c2kbr-34.pdf.

———. *The Hispanic Population, 2000.* By Betsy Guzmán. Census 2000 Brief, C2KBR/01-3. Washington, DC: Government Printing Office, 2001. http://www.census.gov/prod/2001pubs/c2kbr01-3.pdf.

———. *Historical Census Statistics on Population Totals by Race, 1790 to 1990, and by Hispanic Origin, 1970 to 1990, for Large Cities and Other Urban Places in the United States.* By Campbell Gibson and Kay Jung. Working paper no. 56. Washington, DC: Government Printing Office, 2002.

———. *Historical Census Statistics on Population Totals by Race, 1790 to 1990, and by Hispanic Origin, 1970 to 1990, for Large Cities and Other Urban Places in the United States.* By Campbell Gibson and Kay Jung. Working paper no. 76. Washington, DC: Government Printing Office, 2005.

———. *Historical Census Statistics on Population Totals by Race, 1790 to 1990, and by Hispanic Origin, 1970 to 1990, for the United States, Regions, Divisions, and States.* By Campbell Gibson and Kay Jung. Working paper no. 56. Washington, DC: Government Printing Office, 1998.

———. "How the Census Bureau Measures Poverty." Accessed June 5, 2011. http://www.census.gov/hhes/www/poverty/about/overview /measure.html.

————. *Income, Poverty, and Health Insurance Coverage in the United States: 2010*. By Carmen DeNavas-Walt, Bernadette D. Proctor, and Jessica C. Smith. Current Population Reports, P60-239. Washington, DC: Government Printing Office, 2011.

————. *The Newly Arrived Foreign-Born Population of the United States: 2010*. By Nathan P. Walters and Edward N. Trevelyan. Washington, DC: Government Printing Office, 2011.

————. *Population Estimates by Race and Hispanic Origin for States, Metropolitan Areas, and Selected Counties: 1980 to 1985*. By David L. Word. Current Population Reports, P-25, no. 1040. Washington, DC: Government Printing Office, 1989.

————. *Profile of the Foreign-Born Population in the United States: 2000*. By A. Dianne Schmidley. Current Population Reports, Special Studies, P23-206. Washington, DC: Government Printing Office, 2001.

————. *Projections of the Size and Composition of the U.S. Population: 2014 to 2060*. By Sandra L. Colby and Jennifer M. Ortman. Current Population Reports, P25-1143. Washington, DC: Government Printing Office, 2015. http://www.census.gov/content/dam/Census/library/publications/2015/demo/p25-1143.pdf.

————. *We, the American Hispanics*. Washington, DC: Government Printing Office, 1993.

————. *We the People: American Indians and Alaska Natives in the United States*. By Stella U. Ogunwole. Census 2000 Special Reports, Series CENSR-28. Washington, DC: Government Printing Office, 2006.

————. *We the People: Asians in the United States*. By Terrance J. Reeves and Claudette E. Bennett. Census 2000 Special Reports, Series CENSR-17. Washington, DC: Government Printing Office, 2004.

————. *We the People: Blacks in the United States*. By Jesse D. McKinnon and Claudette E. Bennett. Census 2000 Special Reports, Series CENSR-25. Washington, DC: Government Printing Office, 2005.

————. *We the People: Hispanics in the United States*. By Roberto R. Ramirez. Census 2000 Special Reports, Series CENSR-18. Washington, DC: Government Printing Office, 2004.

U.S. Census Bureau, Population Division. *Historical Census Statistics on Population Totals by Race, 1790 to 1990, and by Hispanic Origin, 1970 to 1990, for the United States, Regions, Divisions, and States by Population Division*. By Campbell Gibson and Kay Jung. Working paper no. 56. Washington, DC: Government Printing Office, 2002.

————. *Historical Census Statistics on the Foreign-Born Population of the United States: 1850 to 2000*. By Campbell Gibson and Kay Jung. Working paper no. 81. Washington, DC: U.S. Government Printing Office, 2006.

————. *Intercensal Estimates of the Total Resident Population of States: 1940 to 1949*. Washington, DC: Government Printing Office, 1996.

————. *Population of Counties by Decennial Census: 1900 to 1990*. By Richard Forstall. 1995. http://www.census.gov/population/www/census data/cencounts/files/1900-90.txt.

————. *Population of the 100 Largest Cities and Other Urban Places in the United States: 1790 to 1990*. By Campbell Gibson. Working paper no. 27. Washington, DC: Government Printing Office, 1998.

————. *Statistical Abstract of the United States: 2001*. Washington, DC: Government Printing Office, 2001.

U.S. Commission on Civil Rights. *The Economic Progress of Black Men in America*. Washington, DC: Government Printing Office, 1986.

U.S. Commission on Law Enforcement and Administration of Justice. *The Challenge of Crime in a Free Society*. Washington, DC: Government Printing Office, 1967.

U.S. Department of Agriculture. "Minority Counties are Geographically Clustered." By Douglas E. Bowers and Peggy Cook. *Rural Conditions and Trends* 9 (1999): 14–19. http://webarchives.cdlib.org /sw1bc3ts3z/http://ers.usda.gov/Publications/RCAT/RCAT92/.

U.S. Department of Commerce, Bureau of the Census. *Historical Statistics of the United States, Colonial Times to 1970, Bicentennial Edition*. Parts 1 and 2. Washington, DC: Government Printing Office, 1975.

————. *The Social and Economic Status of the Black Population in the United States: An Historical View, 1790–1978*. Current Population Reports, Special Studies, Series P-23, no. 80. Washington, DC: Government Printing Office, 1979.

————. *Statistical Abstract of the United States, 1958*. Washington, DC: Government Printing Office, 1958.

————. *Statistical Abstract of the United States, 1965*. Washington, DC: Government Printing Office, 1965.

————. *Statistical Abstract of the United States, 1969*. Washington, DC: Government Printing Office, 1969.

————. *Statistical Abstract of the United States, 1970*. Washington, DC: Government Printing Office, 1970.

————. *Statistical Abstract of the United States, 1974.* Washington, DC: Government Printing Office, 1974.

————. *Statistical Abstract of the United States, 1976.* Washington, DC: Government Printing Office, 1976.

————. *Statistical Abstract of the United States: 1982–83.* Washington, DC: Government Printing Office, 1982.

————. *The 2012 Statistical Abstract.* 2011. Page last modified June 26, 2014. https://www.census.gov/library/publications/2011/compendia /statab/131edition.html.

————. *Vital Statistics of the United States, 1940.* Part 1. Washington, DC: Government Printing Office, 1943.

————. *Vital Statistics of the United States, 1941.* Part 1. Washington, DC: Government Printing Office, 1943.

————. *Vital Statistics of the United States, 1942.* Part 1. Washington, DC: Government Printing Office, 1944.

————. *Vital Statistics of the United States, 1944.* Part 1. Washington, DC: Government Printing Office, 1946.

————. *Vital Statistics of the United States, 1945.* Part 1. Washington, DC: Government Printing Office, 1947.

————. *Vital Statistics of the United States, 1946.* Part 1. Washington, DC: Government Printing Office, 1948.

————. *Vital Statistics of the United States, 1947.* Part 1. Washington, DC: Government Printing Office, 1949.

————. *Vital Statistics of the United States, 1948.* Part 1. Washington, DC: Government Printing Office, 1950.

————. *Vital Statistics of the United States, 1949.* Part 1. Washington, DC: Government Printing Office, 1951.

U.S. Department of Commerce and Labor, Bureau of the Census. *Prisoners and Juvenile Delinquents in Institutions, 1904.* Washington, DC: Government Printing Office, 1907.

U.S. Department of Education. *Dropout Rates in the United States: 2005.* By Jennifer Laird, Gregory Kienzl, Matthew DeBell, and Chris Chapman. NCES 2007-059. 2007. Accessed October 31, 2011. http:// nces.ed.gov/pubs2007/2007059.pdf.

————. *Status and Trends in the Education of Racial and Ethnic Minorities.* By Angelina KewalRamani, Lauren Gilbertson, Mary Ann Fox, and Stephen Provasnik. NCES 2007-039. 2007. Accessed January 8, 2013. http://nces.ed.gov/pubs2007/2007039.pdf.

U.S. Department of Health and Human Services, Centers for Disease

Control and Prevention. "About Underlying Cause of Death, 1999–2010." Accessed June 8, 2012. http://wonder.cdc.gov/ucd-icd10.html.

———. *Deaths: Final Data for 2006*. National Vital Statistics Reports, vol. 57, no. 14. April 17, 2009. http://www.cdc.gov/nchs/data/nvsr /nvsr57/nvsr57_14.pdf.

———. "Multiple Cause of Death Data." Accessed January 16, 2017. https://wonder.cdc.gov/mcd.html.

U.S. Department of Health and Human Services, National Institute on Drug Abuse. "DrugFacts: Cocaine." Revised April 2013. Accessed June 22, 2012. http://www.drugabuse.gov/publications/drugfacts /cocaine.

U.S. Department of Health, Education, and Welfare. *Vital Statistics of the United States, 1950*. Vol. 1. Washington, DC: Government Printing Office, 1953.

———. *Vital Statistics of the United States, 1960*. Vol. 2. Washington, DC: Government Printing Office, 1963.

U.S. Department of Homeland Security. *Estimates of the Unauthorized Immigrant Population Residing in the United States: January 2010*. Washington, DC: Government Printing Office, 2011.

U.S. Department of Justice, Bureau of Justice Statistics. *American Indians and Crime*. By Lawrence A. Greenfeld and Steven K. Smith. Washington, DC: Government Printing Office, 1999.

———. *Arrest in the United States, 1980–2009*. By Howard N. Snyder. Washington, DC: Government Printing Office, 2011.

———. *Correctional Populations in the United States, 1997*. Washington, DC: Government Printing Office, 2000.

———. *Crime and Victimization in the Three Largest Metropolitan Areas, 1980–98*. By Janet L. Lauritsen and Robin J. Schaum. Washington, DC: Government Printing Office, 2005.

———. *Criminal Victimization, 2011*. By Jennifer L. Truman and Michael Planty. Washington, DC: Government Printing Office, 2012.

———. *Criminal Victimization in the United States: 1973–88 Trends*. Washington, DC: Government Printing Office, 1991.

———. *Criminal Victimization in the United States, 1987*. Washington, DC: Government Printing Office, 1989.

———. *Criminal Victimization in the United States, 1988*. Washington, DC: Government Printing Office, 1989.

———. *Criminal Victimization in the United States, 1989*. Washington, DC: Government Printing Office, 1990.

————. *Criminal Victimization in the United States, 1990.* Washington, DC: Government Printing Office, 1992.

————. *Criminal Victimization in the United States, 1991.* Washington, DC: Government Printing Office, 1992.

————. *Criminal Victimization in the United States, 1992.* Washington, DC: Government Printing Office, 1993.

————. *Felony Case Processing in State Courts, 1986.* By Carla K. Gaskins. Washington, DC: Government Printing Office, 1990.

————. *Felony Defendants in Large Urban Counties, 2004.* Washington, DC: Government Printing Office, 2008.

————. "Felony Defendants in Large Urban Counties, 2004—Statistical Tables." By Tracey Kyckelhahn and Thomas H. Cohen. 2008. http://bjs.ojp.usdoj.gov/content/pub/html/fdluc/2004/fdluc04st.pdf.

————. *Highlights from 20 Years of Surveying Crime Victims: The National Crime Victimization Survey, 1973–92.* By Marianne W. Zawitz, Patsy A. Klaus, Ronet Bachman, Lisa D. Bastian, Marshall M. DeBerry Jr., Michael R. Rand, and Bruce M. Taylor. Washington, DC: Government Printing Office, 1993.

————. *Hispanic Victims.* By Lisa D. Bastian. Washington, DC: Government Printing Office, 1990.

————. "Homicide Rate Trends." https://web.archive.org/web/2012 1230183805/http://bjs.ojp.usdoj.gov/content/glance/tables/hmrttab .cfm#top.

————. "Homicide Trends in the United States." By James Alan Fox and Marianne W. Zawitz. Washington, DC: Government Printing Office, 2010. http://www.bjs.gov/content/pub/pdf/htius.pdf.

————. *Homicide Trends in the United States, 1980–2008.* By Alexia Cooper and Erica L. Smith. Washington, DC: Government Printing Office, 2011. http://bjs.ojp.usdoj.gov/content/pub/pdf/htus80 08.pdf.

————. *Injuries from Crime.* By Caroline Wolf Harlow. Washington, DC: Government Printing Office, 1989.

————. *Lifetime Likelihood of Victimization.* By Herbert Koppel. Washington, DC: Government Printing Office, 1987.

————. *Murder in Large Urban Counties, 1988.* Washington, DC: Government Printing Office, 1993.

————. "National Corrections Reporting Program: Time Served in State Prison, by Offense, Release Type, Sex, and Race." By Thomas P. Bonczar. Data under 1993 by Doris James Wilson. Accessed May 1, 2012. http://bjs.ojp.usdoj.gov/index.cfm?ty=pbdetail&iid=2045.

———. *Police Departments in Large Cities, 1987.* By Brian A. Reaves. Washington, DC: Government Printing Office, 1989.

———. *Police Departments in Large Cities, 1990–2000.* By Brian A. Reaves and Matthew J. Hickman. Washington, DC: Government Printing Office, 2002.

———. *Prevalence of Imprisonment in the U.S. Population, 1974–2001.* By Thomas P. Bonczar. Washington, DC: Government Printing Office, 2003.

———. *Prison Admissions and Releases, 1982.* By Stephanie Minor-Harper and Lawrence A. Greenfeld. Washington, DC: Government Printing Office, 1985.

———. *Prisoners in 1990.* Washington, DC: Government Printing Office, 1991.

———. *Prisoners in 1997.* By Darrell K. Gilliard and Allen J. Beck. Washington, DC: Government Printing Office, 1998.

———. *Prisoners in 2015.* By E. Ann Carson and Elizabeth Anderson. Washington, DC: Government Printing Office, 2016.

———. *Probation and Parole in the United States, 2005.* By Lauren E. Glaze and Thomas P. Bonczar. Washington, DC: Government Printing Office, 2007.

———. *Race of Prisoners Admitted to State and Federal Institutions, 1926–86.* By Patrick A. Langan. Washington, DC: Government Printing Office, 1991.

———. *Rape and Sexual Assault Victimization among College-Age Females, 1995–2013.* By Sofi Sinozich and Lynn Langton. Washington, DC: Government Printing Office, 2014.

———. *Recidivism of Prisoners Released in 1994.* By Patrick A. Langan and David J. Levin. Washington, DC: Government Printing Office, 2002.

———. *Report to the Nation on Crime and Justice.* 2nd ed. Washington, DC: Government Printing Office, 1988.

———. *Sourcebook of Criminal Justice Statistics, 1990.* Edited by Kathleen Maguire and Timothy J. Flanagan. Washington, DC: Government Printing Office, 1991.

———. *State Corrections Expenditures, FY 1982–2010.* By Tracey Kyckelhahn. Washington, DC: Government Printing Office, 2012.

———. *Survey of State Prison Inmates, 1991.* By Allen Beck, Darrell Gilliard, Lawrence Greenfeld, Caroline Harlow, Thomas Hester, Louis Jankowski, Tracy Snell, James Stephan, and Danielle Morton. Washington, DC: Government Printing Office, 1993.

———. *Truth in Sentencing in State Prisons.* By Paula M. Ditton and Doris James Wilson. Washington, DC: Government Printing Office, 1999.

———. *Violent Crime.* Washington, DC: Government Printing Office, 1994.

———. *Violent Crime by Strangers and Nonstrangers.* By Anita D. Timrots and Michael R. Rand. Washington, DC: Government Printing Office, 1987.

U.S. Department of Justice, Office of Community Oriented Policing Services. *Attorney General's Report to Congress.* 2000. http://www.cops.usdoj.gov/pdf/e12990066_f.pdf.

U.S. Department of Labor. *The Negro Family: The Case for National Action.* [The Moynihan Report.] Washington, DC: Government Printing Office, 1965.

———. *The Recession of 2007–2009.* February 2012. Accessed January 8, 2013. http://www.bls.gov/spotlight/2012/recession/pdf/recession_bls_spotlight.pdf.

U.S. Department of War. *Is a Crime Wave Coming?* By Thorsten Sellin. American Historical Association, 1946. Accessed May 15, 2011. http://www.historians.org/about-aha-and-membership/aha-history-and-archives/gi-roundtable-series/pamphlets/is-a-crime-wave-coming.

U.S. Government Accountability Office. *Criminal Alien Statistics: Information on Incarcerations, Arrests, and Costs.* GAO-11-187. March 2011. Washington, DC. http://www.gao.gov/new.items/d11187.pdf.

U.S. Office of Management and Budget. "Revisions to the Standards for the Classification of Federal Data on Race and Ethnicity." October 30, 1997. Accessed July 15, 2011. http://www.whitehouse.gov/omb/fedreg_1997standards.

———. *Social Indicators, 1973.* Washington, DC: Government Printing Office, 1973.

U.S. Public Health Service, National Office of Vital Statistics. *Vital Statistics Rates in the United States, 1900–1940.* By Forrest E. Linder and Robert D. Grove. Washington, DC: Government Printing Office, 1947.

U.S. Senate, Committee on the Judiciary, Subcommittee to Investigate the Administration of the Internal Security Act and Other Internal Security Laws. *State Department Bombing by Weatherman Underground.* Washington, DC: Government Printing Office, 1975.

U.S. Sentencing Commission. *Cocaine and Federal Sentencing Policy.*

Report to the Congress, May 2007. http://www.ussc.gov/Legisla
tive_and_Public_Affairs/Congressional_Testimony_and_Reports
/Drug_Topics/200705_RtC_Cocaine_Sentencing_Policy.pdf.

Useem, Bert, and Anne Morrison Piehl. *Prison State: The Challenge of Mass Incarceration*. New York: Cambridge University Press, 2008.

von Hentig, Hans. *Crime: Causes and Conditions*. New York: McGraw-Hill, 1947.

Voss, Harwin L. "Ethnic Differentials in Delinquency in Honolulu." *Journal of Criminal Law, Criminology, and Police Science* 54 (1963): 322–27.

Wadsworth, Tim. "Is Immigration Responsible for the Crime Drop? An Assessment of the Influence of Immigration on Changes in Violent Crime between 1990 and 2000." *Social Science Quarterly* 91 (2010): 531–53.

Wakefield, Dan. *Island in the City: Puerto Ricans in New York*. New York: Citadel Press, 1959.

Waldron, Martin. "Shot Kills Indian at Wounded Knee." *New York Times*, April 28, 1973.

Walker, Samuel, Cassia Spohn, and Miriam DeLone. *The Color of Justice: Race, Ethnicity, and Crime in America*. 3rd and 5th eds. Belmont, CA: Wadsworth, 2004 and 2012.

Washington Post. "991 People Shot Dead by Police in 2015." Accessed July 16, 2016. https://www.washingtonpost.com/graphics/national /police-shootings.

Wellford, Charles F. "Age Composition and the Increase in Recorded Crime." *Criminology* 11 (1973): 61–70.

Whalen, Carmen Teresa, and Víctor Vázquez-Hernández, eds. *The Puerto Rican Diaspora: Historical Perspectives*. Philadelphia: Temple University Press, 2005.

White, Richard. *"It's Your Misfortune and None of My Own": A New History of the American West*. Norman: University of Oklahoma Press, 1991.

Wiegrefe, Klaus. "The Horror of D-Day: A New Openness to Discussing Allied War Crimes in WWII." *Spiegel Online*, May 4, 2010. Accessed May 23, 2011. http://www.spiegel.de/international/world /0,1518,692037,00.html.

Wilbanks, William. "Is Violent Crime Intraracial?" *Crime & Delinquency* 31 (1985): 117–28.

———. *The Myth of a Racist Criminal Justice System*. Monterey, CA: Brooks/Cole, 1987.

Wilkerson, Isabel. *In the Warmth of Other Suns*. New York: Random House, 2010.

Willbach, Harry. "The Trend of Crime in Chicago." *American Institute of Criminal Law & Criminology* 31 (1940–41): 720–27.

Wilson, James Q. *Thinking about Crime*. New York: Basic Books, 1983. First published in 1975.

Wilson, James Q., and Philip J. Cook. "Unemployment and Crime: What Is the Connection?" *The Public Interest* 79 (1985): 3–8.

Wilson, James Q., and Richard J. Herrnstein. *Crime and Human Nature*. New York: Free Press, 1985.

Wilson, James Q., and George L. Kelling. "Broken Windows." *Atlantic Monthly*, March, 1982, 29–38.

Wilson, William Julius. "Another Look at *The Truly Disadvantaged*." *Political Science Quarterly* 106 (1991–92): 639–56.

———. "Being Poor, Black, and American: The Impact of Political, Economic, and Cultural Forces." *American Educator* 35 (2011): 1–23, 46.

———. *The Truly Disadvantaged: The Inner City, the Underclass, and Public Policy*. Chicago: University of Chicago Press, 1987.

———. *When Work Disappears: The World of the New Urban Poor*. New York: Alfred A. Knopf, 1996.

Winkler, Allan M. *Home Front U.S.A.: America during World War II*. 2nd ed. Wheeling, IL: Harlan Davidson, 2000.

Wintemute, Garen. "Guns and Gun Violence." In *The Crime Drop in America*, edited by Alfred Blumstein and Joel Wallman, 45–96. Cambridge: Cambridge University Press, 2000.

Witt, Linda, Judith Bellafaire, Britta Granrud, and Mary Jo Binker. *"A Defense Weapon Known to Be of Value": Servicewomen of the Korean War Era*. Lebanon, NH: University Press of New England, 2005.

Wolfgang, Marvin E. "Crime in a Birth Cohort." *Proceedings of the American Philosophical Society* 117 (1973): 404–11.

———. "Suicide by Means of Victim-Precipitated Homicide." *Journal of Clinical and Experimental Psychopathology and Quarterly Review of Psychiatry and Neurology* 20 (1959): 335–49.

Wolfgang, Marvin E., and Franco Ferracuti. *The Subculture of Violence: Towards an Integrated Theory in Criminology*. London: Tavistock Publications, 1967.

Wren, Christopher S. "McVeigh Is Executed for Oklahoma City Bombing." *New York Times*, June 11, 2001. http://www.nytimes.com/2001/06/11/national/11CND-EXECUTE.html.

Wright, Lawrence. *The Looming Tower: Al-Qaeda and the Road to 9/11*. New York: Vintage, 2006.

Wu, Bohsiu. "Homicide Victimization in California: An Asian and Non-Asian Comparison." *Violence and Victims* 23 (2008): 743–57.

Zahn, Margaret A., and Philip C. Sagi. "Stranger Homicides in Nine American Cities." *Journal of Criminal Law and Criminology* 78 (1987): 377–97.

Zimring, Franklin E. *The City That Became Safe: New York's Lessons for Urban Crime and Its Control*. New York: Oxford University Press, 2012.

———. "Determinants of the Death Rate from Robbery: A Detroit Time Study." *Journal of Legal Studies* 6 (1977): 317–32.

———. *The Great American Crime Decline*. New York: Oxford University Press, 2007.

Zimring, Franklin E., and Gordon Hawkins. *Crime Is Not the Problem: Lethal Violence in America*. New York: Oxford University Press, 1997.

Zimring, Franklin E., Gordon Hawkins, and Sam Kamin. *Punishment and Democracy: Three Strikes and You're Out in California*. New York: Oxford University Press, 2001.

Zimring, Franklin E., and James Zuehl. "Victim Injury and Death in Urban Robbery: A Chicago Study." *Journal of Legal Studies* 15 (1986): 1–40.

Index

Abbott, Edith, 39
abortion, 254–55
Adler, Jeffrey, 116
Affluent Society, The (Galbraith), 99–100
African Americans: African immigrants and, 328–29n56; black-on-black crime and, 3, 30, 108, 125–26, 128, 131–32, 134, 216; civil rights movement and, 43–44; crime rates associated with, 10–12, 28–32, 44–45, 73–80, 86–87, 93–97, 125–34, 143–44, 149, 153–54, 171–75, 241, 259–60, 322n148, 335n94, 343n35; cultures of violence and, 75–78, 164–70, 182–84, 269–73, 284n47, 298n85; drugs and, 89, 95–97, 171–82, 233–35, 299n91; economic conditions of, 44, 46–47, 105, 127, 165, 205, 266–67, 282n26, 290n17; fear of crime and, 76–78, 107–9, 128, 131–32, 134, 216; ghettoization of, 56–57; Great Migration of, xii, 3, 10–11, 13–16, 106, 153–54, 164, 210–13, 272–73, 290n20, 320n129; Hispanic crime rates and, 146, 349–50n3; incarceration rates and, xi, 177, 181–82, 222–28, 231–33, 324n14; militancy of, 55, 137–38; Puerto Rican immigrants and, 73–74; rioting and, 15–16, 25, 104, 106, 125–27, 347–48n65; Southern violence and, 167–69; urban centers and, 10–14, 29–32, 47–56, 153–54, 169–70; white fears of, x, xi, 44–45, 52–57, 76–78,